GARDNER'S
ART
THROUGH THE
AGES

GARDNER'S
ART
through the
AGES

THE WESTERN PERSPECTIVE

THIRTEENTH EDITION

BACKPACK EDITION
Antiquity

FRED S. KLEINER

WADSWORTH
CENGAGE Learning

Australia • Brazil • Japan • Korea • Mexico • Singapore • Spain • United Kingdom • United States

WADSWORTH
CENGAGE Learning·

Gardner's Art through the Ages: The Western Perspective, Thirteenth Edition, Antiquity, Book A
Fred S. Kleiner

Publisher: Clark Baxter

Senior Development Editor: Sharon Adams Poore

Assistant Editor: Kimberly Apfelbaum

Editorial Assistant: Nell Pepper

Senior Media Editor: Wendy Constantine

Senior Marketing Manager: Diane Wenckebach

Marketing Communications Manager: Heather Baxley

Senior Project Manager, Editorial Production: Lianne Ames

Senior Art Director: Cate Rickard Barr

Senior Print Buyer: Judy Inouye

Production Service/Layout: Joan Keyes,
   Dovetail Publishing Services

Text Designer: tani hasegawa

Photo Researchers: Sarah Evertson, Stephen Forsling

Cover Designer: tani hasegawa

Cover Image: Sculptors at work, detail of the south wall of
   the main hall of the funerary chapel of Rekhmire, Thebes,
   Egypt, 18th Dynasty, ca. 1425 BCE. Erich Lessing/Art
   Resource, NY.

Compositor: Thompson Type

For product information and technology assistance, contact us at
Cengage Learning Academic Resource Center,
1-800-423-0563
For permission to use material from this text or product, submit all requests online at **www.cengage.com/permissions.**
Further permissions questions can be emailed to
permissionrequest@cengage.com

Library of Congress Control Number: 2008938881

ISBN-13: 978-0-495-79448-6
ISBN-10: 0-495-79448-1

Wadsworth
25 Thomson Place
Boston, MA 02210-1202
USA

Cengage Learning products are represented in Canada by Nelson Education, Ltd.

For your course and learning solutions, visit **academic.cengage.com**

Purchase any of our products at your local college store or at our preferred online store **www.ichapters.com**

Printed in the United States of America
2 3 4 5 6 7 13 12 11 10 09

About the Author

FRED S. KLEINER (Ph.D., Columbia University) is the co-author of the 10th, 11th, and 12th editions of *Art through the Ages* and more than a hundred publications on Greek and Roman art and architecture, including *A History of Roman Art,* also published by Wadsworth. He has taught the art history survey course for more than three decades, first at the University of Virginia and, since 1978, at Boston University, where he is currently Professor of Art History and Archaeology and Chair of the Art History Department. Long recognized for his inspiring lectures and devotion to students, Professor Kleiner won Boston University's Metcalf Award for Excellence in Teaching as well as the College Prize for Undergraduate Advising in the Humanities in 2002 and is a two-time winner of the Distinguished Teaching Prize in the College of Arts and Sciences Honors Program. He was Editor-in-Chief of the *American Journal of Archaeology* from 1985 to 1998.

A History of Roman Art (Wadsworth 2007; ISBN 0534638465)

Gardner's Art through the Ages: Non-Western Perspectives, Thirteenth Edition (Wadsworth 2010; ISBN 0495573671)

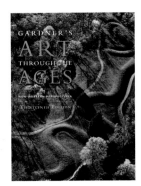

About the Cover Art

Sculptors at work, detail of the south wall of the main hall of the funerary chapel of Rekhmire, Thebes, Egypt, 18th Dynasty, ca. 1425 BCE.

During the reigns of Thutmose III (r. 1458–1425 BCE) and Amenhotep II (r. 1425–1401 BCE), the second most powerful official in Egypt was the vizier Rekhmire, who was the pharaoh's chief administrator. He was also governor of Thebes, where he constructed his funerary chapel on the west bank of the Nile. Rekhmire's chapel is an invaluable source of information about the New Kingdom because of its extensive series of mural paintings depicting Rekhmire's administrative duties, which included the collection of taxes, the receipt of tribute from foreign emissaries, the dispensing of justice, the overseeing of planting and harvesting, and the supervision of the royal metalworkers, jewelers, carpenters, tanners, bricklayers, stonemasons, sculptors, and painters.

The detail reproduced here is the left section of a scene of sculptors at work on three statues of Thutmose III, one depicting him seated, one standing, and the third as a sphinx. The sculptors have completed the cutting of the stone and the refinement of details. Most of the workers are busy polishing the surfaces. One (not shown) is painting the king's standing portrait. The statues are all well over life size, and the sculptors, working in teams, have erected scaffolding to reach the uppermost parts.

In contrast to the modern notion of the artist as a solitary genius, most artists before the 14th century toiled in anonymity in the service of their patrons, whether Egyptian pharaohs, Roman emperors, or medieval bishops. *Art through the Ages* surveys the art of all periods from prehistory to the present and examines how artworks of all kinds, anonymous or signed, have always reflected the historical contexts in which they were created.

CONTENTS

PREFACE

When Helen Gardner published the first edition of *Art through the Ages* in 1926, she could not have imagined that more than 80 years later instructors all over the world would still be using her textbook in their classrooms. Indeed, if she were alive today, she would not recognize the book that long ago became—and remains—the most widely read introduction to the history of art and architecture in the English language. During the past half century, successive authors have constantly reinvented Helen Gardner's groundbreaking survey, always keeping it fresh and current, and setting an ever-higher standard in both content and publication quality with each new edition. I hope both professors and students will agree that this 13th edition lives up to that venerable tradition.

Certainly, this latest edition offers much that is fresh and new (enumerated below), but some things have not changed, including the fundamental belief that guided Helen Gardner—namely, that the primary goal of an introductory art history textbook should be to foster an appreciation and understanding of historically significant works of art of all kinds from all periods. Because of the longevity and diversity of the history of art, it is tempting to assign responsibility for telling its story to a large team of specialists. The Gardner publishers themselves took this approach for the first edition they produced after Helen Gardner's death, and it has now become the norm for introductory art history surveys. But students overwhelmingly say that the very complexity of the history of art makes it all the more important for the story to be told with a consistent voice if they are to master so much diverse material. I think Helen Gardner would be pleased to know that this new edition of *Art through the Ages* once again has a single storyteller.

Along with the late Richard Tansey and my more recent collaborator, Christin Mamiya, with whom I had the honor and pleasure of working on the 10th, 11th, and 12th editions, I continue to believe that the most effective way to tell the story of art through the ages, especially to someone studying art history for the first time, is to organize the vast array of artistic monuments according to the civilizations that produced them and to consider each work in roughly chronological order. This approach has not merely stood the test of time. It is the most appropriate way to narrate the *history* of art. The principle that underlies my approach to every period of art history is that the enormous variation in the form and meaning of the paintings, sculptures, buildings, and other artworks men and women have produced over the past 30,000 years is largely the result of the constantly changing contexts in which artists and architects worked. A historically based

narrative is therefore best suited for a comprehensive history of art because it permits the author to situate each work discussed in its historical, social, economic, religious, and cultural context. That is, after all, what distinguishes art history from art appreciation.

In the first (1926) edition of *Art through the Ages*, Helen Gardner discussed Henri Matisse and Pablo Picasso in a chapter entitled "Contemporary Art in Europe and America." Since then many other artists have emerged on the international scene, and the story of art through the ages has grown longer and even more complex. More important, perhaps, the discipline of art history has changed markedly in recent decades, and so too has Helen Gardner's book. The 13th edition fully reflects the latest art historical research emphases while maintaining the traditional strengths that have made previous editions of *Art through the Ages* so popular. While sustaining attention to style, chronology, iconography, and technique, I also ensure that issues of patronage, function, and context loom large in every chapter. I treat artworks not as isolated objects in sterile 21st-century museum settings but with a view toward their purpose and meaning in the society that produced them at the time they were produced. I examine not only the role of the artist or architect in the creation of a work of art or a building, but also the role of the individuals or groups who paid the artists and influenced the shape the monuments took. Further, I devote more space than previously to the role of women and women artists in diverse societies over time. In every chapter, I have tried to choose artworks and buildings that reflect the increasingly wide range of interests of scholars today, while not rejecting the traditional list of "great" works or the very notion of a "canon." Consequently, the selection of works in this edition encompasses every artistic medium and almost every era and culture in the Western world, and includes many works that until recently art historians would not have considered to be "art" at all.

The 12th edition of *Art through the Ages* was the number-one choice for art history survey courses and the best-selling version of the book in its long history, and for this 13th edition I have retained all of the features that made its predecessor so successful. Once again, this edition, which contains 25 chapters on the Western tradition and its roots in the ancient Near East and Egypt, plus a chapter on Islamic art and architecture, boasts roughly 1,100 photographs, plans, and drawings, virtually all in color and reproduced according to the highest standards of clarity and color fidelity. The 13th edition, however, also features hundreds of new or upgraded photos by a host of new photographers as well as redesigned maps and plans and an extraordinary new set of architectural drawings prepared exclusively for *Art through the Ages* by John Burge.

The captions to the illustrations in this edition of *Art through the Ages*, as before, contain a wealth of information, including the name of the artist or architect, if known; the formal title (printed in italics), if assigned, description of the work, or name of the building; the provenance or place of production of the object or location of the building; the date; the material(s) used; the size; and the current location if the work is in a museum or private collection. As in previous editions, scales accompany all plans, but for the first time scales now also appear next to each photograph of a painting, statue, or other artwork. The works illustrated vary enormously in size, from colossal sculptures carved into mountain cliffs and paintings that cover entire walls or ceilings to tiny figurines, coins, and jewelry that one can hold in the hand. Although the captions contain the pertinent dimensions, it is hard for students who have never seen the paintings or statues in person to translate those dimensions into an appreciation of the real size of the objects. The new scales provide an effective and direct way to visualize how big or how small a given artwork is and its relative size compared with other objects in the same chapter and throughout the book.

Also new to this edition are the Quick-Review Captions that students found so useful when these were introduced in 2006 in the first edition of *Art through the Ages: A Concise History*. These brief synopses of the most significant aspects of each artwork or building illustrated accompany the captions to all images in the book. They have proved invaluable to students preparing for examinations in one-semester art history survey courses, and I am confident they will be equally useful to students enrolled in yearlong courses. In the 13th edition, however, I have provided two additional tools to aid students in reviewing and mastering the material. Each chapter now ends with a full-page feature called The Big Picture, which sets forth in bullet-point format the most important characteristics of each period or artistic movement discussed in the chapter. Small illustrations of characteristic works discussed accompany the summary of major points. Finally, I have attempted to tie all of the chapters together by providing with each copy of *Art through the Ages* a poster-size Global Timeline. This too features illustrations of key monuments of each age and geographical area as well as a brief enumeration of the most important art historical developments during that period. The timeline is global in scope to permit students in Western art courses to place developments in Europe and America in a worldwide context. The poster has four major horizontal bands corresponding to Europe, the Americas, Asia, and Africa, and 34 vertical columns for the successive chronological periods from 30,000 BCE to the present.

Another pedagogical tool not found in any other introductory art history textbook is the *Before 1300* section that appears at the beginning of Books C and D. Because many students taking the second half of a yearlong survey course will not have access to Books A and B, I have provided a special set of concise primers on religion and mythology and on architectural terminology and construction methods in the ancient and medieval worlds—information that is essential for understanding the history of Western art after 1300. The subjects of these special boxes are The Gods and Goddesses of Mount Olympus; The Life of Jesus in Art; Greco-Roman Temple Design and the Classical Orders; Arches and Vaults; and Medieval Church Design.

Boxed essays once again appear throughout the book as well. This popular feature first appeared in the 11th edition of *Art through the Ages*, which won both the Texty and McGuffey Prizes of the Text and Academic Authors Association for the best college textbook of 2001 in the humanities and social sciences. In this edition the essays are more closely tied to the main text than ever before. Consistent with that greater integration, most boxes now incorporate photographs of important artworks discussed in the text proper that also illustrate the theme treated in the boxed essays. These essays fall under six broad categories, one of which is new to the 13th edition.

Architectural Basics boxes provide students with a sound foundation for the understanding of architecture. These discussions are concise explanations, with drawings and diagrams, of the major aspects of design and construction. The information included is essential to an understanding of architectural technology and terminology. The boxes address questions of how and why various forms developed, the problems architects confronted, and the solutions they used to resolve them. Topics discussed include how the Egyptians built the pyramids, the orders of classical architecture, Roman concrete construction, and the design and terminology of mosques and Gothic cathedrals.

Materials and Techniques essays explain the various media artists employed from prehistoric to modern times. Since materials and techniques often influence the character of artworks, these discussions contain essential information on why many monuments appear as they do. Hollow-casting bronze statues; fresco painting; Islamic tile work; embroidery and tapestry; perspective; engraving, etching, and lithography; and daguerreotype and calotype photography are among the many subjects treated.

Religion and Mythology boxes introduce students to the principal elements of great religions, past and present, and to the representation of religious and mythological themes in painting and sculpture of all periods and places. These discussions of belief systems and iconography give readers a richer understanding of some of the greatest artworks ever created. The topics include the gods and goddesses of Egypt, Mesopotamia, Greece, and Rome; the life of Jesus in art; and Muhammad and Islam.

Art and Society essays treat the historical, social, political, cultural, and religious context of art and architecture. In some instances, specific monuments are the basis for a discussion of broader themes, as when the Hegeso stele serves as the springboard for an exploration of the role of women in ancient Greek society. Another essay discusses how people's evaluation today of artworks can differ from those of the society that produced them by examining the problems created by the contemporary market for undocumented archaeological finds. Other subjects include Egyptian mummification, Etruscan women, Byzantine icons and iconoclasm, artistic training in Renaissance Italy, 19th-century academic salons and independent art exhibitions, and public funding of controversial art.

Written Sources present and discuss key historical documents illuminating important monuments of art and architecture throughout the Western world. The passages quoted permit voices from the past to speak directly to the reader, providing vivid and unique insights into the creation of artworks in all media. Examples include Bernard of Clairvaux's treatise on sculpture in medieval churches, Giovanni Pietro Bellori's biographies of Annibale Carracci and Caravaggio, Jean François Marmontel's account of 18th-century salon culture, as well as texts that bring the past to life, such as eyewitness accounts of the volcanic eruption that buried Roman Pompeii and of the fire that destroyed Canterbury Cathedral in medieval England.

A new category is *Artists on Art* in which artists and architects throughout history discuss both their theories and individual works. Examples include Sinan the Great discussing the mosque he designed for Selim II, Leonardo da Vinci and Michelangelo debating the relative merits of painting and sculpture, Artemisia Gentileschi talking about the special problems she confronted as a woman artist, Jacques-Louis David on Neoclassicism, Gustave Courbet on Realism, Henri

Matisse on color, Pablo Picasso on Cubism, Diego Rivera on art for the people, and Judy Chicago on her seminal work *The Dinner Party.*

Instructors familiar with previous editions of *Art through the Ages* will also find that many of the chapters in the 13th edition have been reorganized, especially in volume two. For example, the treatment of European 17th-century art now appears in two discrete chapters, one devoted to Baroque Italy and Spain, the other to Northern Europe. A single chapter is devoted to the 18th century, another to the period from 1800 to 1870, and a third to 1870 to 1900. In addition, in recognition that different instructors at different colleges and universities end the first semester and begin the second semester at different points, for the first time *two* volumes of *Art through the Ages* include Chapter 14 on Italian art from 1200 to 1400. And *The Western Perspective* is now also available in this special backpack edition consisting of four, rather than the traditional two, paperback volumes: Book A (Antiquity: Chapters 1–7), Book B (The Middle Ages: Chapters 8–14), Book C (Renaissance and Baroque: Chapters 14–20), and Book D (Modern Europe and America: Chapters 21–25). These books can also be purchased separately.

Rounding out the features in the book itself is a Glossary containing definitions of all terms introduced in the text in italics and a Bibliography of books in English, including both general works and a chapter-by-chapter list of more focused studies. In this edition I have also taken care to italicize and define in the text all Glossary terms that appear in Books C and D even if they have been used and defined in Books A and B, because many students enrolled in the second semester of a yearlong course will not have taken the first semester and will not be familiar with those terms.

The 13th edition of *Art through the Ages* is not, however, a standalone text, but one element of a complete package of learning tools. In addition to the Global Timeline, every new copy of the book comes with a password to *ArtStudy Online,* a web site with access to a host of multimedia resources that students can employ throughout the entire course, including image flashcards, tutorial quizzes, podcasts, vocabulary, and more. Instructors have access to a host of teaching materials, including digital images with zoom capabilities, video, and Google™ Earth coordinates.

A work as extensive as this history of art could not be undertaken or completed without the counsel of experts in all areas of Western art. As with previous editions, the publisher has enlisted more than a hundred art historians to review every chapter in order to ensure that the text lived up to the Gardner reputation for accuracy as well as readability. I take great pleasure in acknowledging here the invaluable contributions to the 13th edition of *Art through the Ages: The Western Perspective* made by the following for their critiques of various chapters: Charles M. Adelman, University of Northern Iowa; Kirk Ambrose, University of Colorado–Boulder; Susan Ashbrook, Art Institute of Boston; Zainab Bahrani, Columbia University; Susan Bakewell, University of Texas–Austin; James J. Bloom, Florida State University; Suzaan Boettger, Bergen Community College; Colleen Bolton, Mohawk Valley Community College; Angi Elsea Bourgeois, Mississippi State University; Kimberly Bowes, Fordham University; Elizabeth Bredrup, St. Christopher's School; Lawrence E. Butler, George Mason University; Alexandra Carpino, Northern Arizona University; Jane Carroll, Dartmouth College; Hipolito Rafael Chacon, The University of Montana; Catherine M. Chastain, North Georgia College & State University; Violaine Chauvet, Johns Hopkins University; Daniel Connolly, Augustana College; Michael A. Coronel, University of Northern Colorado; Nicole Cox, Rochester Institute of Technology; Jodi Cranston, Boston University; Giovanna De Appolonia, Boston University; Marion de Koning, Grossmont College; John J. Dobbins, University of Virginia; Erika Doss, University of Colorado–Boulder;

B. Underwood DuRette, Thomas Nelson Community College; Lisa Farber, Pace University; James Farmer, Virginia Commonwealth University; Sheila ffolliott, George Mason University; Ferdinanda Florence, Solano Community College; William B. Folkestad, Central Washington University; Jeffery Fontana, Austin College; Mitchell Frank, Carleton University; Sara L. French, Wells College; Norman P. Gambill, South Dakota State University; Elise Goodman, University of Cincinnati; Kim T. Grant, University of Southern Maine; Elizabeth ten Grotenhuis, Silk Road Project; Sandra C. Haynes, Pasadena City College; Valerie Hedquist, The University of Montana; Susan Hellman, Northern Virginia Community College; Marian J. Hollinger, Fairmont State University; Cheryl Hughes, Alta High School; Heidrun Hultgren, Kent State University; Joseph M. Hutchinson, Texas A&M University; Julie M. Johnson, Utah State University; Sandra L. Johnson, Citrus College; Deborah Kahn, Boston University; Fusae Kanda, Harvard University; Catherine Karkov, Miami University; Wendy Katz, University of Nebraska–Lincoln; Nita Kehoe-Gadway, Central Wyoming College; Nancy L. Kelker, Middle Tennessee State University; Cathie Kelly, University of Nevada–Las Vegas; Katie Kempton, Ohio University; John F. Kenfield, Rutgers University; Herbert L. Kessler, Johns Hopkins University; Monica Kjellman-Chapin, Emporia State University; Ellen Konowitz, State University of New York–New Paltz; Kathryn E. Kramer, State University of New York–Cortland; Carol Krinsky, New York University; Lydia Lehr, Atlantic Cape Community College; Krist Lien, Shelton State Community College; Ellen Longsworth, Merrimack College; David A. Ludley, Clayton State University; Henry Luttikhuizen, Calvin College; Christina Maranci, University of Wisconsin–Milwaukee; Dominic Marner, University of Guelph; Jack Brent Maxwell, Blinn College; Anne McClanan, Portland State University; Brian McConnell, Florida Atlantic University; Heather McPherson, University of Alabama–Birmingham; Cynthia Millis, Houston Community College–Southwest; Cynthia Taylor Mills, Brookhaven College; Keith N. Morgan, Boston University; Johanna D. Movassat, San Jose State University; Helen Nagy, University of Puget Sound; Heidi Nickisher, Rochester Institute of Technology; Bonnie Noble, University of North Carolina–Charlotte; Abigail Noonan, Rochester Institute of Technology; Marjorie Och, University of Mary Washington; Karen Michelle O'Day, University of Wisconsin–Eau Claire; Edward J. Olszewski, Case Western Reserve University; Allison Lee Palmer, University of Oklahoma; Martin Patrick, Illinois State University; Glenn Peers, University of Texas–Austin; Jane Peters, University of Kentucky; Julie Anne Plax, University of Arizona; Frances Pohl, Pomona College; Virginia C. Raguin, College of the Holy Cross; Donna Karen Reid, Chemeketa Community College; Albert W. Reischuch, Kent State University; Jonathan Ribner, Boston University; Cynthea Riesenberg, Washington Latin School; James G. Rogers Jr., Florida Southern College; Carey Rote, Texas A&M University–Corpus Christi; David J. Roxburgh, Harvard University; Conrad Rudolph, University of California–Riverside; Catherine B. Scallen, Case Western Reserve University; Denise Schmandt-Besserat, University of Texas–Austin; Natasha Seaman, Berklee College of Music; Malia E. Serrano, Grossmont College; Laura Sommer, Daemen College; Natasha Staller, Amherst College; Nancy Steele-Hamme, Midwestern State University; Andrew Stewart, University of California–Berkeley; Francesca Tronchin, Ohio State University; Frances Van Keuren, University of Georgia; Kelly Wacker, University of Montevallo; Carolynne Whitefeather, Utica College; Nancy L. Wicker, University of Mississippi; Alastair Wright, Princeton University; John G. Younger, University of Kansas; Michael Zell, Boston University.

I am also happy to have this opportunity to express my gratitude to the extraordinary group of people at Wadsworth involved with the editing, production, and distribution of *Art through the Ages.* Some of them I have now worked with on various projects for more than a decade and feel privileged to count among my friends. The success of the Gardner series in all of its various permutations depends in no small part on the expertise and unflagging commitment of these dedicated professionals: Sean Wakely, executive vice president, Cengage Arts and Sciences; P. J. Boardman, vice president, editor-in-chief of Cengage Learning Arts and Sciences; Clark Baxter, publisher; Sharon Adams Poore, senior development editor; Helen Triller-Yambert, development editor; Lianne Ames, senior content project manager; Wendy Constantine, senior media editor; Kimberly Apfelbaum, assistant editor; Nell Pepper, editorial assistant; Cate Rikard Barr, senior art director; Scott Stewart, vice president managing director sales; Diane Wenckebach, senior marketing manager; as well as Kim Adams, Heather Baxley, William Christy, Doug Easton, tani hasegawa, Cara Murphy, Ellen Pettengell, Kathryn Stewart, and Joy Westberg.

I am also deeply grateful to the following for their significant contributions to the 13th edition of *Art through the Ages:* Joan Keyes, Dovetail Publishing Services; Ida May Norton, copy editor; Sarah Evertson and Stephen Forsling, photo researchers; Pete Shanks and Jon Peck, accuracy readers; Pat Lewis, proofreader; John Pierce, Thompson Type; Rick Stanley, Digital Media Inc., U.S.A; Don Larson, Mapping Specialists; Anne Draus, Scratchgravel; Cindy Geiss, Graphic World; and, of course, John Burge, for his superb architectural drawings. I also wish to acknowledge my debt to Edward Tufte for an illuminating afternoon spent discussing publication design and production issues and for his invaluable contribution to the creation of the scales that accompany all reproductions of paintings, sculptures, and other artworks in this edition.

Finally, I owe thanks to my colleagues at Boston University and to the thousands of students and the scores of teaching fellows in my art history courses during the past three decades. From them I have learned much that has helped determine the form and content of *Art through the Ages* and made it a much better book than it otherwise might have been.

Fred S. Kleiner

RESOURCES

FOR FACULTY

PowerLecture with Digital Image Library and JoinIn™ on Turning Point®
ISBN 0495792888

Bring digital images into the classroom with this one-stop lecture and class presentation tool that makes it easy to assemble, edit, and present customized lectures for your course using Microsoft Power-Point™. Available on the PowerLecture DVD, the Digital Image Library provides high-resolution images (maps, illustrations, and fine art images from the text) for lecture presentations, either in an easy-to-use PowerPoint presentation format, or in individual file formats compatible with other image-viewing software. The zoom feature allows you to magnify selected portions of an image for more detailed display, and another setting enables you to show images side by side for purposes of comparison. You can readily customize your classroom presentation by adding your personal visuals to those from the text. The PowerLecture also includes **Google**™**Earth** coordinates that allow you to zoom in on an entire city, as well as key monuments and buildings within it. Also included are panoramic video clips of architectural landmarks in New York City discussed in the text. Using a navigation bar on the video, you can move around the structure and zoom in/out, and right/left, to add a three-dimensional experience to your presentation.

This PowerLecture DVD also includes a Resource Integration Guide, an electronic Instructor's Manual, and a Test Bank with multiple-choice, matching, short-answer, and essay questions in ExamView® computerized format.

Text-specific Microsoft PowerPoint slides have been created for use with JoinIn™ software for classroom personal response systems ("clickers").

WebTutor on Blackboard or WebCT
WebCT ISBN: 0495792608
BlackBoard ISBN: 0495792586

This package allows you to assign preformatted, text-specific content that is available as soon as you log on, or customize the learning environment in any way you choose—from uploading images and other resources, to adding Web links to create your own practice materials.

Contact your Wadsworth representative.

FOR STUDENTS

ArtStudy Online

This tool gives access to a host of multimedia resources, including **flashcards** of works in the text, and a compare-and-contrast feature, where two works are displayed side by side for more in-depth analysis. Other features include critical-thinking questions, interactive

maps, architectural basics materials, big picture overviews, multimedia mini-lectures, video clips of select architectural monuments, museum guide with links, **Google**™**Earth** coordinates, Student Test Packet, audio study tools, vocabulary of art history, a guide to researching art history online, tips on becoming a successful student and links to beneficial Web sites on art, artists, architecture and more, and tips on becoming a successful student of art and art history.

Slide Guide   *Contact your Wadsworth representative.*

This lecture companion allows students to take notes alongside representations of the art images shown in class. New to this edition's slide guide are two features—the use of **Google**™**Earth** coordinates to link satellite images of historic sites and images to textual references, and end-of-chapter questions.

Web Site

Instructors and students have access to a comprehensive array of teaching and learning resources, including chapter-by-chapter online tutorial quizzes, a final exam, chapter reviews, chapter-by-chapter Web links, glossary flashcards, and more.

If you are interested in bundling any of the preceding student resources with the text, contact your Wadsworth sales representative.

To order student editions packaged with the Timeline and ArtStudy Online at no extra cost to students, use the following ISBNs:

Gardner's Art through the Ages: The Western Perspective, 13e
ISBN: 0495573558

Gardner's Art through the Ages: The Western Perspective, 13e
Volume I
ISBN: 0495573604

Gardner's Art through the Ages: The Western Perspective, 13e
Volume II
ISBN: 0495573647

Gardner's Art through the Ages: The Western Perspective, 13e
Backpack edition
ISBN: 049579442

To order the Backpack edition (Books A, B, C, and D):

Gardner's Art through the Ages: The Western Perspective, 13e
Book A   *Antiquity*
ISBN: 0495794481

Gardner's Art through the Ages: The Western Perspective, 13e
Book B   *The Middle Ages*
ISBN: 049579452X

Gardner's Art through the Ages: The Western Perspective, 13e
Book C   *Renaissance and Baroque*
ISBN: 0495794562

Gardner's Art through the Ages: The Western Perspective, 13e
Book D   *Modern Europe and America*
ISBN: 0495794627

GARDNER'S
ART
THROUGH THE
AGES

1 ft.

I-1 Clyfford Still, *1948-C, PH-15*, 1948. Oil on canvas, 6′ 8 7/8″ × 5′ 10 3/4″. Hirshhorn Museum and Sculpture Garden, Smithsonian Institution, Washington, D.C. (purchased with funds of Joseph H. Hirshhorn, 1992).

Clyfford Still painted this abstract composition without knowing who would purchase it or where it would be displayed, but throughout history most artists created works for specific patrons and settings.

INTRODUCTION: WHAT IS ART HISTORY?

Except when referring to the modern academic discipline, people do not often juxtapose the words "art" and "history." They tend to think of history as the record and interpretation of past human actions, particularly social and political actions. Most think of art, quite correctly, as part of the present— as something people can see and touch. Of course, people cannot see or touch history's vanished human events, but a visible, tangible artwork is a kind of persisting event. One or more artists made it at a certain time and in a specific place, even if no one today knows just who, when, where, or why. Although created in the past, an artwork continues to exist in the present, long surviving its times. The first painters and sculptors died 30,000 years ago, but their works remain, some of them exhibited in glass cases in museums built only a few years ago.

Modern museum visitors can admire these objects from the remote past—and countless others humankind has produced over the millennia—without any knowledge of the circumstances that led to the creation of those works. The beauty or sheer size of an object can impress people, the artist's virtuosity in the handling of ordinary or costly materials can dazzle them, or the subject depicted can move them. Viewers can react to what they see, interpret the work in the light of their own experience, and judge it a success or a failure. These are all valid responses to a work of art. But the enjoyment and appreciation of artworks in museum settings are relatively recent phenomena, as is the creation of artworks solely for museum-going audiences to view.

Today, it is common for artists to work in private studios and to create paintings, sculptures, and other objects commercial art galleries will offer for sale. This is what the American painter CLYFFORD STILL (1904–1980) did when he created large canvases of pure color (FIG. I-1) titled simply with the year of their creation. Usually, someone the artist has never met will purchase the artwork and display it in a setting the artist has never seen. This practice is not a new phenomenon in the history of art—an ancient potter decorating a vase for sale at a village market stall probably did not know who would buy the pot or where it would be housed—but it is not at all typical. In fact, it is exceptional. Throughout history, most artists created paintings, sculptures, and other objects for specific patrons and settings and to fulfill a specific purpose, even if today no one knows the original contexts of most of those works. Museum visitors can appreciate the visual and tactile qualities of these objects, but they cannot understand why they were made or why they appear as they do without knowing the circumstances of their creation. Art *appreciation* does not require knowledge of the historical context of an artwork (or a building). Art *history* does.

Thus, a central aim of art history is to determine the original context of artworks. Art historians seek to achieve a full understanding not only of why these "persisting events" of human history look the way they do but also of why the artistic events happened at all. What unique set of circumstances gave rise to the erection of a particular building or led an individual patron to commission a certain artist to fashion a singular artwork for a specific place? The study of history is therefore vital to art history. And art history is often very important to the study of history. Art objects and buildings are historical documents that can shed light on the peoples who made them and on the times of their creation in a way other historical documents cannot. Furthermore, artists and architects can affect history by reinforcing or challenging cultural values and practices through the objects they create and the structures they build. Thus, the history of art and architecture is inseparable from the study of history, although the two disciplines are not the same.

The following pages introduce some of the distinctive subjects art historians address and the kinds of questions they ask, and explain some of the basic terminology they use when answering these questions. Readers armed with this arsenal of questions and terms will be ready to explore the multifaceted world of art through the ages.

ART HISTORY IN THE 21ST CENTURY

Art historians study the visual and tangible objects humans make and the structures humans build. Scholars traditionally have classified such works as architecture, sculpture, the pictorial arts (painting, drawing, printmaking, and photography), and the craft arts, or arts of design. The craft arts comprise utilitarian objects, such as ceramics, metalwork, textiles, jewelry, and similar accessories of ordinary living. Artists of every age have blurred the boundaries among these categories, but this is especially true today, when multimedia works abound.

From the earliest Greco-Roman art critics on, scholars have studied objects that their makers consciously manufactured as "art" and to which the artists assigned formal titles. But today's art historians also study a vast number of objects that their creators and owners almost certainly did not consider to be "works of art." Few ancient Romans, for example, would have regarded a coin bearing their emperor's portrait as anything but money. Today, an art museum may exhibit that coin in a locked case in a climate-controlled room, and scholars may subject it to the same kind of art historical analysis as a portrait by an acclaimed Renaissance or modern sculptor or painter.

The range of objects art historians study is constantly expanding and now includes, for example, computer-generated images, whereas in the past almost anything produced using a machine would not have been regarded as art. Most people still consider the performing arts—music, drama, and dance—as outside art history's realm because these arts are fleeting, impermanent media. But recently even this distinction between "fine art" and "performance art" has become blurred. Art historians, however, generally ask the same kinds of questions about what they study, whether they employ a restrictive or expansive definition of art.

The Questions Art Historians Ask

HOW OLD IS IT? Before art historians can construct a history of art, they must be sure they know the date of each work they study. Thus, an indispensable subject of art historical inquiry is *chronology*,

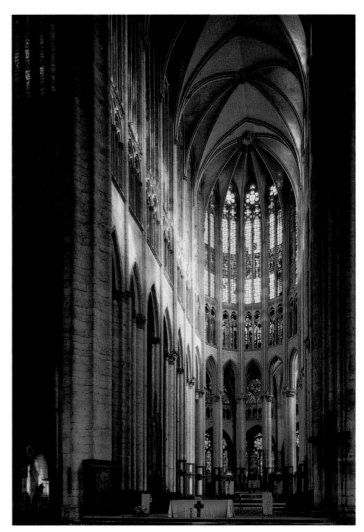

I-2 Choir of Beauvais Cathedral, Beauvais, France, rebuilt after 1284.

The style of an object or building often varies from region to region. This cathedral has towering stone vaults and large stained-glass windows typical of 13th-century French architecture.

the dating of art objects and buildings. If researchers cannot determine a monument's age, they cannot place the work in its historical context. Art historians have developed many ways to establish, or at least approximate, the date of an artwork.

Physical evidence often reliably indicates an object's age. The material used for a statue or painting—bronze, plastic, or oil-based pigment, to name only a few—may not have been invented before a certain time, indicating the earliest possible date someone could have fashioned the work. Or artists may have ceased using certain materials—such as specific kinds of inks and papers for drawings—at a known time, providing the latest possible dates for objects made of those materials. Sometimes the material (or the manufacturing technique) of an object or a building can establish a very precise date of production or construction. Studying tree rings, for instance, usually can help scholars determine within a narrow range the date of a wood statue or a timber roof beam.

Documentary evidence can help pinpoint the date of an object or building when a dated written document mentions the work. For example, official records may note when church officials commissioned a new altarpiece—and how much they paid to which artist.

Internal evidence can play a significant role in dating an artwork. A painter might have depicted an identifiable person or a kind of hairstyle, clothing, or furniture fashionable only at a certain

I-3 Interior of Santa Croce, Florence, Italy, begun 1294.

In contrast to Beauvais Cathedral (FIG. I-2), this contemporaneous Florentine church conforms to the quite different regional style of Italy. The building has a low timber roof and small windows.

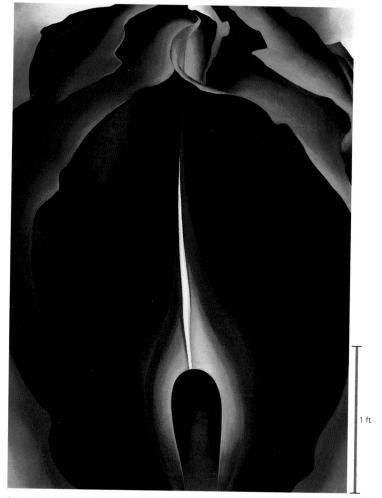

1 ft.

I-4 GEORGIA O'KEEFFE, *Jack-in-the-Pulpit No. 4*, 1930. Oil on canvas, 3′ 4″ × 2′ 6″. National Gallery of Art, Washington, D.C. (Alfred Stieglitz Collection, bequest of Georgia O'Keeffe).

O'Keeffe's paintings feature close-up views of petals and leaves in which the organic forms become powerful abstract compositions. This approach to painting typifies the artist's distinctive personal style.

time. If so, the art historian can assign a more accurate date to that painting.

Stylistic evidence is also very important. The analysis of *style*—an artist's distinctive manner of producing an object—is the art historian's special sphere. Unfortunately, because it is a subjective assessment, stylistic evidence is by far the most unreliable chronological criterion. Still, art historians find style a very useful tool for establishing chronology.

WHAT IS ITS STYLE? Defining artistic style is one of the key elements of art historical inquiry, although the analysis of artworks solely in terms of style no longer dominates the field as it once did. Art historians speak of several different kinds of artistic styles.

Period style refers to the characteristic artistic manner of a specific time, usually within a distinct culture, such as "Archaic Greek" or "Late Byzantine." But many periods do not manifest any stylistic unity at all. How would someone define the artistic style of the opening decade of the new millennium in North America? Far too many crosscurrents exist in contemporary art for anyone to describe a period style of the early 21st century—even in a single city such as New York.

Regional style is the term art historians use to describe variations in style tied to geography. Like an object's date, its *provenance,* or place of origin, can significantly determine its character. Very often two artworks from the same place made centuries apart are more similar than contemporaneous works from two different regions. To cite one example, usually only an expert can distinguish between an Egyptian statue carved in 2500 BCE and one made in 500 BCE. But no

one would mistake an Egyptian statue of 500 BCE for one of the same date made in Greece or Mexico.

Considerable variations in a given area's style are possible, however, even during a single historical period. In late medieval Europe, French architecture differed significantly from Italian architecture. The interiors of Beauvais Cathedral (FIG. I-2) and the Florentine church of Santa Croce (FIG. I-3) typify the architectural styles of France and Italy, respectively, at the end of the 13th century. The rebuilding of the east end of Beauvais Cathedral began in 1284. Construction commenced on Santa Croce only 10 years later. Both structures employ the *pointed arch* characteristic of this era, yet the two churches differ strikingly. The French church has towering stone ceilings and large expanses of colored windows, whereas the Italian building has a low timber roof and small, widely separated windows. Because the two contemporaneous churches served similar purposes, regional style mainly explains their differing appearance.

Personal style, the distinctive manner of individual artists or architects, often decisively explains stylistic discrepancies among monuments of the same time and place. In 1930 the American painter GEORGIA O'KEEFFE (1887–1986) produced a series of paintings of flowering plants. One of them was *Jack-in-the-Pulpit No. 4* (FIG. I-4), a sharply focused close-up view of petals and leaves. O'Keeffe captured the growing plant's slow, controlled motion while converting

1 ft.

I-5 BEN SHAHN, *The Passion of Sacco and Vanzetti,* 1931–1932. Tempera on canvas, 7′ $\frac{1}{2}$″ × 4′. Whitney Museum of American Art, New York (gift of Edith and Milton Lowenthal in memory of Juliana Force).

A contemporary of O'Keeffe's, Shahn developed a style of painting that differed markedly from hers. His paintings are often social commentaries on current events and incorporate readily identifiable people.

the plant into a powerful abstract composition of lines, forms, and colors (see the discussion of art historical vocabulary in the next section). Only a year later, another American artist, BEN SHAHN (1898–1969), painted *The Passion of Sacco and Vanzetti* (FIG. I-5), a stinging commentary on social injustice inspired by the trial and execution of two Italian anarchists, Nicola Sacco and Bartolomeo Vanzetti. Many people believed Sacco and Vanzetti had been unjustly convicted of killing two men in a holdup in 1920. Shahn's painting compresses time in a symbolic representation of the trial and its aftermath. The two executed men lie in their coffins. Presiding over them are the three members of the commission (headed by a college president wearing academic cap and gown) that declared the original trial fair and cleared the way for the executions. Behind, on the wall of a stately government building, hangs the framed portrait of the judge who pronounced the

I-6 GISLEBERTUS, The weighing of souls, detail of Last Judgment (FIG. 12-12), west tympanum of Saint-Lazare, Autun, France, ca. 1120–1135.

In this high relief portraying the weighing of souls on Judgment Day, Gislebertus used disproportion and distortion to dehumanize the devilish figure yanking on the scales of justice.

initial sentence. Personal style, not period or regional style, sets Shahn's canvas apart from O'Keeffe's. The contrast is extreme here because of the very different subjects the artists chose. But even when two artists depict the same subject, the results can vary widely. The *way* O'Keeffe painted flowers and the *way* Shahn painted faces are distinctive and unlike the styles of their contemporaries. (See the "Who Made It?" discussion on page xxiii.)

The different kinds of artistic styles are not mutually exclusive. For example, an artist's personal style may change dramatically during a long career. Art historians then must distinguish among the different period styles of a particular artist, such as the "Blue Period" and the "Cubist Period" of the prolific 20th-century artist Pablo Picasso.

WHAT IS ITS SUBJECT? Another major concern of art historians is, of course, subject matter, encompassing the story, or narrative; the scene presented; the action's time and place; the persons involved; and the environment and its details. Some artworks, such as modern abstract paintings (FIG. I-1), have no subject, not even a setting. The "subject" is the artwork itself. But when artists represent people, places, or actions, viewers must identify these aspects to achieve complete understanding of the work. Art historians traditionally separate pictorial subjects into various categories, such as religious, historical, mythological, *genre* (daily life), portraiture, *landscape* (a depiction of a place), *still life* (an arrangement of inanimate objects), and their numerous subdivisions and combinations.

Iconography—literally, the "writing of images"—refers both to the content, or subject of an artwork, and to the study of content in art. By extension, it also includes the study of *symbols,* images that stand for other images or encapsulate ideas. In Christian art, two intersecting

I-7 The four evangelists, folio 14 verso of the *Aachen Gospels*, ca. 810. Ink and tempera on vellum, 1' × 9½". Cathedral Treasury, Aachen.

Artists depict figures with attributes in order to identify them for viewers. The authors of the four gospels have distinctive attributes—John an eagle, Luke an ox, Mark a lion, and Matthew a winged man.

I-8 ALBRECHT DÜRER, *The Four Horsemen of the Apocalypse*, ca. 1498. Woodcut, 1' 3¼" × 11". Metropolitan Museum of Art, New York (gift of Junius S. Morgan, 1919).

Personifications are abstract ideas codified in human form. Here, Albrecht Dürer represented Death, Famine, War, and Pestilence as four men on charging horses, each carrying an identifying attribute.

lines of unequal length or a simple geometric cross can serve as an emblem of the religion as a whole, symbolizing the cross of Jesus Christ's crucifixion. A symbol also can be a familiar object the artist imbued with greater meaning. A balance or scale, for example, may symbolize justice or the weighing of souls on Judgment Day (FIG. I-6).

Artists may depict figures with unique *attributes* identifying them. In Christian art, for example, each of the authors of the New Testament Gospels, the four evangelists (FIG. I-7), has a distinctive attribute. People can recognize Saint John by the eagle associated with him, Luke by the ox, Mark by the lion, and Matthew by the winged man.

Throughout the history of art, artists have used *personifications*—abstract ideas codified in human form. Worldwide, people visualize Liberty as a robed woman with a torch because of the fame of the colossal statue set up in New York City's harbor in the 19th century. *The Four Horsemen of the Apocalypse* (FIG. I-8) is a terrifying late-15th-century depiction of the fateful day at the end of time when, according to the Bible's last book, Death, Famine, War, and Pestilence will annihilate the human race. The German artist ALBRECHT DÜRER (1471–1528) personified Death as an emaciated old man with a pitchfork. Dürer's Famine swings the scales that will weigh human souls (compare FIG. I-6), War wields a sword, and Pestilence draws a bow.

Even without considering style and without knowing a work's maker, informed viewers can determine much about the work's period and provenance by iconographical and subject analysis alone. In *The Passion of Sacco and Vanzetti* (FIG. I-5), for example, the two

coffins, the trio headed by an academic, and the robed judge in the background are all pictorial clues revealing the painting's subject. The work's date must be after the trial and execution, probably while the event was still newsworthy. And because the two men's deaths caused the greatest outrage in the United States, the painter–social critic was probably American.

WHO MADE IT? If Ben Shahn had not signed his painting of Sacco and Vanzetti, an art historian could still assign, or *attribute* (make an *attribution* of), the work to him based on knowledge of the artist's personal style. Although signing (and dating) works is quite common (but by no means universal) today, in the history of art countless works exist whose artists remain unknown. Because personal style can play a large role in determining the character of an artwork, art historians often try to attribute anonymous works to known artists. Sometimes they assemble a group of works all thought to be by the same person, even though none of the objects in the group is the known work of an artist with a recorded name. Art historians thus reconstruct the careers of artists such as "the Achilles Painter," the anonymous ancient Greek vase painter whose masterwork is a depiction of the hero Achilles. Scholars base their attributions on internal evidence, such as the distinctive way an artist draws or carves drapery folds, earlobes, or flowers. It requires a keen, highly trained eye and long experience to become a *connoisseur*, an expert in

I-9 Augustus wearing the corona civica, early first century CE. Marble, 1′ 5″ high. Glyptothek, Munich.

Patrons frequently dictate the form their portraits will take. The Roman emperor Augustus demanded that he always be portrayed as a young, godlike head of state even though he lived to age 76.

assigning artworks to "the hand" of one artist rather than another. Attribution is subjective, of course, and ever open to doubt. At present, for example, international debate rages over attributions to the famous 17th-century Dutch painter Rembrandt.

Sometimes a group of artists works in the same style at the same time and place. Art historians designate such a group as a *school.* "School" does not mean an educational institution. The term connotes only chronological, stylistic, and geographic similarity. Art historians speak, for example, of the Dutch school of the 17th century and, within it, of subschools such as those of the cities of Haarlem, Utrecht, and Leyden.

WHO PAID FOR IT? The interest many art historians show in attribution reflects their conviction that the identity of an artwork's maker is the major reason the object looks the way it does. For them, personal style is of paramount importance. But in many times and places, artists had little to say about what form their work would take. They toiled in obscurity, doing the bidding of their *patrons,* those who paid them to make individual works or employed them on a continuing basis. The role of patrons in dictating the content and shaping the form of artworks is also an important subject of art historical inquiry.

In the art of portraiture, to name only one category of painting and sculpture, the patron has often played a dominant role in deciding how the artist represented the subject, whether that person was the patron or another individual, such as a spouse, son, or mother. Many Egyptian pharaohs and some Roman emperors, for example, insisted that artists depict them with unlined faces and perfect youthful bodies no matter how old they were when portrayed. In these cases, the state employed the sculptors and painters, and the artists had no choice but to depict their patrons in the officially approved manner. This is why Augustus, who lived to age 76, looks so young in his portraits (FIG. I-9). Although Roman emperor for more than 40 years, Augustus demanded that artists always represent him as a young, godlike head of state.

All modes of artistic production reveal the impact of patronage. Learned monks provided the themes for the sculptural decoration of medieval church portals (FIG. I-6). Renaissance princes and popes dictated the subject, size, and materials of artworks destined for buildings constructed according to their specifications. An art historian could make a very long list of commissioned works, and it would indicate that throughout the history of art, patrons have had diverse tastes and needs and demanded different kinds of art. Whenever a patron contracts an artist or architect to paint, sculpt, or build in a prescribed manner, personal style often becomes a very minor factor in the ultimate appearance of the painting, statue, or building. In these cases, the identity of the patron reveals more to art historians than does the identity of the artist or school. The portrait of Augustus wearing a *corona civica,* or civic crown (FIG. I-9), was the work of a virtuoso sculptor, a master wielder of hammer and chisel. But scores of similar portraits of that emperor exist today. They differ in quality but not in kind from this one. The patron, not the artist, determined the character of these artworks. Augustus's public image never varied.

The Words Art Historians Use

Like all specialists, art historians have their own specialized vocabulary. That vocabulary consists of hundreds of words, but certain basic terms are indispensable for describing artworks and buildings of any time and place. They make up the essential vocabulary of *formal analysis,* the visual analysis of artistic form. Definitions of the most important of these art historical terms follow.

FORM AND COMPOSITION *Form* refers to an object's shape and structure, either in two dimensions (for example, a figure painted on a canvas) or in three dimensions (such as a statue carved from a marble block). Two forms may take the same shape but may differ in their color, texture, and other qualities. *Composition* refers to how an artist organizes (*composes*) forms in an artwork, either by placing shapes on a flat surface or by arranging forms in space.

MATERIAL AND TECHNIQUE To create art forms, artists shape materials (pigment, clay, marble, gold, and many more) with tools (pens, brushes, chisels, and so forth). Each of the materials and tools available has its own potentialities and limitations. Part of all artists' creative activity is to select the *medium* and instrument most suitable to the artists' purpose—or to develop new media and tools, such as bronze and concrete in antiquity and cameras and computers in modern times. The processes artists employ, such as applying paint to canvas with a brush, and the distinctive, personal ways they handle materials constitute their *technique.* Form, material, and technique interrelate and are central to analyzing any work of art.

LINE Among the most important elements defining an artwork's shape or form is *line.* A line can be understood as the path of a point moving in space, an invisible line of sight. More commonly, however, artists and architects make a line tangible by drawing (or chiseling) it on a *plane,* a flat surface. A line may be very thin, wirelike, and delicate. It may be thick and heavy. Or it may alternate quickly from broad to narrow, the strokes jagged or the outline broken. When a continuous line defines an object's outer shape, art historians call it a *contour line.* All of these line qualities are present in Dürer's *Four Horsemen of the Apocalypse* (FIG. I-8). Contour lines define the basic shapes of clouds, human and animal limbs, and weapons. Within the forms, series of short broken lines create shadows and textures. An overall pattern of long parallel strokes suggests the dark sky on the frightening day when the world is about to end.

COLOR Light reveals all colors. Light in the world of the painter and other artists differs from natural light. Natural light, or sunlight, is whole or *additive light.* As the sum of all the wavelengths composing the visible *spectrum,* natural light may be disassembled or fragmented into the individual colors of the spectral band. The painter's light in art—the light reflected from pigments and objects—is *subtractive light.* Paint pigments produce their individual colors by reflecting a segment of the spectrum while absorbing all the rest. Green pigment, for example, subtracts or absorbs all the light in the spectrum except that seen as green.

Hue is the property that gives a color its name. Although the spectrum colors merge into each other, artists usually conceive of their hues as distinct from one another. Color has two basic variables—the apparent amount of light reflected and the apparent purity. A change in one must produce a change in the other. Some terms for these variables are *value,* or *tonality* (the degree of lightness or darkness), and *intensity,* or *saturation* (the purity of a color, or its brightness or dullness).

Artists call the three basic colors—red, yellow, and blue—the *primary colors.* The *secondary colors* result from mixing pairs of primaries: orange (red and yellow), purple (red and blue), and green (yellow and blue). *Complementary colors* represent the pairing of a primary color and the secondary color created from mixing the two other primary colors—red and green, yellow and purple, and blue and orange. They "complement," or complete, each other, one absorbing colors the other reflects.

Artists can manipulate the appearance of colors, however. One artist who made a systematic investigation of the formal aspects of art, especially color, was JOSEF ALBERS (1888–1976), a German-born artist who emigrated to the United States in 1933. In connection with his studies, Albers created the series *Homage to the Square*—hundreds of paintings, most of which are color variations on the same composition of concentric squares, as in the illustrated example (FIG. I-10). The series reflected Albers's belief that art originates in "the discrepancy between physical fact and psychic effect."[1] Because the composition in most of these paintings remains constant, the works succeed in revealing the relativity and instability of color perception. Albers varied the hue, saturation, and value of each square in the paintings in this series. As a result, the sizes of the squares from painting to painting appear to vary (although they remain the same), and the sensations emanating from the paintings range from clashing dissonance to delicate serenity. Albers explained his motivation for focusing on color juxtapositions:

> They [the colors] are juxtaposed for various and changing visual effects. . . . Such action, reaction, interaction . . . is sought in order to make obvious how colors influence and change each other; that the same color, for instance—with different grounds or neighbors— looks different. . . . Such color deceptions prove that we see colors almost never unrelated to each other.[2]

Albers's quotation is only one example of how artists' comments on their own works are often invaluable to art historians. In *Art through*

I-10 JOSEF ALBERS, *Homage to the Square: "Ascending,"* 1953. Oil on composition board, 3′ 7½″ × 3′ 7½″. Whitney Museum of American Art, New York.

Josef Albers painted hundreds of canvases with the same composition but employed variations in hue, saturation, and value in order to reveal the relativity and instability of color perception.

the Ages: The Western Perspective, artist commentaries appear frequently in boxed features called "Artists on Art."

TEXTURE The term *texture* refers to the quality of a surface, such as rough or shiny. Art historians distinguish between true texture, or the tactile quality of the surface, and represented texture, as when painters depict an object as having a certain texture even though the pigment is the true texture. Sometimes artists combine different materials of different textures on a single surface, juxtaposing paint with pieces of wood, newspaper, fabric, and so forth. Art historians refer to this mixed-media technique as *collage.* Texture is, of course, a key determinant of any sculpture's character. A viewer's first impulse is usually to handle a piece of sculpture—even though museum signs often warn "Do not touch!" Sculptors plan for this natural human response, using surfaces varying in texture from rugged coarseness to polished smoothness. Textures are often intrinsic to a material, influencing the type of stone, wood, plastic, clay, or metal sculptors select.

SPACE, MASS, AND VOLUME *Space* is the bounded or boundless "container" of objects. For art historians, space can be the literal three-dimensional space occupied by a statue or a vase or contained within a room or courtyard. Or space can be *illusionistic,* as when painters depict an image (or illusion) of the three-dimensional spatial world on a two-dimensional surface.

Mass and *volume* describe three-dimensional objects and space. In both architecture and sculpture, mass is the bulk, density, and weight of matter in space. Yet the mass need not be solid. It can be the exterior form of enclosed space. Mass can apply to a solid Egyptian pyramid or stone statue, to a church, synagogue, or mosque—architectural shells enclosing sometimes vast spaces—and to a hollow metal statue or baked clay pot. Volume is the space that mass organizes, divides, or encloses. It may be a building's interior spaces, the

I-11 CLAUDE LORRAIN, *Embarkation of the Queen of Sheba,* 1648. Oil on canvas, 4′ 10″ × 6′ 4″. National Gallery, London.

To create the illusion of a deep landscape, Claude Lorrain employed perspective, reducing the size of and blurring the most distant forms. Also, all diagonal lines converge on a single point.

1 ft.

intervals between a structure's masses, or the amount of space occupied by three-dimensional objects such as sculpture, pottery, or furniture. Volume and mass describe both the exterior and interior forms of a work of art—the forms of the matter of which it is composed and the spaces immediately around the work and interacting with it.

PERSPECTIVE AND FORESHORTENING *Perspective* is one of the most important pictorial devices for organizing forms in space. Throughout history, artists have used various types of perspec-

tive to create an illusion of depth or space on a two-dimensional surface. The French painter CLAUDE LORRAIN (1600–1682) employed several perspectival devices in *Embarkation of the Queen of Sheba* (FIG. **I-11**), a painting of a biblical episode set in a 17th-century European harbor with a Roman ruin in the left foreground. For example, the figures and boats on the shoreline are much larger than those in the distance. Decreasing the size of an object makes it appear farther away. Also, the top and bottom of the port building at the painting's right side are not parallel horizontal lines, as they are

1 ft.

I-12 OGATA KORIN, *White and Red Plum Blossoms,* Edo period, ca. 1710–1716. Pair of twofold screens. Ink, color, and gold leaf on paper, each screen 5′ 1⅝″ × 5′ 7⅞″. MOA Art Museum, Shizuoka-ken.

Ogata Korin was more concerned with creating an interesting composition of shapes on a surface than with locating objects in space. Asian artists rarely employed Western perspective.

I-13 PETER PAUL RUBENS, *Lion Hunt*, 1617–1618. Oil on canvas, 8′ 2″ × 12′ 5″. Alte Pinakothek, Munich.

Foreshortening—the representation of a figure or object at an angle to the picture plane—is a common device in Western art for creating the illusion of depth. Foreshortening is a type of perspective.

in a real building. Instead, the lines converge beyond the structure, leading viewers' eyes toward the hazy, indistinct sun on the horizon. These perspectival devices—the reduction of figure size, the convergence of diagonal lines, and the blurring of distant forms—have been familiar features of Western art since the ancient Greeks. But it is important to note at the outset that all kinds of perspective are only pictorial conventions, even when one or more types of perspective may be so common in a given culture that people accept them as "natural" or as "true" means of representing the natural world.

In *White and Red Plum Blossoms* (FIG. I-12), a Japanese landscape painting on two folding screens, OGATA KORIN (1658–1716) used none of these Western perspective conventions. He showed the two plum trees as seen from a position on the ground, but viewers look down on the stream between them from above. Less concerned with locating the trees and stream in space than with composing shapes on a surface, the painter played the water's gently swelling curves against the jagged contours of the branches and trunks. Neither the French nor the Japanese painting can be said to project "correctly" what viewers "in fact" see. One painting is not a "better" picture of the world than the other. The European and Asian artists simply approached the problem of picture-making differently. Claude Lorrain's approach is, however, one of the most distinctive features of the Western tradition in art examined exclusively in this book.

Artists also represent single figures in space in varying ways. When the Flemish artist PETER PAUL RUBENS (1577–1640) painted *Lion Hunt* (FIG. I-13), he used *foreshortening* for all the hunters and animals—that is, he represented their bodies at angles to the picture plane. When in life one views a figure at an angle, the body appears to contract as it extends back in space. Foreshortening is a kind of perspective. It produces the illusion that one part of the body is farther away than another, even though all the forms are on the same surface. Especially noteworthy in *Lion Hunt* are the gray horse at the left, seen from behind with the bottom of its left rear hoof facing viewers and most of its head hidden by its rider's shield, and the fallen hunter at the painting's lower right corner, whose barely visible legs and feet recede into the distance.

The artist who carved the portrait of the ancient Egyptian official Hesire (FIG. I-14) did not employ foreshortening. That artist's purpose was to present the various human body parts as clearly as possible, without overlapping. The lower part of Hesire's body is in

I-14 Hesire, relief from his tomb at Saqqara, Egypt, Third Dynasty, ca. 2650 BCE. Wood, 3′ 9″ high. Egyptian Museum, Cairo.

Egyptian artists combined frontal and profile views to give a precise picture of the parts of the human body, as opposed to depicting how an individual body appears from a specific viewpoint.

1 in.

I-15 King on horseback with attendants, from Benin, Nigeria, ca. 1550–1680. Bronze, 1′ 7½″ high. Metropolitan Museum of Art, New York (Michael C. Rockefeller Memorial Collection, gift of Nelson A. Rockefeller).

This African artist used hierarchy of scale to distinguish the relative rank of the figures, making the king the largest. The sculptor created the relief by casting (pouring bronze into a mold).

ures, constituent parts of buildings, and so forth. In ancient Greece, many sculptors devised canons of proportions so strict and all-encompassing that they calculated the size of every body part in advance, even the fingers and toes, according to mathematical ratios.

Proportional systems can differ sharply from period to period, culture to culture, and artist to artist. Part of the task art history students face is to perceive and adjust to these differences. In fact, many artists have used disproportion and distortion deliberately for expressive effect. In the medieval French depiction of the weighing of souls on Judgment Day (FIG. I-6), the devilish figure yanking down on the scale has distorted facial features and stretched, lined limbs with animal-like paws for feet. Disproportion and distortion make him appear "inhuman," precisely as the sculptor intended.

In other cases, artists have used disproportion to focus attention on one body part (often the head) or to single out a group member (usually the leader). These intentional "unnatural" discrepancies in proportion constitute what art historians call *hierarchy of scale*, the enlarging of elements considered the most important. On a bronze plaque from Benin, Nigeria (FIG. I-15), the sculptor enlarged all the heads for emphasis and also varied the size of each figure according to its social status. Central, largest, and therefore most important is the Benin king, mounted on horseback. The horse has been a symbol of power and wealth in many societies from prehistory to the present. That the Benin king is disproportionately larger than his horse, contrary to nature, further aggrandizes him. Two large attendants fan the king. Other figures of smaller size and status at the Benin court stand on the king's left and right and in the plaque's upper corners. One tiny figure next to the horse is almost hidden from view beneath the king's feet.

One problem that students of art history—and professional art historians too—confront when studying illustrations in art history books is that although the relative sizes of figures and objects in a painting or sculpture are easy to discern, it is impossible to determine the absolute size of the works reproduced because they all appear at approximately the same size on the page. Readers of *Art through the Ages* can learn the size of all artworks from the dimensions given in the captions and, more intuitively, from the scales that appear—for the first time in this 13th edition—at the lower left or right corner of the illustration.

CARVING AND CASTING Sculptural technique falls into two basic categories, *subtractive* and *additive*. *Carving* is a subtractive technique. The final form is a reduction of the original mass of a block of stone, a piece of wood, or another material. Wooden statues were once tree trunks, and stone statues began as blocks pried from mountains. An unfinished marble statue of a bound slave (FIG. I-16) by the Italian artist MICHELANGELO BUONARROTI (1475–1564) clearly reveals the original shape of the stone block. Michelangelo thought of sculpture as a process of "liberating" the statue within the block. All sculptors of stone or wood cut away (subtract) "excess material." When they finish, they "leave behind" the statue—in this example, a twisting nude male form whose head Michelangelo never freed from the stone block.

In additive sculpture, the artist builds up the forms, usually in clay around a framework, or *armature*. Or a sculptor may fashion a *mold*, a hollow form for shaping, or *casting*, a fluid substance such as bronze or plaster. The ancient Greek sculptor who made the bronze statue of a warrior found in the sea near Riace, Italy, cast the head (FIG. I-17), limbs, torso, hands, and feet in separate molds and then *welded* them together (joined them by heating). Finally, the artist added features, such as the pupils of the eyes (now missing), in other materials. The warrior's teeth are silver, and his lower lip is copper.

profile to give the most complete view of the legs, with both the heels and toes of the foot visible. The frontal torso, however, allows viewers to see its full shape, including both shoulders, equal in size, as in nature. (Compare the shoulders of the hunter on the gray horse or those of the fallen hunter in *Lion Hunt*'s left foreground.) The result, an "unnatural" 90-degree twist at the waist, provides a precise picture of human body parts. Rubens and the Egyptian sculptor used very different means of depicting forms in space. Once again, neither is the "correct" manner, although foreshortening, like perspective, is one of the characteristic features of the Western artistic tradition.

PROPORTION AND SCALE *Proportion* concerns the relationships (in terms of size) of the parts of persons, buildings, or objects. People can judge "correct proportions" intuitively ("that statue's head seems the right size for the body"). Or proportion can be a mathematical relationship between the size of one part of an artwork or building and the other parts within the work. Proportion in art implies using a *module*, or basic unit of measure. When an artist or architect uses a formal system of proportions, all parts of a building, body, or other entity will be fractions or multiples of the module. A module might be a *column*'s diameter, the height of a human head, or any other component whose dimensions can be multiplied or divided to determine the size of the work's other parts.

In certain times and places, artists have formulated *canons*, or systems, of "correct" or "ideal" proportions for representing human fig-

I-16 MICHELANGELO BUONARROTI, unfinished captive, 1527–1528. Marble, 8′ 7½″ high. Galleria dell'Accademia, Florence.

Carving a freestanding figure from stone or wood is a subtractive process. Michelangelo thought of sculpture as a process of "liberating" the statue within the block of marble.

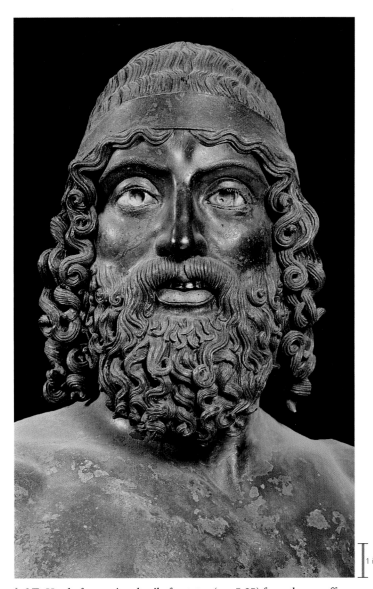

I-17 Head of a warrior, detail of a statue (FIG. 5-35) from the sea off Riace, Italy, ca. 460–450 BCE. Bronze, full statue 6′ 6″ high. Museo Nazionale della Magna Grecia, Reggio Calabria.

The sculptor of this life-size statue of a bearded Greek warrior cast the head, limbs, torso, hands, and feet in separate molds, then welded the pieces together and added the eyes in a different material.

RELIEF SCULPTURE *Statues* that exist independent of any architectural frame or setting and that viewers can walk around are *freestanding* sculptures, or *sculptures in the round*, whether the artist produced the piece by carving (FIG. I-9) or casting (FIG. I-17). In *relief* sculpture, the subjects project from the background but remain part of it. In *high-relief* sculpture, the images project boldly. In the medieval weighing-of-souls scene (FIG. I-6), the relief is so high that not only do the forms cast shadows on the background, but some parts are even in the round, which explains why some pieces, for example the arms of the scale, broke off centuries ago. In *low relief*, or *bas-relief*, such as the portrait of Hesire (FIG. I-14), the projection is slight. Relief sculpture, like sculpture in the round, can be produced either by carving or casting. The plaque from Benin (FIG. I-15) is an example of bronze casting in high relief.

ARCHITECTURAL DRAWINGS Buildings are groupings of enclosed spaces and enclosing masses. People experience architecture both visually and by moving through and around it, so they perceive architectural space and mass together. Architects can represent these spaces and masses graphically in several ways, including as plans, sections, elevations, and cutaway drawings.

A *plan*, essentially a map of a floor, shows the placement of a structure's masses and, therefore, the spaces they circumscribe and enclose. A *section*, like a vertical plan, depicts the placement of the masses as if someone cut through the building along a plane. Drawings showing a theoretical slice across a structure's width are *lateral sections*. Those cutting through a building's length are *longitudinal sections*. Illustrated here are the plan and lateral section of Beauvais Cathedral (FIG. I-18), which may be compared to the photograph of the church's *choir* (FIG. I-2). The plan shows not only the choir's shape and the location of the *piers* dividing the *aisles* and supporting the *vaults* above but also the pattern of the crisscrossing vault *ribs*. The lateral section shows both the interior of the choir with its vaults and tall *stained-glass* windows as well as the roof structure and the form of the exterior *flying buttresses* that hold the vaults in place.

I-18 Plan (*left*) and lateral section (*right*) of Beauvais Cathedral, Beauvais, France, rebuilt after 1284.

Architectural drawings are indispensable aids for the analysis of buildings. Plans are maps of floors, recording the structure's masses. Sections are vertical "slices," across either a building's width or length.

Other types of architectural drawings appear throughout this book. An *elevation* drawing is a head-on view of an external or internal wall. A *cutaway* combines in a single drawing an exterior view with an interior view of part of a building.

This overview of the art historian's vocabulary is not exhaustive, nor have artists used only painting, drawing, sculpture, and architecture as media over the millennia. Ceramics, jewelry, textiles, photography, and computer art are just some of the numerous other arts. All of them involve highly specialized techniques described in distinct vocabularies. As in this introductory chapter, new terms are in *italics* where they first appear. The comprehensive Glossary at the end of the book contains definitions of all italicized terms.

Art History and Other Disciplines

By its very nature, the work of art historians intersects with that of others in many fields of knowledge, not only in the humanities but also in the social and natural sciences. To do their job well today, art historians regularly must go beyond the boundaries of what the public and even professional art historians of previous generations traditionally considered the specialized discipline of art history. In short, art historical research in the 21st century is typically interdisciplinary in nature. To cite one example, in an effort to unlock the secrets of a particular statue, an art historian might conduct archival research hoping to uncover new documents shedding light on who paid for the work and why, who made it and when, where it originally stood, how its contemporaries viewed it, and a host of other questions. Realizing, however, that the authors of the written documents often were not objective recorders of fact but rather observers with their own biases and agendas, the art historian may also use methodologies developed in such fields as literary criticism, philosophy, sociology, and gender studies to weigh the evidence the documents provide.

At other times, rather than attempt to master many disciplines at once, art historians band together with other specialists in multidisciplinary inquiries. Art historians might call in chemists to date an artwork based on the composition of the materials used or might ask geologists to determine which quarry furnished the stone for a particular statue. X-ray technicians might be enlisted in an attempt to establish whether a painting is a forgery. Of course, art historians often reciprocate by contributing their expertise to the solution of problems in other disciplines. A historian, for example, might ask an art historian to determine—based on style, material, iconography, and other criteria—if any of the portraits of a certain king date to after his death. That would help establish the ruler's continuing prestige during the reigns of his successors. (Some portraits of Augustus, FIG. I-9, the founder of the Roman Empire, postdate his death by decades, even centuries.)

DIFFERENT WAYS OF SEEING

The history of art can be a history of artists and their works, of styles and stylistic change, of materials and techniques, of images and themes and their meanings, and of contexts and cultures and patrons. The best art historians analyze artworks from many viewpoints. But no art historian (or scholar in any other field), no matter how broad-minded in approach and no matter how experienced, can be truly objective. Like artists, art historians are members of a society, participants in its culture. How can scholars (and museum visitors and travelers to foreign locales) comprehend cultures unlike their own? They can try to reconstruct the original cultural contexts of artworks, but they are limited by their distance from the thought

I-19 *Left:* John Henry Sylvester, *Portrait of Te Pehi Kupe* (detail), 1826. Watercolor, $8\frac{1}{4}'' \times 6\frac{1}{4}''$. National Library of Australia, Canberra (Rex Nan Kivell Collection). *Right:* Te Pehi Kupe, *Self-Portrait*, 1826. From Leo Frobenius, *The Childhood of Man* (New York: J. B. Lippincott, 1909).

These strikingly different portraits of the same Maori chief reveal how differently Western and non-Western artists "see" a subject. Understanding the cultural context of artworks is vital to art history.

patterns of the cultures they study and by the obstructions to understanding—the assumptions, presuppositions, and prejudices peculiar to their own culture—their own thought patterns raise. Art historians may reconstruct a distorted picture of the past because of culture-bound blindness.

A single instance underscores how differently people of diverse cultures view the world and how various ways of seeing can cause sharp differences in how artists depict the world. Illustrated here are two contemporaneous portraits of a 19th-century Maori chieftain (FIG. I-19)—one by an Englishman, John Sylvester (active early 19th century), and the other by the New Zealand chieftain himself, Te Pehi Kupe (d. 1829). Both reproduce the chieftain's facial tattooing. The European artist (FIG. I-19, *left*) included the head and shoulders and underplayed the tattooing. The tattoo pattern is one aspect of the likeness among many, no more or less important than the chieftain's European attire. Sylvester also recorded his subject's momentary glance toward the right and the play of light on his hair, fleeting aspects that have nothing to do with the figure's identity.

In contrast, Te Pehi Kupe's self-portrait (FIG. I-19, *right*)—made during a trip to Liverpool, England, to obtain European arms to take back to New Zealand—is not a picture of a man situated in space and bathed in light. Rather, it is the chieftain's statement of the supreme importance of the tattoo design that symbolizes his rank among his people. Remarkably, Te Pehi Kupe created the tattoo patterns from memory, without the aid of a mirror. The splendidly composed insignia, presented as a flat design separated from the body and even from the head, is Te Pehi Kupe's image of himself. Only by understanding the cultural context of each portrait can viewers hope to understand why the English representation differs so strikingly from the Maori representation.

As noted at the outset, the study of the context of artworks and buildings is one of the central concerns of art historians. Western art differs in many fundamental ways from other artistic traditions, but even within the Western world, each culture and each period is distinctive. Paintings, sculptures, buildings—indeed, all art forms—changed dramatically with each change of culture, locale, and date. *Art through the Ages: The Western Perspective* seeks to present a history of art and architecture that will help readers understand not only the subjects, styles, and techniques of paintings, sculptures, buildings, and other art forms created in the Western world across 30 millennia but also their cultural and historical contexts. That story now begins.

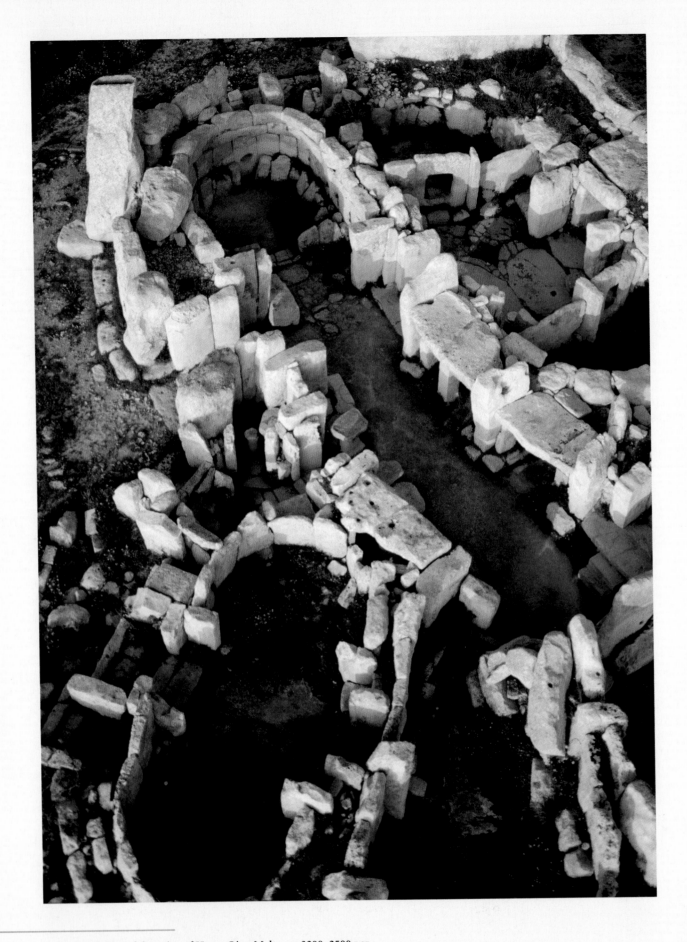

1-1 Aerial view of the ruins of Hagar Qim, Malta, ca. 3200–2500 BCE.

One of the earliest stone temples in the world is on the island of Malta. The 5,000-year-old structure is remarkably sophisticated for its date, especially in the combination of rectilinear and curved forms.

ART BEFORE HISTORY

Humankind seems to have originated in Africa in the very remote past. From that great continent also comes the earliest evidence of human recognition of abstract images in the natural environment, if not the first examples of what people generally call "art." In 1925, explorers of a cave at Makapansgat in South Africa discovered bones of *Australopithecus*, a predecessor of modern humans who lived some three million years ago. Associated with the bones was a waterworn reddish-brown jasperite pebble (FIG. **1-2**) that bears an uncanny resemblance to a human face. The nearest known source of this variety of ironstone is 20 miles away from the cave. One of the early humans who took refuge in the rock shelter at Makapansgat must have noticed the pebble in a streambed and, awestruck by the "face" on the stone, brought it back for safekeeping.

Is the Makapansgat pebble art? In modern times, many artists have created works people universally consider art by removing objects from their normal contexts, altering them, and then labeling them. In 1917, for example, Marcel Duchamp took a ceramic urinal, set it on its side, called it *Fountain* (FIG. **24-27**), and declared his "ready-made" worthy of exhibition among more conventional artworks. But the artistic environment of the past century cannot be projected into the remote past. For art historians to declare a found object such as the Makapansgat pebble an "artwork," it must have been modified by human intervention beyond mere selection—and it was not. In fact, evidence indicates that, with few exceptions, it was not until three million years later, around 30,000 BCE, when large parts of northern Europe were still covered with glaciers during the Ice Age, that humans intentionally manufactured sculptures and paintings. That is when the story of art through the ages really begins.

PALEOLITHIC ART

The several millennia following 30,000 BCE saw a powerful outburst of creativity. The works produced by the peoples of the Old Stone Age or *Paleolithic* period (from the Greek *paleo*, "old," and *lithos*, "stone") are of an astonishing variety. They range from simple shell necklaces to human and animal forms in ivory, clay, and stone to monumental paintings, engravings, and relief sculptures covering the huge wall surfaces of caves. During the Paleolithic period, humankind went beyond the *recognition* of human and animal

1-2 Waterworn pebble resembling a human face, from Makapansgat, South Africa, ca. 3,000,000 BCE. Reddish-brown jasperite, $2\frac{3}{8}''$ wide.

Three million years ago someone recognized a face in this pebble and brought it to a rock shelter for safekeeping, but the stone is not an artwork because it was neither manufactured nor modified.

forms in the natural environment to the *representation* (literally, the presenting again—in different and substitute form—of something observed) of humans and animals. The immensity of this achievement cannot be exaggerated.

Africa

Some of the earliest paintings yet discovered come from Africa, and, like the treasured pebble in the form of a face found at Makapansgat, the oldest African paintings were portable objects.

APOLLO 11 CAVE Between 1969 and 1972, scientists working in the Apollo 11 Cave in Namibia found seven fragments of stone plaques with paint on them, including four or five recognizable images of animals. In most cases, including the example illustrated here (FIG. **1-3**), the species is uncertain, but the forms are always carefully rendered. One plaque depicts a striped beast, possibly a zebra. The charcoal from the archaeological layer in which the Namibian plaques were found has been dated to around 23,000 BCE.

Like every artist in every age in every medium, the painter of the Apollo 11 plaque had to answer two questions before beginning work: *What* shall be my subject? *How* shall I represent it? In Paleolithic art, the almost universal answer to the first question was an animal—bison, mammoth, ibex, and horse were most common. In fact, Paleolithic painters and sculptors depicted humans infrequently and men almost never. In equally stark contrast to today's world, there was also agreement on the best answer to the second question. Artists presented virtually every animal in every Paleolithic, *Mesolithic* (Middle Stone Age), and *Neolithic* (New Stone Age) painting in the same manner—in strict profile. The profile is the only view of an animal wherein the head, body, tail, and all four legs can be seen. A frontal view would have concealed most of the body, and a three-quarter view would not have shown either the front or side fully. Only the profile view is completely informative about the animal's shape, and this is why the Stone Age painter chose it. A very long time passed before artists placed any pre-

1-3 Animal facing left, from the Apollo 11 Cave, Namibia, ca. 23,000 BCE. Charcoal on stone, $5'' \times 4\frac{1}{4}''$. State Museum of Namibia, Windhoek.

Like most other paintings for thousands of years, this very early example from Africa represents an animal in strict profile so that the head, body, tail, and all four legs are clearly visible.

mium on "variety" or "originality," either in subject choice or in representational manner. These are quite modern notions in the history of art. The aim of the earliest painters was to create a convincing image of the subject, a kind of pictorial definition of the animal capturing its very essence, and only the profile view met their needs.

Western Europe

Even older than the Namibian painted plaques are some of the first sculptures and paintings of western Europe (MAP **1-1**), although examples of still greater antiquity may yet be found in Africa, bridging the gap between the Makapansgat pebble and the Apollo 11 painted plaques.

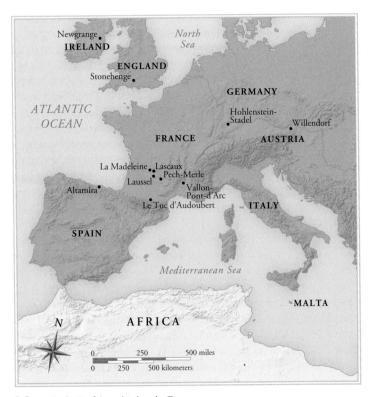

MAP **1-1** Prehistoric sites in Europe.

One of the oldest known sculptures is this large ivory figure of a human with a feline head. It is uncertain whether the work depicts a composite creature or a human wearing an animal mask.

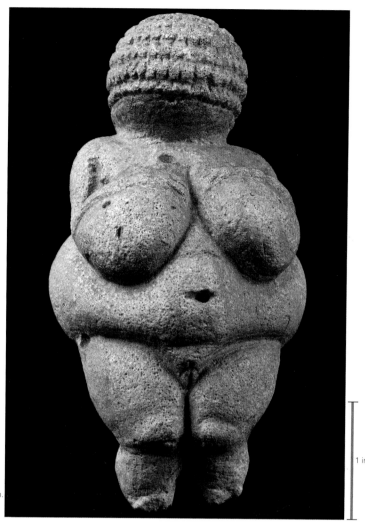

1-5 Nude woman (*Venus of Willendorf*), from Willendorf, Austria, ca. 28,000–25,000 BCE. Limestone, $4\frac{1}{4}''$ high. Naturhistorisches Museum, Vienna.

The anatomical exaggerations in this tiny figurine from Willendorf are typical of Paleolithic representations of women, whose child-bearing capabilities ensured the survival of the species.

HOHLENSTEIN-STADEL

One of the earliest sculptures discovered yet is an extraordinary ivory statuette (FIG. **1-4**), which may date back as far as 30,000 BCE. It was found in fragments inside a cave at Hohlenstein-Stadel in Germany and has been meticulously restored. Carved out of mammoth ivory and nearly a foot tall—a truly huge image for its era—the statuette represents something that existed only in the vivid imagination of the unknown sculptor who conceived it. It is a human (whether male or female is debated) with a feline head. Such composite creatures with animal heads and human bodies (and vice versa) were common in the art of the ancient Near East and Egypt (compare, for example, FIGS. **2-10**, *right,* and **3-36**). In those civilizations, surviving texts usually allow historians to name the figures and describe their role in contemporary religion and mythology. But for Stone Age representations, no one knows what their makers had in mind. The animal-headed humans of Paleolithic art sometimes have been called sorcerers and described as magicians wearing masks. Similarly, Paleolithic human-headed animals have been interpreted as humans dressed up as animals. In the absence of any Stone Age written explanations—this is a time before writing, before (or pre-) history—researchers can only speculate on the purpose and function of a statuette such as that from Hohlenstein-Stadel.

Art historians are certain, however, that these statuettes were important to those who created them, because manufacturing an ivory figure, especially one a foot tall, was a complicated process. First, a tusk had to be removed from the dead animal by cutting into the ivory where it joined the head. The sculptor then cut the tusk to the desired size and rubbed it into its approximate final shape with sandstone. Finally, a sharp stone blade was used to carve the body, limbs, and head, and a stone *burin* (a pointed engraving tool) to *incise* (scratch) lines into the surfaces, as on the Hohlenstein-Stadel creature's arms. All this probably required at least several days of skilled work.

VENUS OF WILLENDORF The composite feline-human from Germany is exceptional for the Stone Age. The vast majority of prehistoric sculptures depict either animals or humans. In the earliest art, humankind consists almost exclusively of women as opposed to men, and the painters and sculptors almost invariably showed them nude, although scholars generally assume that during the Ice Age both women and men wore garments covering parts of their bodies. When archaeologists first discovered Paleolithic statuettes of women, they dubbed them "Venuses," after the Greco-Roman goddess of beauty and love, whom artists usually depicted nude (FIG. **5-62**). The nickname is inappropriate and misleading. It is doubtful that the Old Stone Age figurines represented deities of any kind.

One of the oldest and the most famous of the prehistoric female figures is the tiny limestone figurine of a woman that long has been known as the *Venus of Willendorf* (FIG. **1-5**) after its *findspot* in Austria. Its cluster of almost ball-like shapes is unusual, the result in part of the sculptor's response to the natural shape of the stone selected for carving. The anatomical exaggeration has suggested to many that this and similar statuettes served as fertility images. But other Paleolithic stone women of far more slender proportions exist, and the meaning of these images is as elusive as everything else about Paleolithic art. Yet the preponderance of female over male figures in the Old Stone Age seems to indicate a preoccupation with women, whose child-bearing capabilities ensured the survival of the species.

One thing at least is clear. The *Venus of Willendorf* sculptor did not aim for naturalism in shape and proportion. As with most Paleolithic figures, the sculptor did not carve any facial features. Here the carver suggested only a mass of curly hair or, as some researchers have recently argued, a hat woven from plant fibers—evidence for the art of textile manufacture at a very early date. In either case, the emphasis is on female anatomy. The breasts of the Willendorf woman are enormous, far larger than the tiny forearms and hands that rest upon them. The carver also took pains to scratch into the stone the outline of the pubic triangle. Sculptors often omitted this detail in other early figurines, leading some scholars to question the nature of these figures as fertility images. Whatever the purpose of these statuettes, the makers' intent seems to have been to represent not a specific woman but the female form.

LAUSSEL Because precision in dating is impossible for the Paleolithic era, art historians usually can be no more specific than assigning a range of several thousand years to each artifact. But probably later in date than the *Venus of Willendorf* is a female figure (FIG. 1-6) from Laussel in France. The Willendorf and Hohlenstein-Stadel figures were *sculpted in the round* (that is, they are *freestanding sculptures*). The Laussel woman is one of the earliest *relief sculptures* known. The sculptor employed a stone *chisel* to cut into the relatively flat surface of a large rock and create an image that projects from its background.

Today the Laussel relief is exhibited in a museum, divorced from its original context, a detached piece of what once was a much more imposing monument. When the relief was discovered, the Laussel woman (who is about $1\frac{1}{2}$ feet tall, more than four times larger than the Willendorf statuette) was part of a great stone block that measured about 140 cubic feet. The carved block stood in the open air in front of a Paleolithic rock shelter. Rock shelters were a common type of dwelling for early humans, along with huts and the mouths of caves. The Laussel relief is one of many examples of open-air art in the Old Stone Age. The popular notions that early humans dwelled exclusively in caves and that all Paleolithic art comes from mysterious dark caverns are false.

After chiseling out the female form and incising the details with a sharp burin, the Laussel sculptor applied red ocher, a naturally colored mineral, to the body. (The same color is also preserved on parts of the *Venus of Willendorf.*) Contrary to modern misconceptions about ancient art, stone sculptures were frequently painted in antiquity. The Laussel woman has the same bulbous forms as the earlier Willendorf figurine, with a similar exaggeration of the breasts, abdomen, and hips. The head is once again featureless, but the arms have taken on greater importance. The left arm draws attention to the midsection and pubic area, and the raised right hand holds what most scholars identify as a bison horn. The meaning of the horn is debated.

LE TUC D'AUDOUBERT Paleolithic sculptors sometimes created reliefs by building up forms out of clay rather than by cutting into stone blocks or stone walls. Sometime 12,000 to 17,000 years ago in the low-ceilinged circular space at the end of a succession of cave chambers at Le Tuc d'Audoubert, a master sculptor modeled a pair of bison (FIG. 1-7) in clay against a large, irregular freestanding rock. The two bison, like the much older painted animal (FIG. 1-3) from the Apollo 11 Cave, are in strict profile. Each is about two feet long. They are among the largest Paleolithic sculptures known. The sculptor brought the clay from elsewhere in the cave complex and modeled it by hand into the overall shape of the animals. The artist then

1-6 Woman holding a bison horn, from Laussel, France, ca. 25,000–20,000 BCE. Painted limestone, 1′ 6″ high. Musée d'Aquitaine, Bordeaux.

One of the oldest known relief sculptures depicts a woman who holds a bison horn and whose left arm draws attention to her belly. Scholars continue to debate the meaning of the gesture and the horn.

smoothed the surfaces with a spatula-like tool and finally used fingers to shape the eyes, nostrils, mouths, and manes. The cracks in the two animals resulted from the drying process and probably appeared within days of the sculptures' completion.

LA MADELEINE As already noted, sculptors fashioned ivory mammoth tusks into human and animal (FIG. 1-4) forms from very early times. Prehistoric carvers also used antlers as a sculptural medium, even though it meant they were forced to work on a very small scale. The broken spearthrower (FIG. 1-8) in the form of a bison found at La Madeleine in France is only four inches long and was carved from reindeer antler. The sculptor incised lines into the bison's mane using a sharp burin. Compared to the bison at Le Tuc d'Audoubert, the engraving is much more detailed and extends to the horns, eye, ear, nostrils, mouth, and the hair on the face. Especially interesting is the engraver's decision to represent the bison with the head turned. The small size of the reindeer horn may have been the motivation for this space-saving device. Whatever the reason, it is noteworthy that the sculptor turned the neck a full 180 degrees to maintain the strict profile Paleolithic sculptors and painters insisted on for the sake of clarity and completeness.

1-7 Two bison, reliefs in a cave at Le Tuc d'Audoubert, France, ca. 15,000–10,000 BCE. Clay, each 2′ long.

Representations of animals are far more common than of humans in Paleolithic European art. The sculptor built up these clay bison using a stone spatula-like smoothing tool and fingers to shape the details.

1 ft.

ALTAMIRA The works examined here thus far, whether portable or fixed to rocky outcroppings or cave walls, are all small. They are dwarfed by the "herds" of painted animals that roam the cave walls of southern France and northern Spain, where some of the most spectacular prehistoric art has been discovered (see "Paleolithic Cave Painting," page 6). The first examples of cave paintings were found accidentally by an amateur archaeologist in 1879 at Altamira, Spain. Don Marcelino Sanz de Sautuola was exploring a cave where he had already found specimens of flint and carved bone. His little daughter Maria was with him when they reached a chamber some 85 feet from the cave's entrance. Because it was dark and the ceiling of the debris-filled cavern was only a few inches above the father's head, the child was the first to discern, from her lower vantage point, the shadowy forms of painted beasts on the cave roof (FIG. **1-9**, a detail of a much

1 in.

1 ft.

1-8 Bison with turned head, fragmentary spearthrower, from La Madeleine, France, ca. 12,000 BCE. Reindeer horn, 4″ long.

This fragment of a spearthrower was carved from reindeer antler. Details were incised with a stone burin. The sculptor turned the bison's head a full 180 degrees to maintain the profile view.

1-9 Bison, detail of a painted ceiling in the cave at Altamira, Spain, ca. 12,000–11,000 BCE. Each bison 5′ long.

As in other Paleolithic caves, the painted ceiling at Altamira has no ground line or indication of setting. The artist's sole concern was representing the animals, not locating them in a specific place.

Paleolithic Cave Painting

The caves of Altamira (FIG. 1-9), Pech-Merle (FIG. 1-10), Lascaux (FIGS. 1-11 and 1-13), and other sites in prehistoric Europe are a few hundred to several thousand feet long. They are often choked, sometimes almost impassably, by deposits, such as stalactites and stalagmites. Far inside these caverns, well removed from the cave mouths early humans often chose for habitation, painters sometimes made pictures on the walls. Examples of Paleolithic painting now have been found at more than 200 sites, but prehistorians still regard painted caves as rare occurrences, because the images in them, even if they number in the hundreds, were created over a period of some 10,000 to 20,000 years.

To illuminate the surfaces while working, the Paleolithic painters used stone lamps filled with marrow or fat, with a wick, perhaps, of moss. For drawing, they used chunks of red and yellow ocher. For painting, they ground these same ochers into powders they mixed with water before applying. Recent analyses of the pigments used show that Paleolithic painters employed many different minerals, attesting to a technical sophistication surprising at so early a date.

Large flat stones served as *palettes.* The painters made brushes from reeds, bristles, or twigs, and may have used a blowpipe of reeds or hollow bones to spray pigments on out-of-reach surfaces. Some caves have natural ledges on the rock walls upon which the painters could have stood in order to reach the upper surfaces of the naturally formed chambers and corridors. One Lascaux gallery has holes in one of the walls that once probably anchored a scaffold made of saplings lashed together. Despite the difficulty of making the tools and pigments, modern attempts at replicating the techniques of Paleolithic painting have demonstrated that skilled workers could cover large surfaces with images in less than a day.

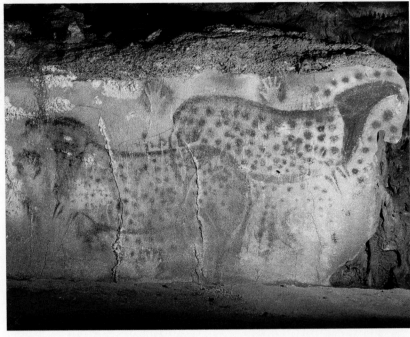

1 ft.

1-10 Spotted horses and negative hand imprints, wall painting in the cave at Pech-Merle, France, ca. 22,000 BCE. 11′ 2″ long.

The purpose and meaning of Paleolithic art are unknown. Some researchers think the painted hands near the Pech-Merle horses are "signatures" of community members or of individual painters.

larger painting approximately 60 feet long). Sanz de Sautuola was certain the bison painted on the ceiling of the cave on his estate dated back to prehistoric times. Professional archaeologists, however, doubted the authenticity of these works, and at the Lisbon Congress on Prehistoric Archaeology in 1880, they officially dismissed the paintings as forgeries. But by the close of the century, other caves had been discovered with painted walls partially covered by mineral deposits that would have taken thousands of years to accumulate. This finally persuaded skeptics that the first paintings were of an age far more remote than they had ever dreamed.

The bison at Altamira are 13,000 to 14,000 years old, but the painters of Paleolithic Spain approached the problem of representing an animal in essentially the same way as the painter of the Namibian stone plaque (FIG. 1-3), who worked in Africa more than 10,000 years earlier. Every one of the Altamira bison is in profile, whether alive and standing or curled up on the ground (probably dead, although this is disputed; one suggestion is that these bison are giving birth). To maintain the profile in the latter case, the painter had to adopt a viewpoint above the animal, looking down, rather than the view a person standing on the ground would have.

Modern critics often refer to the Altamira animals as a "group" of bison, but that is very likely a misnomer. In FIG. 1-9, the several bison do not stand on a common *ground line* (a painted or carved baseline on which figures appear to stand in paintings and reliefs), nor do they share a common orientation. They seem almost to float above viewers' heads, like clouds in the sky. And the dead(?) bison are seen in an "aerial view," while the others are seen from a position on the ground. The painting has no setting, no background, no indication of place. The Paleolithic painter was not at all concerned with *where* the animals were or with how they related to one another, if at all. Instead, several *separate* images of a bison adorn the ceiling, perhaps painted at different times, and each is as complete and informative as possible—even if their meaning remains a mystery (see "Art in the Old Stone Age," page 7).

PECH-MERLE That the paintings did have meaning to the Paleolithic peoples who made and observed them cannot, however, be doubted. In fact, signs consisting of checks, dots, squares, or other arrangements of lines often accompany the pictures of animals. Representations of human hands also are common. At Pech-Merle in France, painted hands accompany representations of spotted horses (FIG. 1-10). These and the majority of painted hands at other sites are "negative;" that is, the painter placed one hand against the wall and then brushed or blew or spat pigment around it. Occasionally,

Art in the Old Stone Age

From the moment in 1879 that cave paintings were discovered at Altamira (FIG. 1-9), scholars have wondered why the hunters of the Old Stone Age decided to cover the walls of dark caverns with animal images like those found at Altamira, Pech-Merle (FIG. 1-10), Lascaux (FIGS. 1-11 and 1-13), and Vallon-Pont-d'Arc (FIG. 1-12). Scholars have proposed various theories including that the painted and engraved animals were mere decoration, but this explanation cannot account for the narrow range of subjects or the inaccessibility of many of the representations. In fact, the remoteness and difficulty of access of many of the images, and indications that the caves were used for centuries, are precisely why many researchers have suggested that the prehistoric hunters attributed magical properties to the images they painted and sculpted. According to this argument, by confining animals to the surfaces of their cave walls, the Paleolithic hunters believed they were bringing the beasts under their control. Some prehistorians have even hypothesized that rituals or dances were performed in front of the images and that these rites served to improve the hunters' luck. Still others have stated that the animal representations may have served as teaching tools to instruct new hunters about the character of the various species they would encounter or even to serve as targets for spears.

In contrast, some scholars have argued that the magical purpose of the paintings and reliefs was not to facilitate the *destruction* of bison and other species. Instead, they believe prehistoric painters and sculptors created animal images to assure the *survival* of the herds on which Paleolithic peoples depended for their food supply and for their clothing. A central problem for both the hunting-magic and food-creation theories is that the animals that seem to have been diet staples of Old Stone Age peoples are not those most frequently portrayed. For example, faunal remains show that the Altamirans ate red deer, not bison.

Other scholars have sought to reconstruct an elaborate mythology based on the cave paintings and sculptures, suggesting that Paleolithic humans believed they had animal ancestors. Still others have equated certain species with men and others with women and postulated various meanings for the abstract signs that sometimes accompany the images. Almost all of these theories have been discredited over time, and most prehistorians admit that no one knows the intent of these representations. In fact, a single explanation for all Paleolithic animal images, even ones similar in subject, style, and *composition* (how the motifs are arranged on the surface), is unlikely to apply universally. The works remain an enigma—and always will, because before the invention of writing, no contemporaneous explanations could be recorded.

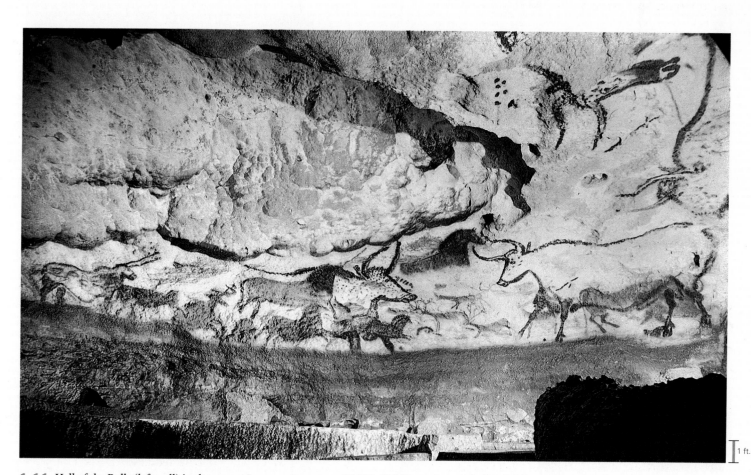

1 ft.

1-11 Hall of the Bulls (left wall) in the cave at Lascaux, France, ca. 15,000–13,000 BCE. Largest bull 11′ 6″ long.

Several species of animals appear together in the Hall of the Bulls. Many are colored silhouettes, but others were created by outline alone—the two basic approaches to painting in the history of art.

The World's Oldest Paintings?

One of the most spectacular archaeological finds of the past century came to light in December 1994 at Vallon-Pont-d'Arc, France, and was announced at a press conference in Paris on January 18, 1995. Unlike some other recent "finds" of prehistoric art that proved to be forgeries, the paintings in the Chauvet Cave (named after the leader of the exploration team, Jean-Marie Chauvet) seemed to be authentic. But no one, including Chauvet and his colleagues, guessed at the time of their discovery that *radiocarbon dating* (a measure of the rate of degeneration of carbon 14 in organic materials) of the paintings might establish that the murals in the cave were more than 15,000 years older than those at Altamira (FIG. 1-9). When the scientific tests were completed, the French archaeologists announced that the Chauvet Cave paintings were the oldest yet found anywhere, datable around 30,000–28,000 BCE.

This new early date immediately caused scholars to reevaluate the scheme of "stylistic development" from simple to more complex forms that had been nearly universally accepted for decades. In the Chauvet Cave, in contrast to Lascaux (FIG. 1-11), the horns of the aurochs (extinct long-horned wild oxen) are shown naturalistically,

one behind the other, not in the twisted perspective thought to be universally characteristic of Paleolithic art. Moreover, the two rhinoceroses at the lower right of FIG. 1-12 appear to confront each other, suggesting to some observers that the artist intended a narrative, another "first" in either painting or sculpture. If the paintings are twice as old as those of Lascaux, Altamira (FIG. 1-9), and Pech-Merle (FIG. 1-10), the assumption that Paleolithic art "evolved" from simple to more sophisticated representations is wrong.

Much research remains to be conducted in the Chauvet Cave, but already the paintings have become the subject of intense controversy. Recently, some archaeologists have contested the early dating of the Chauvet paintings on the grounds that the tested samples were contaminated. If the Chauvet animals were painted later than those at Lascaux, their advanced stylistic features can be more easily explained. The dispute exemplifies the frustration—and the excitement—of studying the art of an age so remote that almost nothing remains and almost every new find causes art historians to reevaluate what had previously been taken for granted.

1-12 Aurochs, horses, and rhinoceroses, wall painting in the Chauvet Cave, Vallon-Pont-d'Arc, France, ca. 30,000–28,000 or ca. 15,000–13,000 BCE.

The date of the Chauvet Cave paintings is the subject of much controversy. If the murals are the oldest paintings known, they exhibit surprisingly advanced features, such as overlapping animal horns.

1 ft.

the painter dipped a hand in the pigment and then pressed it against the wall, leaving a "positive" imprint. These handprints, too, must have had a purpose. Some researchers have considered them "signatures" of cult or community members or, less likely, of individual painters. But like everything else in Paleolithic art, their meaning is unknown.

The *mural* (wall) paintings at Pech-Merle also allow some insight into the reason certain subjects may have been chosen for a specific location. One of the horses (at the right in FIG. 1-10) may have been inspired by the rock formation in the wall surface resembling a horse's head and neck. Old Stone Age painters and sculptors

frequently and skillfully used the caves' naturally irregular surfaces to help give the illusion of real presence to their forms. Many of the Altamira bison (FIG. 1-9), for example, were painted over bulging rock surfaces. In fact, prehistorians have observed that bison and cattle appear almost exclusively on convex surfaces, whereas nearly all horses and hands are painted on concave surfaces. What this signifies has yet to be determined.

LASCAUX Perhaps the best-known Paleolithic cave is that at Lascaux, near Montignac, France. It is extensively decorated, but most of the paintings are hundreds of feet from any entrance, far removed from the daylight. The largest painted area at Lascaux is the so-called Hall of the Bulls (FIG. 1-11), although not all of the animals depicted are bulls. Many are represented using colored silhouettes, as at Altamira (FIG. 1-9) and on the Apollo 11 plaque (FIG. 1-3). Others—such as the great bull at the right in FIG. 1-11—were created by outline alone, as were the Pech-Merle horses (FIG. 1-10). On the walls of the Lascaux cave one sees, side by side, the two basic approaches to drawing and painting found repeatedly in the history of art. These differences in style and technique alone suggest that the animals in the Hall of the Bulls were painted at different times, and the modern impression of a rapidly moving herd of beasts was probably not the original intent. In any case, the "herd" consists of several different kinds of animals of various sizes moving in different directions.

Another feature of the Lascaux paintings deserves attention. The bulls there show a convention of representing horns that has been called *twisted perspective* or a *composite view,* because viewers see the heads in profile but the horns from the front. Thus, the painter's approach is not strictly or consistently optical (seen from a fixed viewpoint). Rather, the approach is descriptive of the fact that cattle have two horns. Two horns are part of the concept "bull." In strict optical-perspective profile, only one horn would be visible, but to paint the animal in that way would amount to an incomplete definition of it. This kind of twisted perspective was the norm in prehistoric painting, but it was not universal. In fact, the recent discovery at Vallon-Pont-d'Arc in France of Paleolithic paintings (FIG. 1-12) in the Chauvet Cave, where the painters represented horns in a more natural way, has caused art historians to rethink many of the assumptions they had made about Paleolithic art (see "The World's Oldest Paintings?" page 8).

Perhaps the most perplexing painting (FIG. 1-13) in the Paleolithic caves of Europe is deep in a well shaft at Lascaux, where man (as opposed to woman) makes one of his earliest appearances in prehistoric art. At the left, and moving to the left, is a rhinoceros, rendered with all the skilled attention to animal detail customarily seen in cave art. Beneath its tail are two rows of three dots of uncertain significance. At the right is a bison, also facing left but more schematically painted, probably by someone else. The second painter nonetheless successfully suggested the bristling rage of the animal, whose bowels are hanging from it in a heavy coil. Between the two beasts is a bird-faced (masked?) man (compare the feline-headed human, FIG. 1-4, from Hohlenstein-Stadel) with outstretched arms and hands with only four fingers. The man is depicted with far less care and detail than either animal, but the painter made the hunter's gender explicit by the prominent penis. The position of the man is ambiguous. Is he wounded or dead or merely tilted back and unharmed? Do the staff(?) with the bird on top and the spear belong to him? Is it he or the rhinoceros who has gravely wounded the bison—or neither? Which animal, if either, has knocked the man down, if indeed he is on the ground? Are these three images related at all? Researchers can be sure of nothing, but if the painter placed the figures beside each other to tell a story, then this is evidence for the creation of complex narrative compositions involving humans and animals at a much earlier date than anyone had imagined only a few generations ago. Yet it is important to remember that even if the artist intended to tell a story, very few people would have been able to "read" it. The painting, in a deep shaft, is very difficult to reach and could have been viewed only in flickering lamplight. Like all Paleolithic art, the scene in the Lascaux well shaft remains enigmatic.

1-13 Rhinoceros, wounded man, and disemboweled bison, painting in the well of the cave at Lascaux, France, ca. 15,000–13,000 BCE. Bison 3′ 8″ long.

If these paintings of two animals and a bird-faced (masked?) man deep in a Lascaux well shaft depict a hunting scene, they constitute the earliest example of narrative art ever discovered.

NEOLITHIC ART

Around 9000 BCE, the ice that covered much of northern Europe during the Paleolithic period melted as the climate grew warmer. The sea level rose more than 300 feet, separating England from continental Europe and Spain from Africa. The reindeer migrated north, and the woolly mammoth disappeared. The Paleolithic gave way to a transitional period, the Mesolithic, and then, for several thousand years at different times in different parts of the globe, a great new age, the Neolithic, dawned. Human beings began to domesticate plants and animals and to settle in fixed abodes. Their food supply assured, many groups changed from hunters to herders, to farmers, and finally to townspeople. Wandering hunters settled down to organized community living in villages surrounded by cultivated fields.

The basis for the conventional division of prehistory into the Paleolithic, Mesolithic, and Neolithic periods is the development of stone implements. However, a different kind of distinction may be made between an age of food gathering and an age of food production. In this scheme, the Paleolithic period corresponds roughly to the age of food gathering, and the Mesolithic period, the last phase of that age, is marked by intensified food gathering and the taming of the dog. In the Neolithic period, agriculture and stock raising became humankind's major food sources. The transition to the Neolithic occurred first in the ancient Near East.

Ancient Near East

The remains of the oldest known settled communities have been found in the grassy foothills of the Antilebanon, Taurus, and Zagros mountains in present-day Turkey, Syria, Iraq, and Iran (MAP 1-2). These regions provided the necessary preconditions for the development of agriculture. Species of native plants, such as wild wheat and barley, were plentiful, as were herds of animals (goats, sheep, and pigs) that could be domesticated. Sufficient rain occurred for the raising of crops. When village farming life was well developed, some settlers, attracted by the greater fertility of the soil and perhaps also by the need to find more land for their rapidly growing populations, moved into the valleys and deltas of the Tigris and Euphrates rivers.

In addition to systematic agriculture, the new sedentary societies of the Neolithic Age originated weaving, metalworking, pottery, and counting and recording with clay tokens. Soon, these innovations spread with remarkable speed throughout the Near East. Village farming communities such as Jarmo in Iraq and Çatal Höyük in southern Anatolia date back to the mid-seventh millennium BCE. The remarkable fortified town of Jericho, before whose walls the biblical Joshua appeared thousands of years later, is even older. Archaeologists are constantly uncovering surprises, and the discovery and exploration of new sites each year are compelling them to revise their views about the emergence of Neolithic society. But three sites known for some time—Jericho, Ain Ghazal, and Çatal Höyük—offer a fascinating picture of the rapid and exciting transformation of human society and of art during the Neolithic period.

JERICHO By 7000 BCE, agriculture was well established from Anatolia to ancient Palestine and Iran. Its advanced state by this date presupposes a long development. Indeed, the very existence of a major settlement such as Jericho gives strong support to this assumption. The site of Jericho—a plateau in the Jordan River valley with a spring that provided a constant water supply—was occupied by a small village as early as the ninth millennium BCE. This village

MAP 1-2 Neolithic sites in Anatolia and the Near East.

underwent spectacular development around 8000 BCE, when the inhabitants built a new Neolithic settlement covering about 10 acres. Its mud-brick houses sat on round or oval stone foundations and had roofs of branches covered with earth.

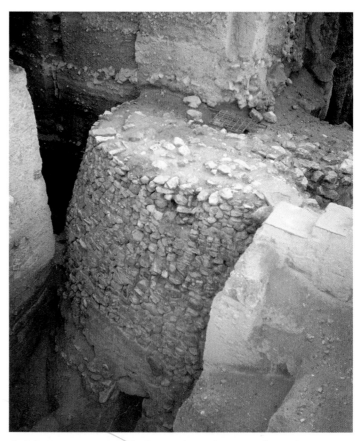

1-14 Great stone tower built into the settlement wall, Jericho, ca. 8000–7000 BCE.

Neolithic Jericho was protected by 5-foot-thick walls and at least one stone tower 30 feet high and 33 feet in diameter—an outstanding achievement that marks the beginning of monumental architecture.

As Jericho's wealth grew, the need for protection against marauding nomads resulted in the first known permanent stone fortifications. By approximately 7500 BCE, a wide rock-cut ditch and a 5-foot-thick wall surrounded the town, estimated to have had a population of more than 2,000 people. Into the circuit wall, which has been preserved to a height of almost 13 feet, was built a great circular tower (FIG. 1-14) of roughly shaped stones laid without mortar and originally about 30 feet high. Almost 33 feet in diameter at the base, the tower has an inner stairway leading to its summit. (Today, a grate covers the entrance to the stairway.) Not enough of the site has been excavated to determine whether this tower was solitary or one of several similar towers that formed a complete defense system. In either case, a structure as large as this was a tremendous technological achievement and a testimony to the builders' ability to organize a significant workforce. The walls and tower(s) of Jericho mark the beginning of the long history of monumental architecture.

AIN GHAZAL Near Amman, Jordan, the construction of a highway in 1974 revealed another important Neolithic settlement in ancient Palestine at the site of Ain Ghazal, occupied from ca. 7200 to ca. 5000 BCE. The inhabitants built houses of irregularly shaped stones, but carefully plastered and then painted their floors and walls red. The most striking finds at Ain Ghazal, however, are two caches containing three dozen plaster statuettes (FIG. 1-15) and busts, some with two heads, datable to ca. 6500 BCE. The sculptures appear to have been ritually buried. The figures were fashioned of white plaster, which was built up over a core of reeds and twine. The sculptors used black bitumen, a tarlike substance, to delineate the pupils of the eyes. On some of the later figures painters added clothing. Only rarely did the artists indicate the gender of the figures. Whatever their purpose, by their size (as much as three feet tall) and sophisticated technique, the Ain Ghazal statuettes and busts are distinguished from Paleolithic figurines such as the tiny *Venus of Willendorf* (FIG. 1-5) and even the foot-tall Hohlenstein-Stadel ivory statuette (FIG. 1-4). They mark the beginning of monumental sculpture in the ancient Near East.

ÇATAL HÖYÜK Remarkable discoveries also have been made in Anatolia. Excavations at Hacilar, Çatal Höyük, and elsewhere have shown that the central Anatolian plateau was the site of a flourishing Neolithic culture between 7000 and 5000 BCE. Twelve successive building levels excavated at Çatal Höyük between 1961 and 1965 have been dated between 6500 and 5700 BCE. On a single site, it is possible to retrace the evolution of a Neolithic culture over a period of 800 years. An

1-15 Human figure, from Ain Ghazal, Jordan, ca. 6750–6250 BCE. Plaster, painted and inlaid with bitumen, 3′ 5⅜″ high. Louvre, Paris.

The dozens of large white plaster statuettes, some with two heads and with details added in paint, found at Ain Ghazal date to the mid-seventh millennium BCE and are the earliest large sculptures known.

1 ft.

important source of Çatal Höyük's wealth was trade, especially in obsidian, a glasslike volcanic stone Neolithic toolmakers and weapon makers valued highly because it could be chipped into fine cutting edges. Along with Jericho, Çatal Höyük seems to have been one of the first experiments in urban living. The regularity of its plan suggests that the town was built according to some predetermined scheme. A peculiar feature is the settlement's complete lack of streets. The houses adjoin one another and have no doors (FIG. 1-16). Openings in the roofs provided access to the interiors. The openings also served as chimneys to ventilate the hearth in the combination living room and kitchen that

1-16 Restored view of a section of Level VI, Çatal Höyük, Turkey, ca. 6000–5900 BCE (John Swogger).

Archaeologists have discovered 12 successive building levels at Çatal Höyük. The houses in this early city adjoined one another and had no doors. Openings in the roofs provided access to the interiors.

formed the core of the house. Impractical as such an arrangement may appear today, it did offer some advantages. The attached buildings were more stable than freestanding structures and, at the limits of the town site, formed a defensive perimeter wall. If enemies managed to breach the exterior wall, they would find themselves not inside the town but above the houses with the defenders waiting there on the roof.

The houses, constructed of mud brick strengthened by sturdy timber frames, varied in size but repeated the same basic plan. Walls and floors were plastered and painted, and platforms along walls served as sites for sleeping, working, and eating. The dead were buried beneath the same platforms. A great number of decorated rooms have been found at Çatal Höyük. The excavators called these rooms shrines, but their function is uncertain. Their number suggests that these rooms played an important role in the life of Çatal Höyük's inhabitants.

The "shrines" are distinguished from the house structures by the greater richness of their interior decoration, which consisted of wall paintings, plaster reliefs, animal heads, and *bucrania* (bovine skulls). Bulls' horns, widely thought to be symbols of masculine potency, are the most common motif in these rooms. In some cases they are displayed next to plaster breasts, symbols of female fertility, projecting from the walls. Many statuettes of stone or *terracotta* (baked clay) also have been found at Çatal Höyük. Most are quite small (2 to 8 inches high) and primarily depict female figures. A few reach 12 inches.

Although animal husbandry was well established, hunting continued to play an important part in the early Neolithic economy of Çatal Höyük. The importance of hunting as a food source (until about 5700 BCE) is reflected also in wall paintings, where, in the older decorated rooms, hunting scenes predominate. In style and concept, however, the deer hunt mural (FIG. 1-17) at Çatal Höyük is worlds apart from the wall paintings the hunters of the Paleolithic period produced. Perhaps what is most strikingly new about the Çatal Höyük painting and others like it is the regular appearance of the human figure—not only singly but also in large, coherent groups with a wide variety of poses, subjects, and settings. As noted earlier, humans were unusual in Paleolithic cave paintings, and pictorial narratives have almost never been found. Even the "hunting scene" (FIG. 1-13) in the well at Lascaux is doubtful as a narrative. In Neolithic paintings, human themes and concerns and action scenes with humans dominating animals are central.

In the Çatal Höyük hunt, the group of hunters—and no one doubts it is, indeed, an organized hunting party, not a series of individual figures—shows a tense exaggeration of movement and a rhythmic repetition of basic shapes customary for the period. The painter took care to distinguish important descriptive details—for example, bows, arrows, and garments—and the heads have clearly defined noses, mouths, chins, and hair. The Neolithic painter placed all the heads in profile for the same reason Paleolithic painters universally chose the profile view for representations of animals. Only the side view of the human head shows all its shapes clearly. However, at Çatal Höyük the torsos are presented from the front—again, the most informative viewpoint—whereas the painter chose the profile view for the legs and arms. This composite view of the human body is quite artificial because the human body cannot make an abrupt 90-degree shift at the hips. But it is very descriptive of what a human body is—as opposed to what it looks like from a particular viewpoint. The technique of painting also changed dramatically since Paleolithic times. The pigments were applied with a brush to a white background of dry plaster. The careful preparation of the wall surface is in striking contrast to the direct application of pigment to the irregularly shaped walls and ceilings of caves.

More remarkable still is a painting (FIG. 1-18 is a watercolor copy) in one of the older rooms at Çatal Höyük that art historians generally have acclaimed as the world's first *landscape* (a picture of a natural setting in its own right, without any narrative content). As such, it remained unique for thousands of years. According to radiocarbon dating, the painting was executed around 6150 BCE. The foreground has been interpreted as a town with rectangular houses neatly laid out side by side, probably representing Çatal Höyük itself.

1-17 Deer hunt, detail of a wall painting from Level III, Çatal Höyük, Turkey, ca. 5750 BCE. Museum of Anatolian Civilization, Ankara.

This Neolithic painter depicted human figures as a composite of frontal and profile views, the most descriptive picture of the shape of the human body. This format would become the rule for millennia.

1-18 Landscape with volcanic eruption(?), watercolor copy of a wall painting from Level VII, Çatal Höyük, Turkey, ca. 6150 BCE.

This late-seventh-millennium BCE mural painting may represent Çatal Höyük during a volcanic eruption. It is the first known landscape painting in which neither humans nor animals appear.

Behind the town appears a mountain with two peaks. Many archaeologists think that the dots and lines issuing from the higher of the two cones represent a volcanic eruption, and have suggested that the mountain is the 10,600-foot-high Hasan Dağ. It is located within view of Çatal Höyük and is the only twin-peaked volcano in central Anatolia. The conjectured volcanic eruption shown in the mural does not necessarily depict a specific historical event. If, however, the Çatal Höyük painting relates a story, even a recurring one, then it cannot be considered a pure landscape. Nonetheless, this mural is the first depiction of a place devoid of both humans and animals.

The rich finds at Çatal Höyük give the impression of a prosperous and well-ordered society that practiced a great variety of arts and crafts. In addition to painting and sculpture, weaving and pottery were well established, and even the technique of smelting lead in small quantities was known before 6000 BCE. The conversion to an agricultural economy appears to have been completed by about 5700 BCE.

Western Europe

In western Europe, where Paleolithic paintings and sculptures abound, no comparably developed towns of the time of Çatal Höyük have been found. However, in succeeding millennia, perhaps as early as 4000 BCE, the local Neolithic populations in several areas developed a monumental architecture employing massive rough-cut stones. The very dimensions of the stones, some as high as 17 feet and weighing as much as 50 tons, have prompted historians to call them *megaliths* (great stones) and to designate Neolithic architecture employing megaliths as *megalithic*.

NEWGRANGE One of the most impressive megalithic monuments in Europe is also one of the oldest. The megalithic tomb at Newgrange in Ireland, north of Dublin, may have been constructed as early as 3200 BCE and is one of the oldest burial monuments in Europe. It takes the form of a *passage grave*, that is, a tomb with a long stone corridor (FIG. **1-19**) leading to a burial chamber, all covered by a great *tumulus* (earthen burial mound). Passage graves have been found also in England, France, Spain, and Scandinavia. All attest to the importance of honoring the dead in Neolithic society. Some mounds contain more than one passage grave. The Newgrange

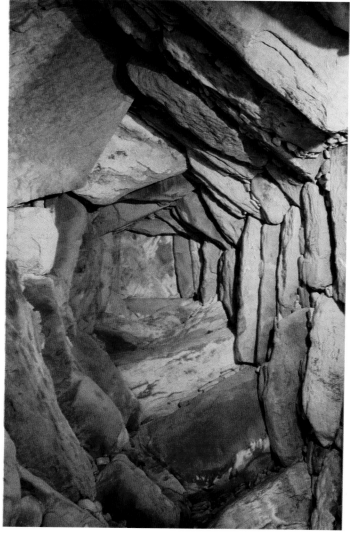

1-19 Gallery leading to the main chamber of the passage grave, Newgrange, Ireland, ca. 3200–2500 BCE.

The Newgrange passage grave is an early example of corbeled vaulting. The megaliths of the corridor leading to the burial chamber beneath the tumulus are held in place by their own weight.

Neolithic Art **13**

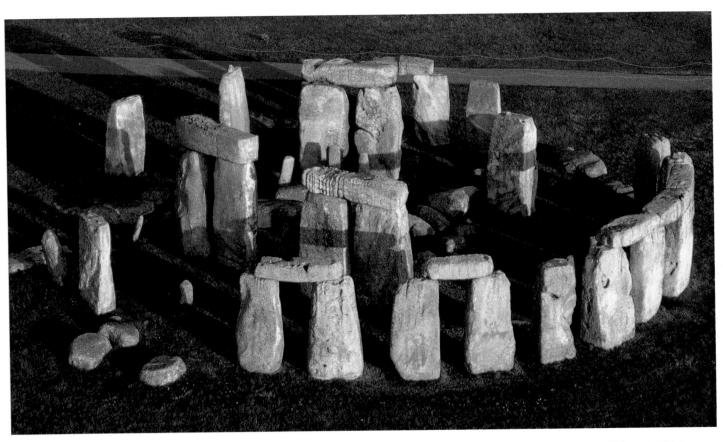

1-20 Aerial view (looking northwest) of Stonehenge, Salisbury Plain, England, ca. 2550–1600 BCE. Circle is 97′ in diameter; trilithons 24′ high.

The circles of trilithons at Stonehenge probably functioned as an astronomical observatory and solar calendar. The sun rises over its "heel stone" at the summer solstice. Some of the megaliths weigh 50 tons.

tumulus is 280 feet in diameter and 44 feet tall. Its passageway is 62 feet long and is an early example of a construction technique used in other later ancient cultures and even today—the *corbeled vault* (FIGS. 4-16 and 4-17*b*). At Newgrange, huge megaliths form the ceiling of the passage and the burial chamber. The stones are held in place by their own weight, those on one side countering the weight of the megaliths on the other side of the passageway. Some of the stones are decorated with incised spirals and other abstract motifs (not visible in FIG. 1-19). A special feature of the Newgrange tomb is that at the winter solstice the sun illuminates the passageway and the burial chamber.

HAGAR QIM Contemporary with Newgrange but on an island far to the south is the megalithic temple (FIG. 1-1) of Hagar Qim, one of many constructed on Malta between 3200 and 2500 BCE and one of the oldest stone temples anywhere in the world. The Maltese builders constructed their temples by piling carefully cut stone blocks in *courses* (stacked horizontal rows). The doorways at Hagar Qim were built using the *post-and-lintel* system (FIG. 4-17*a*) in which two upright stones (posts) support a horizontal beam (*lintel*). The layout of this and other Neolithic Maltese temples is especially noteworthy for the combination of rectilinear and curved forms, including multiple *apses* (semicircular recesses). Inside the Hagar Qim temple archaeologists found altars (hence the identification of the structure as a religious shrine) and several stone statues of headless nude women, one standing, the others seated. The level of architectural and sculptural sophistication seen on this isolated island at so early a date is extraordinary.

STONEHENGE The most famous megalithic monument in Europe is Stonehenge (FIG. 1-20) on the Salisbury Plain in southern England. A *henge* is an arrangement of megalithic stones in a circle, often surrounded by a ditch. The type is almost entirely limited to Britain. Stonehenge is a complex of rough-cut sarsen (a form of sandstone) stones and smaller "bluestones" (various volcanic rocks) built in several stages over hundreds of years. The final henge took the form of concentric post-and-lintel circles. The outer ring, almost 100 feet in diameter, consists of huge sarsen megaliths. Inside is a ring of bluestones, which in turn encircle a horseshoe (open end facing east) of *trilithons* (three-stone constructions)—five lintel-topped pairs of the largest sarsens, each weighing 45 to 50 tons. Standing apart and to the east (outside the aerial view in FIG. 1-20) is the "heel stone," which, for a person looking outward from the center of the complex, would have marked the point where the sun rose at the summer solstice. Stonehenge seems to have been a kind of astronomical observatory and a remarkably accurate solar calendar.

The megalithic tombs, temples, and henges of Europe are enduring testaments to the rapidly developing intellectual powers of Neolithic humans as well as to their capacity for heroic physical effort.

ART BEFORE HISTORY

PALEOLITHIC (OLD STONE AGE) ART, ca. 30,000–9000 BCE

■ The first sculptures and paintings antedate the invention of writing by tens of thousands of years. Paleolithic humans' decision to represent the world around them initiated an intellectual revolution of enormous consequences.

■ No one knows why humans began to paint and carve images or what role those images played in the lives of Paleolithic hunters. Women were far more common subjects than men, but animals, not humans, dominate Paleolithic art.

■ The works created range in size from tiny figurines like the so-called *Venus of Willendorf* to painted walls and ceilings covered with over-life-size animals, as in the cave at Lascaux.

■ Artists always depicted animals in profile so that the image was complete, including the head, body, tail, and all four legs. This format persisted for millennia.

Nude woman (*Venus of Willendorf*),
ca. 28,000–25,000 BCE

Hall of the Bulls, Lascaux,
ca. 15,000–13,000 BCE

NEOLITHIC (NEW STONE AGE) ART, ca. 8000–2300 BCE

■ Around 9000 BCE, the ice that had covered much of northern Europe for millennia receded. After a transitional period, the Neolithic Age began, but at different times in different places. It also continued longer in remote places like Stonehenge in England and Hagar Qim on Malta.

■ The Neolithic Age revolutionized human life with the beginning of agriculture and the formation of the first settled communities, like that at Çatal Höyük in Anatolia.

■ In art, the Neolithic period saw the birth of monumental sculpture, notably the painted plaster figurines from Ain Ghazal, and of monumental stone architecture in the walls and tower(s) of Jericho.

■ In painting, coherent narratives became common and artists began to represent human figures as composites of frontal and profile views—another formula that would remain universal for a very long time.

Plaster figurine, Ain Ghazal,
ca. 6750–6250 BCE

Stonehenge, Salisbury Plain,
ca. 2550–1600 BCE

1 in.

2-1 Hammurabi and Shamash, detail of the stele of Hammurabi (FIG. 2-17), from Susa, Iran, ca. 1780 BCE.

The relationship between king and god in the ancient Near East is set out on this Babylonian stele representing the sun god extending to Hammurabi the symbols of his authority to govern and enact laws.

THE ANCIENT
NEAR EAST

When humans first gave up the dangerous and uncertain life of the hunter and gatherer for the more predictable and stable life of the farmer and herder, the change in human society was so significant that it justly has been called the Neolithic Revolution. This fundamental change in the nature of daily life first occurred in Mesopotamia—a Greek word that means "the land between the [Tigris and Euphrates] rivers." Mesopotamia is at the core of the region often called the Fertile Crescent, a land mass that forms a huge arc from the mountainous border between Turkey and Syria through Iraq to Iran's Zagros Mountains (MAP 2-1). There, humans first learned how to use the wheel and the plow and how to control floods and construct irrigation canals. The land became a giant oasis, the presumed locale of the biblical Garden of Eden.

As the region that gave birth to three of the world's great modern faiths—Judaism, Christianity, and Islam—the Near East has long been of interest to historians. But not until the 19th century did systematic excavation open the public's eyes to the extraordinary art and architecture of the ancient land between the rivers. After the first discoveries, the great museums of Europe, consistent with the treasure-hunting spirit of the era, began to acquire Mesopotamian artworks as quickly as possible. The instructions the British Museum gave to Austen Henry Layard, one of the pioneers of Near Eastern archaeology, were typical: Obtain as many well-preserved artworks as you can while spending the least possible amount of time and money doing so. Interest heightened with each new find, and soon North American museums also began to collect Near Eastern art.

The most popular 19th-century acquisitions were the stone reliefs depicting warfare and hunting (FIGS. 2-22 and 2-23) and the colossal statues of monstrous human-headed bulls (FIG. 2-21) from the palaces of the Assyrians, rulers of a northern Mesopotamian empire during the ninth to the seventh centuries BCE. But nothing that emerged from the Near Eastern soil attracted as much attention as the treasures Leonard Woolley discovered in the 1920s at the Royal Cemetery at Ur in southern Mesopotamia. The interest in the lavish third-millennium Sumerian burials he unearthed rivaled the fascination with the 1922 discovery of the tomb of the Egyptian boy-king Tutankhamen (see Chapter 3). The Ur cemetery yielded gold objects, jewelry, artworks, and musical instruments (FIGS. 2-8 to 2-11) of the highest quality.

SUMER

The discovery of the treasures of ancient Ur put the Sumerians once again in a prominent position on the world stage. They had been absent for more than 4,000 years. The Sumerians were the people who in the fourth millennium BCE transformed the vast and previously sparsely inhabited valley between the Tigris and Euphrates into the Fertile Crescent of the ancient world. Ancient Sumer, which roughly corresponds to southern Iraq today, was not a unified nation. Rather, it was made up of a dozen or so independent *city-states*. Each was thought to be under the protection of a different Mesopotamian deity (see "The Gods and Goddesses of Mesopotamia," page 19). The Sumerian rulers were the gods' representatives on earth and the stewards of their earthly treasure.

The rulers and priests directed all communal activities, including canal construction, crop collection, and food distribution. The development of agriculture to the point that only a portion of the population had to produce food meant that some members of the community could specialize in other activities, including manufacturing, trade, and administration. Specialization of labor is a hallmark of the first complex urban societies. In the city-states of ancient Sumer, activities that once had been individually initiated became institutionalized for the first time. The community, rather than the family, assumed functions such as defense against enemies and against the caprices of nature. Whether ruled by a single person or a council chosen from among the leading families, these communities gained permanent identities as discrete cities. The city-state was one of the great Sumerian inventions.

Another was writing. The oldest written documents known are Sumerian records of administrative acts and commercial transactions. At first, around 3400–3200 BCE, the Sumerians made inventories of cattle, food, and other items by scratching *pictographs* (simplified pictures standing for words) into soft clay with a sharp tool, or *stylus*. The clay plaques hardened into breakable, yet nearly indestructible, tablets. Thousands of these plaques dating back nearly five millennia exist today. The Sumerians wrote their pictorial signs from the top down and arranged them in boxes they read from right to left. By 3000–2900 BCE, they had further simplified the pictographic signs by reducing them to a group of wedge-shaped (*cuneiform*) signs

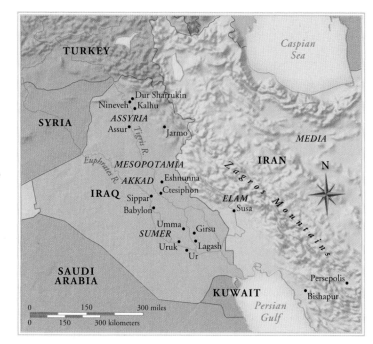

MAP 2-1 The ancient Near East.

(FIG. 2-7 is an early example; see also FIGS. 2-1, 2-16, and 2-17). The development of cuneiform marked the beginning of writing, as historians strictly define it. The surviving cuneiform tablets testify to the far-flung network of Sumerian contacts reaching from southern Mesopotamia eastward to the Iranian plateau, northward to Assyria, and westward to Syria. Trade was essential for the Sumerians, because despite the fertility of their land, it was poor in such vital natural resources as metal, stone, and wood.

The Sumerians also produced great literature. Their most famous work, known from fragmentary cuneiform texts, is the late-third-millennium *Epic of Gilgamesh*, which antedates Homer's *Iliad* and *Odyssey* by some 1,500 years. It recounts the heroic story of Gilgamesh, legendary king of Uruk and slayer of the monster Huwawa. Translations of the Sumerian epic into several other ancient Near Eastern languages attest to the fame of the original version.

2-2 White Temple and ziggurat, Uruk (modern Warka), Iraq, ca. 3200–3000 BCE.

Using only mud bricks, the Sumerians erected temple platforms called ziggurats several centuries before the Egyptians built stone pyramids. The most famous ziggurat was the biblical Tower of Babel.

The Gods and Goddesses of Mesopotamia

The Sumerians and their successors in the ancient Near East worshiped numerous deities, mostly nature gods. Listed here are the Mesopotamian gods and goddesses discussed in this chapter.

▌ *Anu.* The chief deity of the Sumerians, Anu was the god of the sky and of the city of Uruk. One of the earliest Sumerian temples (FIGS. 2-2 and 2-3) may have been dedicated to his worship.

▌ *Enlil.* Anu's son, Enlil was the lord of the winds and the earth. He eventually replaced his father as king of the gods.

▌ *Inanna.* The Sumerian goddess of love and war, Inanna was later known as *Ishtar.* She is the most important female deity in all periods of Mesopotamian history. As early as the fourth millennium BCE, the Sumerians constructed a sanctuary to Inanna at Uruk. Amid the ruins, excavators uncovered fourth-millennium statues and reliefs (FIGS. 2-4 and 2-5) connected with her worship.

▌ *Nanna.* The moon god, Nanna was also known as *Sin.* He was the chief deity of Ur, where his most important shrine was located.

▌ *Utu.* The sun god, Utu was known later as *Shamash* and was especially revered at Sippar. On a Babylonian stele (FIG. 2-1) of ca. 1780 BCE, King Hammurabi presents his law code to Shamash, who is depicted with flames radiating from his shoulders.

▌ *Marduk, Nabu,* and *Adad.* Marduk was the chief god of the Babylonians. His son Nabu was the god of writing and wisdom. Adad was the Babylonian god of storms. Representations of Marduk and Nabu's dragon and Adad's sacred bull adorn the sixth-century BCE Ishtar Gate (FIG. 2-24) at Babylon.

▌ *Ningirsu.* The local god of Lagash and Girsu, Ningirsu helped Eannatum, one of the early rulers of Lagash, defeat an enemy army. Ningirsu's role in the victory is recorded on the *Stele of the Vultures* (FIG. 2-7) of ca. 2600–2500 BCE. Gudea (FIG. 2-16), one of Eannatum's Neo-Sumerian successors, built a great temple about 2100 BCE in honor of Ningirsu after the god instructed him to do so in a dream.

▌ *Ashur.* The local deity of Assur, the city that took his name, Ashur became the king of the Assyrian gods. He sometimes is identified with Enlil.

WHITE TEMPLE, URUK The layout of Sumerian cities reflected the central role of the gods in daily life. The main temple to each state's chief god formed the city's monumental nucleus. In fact, the temple complex was a kind of city within a city, where a staff of priests and scribes carried on official administrative and commercial business, as well as oversaw all religious functions.

The outstanding preserved example of early Sumerian temple architecture is the 5,000-year-old White Temple (FIG. 2-2) at Uruk, a city that in the late fourth millennium BCE had a population of about 40,000. Usually only the foundations of early Mesopotamian temples can still be recognized. The White Temple is a rare exception. Sumerian builders did not have access to stone quarries and instead formed mud bricks for the superstructures of their temples and other buildings. Almost all these structures have eroded over the course of time. The fragile nature of the building materials did not, however, prevent the Sumerians from erecting towering works, such as the Uruk temple, several centuries before the Egyptians built their famous stone pyramids. This says a great deal about the Sumerians' desire to provide monumental settings for the worship of their deities.

Enough of the Uruk complex remains to permit a fairly reliable reconstruction (FIG. 2-3). The temple (whose whitewashed walls lend it its modern nickname) stands atop a high platform, or *ziggurat,* 40 feet above street level in the city center. A stairway on one side leads to the top but does not end in front of any of the temple doorways, necessitating two or three angular changes in direction. This *bent-axis plan* is the standard arrangement for Sumerian temples, a striking contrast to the linear approach the Egyptians preferred for their temples and tombs (see Chapter 3).

Like other Sumerian temples, the corners of the White Temple are oriented to the cardinal points of the compass. The building, probably dedicated to Anu, the sky god, is of modest proportions (61 × 16 feet). By design, it did not accommodate large throngs of worshipers but only a select few, the priests and perhaps the leading community members. The temple has several chambers. The central hall, or *cella,* was set aside for the divinity and housed a stepped altar. The Sumerians referred to their temples as "waiting rooms," a reflection of their belief that the deity would descend from the heavens to appear before the priests in the cella. Whether the Uruk temple had a roof and, if it did, what kind, are uncertain.

The Sumerian idea that the gods reside above the world of humans is central to most of the world's religions. Moses ascended Mount Sinai to receive the Ten Commandments from the Hebrew God, and the Greeks placed the home of their gods and goddesses on Mount Olympus. The elevated placement of Mesopotamian temples on giant platforms reaching toward the sky is consistent with this widespread religious concept. Eroded ziggurats still dominate most of the ruined cities of Sumer. The loftiness of the great temple platforms made a profound impression on the peoples of the ancient Near East. The tallest ziggurat of all, at Babylon, was about 270 feet high. Known to the Hebrews as the Tower of Babel, it became the centerpiece of a biblical story about the insolent pride of humans (see "Babylon, City of Wonders," page 34).

2-3 Reconstruction drawing of the White Temple and ziggurat, Uruk (modern Warka), Iraq, ca. 3200–3000 BCE.

The White Temple at Uruk was probably dedicated to Anu, the sky god. It has a central hall (cella) with a stepped altar where the Sumerian priests would await the apparition of the deity.

INANNA A fragmentary white marble female head (FIG. 2-4) from Uruk is also an extraordinary achievement at so early a date. The head, one of the treasures of the Iraq Museum in Baghdad, disappeared during the Iraq war of 2003 but was later recovered. (FIG. 2-4, which shows the head during its presentation at a press conference after its recovery, gives an excellent idea of its size. Other missing items from the museum that were later recovered, in some cases damaged, include FIGS. 2-5 and 2-12.) The lustrous hard stone used to carve the head had to be brought to Uruk at great cost, and the Sumerians used the stone sparingly. The "head" is actually only a face with a flat back. It has drilled holes for attachment to the rest of the head and the body, which may have been wood. Although found in the sacred precinct of the goddess Inanna, the subject is unknown. Many scholars have suggested that the face is an image of Inanna, but a mortal woman, perhaps a priestess, may be portrayed.

Often the present condition of an artwork can be very misleading, and the Uruk head is a dramatic example. Its original appearance would have been much more vibrant than the pure white fragment preserved today. Colored shell or stone filled the deep recesses for the eyebrows and the large eyes. The deep groove at the top of the head anchored a wig, probably made of gold leaf. The hair strands engraved in the metal fell in waves over the forehead and sides of the face. The bright coloration of the eyes, brows, and hair likely overshadowed the soft modeling of the cheeks and mouth. The missing body was probably clothed in expensive fabrics and bedecked with jewels.

WARKA VASE The Sumerians, pioneers in so many areas, also may have been the first to use pictures to tell coherent stories. Sumerian narrative art goes far beyond the Stone Age artists' tentative efforts at storytelling. The so-called *Warka Vase* (FIG. 2-5) from Uruk (modern Warka) is the first great work of narrative relief

2-4 Female head (Inanna?), from Uruk (modern Warka), Iraq, ca. 3200–3000 BCE. Marble, 8″ high. Iraq Museum, Baghdad.

The Sumerians imported the marble for this head at great cost. It may represent the goddess Inanna and originally had inlaid colored shell or stone eyes and brows, and a wig, probably of gold leaf.

2-5 Presentation of offerings to Inanna (*Warka Vase*), from Uruk (modern Warka), Iraq, ca. 3200–3000 BCE. Alabaster, 3′ ¼″ high. Iraq Museum, Baghdad.

In this oldest known example of Sumerian narrative art, the sculptor divided the tall stone vase's reliefs into registers, a significant break with the haphazard figure placement found in earlier art.

sculpture known. Found within the Inanna temple complex, it depicts a religious festival in honor of the goddess.

The sculptor divided the vase's reliefs into several bands (also called *registers* or *friezes*), and the figures stand on a *ground line* (the horizontal base of the composition). This new kind of composition marks a significant break with the haphazard figure placement found in earlier art. The register format for telling a story was to have a very long future. In fact, artists still employ registers today in modified form in comic books.

The lowest band on the *Warka Vase* shows crops above a wavy line representing water. Then comes a register with ewes and rams—in strict profile, consistent with an approach to representing animals that was then some 20,000 years old. The crops and the alternating male and female animals were the staple commodities of the Sumerian economy, but they were also associated with fertility. They underscore that Inanna had blessed Uruk's inhabitants with good crops and increased herds.

A procession of naked men fills the band at the center of the vase. The men carry baskets and jars overflowing with the earth's abundance. They will present their bounty to the goddess as a *votive offering* (gift of gratitude to a deity usually made in fulfillment of a vow) and will deposit it in her temple. The spacing of each figure involves no overlapping. The Uruk men, like the Neolithic deer hunters at Çatal Höyük (FIG. 1-17), are a composite of frontal and profile views, with large staring frontal eyes in profile heads. The artist indicated those human body parts necessary to communicate the human form and avoided positions, attitudes, or views that would conceal the characterizing parts. For example, if the figures were in strict profile, an arm and perhaps a leg would be hidden. The body would appear to have only half its breadth. And the eye would not "read" as an eye at all, because it would not have its distinctive oval shape. Art historians call this characteristic early approach to representation *conceptual* (as opposed to optical) because artists who used it did not record the immediate, fleeting aspect of figures. Instead, they rendered the human body's distinguishing and fixed properties. The fundamental forms of figures, not their accidental appearance, dictated the artist's selection of the composite view as the best way to represent the human body.

In the uppermost (and tallest) band is a female figure with a tall horned headdress next to two large poles that are the sign of the goddess Inanna. (Some scholars think the woman is a priestess and not the goddess herself.) A nude male figure brings a large vessel brimming with offerings to be deposited in the goddess's shrine. At the far right and barely visible in FIG. 2-5 is an only partially preserved clothed man. Near him is the early pictograph for the Sumerian official that is usually, if ambiguously, called a "priest-king," that is, both a religious and secular leader. The greater height of the priest-king and Inanna compared to the offering bearers indicates their greater importance, a convention called *hierarchy of scale*. Some scholars interpret the scene as a symbolic marriage between the priest-king and the goddess, ensuring her continued goodwill—and reaffirming the leader's exalted position in society.

ESHNUNNA STATUETTES Further insight into Sumerian religious beliefs and rituals comes from a cache of sculptures reverently buried beneath the floor of a temple at Eshnunna (modern Tell Asmar) when the structure was remodeled. Carved of soft gypsum and inlaid with shell and black limestone, the statuettes range in size from well under a foot to about 30 inches tall. The two largest figures are shown in FIG. 2-6. All of the statuettes represent mortals, rather than deities, with their hands folded in front of their chests in a ges-

ture of prayer, usually holding the small beakers the Sumerians used in religious rites. Hundreds of similar goblets have been found in the temple complex at Eshnunna. The men wear belts and fringed skirts. Most have beards and shoulder-length hair. The women wear long robes, with the right shoulder bare. Similar figurines from other sites bear inscriptions giving information such as the name of the donor and the god or even specific prayers to the deity on the owner's behalf. With their heads tilted upward, they wait in the Sumerian "waiting room" for the divinity to appear.

The sculptors of the Eshnunna statuettes employed simple forms, primarily cones and cylinders, for the figures. The statuettes are not portraits in the strict sense of the word, but the sculptors did distinguish physical types. At least one child was portrayed—next to the woman in FIG. 2-6 are the remains of two small legs. Most striking is the disproportionate relationship between the inlaid oversized eyes and the tiny hands. Scholars have explained the exaggeration of the eye size in various ways. But because the purpose of these votive figures was to offer constant prayers to the gods on their donors' behalf, the open-eyed stares most likely symbolize the eternal wakefulness necessary to fulfill their duty.

1 ft.

2-6 Statuettes of two worshipers, from the Square Temple at Eshnunna (modern Tell Asmar), Iraq, ca. 2700 BCE. Gypsum inlaid with shell and black limestone, male figure 2′ 6″ high. Iraq Museum, Baghdad.

The oversized eyes probably symbolized the perpetual wakefulness of these substitute worshipers offering prayers to the deity. The beakers the figures hold were used to pour libations in honor of the gods.

STELE OF THE VULTURES The city-states of ancient Sumer were often at war with one another, and warfare is the theme of the so-called *Stele of the Vultures* (FIG. 2-7) from Girsu. A *stele* is a carved stone slab erected to commemorate a historical event or, in some cultures, to mark a grave. The Girsu stele presents a labeled historical narrative with cuneiform inscriptions filling almost every blank space on the stele. (It is not, however, the first historical representation in the history of art. That honor belongs—at the moment—to an Egyptian relief (FIG. 3-3) carved more than three centuries earlier.) The inscriptions reveal that the *Stele of the Vultures* celebrates the victory of Eannatum, the *ensi* (ruler; king?) of Lagash, over the neighboring city-state of Umma. The stele has reliefs on both sides and takes its nickname from a fragment with a gruesome scene of vultures carrying off the severed heads and arms of the defeated enemy soldiers. Another fragment shows the giant figure of the local god Ningirsu holding tiny enemies in a net and beating one of them on the head with a mace.

The fragment in FIG. 2-7 depicts Eannatum leading an infantry battalion into battle (above) and attacking from a war chariot (below). The foot soldiers are protected behind a wall of shields and trample naked enemies as they advance. (The fragment that shows vultures devouring corpses belongs just to the right in the same register.) Both on foot and in a chariot, Eannatum is larger than anyone else, except Ningirsu on the other side of the stele. The artist presented him as the fearless general who paves the way for his army. Lives were lost, however, and Eannatum himself was wounded in the campaign, but the outcome was never in doubt because Ningirsu fought with the men of Lagash.

Despite its fragmentary state, the *Stele of the Vultures* is an extraordinary document, not only as a very early effort to record historical events in relief but also for the insight it yields about Sumerian society. Through both words and pictures, it provides information about warfare and the special nature of the Sumerian ruler. Eannatum was greater in stature than other men, and Ningirsu watched over him. According to the text, the ensi was born from the god Enlil's semen, which Ningirsu implanted in the womb. When Eannatum was wounded in battle, it says, the god shed tears for him. He was a divinely chosen ruler who presided over all aspects of his city-state, both in war and in peace. This also seems to have been the role of the ensi in the other Sumerian city-states.

STANDARD OF UR Agriculture and trade brought considerable wealth to some of the city-states of ancient Sumer. Nowhere is this clearer than in the so-called Royal Cemetery at Ur, the city that was home to the biblical Abraham. In the third millennium BCE, the leading families of Ur buried their dead in chambers beneath the earth. Scholars still debate whether these deceased were true kings and queens or simply aristocrats and priests, but the Sumerians laid them to rest in regal fashion. Archaeologists exploring the Ur cemetery uncovered gold helmets and daggers with handles of lapis lazuli (a rich azure-blue stone imported from Afghanistan), golden beakers and bowls, jewelry of gold and lapis, musical instruments, chariots, and other luxurious items. Dozens of bodies were also found in the richest tombs. A retinue of musicians, servants, charioteers, and soldiers was sacrificed in order to accompany the "kings and queens" into the afterlife. (Comparable rituals are documented in other societies, for example, in ancient America.)

Not the costliest object found in the "royal" graves, but probably the most significant from the viewpoint of the history of art, is the so-called *Standard of Ur* (FIGS. 2-8 and 2-9). This rectangular box of uncertain function has sloping sides inlaid with shell, lapis lazuli, and red limestone. The excavator, Leonard Woolley, thought the object was

2-7 Fragment of the victory stele of Eannatum (*Stele of the Vultures*), from Girsu (modern Telloh), Iraq, ca. 2600–2500 BCE. Limestone, fragment 2′ 6″ high, full stele 5′ 11″ high. Louvre, Paris.

Cuneiform inscriptions on this stele describe the victory of Eannatum of Lagash over the city of Umma. This fragment shows Eannatum leading his army into battle. The artist depicted the king larger than his soldiers.

1 ft.

2-8 War side of the *Standard of Ur,* from tomb 779, Royal Cemetery, Ur (modern Tell Muqayyar), Iraq, ca. 2600 BCE. Wood inlaid with shell, lapis lazuli, and red limestone, 8″ × 1′ 7″. British Museum, London.

Using a mosaic-like technique, this Sumerian artist depicted a battlefield victory in three registers. In the top band, soldiers present bound captives to a kinglike figure who is larger than everyone else.

2-9 Peace side of the *Standard of Ur,* from tomb 779, Royal Cemetery, Ur (modern Tell Muqayyar), Iraq, ca. 2600 BCE. Wood inlaid with shell, lapis lazuli, and red limestone, 8″ × 1′ 7″. British Museum, London.

The feast on the peace side of the *Standard of Ur* may be a victory celebration. The narrative again reads from bottom to top, and the size of the figures varies with their importance in Sumerian society.

originally mounted on a pole, and he considered it a kind of military standard—hence its nickname. Art historians usually refer to the two long sides of the box as the "war side" and "peace side," but the two sides may represent the first and second parts of a single narrative. The artist divided each into three horizontal bands. The narrative reads from left to right and bottom to top. On the war side (FIG. 2-8), four ass-drawn four-wheeled war chariots mow down enemies, whose bodies appear on the ground in front of and beneath the animals. The gait of the asses accelerates along the band from left to right. Above, foot soldiers gather up and lead away captured foes. In the uppermost register, soldiers present bound captives (who have been stripped naked to degrade them) to a kinglike figure, who has stepped out of his chariot. His central place in the composition and his greater stature (his head breaks through the border at the top) set him apart from all the other figures.

In the lowest band on the peace side (FIG. 2-9), men carry provisions, possibly war booty, on their backs. Above, attendants bring animals, perhaps also spoils of war, and fish for the great banquet depicted in the uppermost register. There, seated dignitaries and a larger-than-life "king" (third from the left) feast, while a lyre player and singer entertain the group. Art historians have interpreted the scene both as a victory celebration and as a banquet in connection with cult ritual. The two are not necessarily incompatible. The absence of an inscription prevents connecting the scenes with a specific event or person, but the *Standard of Ur* undoubtedly is another early example of historical narrative.

BULL-HEADED LYRE From the "King's Grave" at Ur comes a fragmentary lyre (FIG. **2-10**) that, when intact, probably resembled the instrument depicted in the feast scene (FIG. **2-9**, *top right*) on the *Standard of Ur*. A magnificent bull's head (FIG. **2-10**, *left*) caps the instrument's sound box. It is fashioned of gold leaf over a wooden core. The hair, beard, and details are lapis lazuli. The sound box (FIG. **2-10**, *right*) also features bearded—but here human-headed—bulls in the uppermost of its four inlaid panels. Imaginary composite creatures are commonplace in the art of the ancient Near East and Egypt. On the Ur lyre, a heroic figure embraces the two man-bulls in a *heraldic composition* (symmetrical on either side of a central figure). His body and that of the scorpion-man in the lowest panel are in composite view. The animals are, equally characteristically, solely in profile: the dog wearing a dagger and carrying a laden table, the lion bringing in the beverage service, the ass playing the lyre, the jackal playing the zither, the bear steadying the lyre (or perhaps dancing), and the gazelle bearing goblets. The banquet animals almost seem to be burlesquing the kind of regal feast reproduced on the peace side of the *Standard of Ur*. The meaning of the sound-box scenes is unclear. Some scholars have suggested, for example, that the creatures inhabit the land of the dead and that the narrative has a funerary significance. In any event, the sound box is a very early specimen of the recurring theme in both literature and art of animals acting as people. Later examples include Aesop's fables in ancient Greece, medieval *bestiaries,* and Walt Disney's cartoon animal actors.

CYLINDER SEALS A banquet is also the subject of a *cylinder seal* (FIG. **2-11**) found in the tomb of "Queen" Pu-abi and inscribed with her name. (Many historians prefer to designate her more conservatively and ambiguously as "Lady" Pu-abi.) The seal is typical of the period, consisting of a cylindrical piece of stone engraved to produce a raised impression when rolled over clay (see "Mesopotamian Seals," page 25). In the upper zone, a woman, probably Pu-abi, and a man sit and drink from beakers, attended by servants. Below, male attendants serve two more seated men. Even in miniature and in a medium very different from that of the *Standard of Ur,* the Sumerian artist employed the same figure types and followed the same compositional rules. All the figures are in composite views with large frontal eyes in profile heads, and the seated dignitaries are once again larger in scale to underscore their elevated position in the social hierarchy.

2-10 Bull-headed lyre from tomb 789 ("King's Grave"), Royal Cemetery, Ur (modern Tell Muqayyar), Iraq, ca. 2600 BCE. Lyre (*left*): Gold leaf and lapis lazuli over a wooden core, 5′ 5″ high. Sound box (*right*): Wood with inlaid gold, lapis lazuli, and shell, 1′ 7″ high. University of Pennsylvania Museum of Archaeology and Anthropology, Philadelphia.

This lyre from a royal grave at Ur is adorned with a bearded bull's head of gold leaf and lapis lazuli, and inlaid figures of a Gilgamesh-like hero and animals acting out scenes of uncertain significance.

1 ft.

1 ft.

Mesopotamian Seals

Seals have been unearthed in great numbers at sites throughout Mesopotamia. Generally made of stone, seals of ivory, glass, and other materials also survive. The seals take two forms: flat *stamp seals* and *cylinder seals*. The latter have a hole drilled lengthwise through the center of the cylinder so that they could be strung and worn around the neck or suspended from the wrist. Cylinder seals (FIG. 2-11) were prized possessions, signifying high positions in society, and they frequently were buried with the dead.

The primary function of cylinder seals, however, like the earlier stamp seals, was not to serve as items of adornment. The Sumerians (and other peoples of the Near East) used both stamp and cylinder seals to identify their documents and protect storage jars and doors against unauthorized opening. The oldest seals predate the invention of writing and conveyed their messages with pictographs that ratified ownership. Later seals often bear long cuneiform inscriptions and record the names and titles of rulers, bureaucrats, and deities. Although sealing is increasingly rare, the tradition lives on today whenever a letter is sealed with a lump of wax and then stamped with a monogram or other identifying mark. Customs officials often still seal packages and sacks with official stamps when goods cross national borders.

In the ancient Near East, artists decorated both stamp and cylinder seals with incised designs, producing a raised pattern when the seal was pressed into soft clay. (Cylinder seals largely displaced stamp seals because they could be rolled over the clay and thus cover a greater area more quickly.) FIG. 2-11 shows a cylinder seal from the Royal Cemetery at Ur and a modern impression made from it. Note how cracks in the stone cylinder become raised lines in the impression and how the engraved figures, chairs, and cuneiform characters appear in relief. Continuous rolling of the seal over a clay strip results in a repeating design, as the illustration also demonstrates at the edges.

The miniature reliefs the seals produce are a priceless source of information about Mesopotamian religion and society. Without them, archaeologists would know much less about how Mesopotamians dressed and dined; what their shrines looked like; how they depicted their gods, rulers, and mythological figures; how they fought wars; and what role women played in ancient Near Eastern society. Clay seal impressions excavated in architectural contexts shed a welcome light on the administration and organization of Mesopotamian city-states. Mesopotamian seals are also an invaluable resource for art historians, providing them with thousands of miniature examples of relief sculpture that span roughly 3,000 years.

1 in.

2-11 Banquet scene, cylinder seal (*left*) and its modern impression (*right*), from the tomb of Pu-abi (tomb 800), Royal Cemetery, Ur (modern Tell Muqayyar), Iraq, ca. 2600 BCE. Lapis lazuli, 2″ high. British Museum, London.

Seals were widely used in Mesopotamia to identify and secure goods. Artists incised designs into stone cylinders and then rolled them over clay to produce miniature artworks like this banquet scene.

AKKAD AND THE THIRD DYNASTY OF UR

In 2332 BCE, the loosely linked group of cities known as Sumer came under the domination of a great ruler, Sargon of Akkad (r. 2332–2279 BCE). Archaeologists have yet to locate the specific site of the city of Akkad, but it was in the vicinity of Babylon. The Akkadians were Semitic in origin—that is, they were a Near Eastern people who spoke a language related to Hebrew and Arabic. Their language,

Akkadian, was entirely different from the language of Sumer, but they used the Sumerians' cuneiform characters for their written documents. Under Sargon (whose name means "true king") and his followers, the Akkadians introduced a new concept of royal power based on unswerving loyalty to the king rather than to the city-state. During the rule of Sargon's grandson, Naram-Sin (r. 2254–2218 BCE), governors of cities were considered mere servants of the king, who in turn called himself "King of the Four Quarters"—in effect, ruler of the earth, akin to a god.

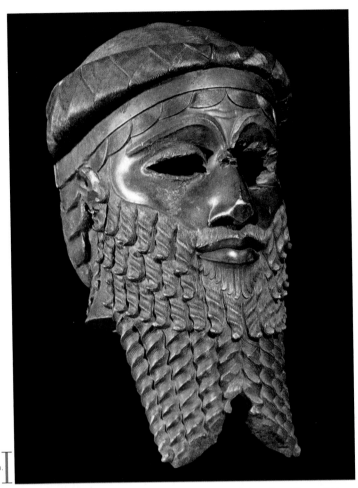

1 in.

2-12 Head of an Akkadian ruler, from Nineveh (modern Kuyunjik), Iraq, ca. 2250–2200 BCE. Copper, 1′ 2¾″ high. Iraq Museum, Baghdad.

The sculptor of this first known life-size hollow-cast head captured the distinctive features of the ruler while also displaying a keen sense of abstract pattern. The head was vandalized in antiquity.

1 ft.

2-13 Victory stele of Naram-Sin, from Susa, Iran, 2254–2218 BCE. Pink sandstone, 6′ 7″ high. Louvre, Paris.

To commemorate his conquest of the Lullubi, Naram-Sin set up this stele showing him leading his army up a mountain. The sculptor staggered the figures, abandoning the traditional register format.

AKKADIAN PORTRAITURE A magnificent copper head of an Akkadian king (FIG. 2-12) found at Nineveh embodies this new concept of absolute monarchy. The head is all that survives of a statue that was knocked over in antiquity, perhaps when the Medes, a people that occupied the land south of the Caspian Sea (MAP 2-1), sacked Nineveh in 612 BCE. But the damage to the portrait was not due solely to the statue's toppling. There are also signs of deliberate mutilation. To make a political statement, the enemy gouged out the eyes (once inlaid with precious or semiprecious stones), broke off the lower part of the beard, and slashed the ears of the royal portrait. Nonetheless, the king's majestic serenity, dignity, and authority are evident. So, too, is the masterful way the sculptor balanced naturalism and abstract patterning. The artist carefully observed and recorded the man's distinctive features—the profile of the nose and the long, curly beard—and brilliantly communicated the differing textures of flesh and hair, even the contrasting textures of the mustache, beard, and braided hair on the top of the head. The coiffure's triangles, lozenges, and overlapping disks of hair and the great arching eyebrows that give so much character to the portrait reveal that the sculptor was also sensitive to formal pattern.

No less remarkable is the fact this is a life-size, hollow-cast metal sculpture (see "Hollow-Casting Life-Size Bronze Statues," Chapter 5, page 108), one of the earliest known. The head demonstrates the artisan's sophisticated skill in casting and polishing copper and in engraving the details. The portrait is the earliest known great monumental work of hollow-cast sculpture.

NARAM-SIN STELE The godlike sovereignty the kings of Akkad claimed is also evident in the victory stele (FIG. 2-13) Naram-Sin set up at Sippar. The stele commemorates his defeat of the Lullubi, a people of the Iranian mountains to the east. It is inscribed twice, once in honor of Naram-Sin and once by an Elamite king who had captured Sippar in 1157 BCE and taken the stele as booty back to Susa in southwestern Iran (MAP 2-1), where it was found. On the stele, the grandson of Sargon leads his victorious army up the slopes of a wooded mountain. His routed enemies fall, flee, die, or beg for mercy. The king stands alone, far taller than his men, treading on the bodies of two of the fallen Lullubi. He wears the horned helmet signifying divinity—the first time a king appears as a god in Mesopotamian art. At least three favorable stars (the stele is damaged at the top) shine on his triumph.

By storming the mountain, Naram-Sin seems also to be scaling the ladder to the heavens, the same conceit that lies behind the great ziggurat towers of the ancient Near East. His troops march up the mountain behind him in orderly files, suggesting the discipline and organization of the king's forces. The enemy, in contrast, is in disarray, depicted in a great variety of postures—one falls headlong down

Enheduanna, Priestess and Poet

In the man's world of ancient Akkad, one woman stands out prominently—Enheduanna, daughter of King Sargon and priestess of the moon god Nanna at Ur. Her name appears in several inscriptions, and she was the author of a series of hymns in honor of the goddess Inanna. Enheduanna's is the oldest recorded name of a poet, male or female. Indeed, hers is the earliest known name of the author of any literary work in world history.

The most important surviving object associated with Enheduanna is the alabaster disk (FIG. 2-14) found at Ur in several fragments in the residence of the priestess of Nanna. The reverse bears a cuneiform inscription identifying Enheduanna as the "wife of Nanna" and "daughter of Sargon, king of the world" and credits Enheduanna with erecting an altar to Nanna in his temple. The dedication of the relief to the moon god explains its unusual round format, which corresponds to the shape of the full moon. The front of the disk shows four figures approaching a four-story ziggurat. The first figure is a nude man who is either a priest or Enheduanna's assistant. He pours a libation into a plant stand. The second figure, taller than the rest and wearing the headgear of a priestess, is Enheduanna herself. She raises her right hand in a gesture of greeting and respect for the god. Two figures, probably female attendants, follow her.

Artworks created to honor women are rare in Mesopotamia and in the ancient world in general, and Enheduanna's is the oldest known. Enheduanna was, however, a princess and priestess, not a ruler in her own right, and her disk pales in comparison to the monuments erected almost a thousand years later in honor of Queen Hatshepsut of Egypt (see "Hatshepsut," Chapter 3, page 54).

2-14 Votive disk of Enheduanna, from Ur (modern Tell Muqayyar), Iraq, ca. 2300–2275 BCE. Alabaster, diameter 10″. University of Pennsylvania Museum of Archaeology and Anthropology, Philadelphia.

Enheduanna, daughter of Sargon of Akkad and priestess of Nanna at Ur, is the first author whose name is known. She is the tallest figure on this disk that she dedicated in honor of the moon god.

the mountainside. The Akkadian artist adhered to older conventions in many details, especially by portraying the king and his soldiers in composite views and by placing a frontal two-horned helmet on Naram-Sin's profile head. But the sculptor showed daring innovation in creating a landscape setting for the story and placing the figures on successive tiers within that landscape. For the first time, an artist rejected the standard way of telling a story in a series of horizontal registers, the compositional formula that had been the rule for a millennium. The traditional frieze format was used, however, for an alabaster disk (FIG. 2-14) that is in other respects one of the

most remarkable discoveries ever made in the ancient Near East (see "Enheduanna, Priestess and Poet," above).

ZIGGURAT, UR Around 2150 BCE, a mountain people, the Gutians, brought Akkadian power to an end. The cities of Sumer, however, soon united in response to the alien presence, drove the Gutians out of Mesopotamia, and established a Neo-Sumerian state ruled by the kings of Ur. This age, which historians call the Third Dynasty of Ur, saw the construction of the ziggurat (FIG. 2-15) at Ur, one of the largest in Mesopotamia. Built about a millennium later than that at

2-15 Ziggurat (northeastern facade with restored stairs), Ur (modern Tell Muqayyar), Iraq, ca. 2100 BCE.

The Ur ziggurat is one of the largest in Mesopotamia. It has three ramplike stairways of a hundred steps each that originally ended at a gateway to a brick temple, which does not survive.

Akkad and the Third Dynasty of Ur **27**

The Piety of Gudea

One of the central figures of the Neo-Sumerian age was Gudea of Lagash. Nearly two dozen portraits of him survive. All stood in temples where they could render perpetual service to the gods and intercede with the divine powers on his behalf. Although a powerful ruler, Gudea rejected the regal trappings of Sargon of Akkad and his successors in favor of a return to the Sumerian votive tradition of the Eshnunna statuettes (FIG. 2-6). Like the earlier examples, many of Gudea's statues are inscribed with messages to the gods of Sumer. One from Girsu says, "I am the shepherd loved by my king [Ningirsu, the god of Girsu]; may my life be prolonged." Another, also from Girsu, as if in answer to the first, says, "Gudea, the builder of the temple, has been given life." Some of the inscriptions help explain why Gudea was portrayed the way he was. For example, his large chest is a sign that the gods have given him fullness of life and his muscular arms reveal his god-given strength. Other inscriptions underscore that his large eyes signify that his gaze is perpetually fixed on the gods (compare FIG. 2-6).

Gudea built or rebuilt, at great cost, all the temples in which he placed his statues. One characteristic portrait (FIG. 2-16) depicts the pious ruler of Lagash seated with his hands clasped in front of him in a gesture of prayer. The head is unfortunately lost, but the statue is of unique interest because Gudea has a temple plan drawn on a tablet on his lap. It is the plan for a new temple dedicated to Ningirsu. Gudea buried accounts of his building enterprises in the temple foundations. The surviving texts describe how the Neo-Sumerians prepared and purified the sites, obtained the materials, and dedicated the completed temples. They also record Gudea's dreams of the gods asking him to erect temples in their honor, promising him prosperity if he fulfilled his duty. In one of these dreams, Ningirsu addresses Gudea:

> When, O faithful shepherd Gudea, thou shalt have started work
> for me on Erinnu, my royal abode [Ningirsu's new temple], I will
> call up in heaven a humid wind. It shall bring the abundance from
> on high.... All the great fields will bear for thee; dykes and canals will
> swell for thee; ... good weight of wool will be given in thy time.*

*Translated by Thorkild Jacobsen, in Henri Frankfort, *The Art and Architecture of the Ancient Orient*, 5th ed. (New Haven: Yale University Press, 1996), 98.

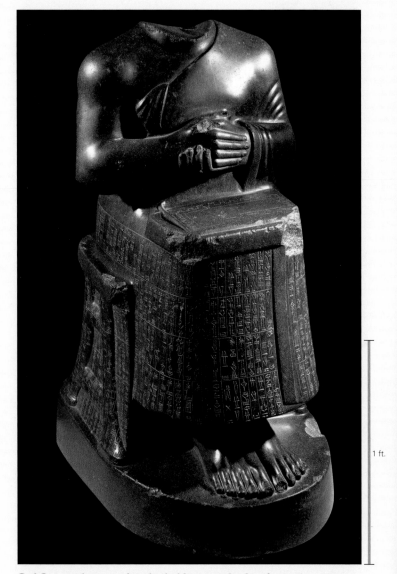

1 ft.

2-16 Seated statue of Gudea holding temple plan, from Girsu (modern Telloh), Iraq, ca. 2100 BCE. Diorite, 2′ 5″ high. Louvre, Paris.

Gudea of Lagash built or rebuilt many temples and placed statues of himself in all of them. In this seated portrait, Gudea has on his lap a plan of the new temple he erected to Ningirsu.

Uruk (FIGS. 2-2 and 2-3), the Ur ziggurat is much grander. The base is a solid mass of mud brick 50 feet high. The builders used baked bricks laid in bitumen, an asphaltlike substance, for the facing of the entire monument. Three ramplike stairways of a hundred steps each converge on a tower-flanked gateway. From there another flight of steps probably led to the temple proper, which does not survive.

GUDEA OF LAGASH The most conspicuous preserved sculptural monuments of the Neo-Sumerian age portray Gudea, the ensi of Lagash around 2100 BCE (see "The Piety of Gudea," above). His statues (FIG. 2-16) show him seated or standing, hands tightly clasped, head shaven, sometimes wearing a woolen brimmed hat, and always dressed in a long garment that leaves one shoulder and arm exposed. Gudea was zealous in granting the gods their due, and the numerous statues he commissioned are an enduring testimony to his piety—and to his wealth and pride. All his portraits are of polished diorite, a rare and costly dark stone that had to be imported. Diorite is also extremely hard and difficult to carve. The prestige of the material—which in turn lent prestige to Gudea's portraits—is evident from an inscription on one of Gudea's statues: "This statue has not been made from silver nor from lapis lazuli, nor from copper nor from lead, nor yet from bronze; it is made of diorite."

Hammurabi's Law Code

In the early 18th century BCE, King Hammurabi of Babylon formulated a comprehensive law code for his people. At the time, parts of Europe were still in the Stone Age. Even in Greece, it was not until more than 1,000 years later that Draco provided Athens with its first written set of laws. Two earlier Sumerian law codes survive in part, but Hammurabi's laws are the only ones known in great detail, thanks to the chance survival of a tall black-basalt stele (FIG. 2-17) that was carried off as booty to Susa in 1157 BCE, together with the Naram-Sin stele (FIG. 2-13). At the top (FIG. 2-1) is a representation in high relief of Hammurabi in the presence of Shamash, the flame-shouldered sun god. The king raises his hand in respect. The god extends to Hammurabi the rod and ring that symbolize authority. The symbols derive from builders' tools—measuring rods and coiled rope—and connote the ruler's capacity to build the social order and to measure people's lives, that is, to render judgments and enforce the laws spelled out on the stele. The judicial code, written in Akkadian, was inscribed in 3,500 lines of cuneiform characters. Hammurabi's laws governed all aspects of Babylonian life, from commerce and property to murder and theft to marital fidelity, inheritances, and the treatment of slaves.

Here is a small sample of the infractions described and the penalties imposed (which vary with the person's standing in society):

- If a man puts out the eye of another man, his eye shall be put out.
- If he kills a man's slave, he shall pay one-third of a mina.
- If someone steals property from a temple, he will be put to death, as will the person who receives the stolen goods.
- If a man rents a boat and the boat is wrecked, the renter shall replace the boat with another.
- If a married woman dies before bearing any sons, her dowry shall be repaid to her father, but if she gave birth to sons, the dowry shall belong to them.
- If a man's wife is caught in bed with another man, both will be tied up and thrown in the water.

Hammurabi's stele is noteworthy artistically as well. The sculptor depicted Shamash (FIG. 2-1) in the familiar convention of combined front and side views, but with two important exceptions. His great headdress with its four pairs of horns is in true profile so that only four, not all eight, of the horns are visible. And the artist seems to have tentatively explored the notion of *foreshortening*—a means of suggesting depth by representing a figure or object at an angle, instead of frontally or in profile. Shamash's beard is a series of diagonal rather than horizontal lines, suggesting its recession from the picture plane, and the sculptor represented the side of his throne at an angle.

2-17 Stele with law code of Hammurabi, from Susa, Iran, ca. 1780 BCE. Basalt, 7′ 4″ high. Louvre, Paris.

The stele that records Hammurabi's remarkably early law code also is one of the first examples of an artist employing foreshortening—the representation of a figure or object at an angle (compare FIG. 2-1).

1 ft.

SECOND MILLENNIUM BCE

The resurgence of Sumer was short-lived. The last of the kings of the Third Dynasty of Ur fell at the hands of the Elamites, who ruled the territory east of the Tigris River. The following two centuries witnessed the reemergence of the traditional Mesopotamian political pattern of several independent city-states existing side by side.

HAMMURABI Babylon was one of those city-states until its most powerful king, Hammurabi (r. 1792–1750 BCE), reestablished a centralized government in southern Mesopotamia. Perhaps the most renowned king in Mesopotamian history, Hammurabi was famous for his conquests. But he is best known today for his law code (FIGS. 2-1 and 2-17), which prescribed penalties for everything from adultery and murder to the cutting down of a neighbor's trees (see "Hammurabi's Law Code," above).

LION GATE, HATTUSA The Babylonian Empire toppled in the face of an onslaught by the Hittites, an Anatolian people who conquered and sacked Babylon around 1595 BCE. They then retired to their homeland, leaving Babylon in the hands of the Kassites. Remains of the strongly fortified capital city of the Hittites still may be seen at Hattusa near modern Boghazköy, Turkey. Constructed of large blocks

2-18 Lion Gate, Hattusa (modern Boghazköy), Turkey, ca. 1400 BCE.

The Hittites conquered and sacked Babylon around 1595 BCE. Their fortified capital at Boghazköy in Anatolia had seven-foot-tall stone lions guarding the main gateway (compare FIGS. 2-21 and 4-19).

of heavy stone—a striking contrast to the brick architecture of Mesopotamia—the walls and towers of the Hittites effectively protected them from attack. Symbolically guarding the gateway (FIG. 2-18) to the Hattusa citadel are two huge (seven-foot-high) lions. Their simply carved forequarters project from massive stone blocks on either side of the entrance. These Hittite guardian beasts are early examples of a theme that was to be echoed on many Near Eastern gates. Notable are those of Assyria (FIG. 2-21), one of the greatest empires of the ancient world, and of the reborn Babylon (FIG. 2-24) in the first millennium BCE. But the idea of protecting a city, palace, temple, or tomb from evil by placing wild beasts or fantastic monsters before an entranceway was not unique to the Near Eastern world. Examples abound in Egypt, Greece, Italy, and elsewhere.

NAPIR-ASU OF ELAM To the east of Sumer, Akkad, and Babylon was Elam, which appears in the Bible as early as Genesis 10:22. During the second half of the second millennium BCE, Elam reached the height of its political and military power. At this time the Elamites were strong enough to plunder Babylonia and to carry off the stelae of Naram-Sin and Hammurabi (FIGS. 2-13 and 2-17) and display them as war booty at their capital city, Susa.

In the ruins of Susa, archaeologists discovered a life-size bronze-and-copper statue (FIG. 2-19) of Queen Napir-Asu, wife of one of the most powerful Elamite kings, Untash-Napirisha. The statue weighs 3,760 pounds even in its fragmentary and mutilated state, because the sculptor, incredibly, cast the statue with a solid bronze core inside a hollow-cast copper shell. The bronze core increased the cost of the statue enormously, but the queen wished her portrait to be a permanent, immovable votive offering in the temple where it was found. In fact, the Elamite inscription on the queen's skirt explicitly asks the gods to protect the statue:

> He who would seize my statue, who would smash it, who would destroy its inscription, who would erase my name, may he be smitten by the curse of [the gods], that his name shall become extinct, that his offspring be barren. . . . This is Napir-Asu's offering.[1]

Napir-Asu's portrait thus falls within the votive tradition going back to the third-millennium BCE Eshnunna figurines (FIG. 2-6). In the Elamite statue, the Mesopotamian instinct for cylindrical volume is again evident. The tight silhouette, strict frontality, and firmly crossed hands held close to the body are all enduring characteristics common to the Sumerian statuettes. Yet within these rigid conventions of form and pose, the Elamite artist managed to create refinements that must have come from close observation. The sculptor conveyed the feminine softness of arm and bust, the grace and elegance of the long-fingered hands, the supple and quiet bend of the wrist, the ring and bracelets, and the gown's patterned fabric. The loss of the head is especially unfortunate. The figure presents a portrait of the ideal queen. The hands crossed over the belly may allude to fertility and the queen's role in assuring peaceful dynastic succession.

2-19 Statue of Queen Napir-Asu, from Susa, Iran, ca. 1350–1300 BCE. Bronze and copper, 4′ 2¾″ high. Louvre, Paris.

This life-size bronze-and-copper statue of the wife of one of the most powerful Elamite kings weighs 3,760 pounds. The queen wanted her portrait to be an immovable votive offering in a temple.

ASSYRIA

During the first half of the first millennium BCE, the fearsome Assyrians vanquished the various warfaring peoples that succeeded the Babylonians and Hittites, including the Elamites, whose capital of Susa they sacked in 641 BCE. The Assyrians took their name from Assur, the city on the Tigris River in northern Iraq named for the god Ashur. At the height of their power, the Assyrians ruled an empire that extended from the Tigris River to the Nile and from the Persian Gulf to Asia Minor.

The royal citadel (FIG. 2-20) of Sargon II (r. 721–705 BCE) at Dur Sharrukin reveals in its ambitious layout the confidence of the Assyrian kings in their all-conquering might. Its strong defensive walls also reflect a society ever fearful of attack during a period of almost constant warfare. The city measures about a square mile in area. The palace, elevated on a mound 50 feet high, covered some 25 acres and had more than 200 courtyards and rooms. Timber-roofed rectangular halls were grouped around square and rectangular courts. Behind the main courtyard, whose sides each measured 300 feet, were the residential quarters of the king, who received foreign emissaries in the long, high, brightly painted throne room. All visitors entered from another large courtyard, where over-life-size figures of the king and his courtiers lined the walls.

Sargon II regarded his city and palace as an expression of his grandeur. The Assyrians cultivated an image of themselves as merciless to anyone who dared oppose them, although they were forgiving to those who submitted to their will. Sargon, for example, wrote in an inscription, "I built a city with [the labors of] the peoples subdued by my hand, whom Ashur, Nabu, and Marduk had caused to lay themselves at my feet and bear my yoke." And in another text, he proclaimed, "Sargon, King of the World, has built a city. Dur Sharrukin he has named it. A peerless palace he has built within it."

In addition to the complex of courtyards, throne room, state chambers, service quarters, and guard rooms that made up the palace, the citadel included a great ziggurat and six sanctuaries for six different gods. The ziggurat at Dur Sharrukin may have had as many as seven stories. Four remain, each 18 feet high and painted a different color. A continuous ramp spiraled around the building from its base to the temple at its summit. Here, the legacy of the Sumerian bent-axis plan may be seen more than two millennia after the erection of the White Temple (FIG. 2-3) on the ziggurat at Uruk.

Guarding the gate to Sargon's palace were colossal limestone monsters (FIG. 2-21), which the Assyrians probably called *lamassu*. These winged, man-headed bulls served to ward off the king's enemies. The task of moving and installing these immense stone sculptures was so daunting that several reliefs in the palace of Sargon's successor celebrate the feat,

2-20 Reconstruction drawing of the citadel of Sargon II, Dur Sharrukin (modern Khorsabad), Iraq, ca. 720–705 BCE (after Charles Altman).

The fortified walls of the vast royal citadel of Sargon II enclosed courtyards, a throne room, service quarters, guard rooms, a great ziggurat, and six sanctuaries for six different gods.

2-21 Lamassu (winged, human-headed bull), from the citadel of Sargon II, Dur Sharrukin (modern Khorsabad), Iraq, ca. 720–705 BCE. Limestone, 13′ 10″ high. Louvre, Paris.

Ancient sculptors insisted on showing complete views of animals. This four-legged Assyrian palace guardian has five legs—two when seen from the front and four in profile view.

1 ft.

2-22 Assyrian archers pursuing enemies, relief from the Northwest Palace of Ashurnasirpal II, Kalhu (modern Nimrud), Iraq, ca. 875–860 BCE. Gypsum, 2′ 10⅝″ high. British Museum, London.

Assyrian palaces were adorned with extensive series of narrative reliefs exalting the king and recounting his great deeds. This one depicts Assyrian archers driving the enemy into the Euphrates River.

showing scores of men dragging lamassu figures with the aid of ropes and sledges. The Assyrian lamassu sculptures are partly in the round, but the sculptor nonetheless conceived them as high reliefs on adjacent sides of a corner. They combine the front view of the animal at rest with the side view of it in motion. Seeking to present a complete picture of the lamassu from both the front and the side, the sculptor gave the monster five legs—two seen from the front, four seen from the side. This sculpture, then, is yet another case of early artists' providing a conceptual picture of an animal or person and of all its important parts, as opposed to an optical view of the lamassu as it actually would stand in space.

PALACE OF ASHURNASIRPAL II For their palace walls the Assyrian kings commissioned extensive series of painted narrative re-

liefs exalting royal power. The degree of documentary detail in the Assyrian reliefs is without parallel in the ancient world before the Roman Empire (see Chapter 7). One of the earliest and most extensive cycles of reliefs comes from the palace of Ashurnasirpal II (r. 883–859 BCE) at Kalhu. Throughout the palace, painted gypsum reliefs sheathed the lower parts of the mud-brick walls below brightly colored plaster. Rich textiles on the floors contributed to the luxurious ambience. Every relief celebrated the king and bore an inscription naming Ashurnasirpal and describing his accomplishments.

FIG. 2-22 probably depicts an episode that occurred in 878 BCE when Ashurnasirpal drove his enemy's forces into the Euphrates River. In the relief, two Assyrian archers shoot arrows at the fleeing foe. Three enemy soldiers are in the water. One swims with an arrow in his back. The other two attempt to float to safety by inflating animal

2-23 Ashurbanipal hunting lions, relief from the North Palace of Ashurbanipal, Nineveh (modern Kuyunjik), Iraq, ca. 645–640 BCE. Gypsum, 5′ 4″ high. British Museum, London.

In addition to ceremonial and battle scenes, the hunt was a common subject of Assyrian palace reliefs. The Assyrians considered the hunting and killing of lions manly royal virtues on a par with victory in warfare.

skins. Their destination is a fort where their compatriots await them. The artist showed the fort as if it were in the middle of the river, but it must, of course, have been on land, perhaps at some distance from where the escapees entered the water. The artist's purpose was to tell the story clearly and economically. In art, distances can be compressed and the human actors enlarged so that they stand out from their environment. Literally interpreted, the defenders of the fort are too tall to walk through its archway. (Compare Naram-Sin and his men scaling a mountain, FIG. 2-13.) The sculptor also combined different viewpoints in the same frame, just as the figures are composites of frontal and profile views. The river is seen from above; the men, trees, and fort from the side. The artist also made other adjustments for clarity. The archers' bowstrings are in front of their bodies but behind their heads in order not to hide their faces. The men will snare their own heads in their bows when they launch their arrows! All these liberties with optical reality result, however, in a vivid and easily legible retelling of a decisive moment in the king's victorious campaign. This was the artist's primary goal.

PALACE OF ASHURBANIPAL Two centuries later, sculptors carved hunting reliefs for the Nineveh palace of the conqueror of Elamite Susa, Ashurbanipal (r. 668–627 BCE). The Assyrians, like many other societies before and after, regarded prowess in hunting as a manly virtue on a par with success in warfare. The royal hunt did not take place in the wild, however, but in a controlled environment, ensuring the king's safety and success. In FIG. 2-23, lions released from cages in a large enclosed arena charge the king, who, in his chariot and with his attendants, thrusts a spear into a savage lion. The animal leaps at the king even though it already has two arrows in its body. All around the royal chariot is a pathetic trail of dead and dying animals, pierced by what appear to be far more arrows than needed to kill them. Blood streams from some of the lions, but they refuse to die. The artist brilliantly depicted the straining muscles, the swelling veins, the muzzles' wrinkled skin, and the flattened ears of the powerful and defiant beasts. Modern sympathies make this scene of carnage a kind of heroic tragedy, with the lions as protagonists. It is unlikely, however, that the king's artists had any intention other than to glorify their ruler by showing the king of men pitting himself against and repeatedly conquering the king of beasts. Portraying Ashurbanipal's beastly foes as possessing courage and nobility as well as the power to kill made the king's accomplishments that much grander.

The Assyrian Empire was never very secure, and most of its kings had to fight revolts in large sections of the Near East. Assyria's conquest of Elam in the seventh century BCE and frequent rebellions in Babylonia apparently overextended its resources. During the last years of Ashurbanipal's reign, the empire began to disintegrate. Under his successors, it collapsed from the simultaneous onslaught of the Medes from the east and the resurgent Babylonians from the south. Neo-Babylonian kings held sway over the former Assyrian Empire until the Persian conquest.

NEO-BABYLONIA AND PERSIA

The most renowned of the Neo-Babylonian kings was Nebuchadnezzar II (r. 604–562 BCE), whose exploits the biblical Book of Daniel recounts. Nebuchadnezzar restored Babylon to its rank as one of the great cities of antiquity. The city's famous hanging gardens were among the Seven Wonders of the ancient world, and the Bible immortalized its enormous ziggurat as the Tower of Babel (see "Babylon, City of Wonders," page 34).

ISHTAR GATE, BABYLON Nebuchadnezzar's Babylon was a mud-brick city, but dazzling blue-glazed bricks faced the most important monuments, such as the Ishtar Gate (FIG. 2-24), actually a pair of gates, one of which has been restored and installed in a German museum. The Ishtar Gate consists of a large *arcuated* (arch-shaped) opening flanked by towers, and features *glazed* bricks with molded reliefs of animals, real and imaginary. Each Babylonian brick was molded and glazed separately, then set in proper sequence on the wall. On the Ishtar Gate, profile figures of Marduk and Nabu's dragon and Adad's bull alternate. Lining the processional way leading up to the gate were reliefs of Ishtar's sacred lion, glazed in yellow, brown, and red against a blue background.

2-24 Ishtar Gate (restored), Babylon, Iraq, ca. 575 BCE. Glazed brick. Vorderasiatisches Museum, Staatliche Museen zu Berlin, Berlin.

Babylon under King Nebuchadnezzar II was one of the greatest cities of the ancient world. Its arcuated Ishtar Gate featured glazed bricks depicting Marduk and Nabu's dragon and Adad's bull.

Babylon, City of Wonders

The uncontested list of the Seven Wonders of the ancient world was not codified until the 16th century. But already in the second century BCE, Antipater of Sidon, a Greek poet, compiled a roster of seven must-see monuments, including six of the seven later Wonders. All of the Wonders were of colossal size and constructed at great expense. Three of them were of great antiquity: the pyramids of Gizeh (FIG. 3-8), which Antipater described as "man-made mountains," and "the hanging gardens" and "walls of impregnable Babylon."

Babylon was the only site on Antipater's list that could boast two Wonders. Later list makers preferred to distribute the Seven Wonders among seven different cities. Most of these Wonders date to Greek times—the Temple of Artemis at Ephesos, with its 60-foot-tall columns; Phidias's colossal gold-and-ivory statue of Zeus at Olympia; the grandiose tomb of Mausolus (the "Mausoleum") at Halikarnassos; the Colossus of Rhodes, a bronze statue of the sun god 110 feet tall; and the lighthouse at Alexandria, perhaps the tallest building in the ancient world. The pyramids are the oldest and the Babylonian gardens the only Wonder in the category of "landscape architecture."

Several ancient texts describe Babylon's gardens. Quintus Curtius Rufus, writing in the mid-first century CE, reported:

On the top of the citadel are the hanging gardens, a wonder celebrated in the tales of the Greeks. . . . Columns of stone were set up to sustain the whole work, and on these was laid a floor of squared blocks, strong enough to hold the earth which is thrown upon it to a great depth, as well as the water with which they irrigate the soil; and the structure supports trees of such great size that the thickness of their trunks equals a measure of eight cubits [about twelve feet]. They tower to a height of fifty feet, and they yield as much fruit as if they were growing in their native soil. . . . To those who look upon [the trees] from a distance, real woods seem to be overhanging their native mountains.*

Not qualifying as a Wonder, but in some ways no less impressive, was Babylon's Marduk ziggurat, the biblical Tower of Babel. According to the Bible, humankind's arrogant desire to build a tower to Heaven angered God. The Lord put an end to it by causing the workers to speak different languages, preventing them from communicating with one another. The fifth-century BCE Greek historian Herodotus described the Babylonian temple complex:

In the middle of the sanctuary [of Marduk] has been built a solid tower . . . which supports another tower, which in turn supports another, and so on: there are eight towers in all. A stairway has been constructed to wind its way up the outside of all the towers; halfway up the stairway there is a shelter with benches to rest on, where people making the ascent can sit and catch their breath. In the last tower there is a huge temple. The temple contains a large couch, which is adorned with fine coverings and has a golden table standing beside it, but there are no statues at all standing there. . . . [The Babylonians] say that the god comes in person to the temple [compare the Sumerian notion of the temple as a "waiting room"] and rests on the couch; I do not believe this story myself.†

*Translated by John C. Rolfe, *Quintus Curtius I* (Cambridge, Mass.: Harvard University Press, 1971), 337–339.
†Translated by Robin Waterfield, *Herodotus: The Histories* (New York: Oxford University Press, 1998), 79–80.

THE PERSIAN EMPIRE Although Nebuchadnezzar, "King of Kings" of the biblical Daniel, had boasted that he "caused a mighty wall to circumscribe Babylon . . . so that the enemy who would do evil would not threaten," Cyrus of Persia (r. 559–529 BCE) captured the city in the sixth century. Cyrus, who may have been descended from an Elamite line, was the founder of the Achaemenid dynasty and traced his ancestry back to a mythical King Achaemenes. Babylon was but one of the Persians' conquests. Egypt fell to them in 525 BCE, and by 480 BCE the Persian Empire was the largest the world had yet known, extending from the Indus River in South Asia to the Danube River in northeastern Europe. Only the successful Greek resistance in the fifth century BCE prevented Persia from embracing southeastern Europe as well. The Achaemenid line ended with the death of Darius III in 330 BCE, after his defeat at the hands of Alexander the Great (FIG. 5-70).

PERSEPOLIS The most important source of knowledge about Persian art and architecture is the ceremonial and administrative complex on the citadel at Persepolis (FIG. 2-25), which the successors of Cyrus, Darius I (r. 522–486 BCE) and Xerxes (r. 486–465 BCE), built between 521 and 465 BCE. Situated on a high plateau, the heavily fortified complex of royal buildings stood on a wide platform overlooking the plain. Alexander the Great razed the site in a gesture symbolizing the destruction of Persian imperial power. Some said it was an act of revenge for the Persian sack of the Athenian Acropolis in the early fifth century BCE (see Chapter 5). But even in ruins, the Persepolis citadel is impressive.

The approach to the citadel led through a monumental gateway called the Gate of All Lands, a reference to the harmony among the peoples of the vast Persian Empire. Assyrian-inspired colossal man-headed winged bulls flanked the great entrance. Broad ceremonial stairways provided access to the platform and the royal audience hall, or *apadana*, a huge hall 60 feet high and 217 feet square, containing 36 colossal columns. An audience of thousands could have stood within the hall.

The reliefs (FIG. 2-26) decorating the walls of the terrace and staircases leading to the apadana represent processions of royal guards, Persian nobles and dignitaries, and representatives from 23 subject nations bringing the king tribute. Every one of the emissaries wears his national costume and carries a typical regional gift for the conqueror. The carving of the Persepolis reliefs is technically superb, with subtly modeled surfaces and crisply chiseled details. Traces of color prove that the reliefs were painted, and the original effect must have been even more striking than it is today. Although the Persepolis sculptures may have been inspired by those in Assyrian palaces, they are different in style. The forms are more rounded, and they project more from the background. Some of the details, notably the treatment of drapery folds, echo forms characteristic of Archaic Greek sculpture (see Chapter 5), and Greek influence seems to be one of the many ingredients of Achaemenid style. Persian art testifies to the active exchange of ideas and artists among all the Mediterranean and Near Eastern civilizations at this date. A building inscription at Susa, for example, names Ionian Greeks, Medes, Egyp-

2-25 Aerial view (looking west) of Persepolis (apadana in the background), Iran, ca. 521–465 BCE.

The heavily fortified complex of Persian royal buildings on a high plateau at Persepolis contained a royal audience hall, or apadana, 60 feet high and 217 feet square with 36 colossal columns.

tians, and Babylonians among those who built and decorated the palace. Under the single-minded direction of its Persian masters, this heterogeneous workforce, with a widely varied cultural and artistic background, created a new and coherent style that perfectly suited the expression of Persian imperial ambitions.

SASANIAN CTESIPHON Alexander the Great's conquest of Persia in 330 BCE marked the beginning of a long period of first Greek and then Roman rule of large parts of the ancient Near East,

beginning with one of Alexander's former generals, Seleucus I (r. 312–281 BCE), founder of the Seleucid dynasty. In the third century CE, however, a new power rose up in Persia that challenged the Romans and sought to force them out of Asia. The new rulers called themselves Sasanians. They traced their lineage to a legendary figure named Sasan, said to be a direct descendant of the Achaemenid kings. Their New Persian Empire was founded in 224 CE, when the first Sasanian king, Artaxerxes I (r. 211–241), defeated the Parthians (another of Rome's eastern enemies).

2-26 Processional frieze (detail) on the terrace of the apadana, Persepolis, Iran, ca. 521–465 BCE. Limestone, 8′ 4″ high.

The reliefs decorating the walls of the terrace and staircases leading up to the Persepolis apadana included depictions of representatives of 23 subject nations bringing tribute to the Persian king.

1 ft.

Neo-Babylonia and Persia **35**

2-27 Palace of Shapur I, Ctesiphon, Iraq, ca. 250 CE.

The last great pre-Islamic civilization of the Near East was that of the Sasanians. Their palace at Ctesiphon, near Baghdad, features a brick audience hall (iwan) covered by an enormous pointed vault.

The son and successor of Artaxerxes, Shapur I (r. 241–272), succeeded in further extending Sasanian territory. He also erected a great palace (FIG. 2-27) at Ctesiphon, the capital his father had established near modern Baghdad in Iraq. The central feature of Shapur's palace was the monumental *iwan,* or brick audience hall, covered by a *vault* (here, a deep arch over an oblong space) that came almost to a point more than 100 feet above the ground. The facade to the left and right of the iwan was divided into a series of horizontal bands made up of *blind arcades,* a series of arches without actual openings, applied as wall decoration. A thousand years later, Islamic architects looked at Shapur's palace and especially its soaring iwan and established it as the standard for judging their own engineering feats (see Chapter 10).

SHAPUR I AND ROME So powerful was the Sasanian army that in 260 CE Shapur I even succeeded in capturing the Roman emperor Valerian near Edessa (Turkey). His victory over Valerian was such a significant event that Shapur commemorated it in a series of rock-cut reliefs in the cliffs of Bishapur in Iran, far from the site of his triumph. FIG. 2-28 reproduces one of the Bishapur reliefs. Shapur appears larger than life, riding in from the right wearing the distinctive tall Sasanian crown, which breaks through the relief 's border and draws attention to the king. At the left, Valerian kneels before Shapur and begs for mercy. Similar scenes of kneeling enemies before triumphant generals are commonplace in Roman art—but at Bishapur the roles are reversed. This appropriation of Roman compositional patterns and motifs in a relief celebrating the Sasanian defeat of the Romans adds another, ironic, level of meaning to the political message in stone.

The New Persian Empire endured more than 400 years, until the Arabs drove the Sasanians out of Mesopotamia in 636 CE, just four years after the death of Muhammad. Thereafter, the greatest artists and architects of Mesopotamia worked in the service of Islam (see Chapter 10).

2-28 Triumph of Shapur I over Valerian, rock-cut relief, Bishapur, Iran, ca. 260 CE.

The Sasanian king Shapur I humiliated the Roman emperor Valerian in 260 CE and commemorated his surrender in over-life-size reliefs cut into the cliffs outside Persepolis.

THE ANCIENT NEAR EAST

SUMERIAN ART, ca. 3500–2332 BCE

▮ The Sumerians founded the world's first city-states in the valley between the Tigris and Euphrates rivers and invented writing in the fourth millennium BCE.

▮ They were also the first to build towering temple platforms, called ziggurats, and to place figures in registers to tell coherent stories.

Standard of Ur, ca. 2600 BCE

AKKADIAN ART, ca. 2332–2150 BCE

▮ The Akkadians were the first Near Eastern rulers to call themselves kings of the world and to assume divine attributes. The earliest recorded name of an author is the Akkadian priestess Enheduanna.

▮ Akkadian artists may have been the first to cast hollow life-size bronze sculptures and to place figures at different levels in a landscape setting.

Portrait of an Akkadian king, ca. 2250–2200 BCE

NEO-SUMERIAN AND BABYLONIAN ART, ca. 2150–1600 BCE

▮ During the Third Dynasty of Ur, the Sumerians rose again to power and constructed one of the largest ziggurats in Mesopotamia at Ur.

▮ Gudea of Lagash (r. ca. 2100 BCE) built numerous temples and placed diorite portraits of himself in all of them as votive offerings to the gods.

▮ Babylon's greatest king, Hammurabi (r. 1792–1750 BCE), established a comprehensive law code for the empire he ruled. Babylonian artists were among the first to experiment with foreshortening.

Stele of Hammurabi, ca. 1780 BCE

ASSYRIAN ART, ca. 900–612 BCE

▮ At the height of their power, the Assyrians ruled an empire that extended from the Persian Gulf to the Nile and Asia Minor.

▮ Assyrian palaces were fortified citadels with gates guarded by monstrous lamassu. Painted reliefs depicting the king in battle and hunting lions decorated the walls of the ceremonial halls.

Lamassu, citadel of Sargon II, Dur Sharrukin, ca. 720–705 BCE

NEO-BABYLONIAN AND PERSIAN ART, ca. 612–330 BCE

▮ In the sixth century BCE, the Babylonians constructed two of the Seven Wonders of the ancient world. The Ishtar Gate, with its colorful glazed brick reliefs, gives an idea of how magnificent Babylon was under Nebuchadnezzar II (r. 604–562 BCE).

▮ The capital of the Achaemenid Persians was at Persepolis, where Darius I (r. 522–486 BCE) and Xerxes (r. 486–465 BCE) built a huge palace complex with an audience hall that could accommodate thousands. Painted reliefs of subject nations bringing tribute decorated the terraces.

▮ Alexander the Great conquered the Persian Empire in 330 BCE.

Ishtar Gate, Babylon, ca. 575 BCE

1 in.

3-1 Death mask of Tutankhamen, from the innermost coffin in his tomb at Thebes, Egypt, 18th Dynasty, ca. 1323 BCE. Gold with inlay of semiprecious stones, 1′ 9¼″ high. Egyptian Museum, Cairo.

The extraordinary treasures in the boy-king Tutankhamen's tomb attest to the wealth the Egyptian pharaohs lavished on preparing for the afterlife. Tutankhamen's mask is gold with inlaid gems.

EGYPT UNDER
THE PHARAOHS

Nearly 2,500 years ago, the Greek historian Herodotus wrote, "Concerning Egypt itself I shall extend my remarks to a great length, because there is no country that possesses so many wonders, nor any that has such a number of works that defy description."[1] Even today, many would agree with this assessment. The ancient Egyptians left to the world a profusion of spectacular monuments dating across three millennia. From the cliffs of the Libyan and Arabian deserts they cut giant blocks of stone and erected grand temples to their immortal gods (see "The Gods and Goddesses of Egypt," page 40). From the same imperishable material that symbolized the timelessness of their world, the Egyptians set up countless statues of their equally immortal god-kings and built thousands of tombs to serve as eternal houses of the dead. The solemn and ageless art of the Egyptians expresses the unchanging order that, for them, was divinely established.

The backbone of Egypt was, and still is, the Nile River, whose annual floods supported all life in that ancient land (MAP **3-1**). Even more than the Tigris and the Euphrates rivers of Mesopotamia, the Nile defined the cultures that developed along its banks. Originating deep in Africa, the world's longest river flows through regions that may not receive a single drop of rainfall in a decade. Yet crops thrive from the rich soil that the Nile brings thousands of miles from the African hills. In the time of the *pharaohs,* the ancient Egyptian kings, the land bordering the Nile consisted of marshes dotted with island ridges. The Egyptians hunted the amphibious animals that swarmed through the tall forests of *papyrus* and rushes in the marshes. Egypt's fertility was famous. When Egypt became a province of the Roman Empire after Queen Cleopatra's death (r. 51–30 BCE), it served as the granary of the Mediterranean world.

Even in the Middle Ages, Egypt's reputation as an ancient land of wonders and mystery lived on. Until the late 18th century, people regarded its undeciphered writing and exotic monuments as treasures of occult wisdom, locked away from any but those initiated in the mystic arts. Scholars knew something of Egypt's history from references in the Old Testament, from Herodotus and other Greco-Roman authors, and from preserved portions of a history of Egypt written in Greek in the third century BCE by an Egyptian high priest named Manetho. Manetho described the succession of pharaohs, dividing them into the still-useful groups called dynasties, but his chronology was inaccurate, and the absolute dates of the pharaohs are still debated. The chronologies scholars have proposed for the earliest Egyptian dynasties

The Gods and Goddesses of Egypt

The worldview of the Egyptians was distinct from those of their neighbors in the ancient Mediterranean and Near Eastern worlds. Egyptians believed that before the beginning of time the primeval waters, called *Nun*, existed alone in the darkness. At the moment of creation, a mound rose out of the limitless waters—just as muddy mounds emerge from the Nile after the annual flood recedes. On this mound the creator god appeared and brought light to the world. In later times, the mound was formalized as a pyramidal stone called the *ben-ben* supporting the supreme god, **Amen,** the god of the sun (*Re*).

The supreme god also created the first of the other gods and goddesses of Egypt. According to one version of the myth, the creator masturbated and produced **Shu** and **Tefnut,** the primary male and female forces in the universe. They coupled to give birth to **Geb** (Earth) and **Nut** (Sky), who bore Osiris, Seth, Isis, and Nephthys. The eldest, **Osiris,** was the god of order and was revered as the king who brought civilization to Egypt. His brother, **Seth,** was his evil opposite, the god of chaos. Seth murdered Osiris and cut him into pieces, which he scattered across Egypt. **Isis,** the sister and consort of Osiris, with the help of **Nephthys,** Seth's wife, succeeded in collecting Osiris's body parts, and with her powerful magic brought him back to life.

The resurrected Osiris fathered a son with Isis—**Horus,** who avenged his father's death and displaced Seth as king of Egypt. Osiris then became the lord of the Underworld. Horus is represented in art either as a falcon, considered the noblest bird of the sky, or as a falcon-headed man. All Egyptian pharaohs were identified with Horus while alive and with Osiris after they died.

Other Egyptian deities included **Mut,** the consort of the sun god Amen, and **Khonsu,** the moon god, who was their son. **Thoth,** another lunar deity and the god of knowledge and writing, appears in art as an ibis, a baboon, or an ibis-headed man crowned with the crescent moon and the moon disk. When Seth tore out Horus's falcon-eye (*wedjat*), Thoth restored it. He, too, was associated with rebirth and the afterlife. **Hathor,** daughter of Re, was a divine mother of the pharaoh, nourishing him with her milk. She appears in Egyptian art as a cow-headed woman or as a woman with a cow's horns. **Anubis,** a jackal or jackal-headed deity, was the god of the Underworld and of mummification. **Maat,** another daughter of Re, was the goddess of truth and justice. Her feather was used to measure the weight of the deceased's heart on Anubis's scales to determine if the *ka* (life force) would be blessed in the afterlife.

---

can vary by as much as two centuries. Exact years cannot be assigned to the reigns of individual pharaohs until 664 BCE (26th Dynasty).[2]

At the end of the 18th century, when Europeans rediscovered Egypt, the land of the Nile became the first subject of archaeological exploration. In 1799, Napoleon Bonaparte, on a military expedition to Egypt, took with him a small troop of scholars, linguists, antiquarians, and artists. The chance discovery of the famed *Rosetta Stone*, now in the British Museum, provided the key to deciphering Egyptian *hiero-glyphic* writing. The stone bears an inscription in three sections: one in Greek, which the Frenchmen easily read; one in *demotic* (Late Egyptian); and one in formal hieroglyphic. On the assumption that the text was the same in all three sections, scholars attempted to decipher the two non-Greek sections. Eventually, Jean-François Champollion deduced that the hieroglyphs were not simply pictographs but the signs of a once-spoken language whose traces survived in Coptic, the language of Christian Egypt. The ability to read hieroglyphic inscriptions revolutionized the study of Egyptian civilization and art.

THE PREDYNASTIC AND EARLY DYNASTIC PERIODS

The Predynastic, or prehistoric, beginnings of Egyptian civilization are chronologically vague. But tantalizing remains of tombs, paintings, pottery, and other artifacts attest to the existence of a sophisticated culture on the banks of the Nile around 3500 BCE.

Painting and Sculpture

In Predynastic times, Egypt was divided geographically and politically into Upper Egypt (the southern, upstream part of the Nile Valley), a narrow tract of grassland that encouraged hunting, and Lower (northern) Egypt, where the rich soil of the Nile Delta islands encouraged agriculture and animal husbandry. The major finds of Predynastic art come from Upper Egypt, especially Hierakonpolis.

TOMB 100, HIERAKONPOLIS Archaeologists exploring the Predynastic cemetery at Hierakonpolis found extraordinary mural paintings on three interior walls of tomb 100. The tomb is no longer preserved, but a watercolor copy (FIG. 3-2) of the murals records

MAP 3-1 Ancient Egypt.

People, boats, and animals, detail of a watercolor copy of a wall painting from tomb 100 at Hierakonpolis, Egypt, Predynastic, ca. 3500–3200 BCE. Paint on plaster, entire painting 16′ 4″ × 3′ 7 3/8″. Egyptian Museum, Cairo.

The oldest Egyptian mural painting depicts boats, a heraldic group of a human and animals, and a man striking prisoners. The random arrangement of the motifs is characteristic of Neolithic painting.

1 ft.

their original appearance. The paintings formed a frieze running around three adjacent walls of the tomb and represented what seems to be, at least in part, a funerary scene with people, animals, and large boats. The stick figures and their apparently random arrangement recall the Neolithic painted hunters (FIG. 1-17) of Çatal Höyük. One black and five white boats, symbolic of the journey down the river of life and death, carry cargo of uncertain significance. The figures include a heraldic grouping of two animals flanking a human figure (at the lower left) and a man striking three prisoners with a mace (lower left corner). The heraldic group, a compositional type usually associated with Mesopotamian art (FIG. 2-10, *right*), suggests that influences from Mesopotamia not only had reached Egypt by this time but

also already had made the thousand-mile journey up the Nile. The second group, however, is characteristically Egyptian, and the motif was to have a long history in Egyptian painting and sculpture alike.

PALETTE OF KING NARMER The Predynastic period ended with the unification of Upper and Lower Egypt, which until recently scholars thought occurred during the rule of the First Dynasty pharaoh Menes, identified by many Egyptologists with King Narmer. Narmer's image and name appear on both sides of a ceremonial *palette* (stone slab with a circular depression) found at Hierakonpolis. The palette (FIG. 3-3) is one of the earliest historical (versus prehistorical) artworks preserved, but Egyptologists still debate

3-3 Palette of King Narmer (*left*, back; *right*, front), from Hierakonpolis, Egypt, Predynastic, ca. 3000–2920 BCE. Slate, 2′ 1″ high. Egyptian Museum, Cairo.

These earliest preserved labeled historical reliefs commemorate the unification of Upper and Lower Egypt. Narmer, the largest figure, effortlessly defeats a foe on one side, and on the other surveys the beheaded enemy.

1 in.

The Predynastic and Early Dynastic Periods   **41**

exactly what event is depicted. No longer regarded as commemorating the foundation of the first of Egypt's 31 dynasties around 2920 BCE (the last ended in 332 BCE), the reliefs probably record the unification of the two kingdoms. Scholars now believe this unification occurred over several centuries, but the palette depicts the creation of the "Kingdom of the Two Lands" as a single great event.

Narmer's palette is an elaborate, formalized version of a utilitarian object commonly used in the Predynastic period to prepare eye makeup. (Egyptians used makeup to protect their eyes against irritation and the glare of the sun.) Narmer's palette is important not only as a document marking the transition from the prehistorical to the historical period in ancient Egypt but also as a kind of early blueprint of the formula for figure representation that characterized most Egyptian art for 3,000 years. At the top of each side of the palette are two heads of a cow with a woman's face, usually identified as the goddess Hathor but sometimes as the sky goddess Bat. Between the two heads is a hieroglyph giving Narmer's name (catfish = nar; chisel = mer) within a frame representing the royal palace, making Narmer's palette the earliest existing labeled work of historical art.

On the back (FIG. 3-3, *left*) of the palette, the king, wearing the high, white, bowling-pin–shaped crown of Upper Egypt and accompanied by an official who carries his sandals, slays an enemy. The motif closely resembles the group at the lower left of the Hierakonpolis mural (FIG. 3-2) and became the standard pictorial formula signifying the inevitable triumph of the Egyptian god-kings over their enemies. Above and to the right, the falcon with human arms is Horus, the king's protector. The falcon-god takes captive a man-headed hieroglyph with a papyrus plant growing from it that stands for the land of Lower Egypt. Below the king are two fallen enemies.

On the front (FIG. 3-3, *right*) of the palette, the elongated necks of two felines form the circular depression that would have held eye makeup in an ordinary palette not made for display. The intertwined necks of the animals (a motif common in Mesopotamian art) may be another pictorial reference to Egypt's unification. In the uppermost register, Narmer, wearing the red crown of Lower Egypt, reviews the beheaded bodies of the enemy. The dead are seen from above, as are the bison (FIG. 1-9) lying on the ground on the ceiling of the Altamira cave. The artist depicted each body with its severed head neatly placed between its legs. By virtue of his superior rank, the king, on both sides of the palette, performs his ritual task alone and towers over his own men and the enemy. The king's superhuman strength is symbolized in the lowest band by a great bull knocking down a rebellious city whose fortress walls also are seen in an "aerial view." Specific historical narrative was not the artist's goal in this work. What was important was the characterization of the king as supreme, isolated from and larger than all ordinary men and solely responsible for the triumph over the enemy. Here, at the very beginning of Egyptian history, is evidence of the state policy that established the pharaoh as a divine ruler.

The artist's portrayal of Narmer on both sides of the palette combines profile views of his head, legs, and arms with front views of his eye and torso—the same composite view of the human figure found in Mesopotamian art and even some Stone Age paintings. Although the proportions of the human figure changed, this composite representation of the body's parts became standard in Egyptian art as well. In the Hierakonpolis painting (FIG. 3-2), the artist scattered the figures across the wall more or less haphazardly. On Narmer's palette, the sculptor subdivided the surface into registers and inserted the pictorial elements into their organized setting in a neat and orderly way. The horizontal lines separating the narratives also define the ground supporting the figures. This too was the preferred mode for narrative art in the ancient Near East. Narmer's palette established it as the norm in Egyptian art for millennia. Egyptian artists who departed from this compositional scheme did so deliberately, usually to express the absence of order, as in a chaotic battle scene (FIG. 3-35).

Architecture

Narmer's palette is exceptional among surviving Egyptian artworks because it is commemorative rather than funerary in nature. Far more typical is the Predynastic mural from Hierakonpolis. In fact, Egyptian tombs provide the principal, if not the exclusive, evidence for the historical reconstruction of Egyptian civilization. The majority of monuments the Egyptians left behind were dedicated to ensuring safety and happiness in the next life (see "Mummification and Immortality," page 43).

The standard tomb type in early Egypt was the *mastaba* (FIG. 3-4). The mastaba (Arabic for "bench") was a rectangular brick or stone structure with sloping sides erected over an underground burial chamber. The form probably developed from earthen mounds that had covered even earlier tombs. Although mastabas originally housed single burials, as in FIG. 3-4, they later accommodated multiple family burials and became increasingly complex. The main feature of the tomb, other than the burial chamber itself, was the

1. Chapel
2. False door
3. Shaft into burial chamber
4. Serdab (chamber for statue of deceased)
5. Burial chamber

3-4 Section (*top*), plan (*center*), and restored view (*bottom*) of typical Egyptian mastaba tombs.

The standard early Egyptian tomb had an underground burial chamber and rooms to house a portrait statue and offerings to the deceased. Scenes of daily life often decorated the interior walls.

Mummification and Immortality

The Egyptians did not make the sharp distinction between body and soul that is basic to many religions. Rather, they believed that from birth a person was accompanied by a kind of other self, the *ka* (life force), which, on the death of the body, could inhabit the corpse and live on. For the ka to live securely, however, the body had to remain as nearly intact as possible. To ensure that it did, the Egyptians developed the technique of embalming (*mummification*) to a high art. Although the Egyptians believed that the god Anubis invented embalming to preserve the body of the murdered Osiris (see "The Gods and Goddesses of Egypt," page 40), they did not practice mummification systematically until the Fourth Dynasty.

The first step in the 70-day process was the surgical removal of the lungs, liver, stomach, and intestines through an incision in the left flank. The Egyptians thought these organs were most subject to decay. The organs were individually wrapped and placed in four containers known as *canopic jars* for eventual deposit in the burial chamber with the corpse. (The jars take their name from the Egyptian port of Canopus, where human-headed jars were worshiped as personifications of Osiris. These jars were not, however, used in embalming.) The brain was extracted through the nostrils and discarded. The Egyptians did not attach any special significance to the brain. But they left in place the heart, necessary for life and regarded as the seat of intelligence.

Next, the body was treated for 40 days with natron, a naturally occurring salt compound that dehydrated the body. Then the corpse was filled with resin-soaked linens, and the embalming incision was closed and covered with a representation of the *wedjat* eye of Horus, a powerful *amulet* (a device to ward off evil and promote rebirth). Finally, the body was treated with lotions and resins and then wrapped tightly with hundreds of yards of linen bandages to maintain its shape. The Egyptians often placed other amulets within the bandages or on the corpse. The most important were heart *scarabs* (gems in the shape of beetles). Spells written on them ensured that the heart would be returned to its owner if it were ever lost. A scroll copy of the *Book of the Dead* (FIG. 3-36) frequently was placed between the legs of the deceased. It contained some 200 spells intended to protect the mummy and the ka in the afterlife. The mummies of the wealthy had their faces covered with funerary masks (FIG. 3-1).

The Egyptian practice of mummification endured for thousands of years, even under Greek and Roman rule. Roman mummies with painted portraits (FIG. 7-62) dating to the first three centuries CE have long been known, but the discovery in 1996 of a cemetery at Bahariya Oasis in the desert southwest of Cairo greatly expanded their number. The site—at least four square miles in size—has come to be called the Valley of the Golden Mummies. The largest tomb found to date contained 32 mummies, but another held 43, some stacked on top of others because the tomb housed several generations of Egyptians and space ran out.

The care with which the Egyptians laid the dead to rest in the Bahariya cemetery varied markedly with the social position and wealth of the deceased. The bodies of the poorer members of the community were carelessly wrapped in linen and have almost completely decayed. The 60 most elaborate mummies, probably those of successful merchants and their families, have gilded *stucco* masks. Some also have gilded chest plates with reliefs depicting Egyptian deities, including Thoth holding Maat's feather (compare the weighing scene in FIG. 3-36). Others have painted decoration, and some have eyes of white marble with black obsidian irises and copper eyelashes. The excavators believe the cemetery was still in use as late as the fourth or fifth century CE.

Preserving the deceased's body by mummification was only the first requirement for immortality in ancient Egypt. Food and drink also had to be provided, as did clothing, utensils, and furniture. Nothing that had been enjoyed on earth was to be lacking. Statuettes called *ushabtis* (answerers) also were placed in the tomb. These figurines performed any labor required of the deceased in the afterlife, answering whenever his or her name was called.

Beginning in the third millennium BCE, the Egyptians also set up statues of the dead in their tombs. The statues were meant to guarantee the permanence of the person's identity by providing substitute dwelling places for the ka in case the mummy disintegrated. Wall paintings and reliefs recorded the recurring round of human activities. The Egyptians hoped and expected that the images and inventory of life, collected within the protective stone walls of the tomb, would ensure immortality.

chapel, which had a false door through which the ka could join the world of the living and partake in the meals placed on an offering table. Some mastabas also had a *serdab*, a small room housing a statue of the deceased.

IMHOTEP AND DJOSER One of the most renowned figures in Egyptian history is IMHOTEP, the builder for King Djoser (r. 2630–2611 BCE) of the Third Dynasty. Imhotep was a man of legendary talent who served also as the pharaoh's chancellor and high priest of the sun god. After his death, the Egyptians revered Imhotep as a god and in time may have inflated the list of his achievements, but his is the first recorded name of an artist in history.

The historian Manetho states that Imhotep designed the Stepped Pyramid of Djoser at Saqqara, the ancient *necropolis* (Greek for "city of the dead") for Memphis, Egypt's capital at the time. Built before 2600 BCE, the pyramid (FIG. 3-5) is one of the oldest stone structures in Egypt and, in its final form, the first truly grandiose royal tomb. Begun as a large mastaba with each of its faces oriented toward one of the cardinal points of the compass, the tomb was enlarged at least twice before taking on its ultimate shape. About 200 feet high, the Stepped Pyramid seems to be composed of a series of mastabas of diminishing size, stacked one atop another to form a structure that resembles the great Mesopotamian ziggurats (FIGS. 2-15 and 2-20, *top center*). Unlike the ziggurats, however, Djoser's pyramid is a tomb, not a temple platform, and its dual function was to protect the mummified king and his possessions and to symbolize, by its gigantic presence, his absolute and godlike power. Beneath the pyramid was a network of several hundred underground rooms and galleries cut out of the Saqqara

3-5 Imhotep, Stepped Pyramid and mortuary precinct of Djoser, Saqqara, Egypt, Third Dynasty, ca. 2630–2611 BCE.

Imhotep, the first artist whose name is recorded, built the first pyramid during the Third Dynasty for King Djoser. Djoser's pyramid resembles a series of stacked mastabas of diminishing size.

3-6 Plan (*top*) and restored view (*bottom*) of the mortuary precinct of Djoser, Saqqara, Egypt, Third Dynasty, ca. 2630–2611 BCE.

Djoser's pyramid was the center-piece of an immense funerary complex that included a mortuary temple, other buildings, and court-yards. Its network of underground galleries resembled a palace.

1. Stepped pyramid
2. Funerary temple of Djoser
3. Court with serdab
4. Large court with altar
5. Entrance portico
6. Heb-Sed court and sham chapels
7. Small temple
8. Court before North Palace
9. North Palace
10. Court before South Palace
11. South Palace
12. South tomb
13. Royal Pavilion
14. Magazines

N   0   100   200   300 feet
     0   50   100 meters

bedrock. The vast subterranean complex resembles a palace. It was to be Djoser's new home in the afterlife.

Befitting the god-king's majesty, Djoser's pyramid (FIG. 3-5) stands near the center of an immense (37-acre) rectangular enclosure (FIG. 3-6) surrounded by a 34-foot-high and 5,400-foot-long wall of white limestone. The huge precinct, with its protective walls and tightly regulated access, stands in sharp contrast to the roughly contemporary Sumerian Royal Cemetery at Ur, where no barriers kept people away from the burial area. Nor did the Mesopotamian cemetery have a temple for the worship of the deified dead. At

Saqqara, a funerary temple (FIG. 3-6, no. 2) stands against the northern face of Djoser's pyramid. Priests performed daily rituals at the temple in celebration of the divine pharaoh.

Djoser's funerary temple was but one of many buildings arranged around several courts. Most of the others were dummy structures (FIG. 3-6, no. 6) with stone walls enclosing fills of rubble, sand, or gravel. The buildings imitated in stone masonry various types of temporary structures made of plant stems and mats erected in Upper and Lower Egypt to celebrate the Jubilee Festival, which perpetually reaffirmed the royal existence in the hereafter. The trans-

3-7 Detail of the facade of the North Palace of the mortuary precinct of Djoser, Saqqara, Egypt, Third Dynasty, ca. 2630–2611 BCE.

The earliest known stone columns are in Djoser's funerary precinct. Those on the North Palace facade are engaged (attached) to the walls and have shafts and capitals resembling papyrus stalks and blossoms.

lation into stone of structural forms previously made out of plants may be seen in the *columns* (FIG. 3-7) of the North Palace (FIG. 3-6, no. 9) of Djoser's funerary precinct. The columns end in *capitals* ("heads") that take the form of the papyrus blossoms of Lower Egypt. The column *shafts* resemble papyrus stalks. Djoser's columns are not freestanding, as are most later columns. They are *engaged* (attached) to walls, but are nonetheless the earliest known stone columns in the history of architecture.

THE OLD KINGDOM

The Old Kingdom is the first of the three great periods of Egyptian history, called the Old, Middle, and New Kingdoms, respectively. Many Egyptologists now begin the Old Kingdom with the first pharaoh of the Fourth Dynasty, Sneferu (r. 2575–2551 BCE), although the traditional division of kingdoms places Djoser and the Third Dynasty in the Old Kingdom. It ended with the demise of the Eighth Dynasty around 2134 BCE.

Architecture

The pharaohs of the Old Kingdom amassed great wealth and expended it on grandiose architectural projects, of which the most spectacular were the Great Pyramids of Gizeh, the oldest of the Seven Wonders of the ancient world (see "Babylon, City of Wonders," Chapter 2, page 34). The prerequisites for membership in this elite club were colossal size and enormous cost.

GREAT PYRAMIDS, GIZEH The three pyramids (FIGS. 3-8 and 3-9) of Gizeh were built in the course of about 75 years (see "Building the Great Pyramids," page 46) as the tombs of the Fourth Dynasty pharaohs Khufu (r. 2551–2528 BCE), Khafre (r. 2520–2494 BCE), and Menkaure (r. 2490–2472 BCE). They represent the culmination of an architectural evolution that began with the mastaba, but the classic pyramid form is not simply a refinement of the stepped pyramid. The new tomb shape probably reflects the influence of Heliopolis, the seat of the powerful cult of Re, whose emblem was a pyramidal stone, the *ben-ben* (see "The Gods and

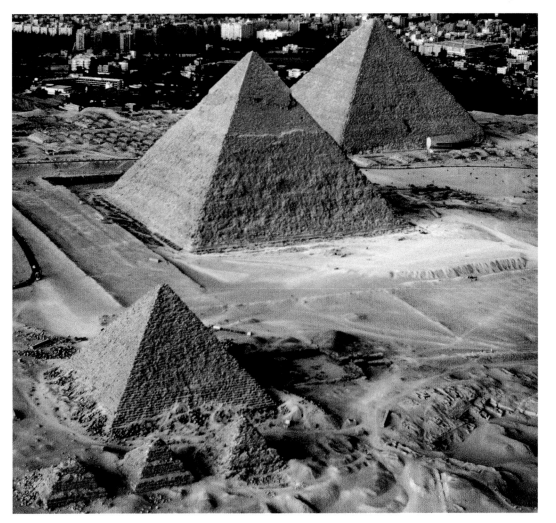

3-8 Great Pyramids, Gizeh, Egypt, Fourth Dynasty. *From bottom:* Pyramids of Menkaure, ca. 2490–2472 BCE; Khafre, ca. 2520–2494 BCE; and Khufu, ca. 2551–2528 BCE.

The Great Pyramids of Gizeh took the shape of the ben-ben, the emblem of the sun, Re. The sun's rays were the ramp the Egyptian pharaohs used to ascend to the heavens after their death and rebirth.

Building the Great Pyramids

The Great Pyramids (FIG. 3-8) across the Nile from modern Cairo attest to the extraordinary engineering and mathematical expertise of the Egyptians of the mid-third millennium BCE. They also are testaments to the Old Kingdom builders' mastery of stone masonry and ability to mobilize, direct, house, and feed a huge workforce engaged in one of the most labor-intensive enterprises ever undertaken. Like all building projects of this type, the process of erecting the pyramids began with the quarrying of stone, in this case primarily the limestone of the Gizeh plateau itself. Teams of skilled workers had to cut into the rock and remove large blocks of roughly equal size using stone or copper chisels and wooden mallets and wedges. Often, the artisans had to cut deep tunnels to find high-quality stone free of cracks and other flaws. To remove a block, the workers cut channels on all sides and partly underneath. Then they pried the stones free from the bedrock with wooden levers.

After workers liberated the stones, the rough blocks had to be transported to the building site and *dressed* (shaped to the exact dimensions required, with smooth faces for a perfect fit). Small blocks could be carried on a man's shoulders or on the back of a donkey, but the massive blocks used to construct the Great Pyramids were moved using wooden rollers and sleds. The artisans dressed the blocks by chiseling and pounding the surfaces and, in the last stage, by rubbing and grinding the surfaces with fine polishing stones. This kind of construction, in which carefully cut and regularly shaped blocks of stone are piled in successive rows, or *courses,* is called *ashlar masonry.*

To set the ashlar blocks in place, workers erected great rubble ramps against the core of the pyramid. Their size and slope were adjusted as work progressed and the tomb grew in height. Scholars debate whether the Egyptians used simple linear ramps inclined at a right angle to one face of the pyramid or zigzag or spiral ramps akin to staircases. Linear ramps would have had the advantage of simplicity and would have left three sides of the pyramid unobstructed. But zigzag ramps placed against one side of the structure or spiral ramps winding around the pyramid would have greatly reduced the slope of the incline and would have made the dragging of the blocks easier. Some scholars also have suggested a combination of straight and spiral ramps.

The Egyptians used ropes, pulleys, and levers both to lift and to lower the stones, guiding each block into its designated place. Finally, the pyramid received a casing of white limestone blocks (FIG. 3-9, no. 1), cut so precisely that the eye could scarcely detect the joints. The reflection of sunlight on the facing would have been dazzling,

underscoring the pyramid's solar symbolism. A few casing stones still can be seen in the cap that covers the Pyramid of Khafre (FIGS. 3-8, *center,* and 3-11, *left*).

Of the three Fourth Dynasty pyramids at Gizeh, the tomb of Khufu (FIGS. 3-9 and 3-10, no. 7) is the oldest and largest. Except for the galleries and burial chamber, it is an almost solid mass of limestone masonry. Some dimensions will suggest the immensity of the Gizeh pyramids: At the base, the length of one side of Khufu's tomb is approximately 775 feet, and its area is some 13 acres. Its present height is about 450 feet (originally 480 feet). The structure contains roughly 2.3 million blocks of stone, each weighing an average of 2.5 tons. Some of the stones at the base weigh about 15 tons. Napoleon's scholars calculated that the blocks in the three Great Pyramids were sufficient to build a wall 1 foot wide and 10 feet high around France.

1. Silhouette with original facing stone
2. Thieves' tunnels
3. Entrance
4. Grand gallery
5. King's chamber
6. So-called Queen's chamber
7. False tomb chamber
8. Relieving blocks
9. Airshafts(?)

3-9 Section of the Pyramid of Khufu, Gizeh, Egypt, Fourth Dynasty, ca. 2551–2528 BCE.

Khufu's pyramid is the largest at Gizeh. Constructed of roughly 2.3 million blocks of stone weighing an average of 2.5 tons, the structure is an almost solid mass of stone quarried from the Gizeh plateau itself.

Goddesses of Egypt," page 40). The Great Pyramids are symbols of the sun. The Pyramid Texts, inscribed on the burial chamber walls of many royal tombs beginning with the Fifth Dynasty Pyramid of Unas (r. 2356–2323 BCE), refer to the sun's rays as the ramp the pharaoh uses to ascend to the heavens. Djoser's Stepped Pyramid (FIG. 3-5) may also have been conceived as a giant stairway. The pyramids were where Egyptian kings were reborn in the afterlife, just as the sun is reborn each day at dawn. As with Djoser's pyramid, the four sides of each of the Great Pyramids are oriented to the cardinal points of the compass. But the funerary temples associated with the three Gizeh pyramids are not placed on the north side, facing

the stars of the northern sky, as was Djoser's temple. The temples sit on the east side, facing the rising sun and underscoring their connection with Re.

From the remains surrounding the Pyramid of Khafre at Gizeh, archaeologists have been able to reconstruct an entire funerary complex (FIG. 3-10). The complex included the pyramid itself with the pharaoh's burial chamber; the *mortuary temple* adjoining the pyramid on the east side, where offerings were made to the dead king, ceremonies performed, and cloth, food, and ceremonial vessels stored; the roofed causeway leading to the mortuary temple; and the *valley temple* at the edge of the floodplain. According to one theory,

3-10 Model of the Fourth Dynasty pyramid complex, Gizeh, Egypt. Harvard University Semitic Museum, Cambridge. 1) Pyramid of Menkaure, 2) Pyramid of Khafre, 3) mortuary temple of Khafre, 4) causeway, 5) Great Sphinx, 6) valley temple of Khafre, 7) Pyramid of Khufu, 8) pyramids of the royal family and mastabas of nobles.

Like Djoser's pyramid (FIG. 3-5), the Great Pyramids were not isolated tombs but parts of funerary complexes with a valley temple, a covered causeway, and a mortuary temple adjoining the pyramid.

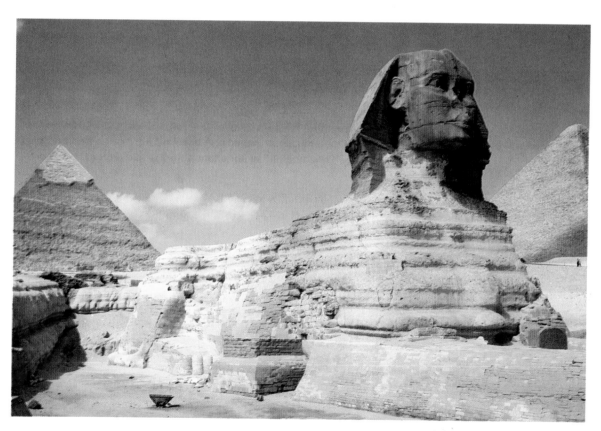

3-11 Great Sphinx (with Pyramid of Khafre in the background at left), Gizeh, Egypt, Fourth Dynasty, ca. 2520–2494 BCE. Sandstone, 65′ × 240′.

Carved out of the Gizeh stone quarry, the Great Sphinx is the largest statue in the Near East. The sphinx is associated with the sun god, and joins the body of a lion with the head of a pharaoh.

the complex served not only as the king's tomb and temple but also as his palace in the afterlife.

GREAT SPHINX Beside the causeway and dominating the valley temple of Khafre rises the Great Sphinx (FIG. **3-11**). Carved from a spur of rock in an ancient quarry, the colossal statue—the largest in the ancient Near East—represents a pharaoh, probably Khafre (origi-nally complete with the pharaoh's ceremonial beard and uraeus head-dress), although some scholars believe it portrays Khufu and was carved before construction of Khafre's complex began. Whoever it portrays, the *sphinx*—a lion with a human head—was associated with the sun god and therefore was an appropriate image for a pharaoh. The composite form suggests that the pharaoh combines human intel-ligence with the immense strength and authority of the king of beasts.

Sculpture

Old Kingdom statues survive in significant numbers because they fulfilled an important function in Egyptian tombs as substitute abodes for the ka (see "Mummification and Immortality," page 43). Although Egyptian sculptors used wood, clay, and other materials, mostly for images of those not of the royal or noble classes, the primary material for funerary statuary was stone.

KHAFRE ENTHRONED The seated statue of Khafre (FIG. 3-12) is one of a series of similar statues carved for the pharaoh's valley temple (FIG. 3-10, no. 6) near the Great Sphinx. The stone is diorite, an exceptionally hard dark stone brought some 400 miles down the Nile from royal quarries in the south. (The Neo-Sumerian ruler Gudea, FIG. 2-16, so admired diorite that he imported it to far-away Girsu.) Khafre wears a simple kilt and sits rigidly upright on a throne formed of two stylized lions' bodies. Intertwined lotus and papyrus plants—symbolic of the united Egypt—appear between the throne's legs. The falcon-god Horus extends his protective wings to shelter the pharaoh's head. Khafre has the royal false beard fastened to his chin and wears the royal linen *nemes* headdress with the *uraeus* cobra of kingship on the front. The headdress covers his forehead and falls in pleated folds over his shoulders. (The head of the Great Sphinx is similarly attired.) As befitting a divine ruler, the sculptor portrayed Khafre with a well-developed, flawless body and a perfect face, regardless of his actual age and appearance. The Egyptians considered ideal proportions appropriate for representing their god-kings, and the statue of Khafre is not a true portrait and was not intended to be. The purpose of pharaonic portraiture was not to record individual features or the distinctive shapes of bodies, but rather to proclaim the divine nature of Egyptian kingship.

The enthroned Khafre radiates serenity. The sculptor created this effect, common to Egyptian royal statues, in part by giving the

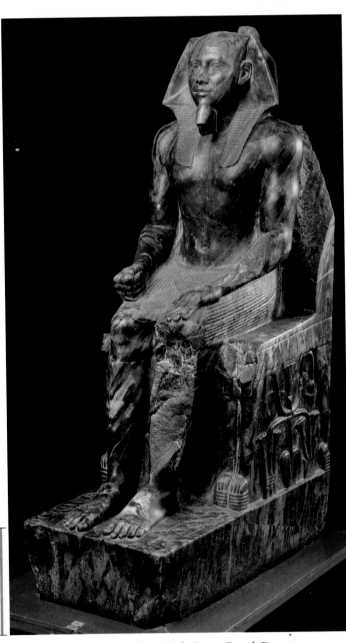

3-12 Khafre enthroned, from Gizeh, Egypt, Fourth Dynasty, ca. 2520–2494 BCE. Diorite, 5′ 6″ high. Egyptian Museum, Cairo.

This portrait from his pyramid complex depicts Khafre as an enthroned divine ruler with a perfect body. The rigidity of the pose creates the effect of eternal stillness, appropriate for the timeless afterlife.

3-13 Menkaure and Khamerernebty(?), from Gizeh, Egypt, Fourth Dynasty, ca. 2490–2472 BCE. Graywacke, 4′ 6½″ high. Museum of Fine Arts, Boston.

The double portrait of Menkaure and his wife displays the conventional postures used for statues designed as substitute homes for the ka. The frozen gestures signify that the man and woman are married.

figure great compactness and solidity, with few projecting, breakable parts. The form manifests the purpose: to last for eternity. Khafre's body is one with the unarticulated slab that forms the back of the king's throne. His arms are held close to the torso and thighs, and his legs are close together. Part of the original stone block still connects the king's legs to his chair. Khafre's pose is frontal, rigid, and *bilaterally symmetrical* (the same on either side of an axis, in this case the vertical axis). The sculptor suppressed all movement and with it the notion of time, creating an eternal stillness.

To produce the statue, the artist first drew the front, back, and two profile views of the pharaoh on the four vertical faces of the stone block. Next, apprentices chiseled away the excess stone on each side, working inward until the planes met at right angles. Finally, the master sculpted the parts of Khafre's body, the falcon, and so forth. The finishing was done by *abrasion* (rubbing or grinding the surface). This *subtractive* method of creating the pharaoh's portrait accounts in large part for the blocklike look of the standard Egyptian statue. Nevertheless, other sculptors, both ancient and modern, with different aims, have transformed stone blocks into dynamic, twisting human forms (for example, FIGS. I-16 and 5-84).

MENKAURE AND KHAMERERNEBTY The seated statue is one of only a small number of basic formulaic types that Old Kingdom sculptors employed to represent the human figure. Another is the image of a person or deity standing, either alone or in a group, for example the double portrait (FIG. 3-13) of Menkaure and one of his wives, probably Khamerernebty. The statue once stood in the valley temple of Menkaure's pyramid complex at Gizeh. Here, too, the figures remain wedded to the stone block from which they were carved. In fact, the statue could be classified as a high-relief sculpture. Menkaure's pose, which is duplicated in countless other Egyptian statues, is rigidly frontal with the arms hanging straight down and close to his well-built body. His hands are clenched into fists with the thumbs forward. His left leg is slightly advanced, but no shift occurs in the angle of the hips to correspond to the uneven distribution of weight. Khamerernebty stands in a similar position. Her right arm, however, encircles the king's waist, and her left hand gently rests on his left arm. This frozen stereotypical gesture indicates their marital status. The husband and wife show no other sign of affection or emotion and look not at each other but out into space. The artist's aim was not to portray living figures, but to suggest the timeless nature of the stone statue that was designed to provide an eternal substitute home for the ka.

SEATED SCRIBE Traces of paint remain on the portraits of Menkaure and Khamerernebty. Most Egyptian statues were painted, although sometimes the stone was left its natural color, enhancing the sense of abstraction and timelessness. A striking example of painted statuary is the seated portrait (FIG. 3-14) of a Fourth Dynasty scribe found at Saqqara. Despite the stiff upright posture and the frontality of head and body, the color lends a lifelike quality to the stone statue. The head displays an extraordinary sensitivity. The sculptor conveyed the personality of a sharply intelligent and alert individual with a penetration and sympathy seldom achieved at this early date. The scribe sits directly on the ground, not on a throne or even on a chair. Although he occupied

3-14 Seated scribe, from Saqqara, Egypt, Fourth Dynasty, ca. 2500 BCE. Painted limestone, 1′ 9″ high. Louvre, Paris.

The idealism that characterizes the portraiture of the Egyptian god-kings did not extend to the portrayal of non-elite individuals. This more realistic painted portrait of a scribe shows clear signs of aging.

1 in.

The Old Kingdom **49**

a position of honor in a largely illiterate society, the scribe was a much lower figure in the Egyptian hierarchy than the pharaoh, whose divinity made him superhuman. In the history of art, especially portraiture, it is almost a rule that as a human subject's importance decreases, formality is relaxed and realism is increased. It is telling that the sculptor portrayed the scribe with sagging chest muscles and a protruding belly. These signs of age would have been disrespectful and wholly inappropriate in a depiction of an Egyptian god-king. But the statue of the scribe is not a true portrait either. Rather, it is a composite of conventional types. Obesity, for example, characterizes many nonroyal Old Kingdom portraits, perhaps because it attested to the comfortable life of the person represented and his relatively high position in society.

TOMB OF TI, SAQQARA In Old Kingdom tombs, images of the deceased also frequently appear in relief sculpture and in mural painting, sometimes alone (FIG. I-14) and sometimes in a narrative context. The painted limestone relief scenes that decorate the walls of the mastaba of a Fifth Dynasty official named Ti typify the subjects Old Kingdom patrons favored for the adornment of their final resting places. Depictions of agriculture and hunting fill Ti's tomb. These activities were associated with the provisioning of the ka in the hereafter, but they also had powerful symbolic overtones. In ancient Egypt, success in the hunt, for example, was a metaphor for triumph over the forces of evil.

On one wall (FIG. 3-15), Ti, his men, and his boats move slowly through the marshes, hunting hippopotami and birds in a dense growth of towering papyrus. The sculptor delineated the reedy stems of the plants with repeated fine grooves that fan out gracefully at the top into a commotion of frightened birds and stalking foxes. The water beneath the boats, signified by a pattern of wavy lines, is crowded with hippopotami and fish. Ti's men seem frantically busy with their spears, while Ti, depicted twice their size, stands aloof. The basic conventions of Egyptian figure representation used a half millennium earlier for the palette of King Narmer (FIG. 3-3) are seen again here. As on the Predynastic palette, the artist exaggerated the size of Ti to announce his rank, and combined frontal and profile views of Ti's body to show its most characteristic parts clearly. This approach to representation was well suited for Egyptian funerary art because it emphasized the essential nature of the deceased, not his accidental appearance. Ti's conventional pose contrasts with the realistically rendered activities of his tiny servants and with the naturalistically carved and painted birds and animals among the papyrus buds. Ti's immobility suggests that he is not an actor in the hunt. He does not *do* anything. He simply *is*, a figure apart from time and an impassive observer of life, like his ka.

The idealized and stiff image of Ti is typical of Egyptian relief sculpture. Egyptian artists regularly ignored the endless variations in body types of real human beings. Painters and sculptors did not sketch their subjects from life but applied a strict *canon*, or system of proportions, to the human figure. They first drew a grid on the wall. Then they placed various human body parts at specific points on the network of squares. The height of a figure, for example, was a fixed number of squares, and the head, shoulders, waist, knees, and other parts of the body also had a predetermined size and place within the scheme. This approach to design lasted for thousands of years. Specific proportions might vary from workshop to workshop and change over time, but the principle of the canon persisted.

On another wall (FIG. 3-16) of Ti's mastaba, the artist represented in two registers goats treading in seeds and cattle fording a canal in the Nile. Once again, the scenes may be interpreted on

3-15 Ti watching a hippopotamus hunt, relief in the mastaba of Ti, Saqqara, Egypt, Fifth Dynasty, ca. 2450–2350 BCE. Painted limestone, 4′ high.

In Egypt, a successful hunt was a metaphor for triumph over evil. In this painted tomb relief, the deceased stands aloof from the hunters busily spearing hippopotami. Ti's size reflects his high rank.

a symbolic as well as a literal level. The fording of the Nile, for example, was a metaphor for the deceased's passage from life to the hereafter. Ti is absent from the scenes, and all the men and animals participate in the narrative. Despite the sculptor's repeated use of similar poses for most of the human and animal figures, the reliefs are full of anecdotal details. Especially charming is the group at the lower right. A youth, depicted in a complex unconventional posture, carries a calf on his back. The animal, not a little afraid, turns its head back a full 180 degrees (compare FIG. 1-8) to seek reassurance from its mother, who returns the calf's gaze. Scenes such as this demonstrate that Egyptian artists could be close observers of daily life. The suppression of the anecdotal (that is, of the time-bound) from their representations of the deceased both in relief and in the round was a deliberate choice. Their primary purpose was to suggest the deceased's eternal existence in the afterlife, not to portray nature.

THE MIDDLE KINGDOM

About 2150 BCE, the Egyptians challenged the pharaohs' power, and for more than a century the land was in a state of civil unrest and near anarchy. But in 2040 BCE, the pharaoh of Upper Egypt, Mentuhotep II (r. 2050–1998 BCE), managed to unite Egypt again under the rule of a single king and established the so-called Middle Kingdom (11th to 14th Dynasties).

3-16 Goats treading seed and cattle fording a canal, reliefs in the mastaba of Ti, Saqqara, Egypt, Fifth Dynasty, ca. 2450–2350 BCE. Painted limestone.

The fording of the Nile was a metaphor for the passage to the afterlife. These reliefs combine stereotypical poses for humans and animals with unconventional postures and anecdotal details.

Sculpture

Although in most respects Middle Kingdom sculptors adhered to the conventions established during the Old Kingdom, there were some notable innovations.

SENUSRET III One of Mentuhotep II's successors was Senusret III (r. 1878–1859 BCE), who fought four brutal military campaigns in Nubia (MAP 3-1). Although Egyptian armies devastated the land and poisoned the wells, Senusret III never fully achieved secure control over the Nubians. In Egypt itself, he attempted, with greater success, to establish a more powerful central government. His portraits (FIG. 3-17) are of special interest because they represent a sharp break from Old Kingdom practice. Although the king's preserved statues have idealized bodies, the sculptors brought a stunning and unprecedented realism to the rendition of Senusret III's features. His pessimistic expression reflects the dominant mood of the time and is echoed in Middle Kingdom literature. The strong mouth, the drooping lines about the nose and eyes, and the shadowy brows show a determined ruler who had also shared in the cares of the world, sunk in brooding meditation. The portrait is different in kind from the typically impassive faces of the Old Kingdom. It is personal, almost intimate, in its revelation of the mark of anxiety that a troubled age might leave on the soul of a king.

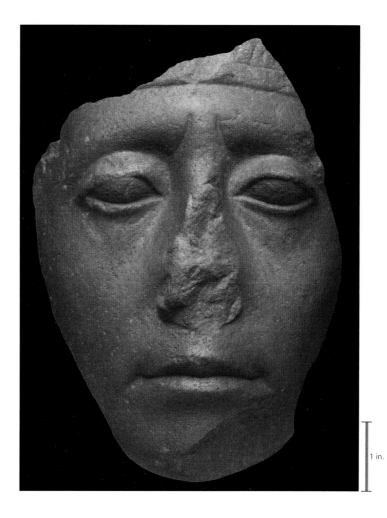

3-17 Fragmentary head of Senusret III, 12th Dynasty, ca. 1860 BCE. Red quartzite, $6\frac{1}{2}''$ high. Metropolitan Museum of Art, New York.

The portraits of Senusret III exhibit an unprecedented realism. The king's brooding expression reflects the dominant mood of the time and contrasts sharply with the impassive faces of Old Kingdom pharaohs.

1 in.

Architecture

Senusret III's tomb, at Dashur, is a mud-brick pyramid, but the most characteristic funerary monuments of the Middle Kingdom are rock-cut tombs. These tombs, which also existed during the Old Kingdom, became especially popular during the Middle Kingdom and largely replaced the mastaba as the standard Egyptian tomb type.

BENI HASAN Some of the best-preserved Middle Kingdom tombs are at Beni Hasan. Hollowed out of the cliffs, these tombs (FIG. 3-18) often have a shallow columnar porch, which led into a columned hall and then into a burial chamber. In the 12th Dynasty tomb of Amenemhet, the columns in the hall (FIG. 3-19) serve no supporting function because, like the porch columns, they are continuous parts of the rock fabric. (Note the broken column in the rear suspended from the ceiling like a stalactite.) The column shafts are *fluted* with vertical channels in a manner similar to later Greek columns, and there is no doubt that the Greeks knew about and emulated many aspects of Egyptian architecture (see Chapter 5). Archaeologists believe fluting derived from the dressing of softwood trunks with the rounded cutting edge of the adze. Fluted stone

3-18 Rock-cut tombs BH 3–5, Beni Hasan, Egypt, 12th Dynasty, ca. 1950–1900 BCE.

The tombs of Beni Hasan are characteristic of the Middle Kingdom. Hollowed out of the cliffs, these tombs often have a shallow columnar porch, which leads into a columned hall and burial chamber.

3-19 Interior hall of the rock-cut tomb of Amenemhet (tomb BH 2), Beni Hasan, Egypt, 12th Dynasty, ca. 1950–1900 BCE.

The columnar hall of Amenemhet's tomb was carved out of the living rock, which explains the suspended broken column at the rear. The shafts are fluted in a manner Greek architects later emulated.

columns are yet another case of Egyptian builders' translating perishable natural forms into permanent architecture. Artists decorated the tomb walls with paintings and painted reliefs, as in former times, and placed statues of the deceased in niches.

THE NEW KINGDOM

Like its predecessor, the Middle Kingdom disintegrated, and power passed to the Hyksos, or shepherd kings, who descended on Egypt from the Syrian and Mesopotamian uplands. They brought with them a new and influential culture and that practical animal, the horse. Their innovations in weaponry and war techniques ironically contributed to their own overthrow by native Egyptian kings of the 17th Dynasty around 1600–1550 BCE. Ahmose I (r. 1550–1525 BCE), final conqueror of the Hyksos and first king of the 18th Dynasty, ushered in the New Kingdom, the most brilliant period in Egypt's long history. At this time, Egypt extended its borders by conquest from the Euphrates River in the east deep into Nubia to the south. A new capital—Thebes, in Upper Egypt—became a great and luxurious metropolis with magnificent palaces, tombs, and temples along both banks of the Nile.

Architecture

If the most impressive monuments of the Old Kingdom are its pyramids, those of the New Kingdom are its grandiose temples, often built to honor pharaohs and queens as well as gods. Great pharaonic mortuary temples arose along the Nile in the Thebes district. These shrines provided the rulers with a place for worshiping their patron gods during their lifetime and then served as temples in their own honor after their death. The temples were elaborate and luxuriously decorated, befitting both the pharaohs and the gods.

TEMPLE OF HATSHEPSUT The most majestic of these royal mortuary temples (FIG. **3-20**), at Deir el-Bahri, honored the female pharaoh Hatshepsut, one of the most remarkable women of the ancient world (see "Hatshepsut, the Woman Who Would Be King," page 54). Some have attributed the temple to SENMUT (FIG. **3-27**), Hatshepsut's chancellor and possible lover, who is described in two inscriptions as royal architect. His association with this project is uncertain, however. Hatshepsut's temple rises from the valley floor in three colonnaded terraces connected by ramps on the central axis. It is remarkable how visually well suited the structure is to its natural setting. The long horizontals and verticals of the *colonnades* and their rhythm of light and dark repeat the pattern of the limestone cliffs above. The colonnade *pillars,* which are either simply rectangular or *chamfered* (beveled, or flattened at the edges) into 16 sides, are well proportioned and rhythmically spaced.

In Hatshepsut's day, the terraces were not the barren places they are now but gardens with frankincense trees and rare plants the pharaoh brought from the faraway "land of Punt" on the Red Sea. Her expedition to Punt figures prominently in the poorly preserved

3-20 Mortuary temple of Hatshepsut (looking west with the Middle Kingdom mortuary temple of Mentuhotep II at left), Deir el-Bahri, Egypt, 18th Dynasty, ca. 1473–1458 BCE.

Hatshepsut was the first great female monarch whose name is recorded. Painted reliefs recounting her divine birth and significant achievements adorned her immense funerary temple.

Hatshepsut, the Woman Who Would Be King

In 1479 BCE, Thutmose II, the fourth pharaoh of the 18th Dynasty (r. 1492–1479 BCE), died. His principal wife (and half sister), Queen Hatshepsut (r. 1473–1458 BCE), had not given birth to any sons who survived, so the title of king went to Thutmose III, son of Thutmose II by a minor wife. Hatshepsut was named regent for the boy-king. Within a few years, however, the queen proclaimed herself pharaoh and insisted that her father Thutmose I had actually chosen her as his successor during his lifetime. Underscoring her claim, one of the reliefs decorating Hatshepsut's enormous funerary complex (FIG. 3-20) depicts Thutmose I crowning his daughter as king in the presence of the Egyptian gods. Hatshepsut is the first great female monarch whose name has been recorded. (In the 12th Dynasty, Sobekneferu was crowned king of Egypt, but she reigned as pharaoh for only a few years.) Hatshepsut boasted of having made the "Two Lands to labor with bowed back" for her, and for two decades she ruled what was then the most powerful and prosperous empire in the world.

Hatshepsut commissioned numerous building projects, and sculptors produced portraits of the female pharaoh in great numbers for display in those complexes. Unfortunately, Thutmose III (r. 1458–1425 BCE), for reasons still not fully understood, late in his reign ordered Hatshepsut's portraits destroyed. In her surviving portraits, Hatshepsut uniformly wears the costume of the male pharaohs, with royal headdress and kilt, and in some cases (FIG. 3-21) even a false ceremonial beard. Many inscriptions refer to Hatshepsut as "*His* Majesty"! In other statues, however, Hatshepsut has delicate features, a slender frame, and breasts, leaving no doubt that artists also represented her as a woman.

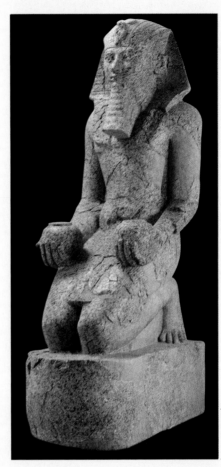

3-21 Hatshepsut with offering jars, from the upper court of her mortuary temple, Deir el-Bahri, Egypt, 18th Dynasty, ca. 1473–1458 BCE. Red granite, 8′ 6″ high. Metropolitan Museum of Art, New York.

Many of Hatshepsut's portraits were destroyed after her death. Conservators reassembled this one, which depicts the queen as a male pharaoh with false beard, consistent with inscriptions calling her "His Majesty."

1 ft.

---

but once brightly painted low reliefs that cover many walls of the complex. In addition to representing great deeds, the reliefs also show Hatshepsut's coronation and divine birth. She was said to be the daughter of the god Amen-Re, whose sanctuary was situated on the temple's uppermost level. The painted reliefs of Hatshepsut's mortuary temple constituted the first great tribute to a woman's achievements in the history of art. Their defacement after her death is therefore especially unfortunate.

HATSHEPSUT'S PORTRAITS As many as 200 statues in the round depicting Hatshepsut in various guises complemented the extensive relief program. On the lowest terrace, to either side of the processional way, Hatshepsut repeatedly appeared as a sphinx. On the uppermost level, sculptors represented the female pharaoh standing or seated or in the form of a mummy. At least eight colossal kneeling statues in red granite lined the way to the entrance of the Amen-Re sanctuary.

The statue in FIG. **3-21** suffered the same fate as most of Hatshepsut's portraits during the reign of Thutmose III. It was smashed and the pieces were thrown in a dump, but the portrait has been skillfully reassembled. Hatshepsut holds a globular offering jar in each hand as she takes part in a ritual in honor of the sun god. (A king kneeled only before a god, never a mortal.) She wears the royal male nemes headdress (compare FIGS. 3-11 to 3-13) and the pharaoh's ceremonial beard. The agents of Thutmose III hacked off

the uraeus cobra that once adorned the front of the headdress. The figure is also anatomically male, although other surviving portraits of Hatshepsut represent her with a woman's breasts. The male imagery is, however, consistent with the queen's formal assumption of the title of king and with the many inscriptions that address her as a man.

TEMPLE OF RAMSES II The sheer size of Hatshepsut's mortuary temple never fails to impress visitors, and this is no less true of the immense rock-cut temple (FIG. **3-22**) of Ramses II (r. 1290–1224 BCE) at Abu Simbel. In 1968, engineers moved the immense Nubian temple nearly 700 feet—an amazing feat in its own right—to save it from submersion in the Aswan High Dam reservoir. Ramses was Egypt's last great warrior pharaoh, and he ruled for two-thirds of a century, an extraordinary accomplishment in an era when life expectancy was far less than it is today. The pharaoh, proud of his many campaigns to restore the empire, proclaimed his greatness by placing four colossal images of himself on the temple *facade*. The portraits are almost eight times as large as Hatshepsut's kneeling statues and, at 65 feet tall, almost a dozen times the height of an ancient Egyptian, even though the pharaoh is seated. Spectacular as they are, the rock-cut statues nonetheless lack the refinement of earlier periods, because much was sacrificed to overwhelming size. This is a characteristic of colossal statuary of every period and every place.

3-22 Facade of the Temple of Ramses II, Abu Simbel, Egypt, 19th Dynasty, ca. 1290–1224 BCE. Sandstone, colossi 65' high.

Four rock-cut images of Ramses II dominate the facade of his mortuary temple at Abu Simbel in Nubia. The colossal portraits are a dozen times the height of a man, even though the pharaoh is seated.

The rock-cut interior (FIG. 3-23) of the temple is also of colossal size. The distance from the facade to the back wall is an astounding 206 feet. In the main gallery there are 32-foot-tall figures of the king in the guise of Osiris, carved as one with the pillars, facing each other across the narrow corridor. The pillars, carved from the cliff like the pharaoh's facade portraits, have no load-bearing function. In this respect, they resemble the columns in the tombs at Beni Hasan (FIG. 3-19). The statue-column, in its male (*atlantid*) or female (*caryatid*) variants, reappears throughout the history of art. Often, as here, the human figure is attached to a column or pier. At other times the figure replaces the architectural member and forms the sole source of support (FIG. 5-54).

FAMILY OF RAMSES Ramses, like other pharaohs, had many wives, and he fathered scores of sons. The pharaoh honored the most important members of his family with immense monuments

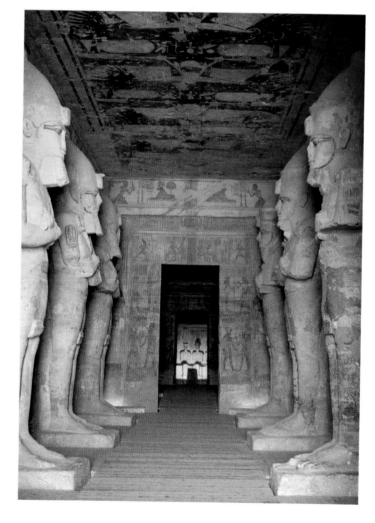

3-23 Interior of the temple of Ramses II, Abu Simbel, Egypt, 19th Dynasty, ca. 1290–1224 BCE. Sandstone, pillar statues 32' high.

Inside Ramses II's mortuary temple are 32-foot-tall figures of the long-reigning pharaoh in the guise of Osiris, carved as one with the pillars, facing each other across the narrow corridor.

3-24 Restored view of the temple of Amen-Re, Karnak, Egypt, begun 15th century BCE (Jean Claude Golvin).

The vast Karnak temple complex contains an artificial lake associated with the primeval waters of the Egyptian creation myth and a pylon temple with a bilaterally symmetrical axial plan.

of their own. At Abu Simbel, for example, north of his own temple, Ramses ordered the construction of a grand temple for his principal wife, Nefertari. Huge rock-cut statues—four standing images of the king and two of the queen—dominated the temple's facade. For his sons, Ramses constructed a huge underground tomb complex in the Valley of the Kings at Thebes, which an American archaeological team rediscovered in 1987. The tomb, however, was looted within a half century of its construction, but the excavators have yet to find the royal burial chambers themselves, so the tomb may one day yield important artworks.

TEMPLE OF AMEN-RE, KARNAK Distinct from the temples honoring pharaohs and queens are the edifices built to honor one or more of the gods. Successive kings often added to them until they reached gigantic size. The temple of Amen-Re (FIG. **3-24**) at Karnak, for example, was largely the work of the 18th Dynasty pharaohs, including Thutmose I and III and Hatshepsut, but Ramses II (19th Dynasty) and others also contributed sections. Chapels were added to the complex as late as the 26th Dynasty. The artificial sacred lake within the precinct of the Karnak temple is a reference to the primeval waters before creation (see "The Gods and Goddesses of Egypt," page 40). The temple rises from the earth as the original sacred mound rose from the waters at the beginning of time.

The New Kingdom temples all had similar *axial plans*. A typical *pylon temple* (the name derives from the simple and massive gateways, or *pylons,* with sloping walls) is bilaterally symmetrical along a single axis that runs from an approaching avenue through a colonnaded court and hall into a dimly lit sanctuary. Only the pharaohs and the priests could enter the sanctuary. A chosen few were admitted to the great columnar hall. The majority of the people were allowed only as far as the open court, and a high wall shut off the site from the outside world. The central feature of the New Kingdom pylon temple

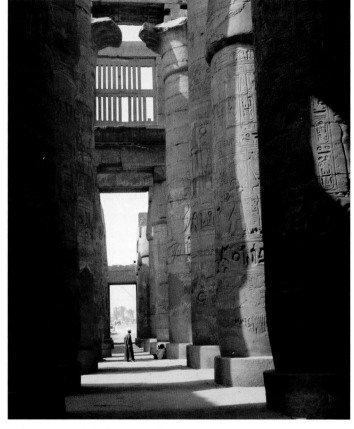

3-25 Hypostyle hall, temple of Amen-Re, Karnak, Egypt, 19th Dynasty, ca. 1290–1224 BCE.

The hypostyle hall of the Amen-Re temple is crowded with columns. The tallest are 66 feet high and have capitals that are 22 feet in diameter. The columns support a roof of stone slabs carried on lintels.

plan—a narrow axial passageway through the complex—is characteristic of much of Egyptian architecture. Axial corridors are also the approaches to the Great Pyramids (FIG. 3-10) and to Hatshepsut's multilevel mortuary temple (FIG. 3-20).

The dominating feature of the statuary-lined approach to a New Kingdom temple was the monumental facade of the pylon, which sculptors routinely covered with reliefs glorifying Egypt's rulers (FIG. 3-38). Inside was an open court with columns on two or more sides, followed by a hall between the court and sanctuary, its long axis placed at right angles to the corridor of the entire building complex. This *hypostyle hall* (one where columns support the roof) was crowded with massive columns, which supported a roof of stone slabs carried on lintels. In Karnak's hypostyle hall (FIGS. 3-25 and 3-26), the columns have bud-cluster or bell-shaped capitals resembling lotus or papyrus, the plants of Upper and Lower Egypt. The central columns are 66 feet high, and the capitals are 22 feet in diameter at the top, large enough to hold a hundred people. The Egyptians, who used no cement, depended on precise cutting of the joints and the weight of the huge stone blocks to hold the columns in place. The two central rows of columns are taller than those at the sides. Raising the roof's central section created a *clerestory*. Openings in the clerestory permitted sunlight to filter into the interior, although the stone grilles (FIG. 3-25) would have blocked much of the light. This method of construction appeared in primitive form in the Old Kingdom valley temple of Khafre at Gizeh. The clerestory is evidently an Egyptian innovation, and its significance hardly can be overstated. Before the invention of the electric light bulb, illuminating a building's interior was always a challenge for architects. The clerestory played a key role in the history of architecture until very recently.

In the hypostyle hall at Karnak, the columns are indispensable structurally, unlike the rock-cut columns of the tombs at Beni Hasan (FIGS. 3-18 and 3-19) and Abu Simbel (FIG. 3-23). But horizontal bands of painted *sunken relief* sculpture almost hide their function as vertical supports. To create these reliefs, the New Kingdom sculptors chiseled deep outlines below the stone's surface, rather than cut back the stone around the figures to make the figures project from the surface. Sunken reliefs preserve the contours of the columns they adorn. Otherwise, the Karnak columns would have had an irregular, wavy profile. Despite this effort to maintain sharp architectural lines, the overwhelming of the surfaces with reliefs indicates that the architects' intention was not to emphasize the functional role of the columns. Instead, they used columns as image- and message-bearing surfaces.

Sculpture and Painting

Although the great temple complexes of the New Kingdom were lavishly decorated with statues and painted reliefs, many of the finest examples of statuary and mural painting were produced for tombs, as in the Old and Middle Kingdoms.

SENMUT AND NEFRURA *Block statues* were extremely popular during the New Kingdom. In these works the idea that the ka could find an eternal home in the cubic stone image of the deceased was expressed in an even more radical simplification of form than was common in Old Kingdom statuary. In the statue (FIG. 3-27) of Senmut and Princess Nefrura, the streamlined design concentrates attention on the heads and treats the two bodies as a single cubic block, given over to inscriptions. Hatshepsut's chancellor holds the pharaoh's daughter by Thutmose II in his "lap" and envelops the

1 ft.

3-27 Senmut with Princess Nefrura, from Thebes, Egypt, 18th Dynasty, ca. 1470–1460 BCE. Granite, 3′ $\frac{1}{2}$″ high. Ägyptisches Museum, Berlin.

New Kingdom block statues exhibit an even more radical simplification of form than do Old Kingdom statues. Here, Hatshepsut's chancellor holds the queen's daughter in his "lap" and envelops her in his cloak.

3-26 Model of the hypostyle hall, temple of Amen-Re, Karnak, Egypt, 19th Dynasty, ca. 1290–1224 BCE. Metropolitan Museum of Art, New York.

The two central rows of columns of Karnak's hypostyle hall are taller than the rest. Raising the roof's central section created a clerestory that admitted light to the interior through windows with stone grilles.

3-28 Fowling scene, from the tomb of Nebamun, Thebes, Egypt, 18th Dynasty, ca. 1400–1350 BCE. Fresco on dry plaster, 2′ 8″ high. British Museum, London.

Nebamun's wife and daughter—depicted smaller than the deceased—accompany him on his hunt for fowl. A painted inscription states that Nebamun is enjoying recreation in his eternal afterlife.

girl in his cloak. The polished stone shape has its own simple beauty, with the surfaces turning subtly about smoothly rounded corners. The work—one of many surviving statues depicting Senmut with Hatshepsut's daughter—is also a reflection of the power of Egypt's female ruler. The frequent depiction of Senmut with Nefrura was meant to enhance Senmut's stature through his association with the princess (he was her tutor) and, by implication, with Hatshepsut herself.

TOMB OF NEBAMUN Some of the best-preserved mural paintings of the New Kingdom come from the 18th Dynasty Theban tomb of Nebamun, whose official titles were "scribe and counter of grain." On one wall (FIG. **3-28**), the painter depicted Nebamun standing in his boat, flushing birds from a papyrus swamp. The hieroglyphic text beneath his left arm says that Nebamun is enjoying recreation in his eternal afterlife. (Here, as elsewhere in Egyptian art, the accompanying text amplifies the message of the picture—and

vice versa.) In contrast to the static pose of Ti watching others hunt hippopotami (FIG. **3-15**), the painter showed Nebamun striding forward and vigorously swinging his throwing stick. In his right hand, he holds three birds he has caught. A wild cat, impossibly perched on a papyrus stem just in front of and below him, has caught two more in its claws and is holding the wings of a third in its teeth. Nebamun's wife and daughter accompany him on this hunt and hold the lotuses they have gathered. The artist scaled down their figures in proportion to their rank, as did Old Kingdom artists. And, as in Ti's tomb, the animals show a naturalism based on careful observation.

The painting technique, also employed in earlier Egyptian tombs, is *fresco secco* (dry fresco), whereby artists let the plaster dry

3-29 Musicians and dancers, from the tomb of Nebamun, Thebes, Egypt, 18th Dynasty, ca. 1400–1350 BCE. Fresco on dry plaster, 1′ × 2′ 3″. British Museum, London.

A second fresco in Nebamun's tomb represents a funerary banquet in which the artist experimented with frontal views of faces and bodies— a relaxation of the Old Kingdom's stiff rules of representation.

before painting on it. This procedure, in contrast to true fresco painting on wet plaster (see "Fresco Painting," Chapter 14, page 382), permitted slower and more meticulous work than painting on wet plaster, which had to be completed before the plaster dried. Fresco secco, however, is not as durable as true fresco painting, because the colors do not fuse with the wall surface.

Another fresco fragment (FIG. 3-29) from Nebamun's tomb shows four noblewomen watching and apparently participating in a musicale and dance where two nimble and almost nude dancing girls perform at a banquet. When Nebamun was buried, his family must have eaten the customary ceremonial meal at his tomb. They would have returned one day each year to partake in a commemorative banquet for the living to commune with the dead. This fresco represents one of these funerary feasts, with an ample supply of wine jars at the right. It also shows that New Kingdom artists did not always adhere to the old standards for figural representation. This painter carefully recorded the dancers' overlapping figures, their facing in opposite directions, and their rather complicated gyrations, producing a pleasing intertwined motif at the same time. The profile view of the dancers is consistent with their lower stature in the Egyptian hierarchy. The painter still reserved the composite view for Nebamun and his family. Of the four seated women, the artist represented the two at the left conventionally, but the other two face the observer in what is a rarely attempted frontal pose. They clap and beat time to the dance, while one of them plays the reeds. The painter took careful note of the soles of their feet as they sat cross-legged and suggested the movement of the women's heads by the loose arrangement of their hair strands. This informality constituted a relaxation of the Old Kingdom's stiff rules of representation.

The frescoes in Nebamun's tomb testify to the luxurious life of the Egyptian nobility, filled with good food and drink, fine musicians, lithe dancers, and leisure time to hunt and fish in the marshes. But, as in the earlier tomb of Ti, the scenes should be read both literally and allegorically. Although Nebamun is shown enjoying himself in the afterlife, the artist symbolically asked viewers to recall how he got there. Hunting scenes reminded Egyptians of Horus, the son of Osiris, hunting down his father's murderer, Seth, the god of disorder. Successful hunts were metaphors for triumphing over death and disorder, ensuring a happy existence in the afterlife. Music and dance were sacred to Hathor, who aided the dead in their passage to the other world. The sensual women at the banquet are a reference to fertility, rebirth, and regeneration.

Akhenaton and the Amarna Period

Not long after Nebamun was laid to rest in his tomb at Thebes, a revolution occurred in Egyptian society and religion. In the mid-14th century BCE, the pharaoh Amenhotep IV, later known as Akhenaton (r. 1353–1335 BCE), abandoned the worship of most of the Egyptian gods in favor of Aton, identified with the sun disk, whom he declared to be the universal and only god. Akhenaton blotted out the name of Amen from all inscriptions and even from his own name and that of his father, Amenhotep III. He emptied the great temples, enraged the priests, and moved his capital downriver from Thebes to a site he named Akhetaton (after his new god), where he built his own city and shrines. It is now called Amarna. The pharaoh claimed to be both the son and sole prophet of Aton. To him alone could the god make revelation. Moreover, in stark contrast to earlier practice, artists represented Akhenaton's god neither in animal nor in human form but simply as the sun disk emitting life-giving rays. The pharaohs who followed Akhenaton reestablished the cult and priesthood of Amen and restored the temples and the inscriptions. The gigantic temple complex at Karnak (FIG. 3-24), for example, was dedicated to the re-

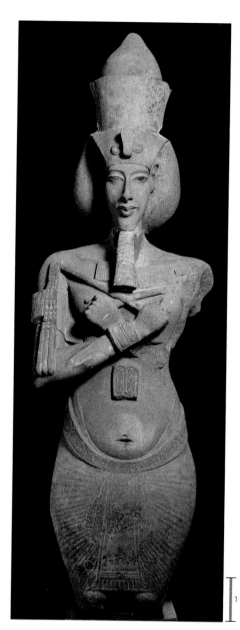

3-30 Akhenaton, from the temple of Aton, Karnak, Egypt, 18th Dynasty, ca. 1353–1335 BCE. Sandstone, 13′ high. Egyptian Museum, Cairo.

Akhenaton initiated a religious revolution, and his art is also a deliberate reaction against tradition. This curious androgynous image may be an attempt to portray the pharaoh as Aton, the sexless sun disk.

1 ft.

newed worship of the Theban god Amen. Akhenaton's brief religious revolution was soon undone, and his new city was largely abandoned.

During the brief heretical episode of Akhenaton, however, profound changes occurred in Egyptian art. A colossal statue (FIG. 3-30) of Akhenaton from Karnak, toppled and buried after his death, retains the standard frontal pose of canonical pharaonic portraits. But the effeminate body, with its curving contours, and the long face with full lips and heavy-lidded eyes are a far cry indeed from the heroically proportioned figures of the pharaoh's predecessors (compare FIG. 3-13). Akhenaton's body is curiously misshapen, with weak arms, a narrow waist, protruding belly, wide hips, and fatty thighs. Modern doctors have tried to explain his physique by attributing a variety of illnesses to the pharaoh. They cannot agree on a diagnosis, and their premise—that the statue is an accurate depiction of a physical deformity—is probably faulty. Some art historians think that Akhenaton's portrait is a deliberate artistic reaction against the established style, paralleling the suppression of traditional religion. They argue that Akhenaton's artists tried to formulate a new androgynous image of the pharaoh as the manifestation of Aton, the sexless sun disk. But no consensus exists other than that the style was revolutionary and short-lived.

1 in.

3-31 Thutmose, Nefertiti, from Amarna, Egypt, 18th Dynasty, ca. 1353–1335 BCE. Painted limestone, 1′ 8″ high. Ägyptisches Museum, Berlin.

Nefertiti, Akhenaton's influential wife, is portrayed here as an elegant beauty, with a pensive expression and a long, delicately curved neck. The unfinished portrait was found in Thutmose's workshop.

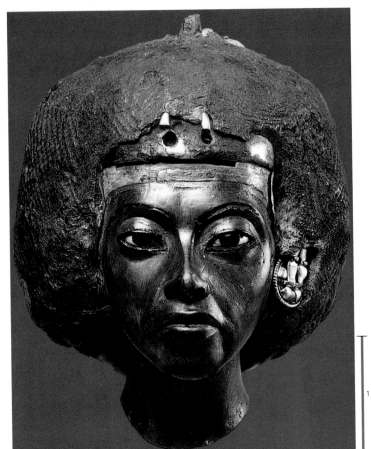

1 in.

3-32 Tiye, from Ghurab, Egypt, 18th Dynasty, ca. 1353–1335 BCE. Wood, with gold, silver, alabaster, and lapis lazuli, $3\frac{3}{4}$″ high. Ägyptisches Museum, Berlin.

This portrait of Akhenaton's mother is carved of dark yew wood, probably to match the queen's complexion. The head was remodeled during her son's reign to remove all references to traditional deities.

NEFERTITI AND TIYE A painted limestone bust (FIG. 3-31) of Akhenaton's queen, Nefertiti (her name means "The Beautiful One Has Come"), exhibits a similar expression of entranced musing and an almost mannered sensitivity and delicacy of curving contour. The piece was found at Amarna in the workshop of the sculptor THUTMOSE and is a deliberately unfinished model very likely by the master's own hand. The left eye socket still lacks the inlaid eyeball, making the portrait a kind of before-and-after demonstration piece. With this elegant bust, Thutmose may have been alluding to a heavy flower on its slender stalk by exaggerating the weight of the crowned head and the length of the almost serpentine neck. The sculptor seems to have adjusted the actual likeness of his subject to meet the era's standard of spiritual beauty.

A moving portrait of old age is preserved in the miniature head (FIG. 3-32) of Queen Tiye, mother of Akhenaton. Although not of royal birth, Tiye was the daughter of a high-ranking official and became the chief wife of Amenhotep III. Her portrait, carved of dark yew wood, probably to match her complexion, was found at Ghurab

with other objects connected with the funerary cult of Amenhotep III. Another artist probably remodeled the work during her son's reign to eliminate all reference to deities of the old religion. That is when the head acquired the present wig of plaster and linen with small blue beads. Tiye is shown as an older woman with lines and furrows, consistent with the new relaxation of artistic rules in the Amarna age. Her heavy-lidded slanting eyes are inlaid with alabaster and ebony, the lips are painted red, and the earrings (one is hidden by the later wig) are of gold and lapis lazuli. The wig covers what was originally a silver-foil headdress. A gold band still adorns the forehead. Such luxurious materials were common for royal portraits.

Both Nefertiti and Tiye figured prominently in the art and life of the Amarna age. Tiye, for example, regularly appeared in art beside her husband during his reign, and she apparently played an important role in his administration as well as her son's. Letters survive from foreign rulers advising the young Akhenaton to seek his mother's counsel in the conduct of international affairs. Nefertiti too was an influential woman. She frequently appears in the decoration of the Aton temple at Karnak, and she not only equals her husband in size but also sometimes wears pharaonic headgear.

FAMILY PORTRAITURE A sunken relief stele (FIG. 3-33), perhaps from a private shrine, provides a rare look at this royal family. The style is familiar from the colossus of Akhenaton (FIG. 3-30) and the portrait head of Nefertiti (FIG. 3-31). Undulating curves replace rigid lines, and the figures possess the prominent bellies that

3-33 Akhenaton, Nefertiti, and three daughters, from Amarna, Egypt, 18th Dynasty, ca. 1353–1335 BCE. Limestone, $1' \frac{1}{4}''$ high. Ägyptisches Museum, Berlin.

In this sunken relief the Amarna artist provided a rare intimate look at the royal family in a domestic setting. Akhenaton, Nefertiti, and three of their daughters bask in the life-giving rays of Aton, the sun disk.

characterize figures of the Amarna period. The pharaoh, his wife, and three of their daughters bask in the life-giving rays of Aton, the sun disk. The mood is informal and anecdotal. Akhenaton lifts one of his daughters in order to kiss her. Another daughter sits on Nefertiti's lap and gestures toward her father while the youngest daughter reaches out to touch a pendant on her mother's crown. This kind of intimate portrayal of the pharaoh and his family is unprecedented in Egyptian art. The political and religious revolution under Akhenaton was matched by an equally radical upheaval in art.

The Tomb of Tutankhamen and the Post-Amarna Period

The most famous figure of the Post-Amarna period is Tutankhamen (r. 1333–1323 BCE), who was probably Akhenaton's son by a minor wife. Tutankhamen ruled for a decade and died at age 18. (Although some people speculated foul play, examination of the king's mummy in 2005 ruled out murder.) Tutankhamen was a very minor figure in Egyptian history, however. The public remembers him today solely because in 1922 Howard Carter, a British archaeologist, discovered the boy-king's tomb with its fabulously rich treasure of sculpture, furniture, and jewelry largely intact.

TOMB OF TUTANKHAMEN The principal item that Carter found in Tutankhamen's tomb is the enshrined body of the pharaoh himself. The royal mummy reposed in the innermost of three coffins, nested one within the other. The innermost coffin (FIG. 3-34) was the most luxurious of the three. Made of beaten gold (about a quarter ton of it) and inlaid with semiprecious stones such as lapis lazuli, turquoise, and carnelian, it is a supreme monument to the sculptor's and goldsmith's crafts. The portrait mask (FIG. 3-1), which covered the king's face, is also made of gold with inlaid semiprecious stones. It is a sensitive portrayal of the serene adolescent king dressed in his official regalia, including the nemes headdress and false beard. The general effects of the mask and of the tomb treasures as a whole are of grandeur and richness expressive of Egyptian power, pride, and affluence.

3-34 Innermost coffin of Tutankhamen, from his tomb at Thebes, Egypt, 18th Dynasty, ca. 1323 BCE. Gold with inlay of enamel and semiprecious stones, 6' 1" long. Egyptian Museum, Cairo.

The boy-king Tutankhamen's fame today is due to the discovery of his treasure-laden tomb. His mummy was encased in three nested coffins. The innermost one, made of gold, portrays the pharaoh as Osiris.

3-35 Painted chest, from the tomb of Tutankhamen, Thebes, Egypt, 18th Dynasty, ca. 1333–1323 BCE. Wood, 1′ 8″ long. Egyptian Museum, Cairo.

Tutankhamen is here represented triumphing over Asian enemies. The artist contrasted the orderly registers of Egyptian chariots with the chaotic pile of foreign soldiers who fall before the king.

Although Tutankhamen probably was considered too young to fight, his position as king required that he be represented as a conqueror. He is shown as such in the panels of a painted chest (FIG. 3-35) deposited in his tomb. The lid panel shows the king as a successful hunter pursuing droves of fleeing animals in the desert, and the side panel shows him as a great warrior. From a war chariot pulled by spirited, plumed horses, the pharaoh, shown larger than all other figures on the chest, draws his bow against a cluster of bearded Asian enemies, who fall in confusion before him. (The absence of a ground line in an Egyptian painting or relief implies chaos and death.) Tutankhamen slays the enemy, like game, in great numbers. Behind him are three tiers of undersized war chariots, which serve to magnify the king's figure and to increase the count of his warriors. The themes are traditional, but the fluid, curvilinear forms are features reminiscent of the Amarna style.

3-36 Last judgment of Hu-Nefer, from his tomb at Thebes, Egypt, 19th Dynasty, ca. 1290–1280 BCE. Painted papyrus scroll, 1′ 6″ high. British Museum, London.

The *Book of the Dead* contained spells and prayers. This scroll depicts the weighing of Hu-Nefer's heart against Maat's feather before the deceased can be brought before Osiris, god of the Underworld.

SCROLL OF HU-NEFER Tutankhamen's mummy case (FIG. 3-34) shows the boy-king in the guise of Osiris, god of the dead and king of the Underworld, as well as giver of eternal life. The ritual of the cult of Osiris is recorded in the so-called *Book of the Dead*, a collection of spells and prayers. Illustrated papyrus scrolls, some as long as 70 feet, containing these texts were the essential equipment of the tombs of well-to-do persons (see "Mummification and Immortality," page 43).

The scroll (FIG. 3-36) of Hu-Nefer, the royal scribe and steward of Seti I, was found in his tomb in the Theban necropolis and represents the final judgment of the deceased. At the left, Anubis, the jackal-headed god of embalming, leads Hu-Nefer into the hall of judgment. The god then adjusts the scales to weigh the dead man's heart against the feather of the goddess Maat, protectress of truth and right. A hybrid crocodile-hippopotamus-lion monster, Ammit, devourer of the sinful, awaits the decision of the scales. If the weighing had been unfavorable to the deceased, the monster would have eaten his heart. The ibis-headed god Thoth records the proceedings. Above, the gods of the Egyptian pantheon are arranged as witnesses, while Hu-Nefer kneels in adoration before them. Having been justified by the scales, Hu-Nefer is brought by Osiris's son, the falcon-headed Horus, into the presence of the green-faced Osiris and his sisters Isis and Nephthys to receive the award of eternal life.

In Hu-Nefer's scroll, the figures have all the formality of stance, shape, and attitude of traditional Egyptian art. Abstract figures and hieroglyphs alike are aligned rigidly. Nothing here was painted in the flexible, curvilinear style suggestive of movement that was evident in the art of Amarna and Tutankhamen. The return to conservatism is unmistakable.

FIRST MILLENNIUM BCE

During the first millennium BCE, Egypt lost the commanding role it once had played in the ancient Near East. The empire dwindled away, and foreign powers invaded, occupied, and ruled the land, until it was taken over by Alexander the Great of Macedon and his Greek successors and, eventually, by the emperors of Rome.

Kingdom of Kush

One of those foreign powers was Egypt's gold-rich neighbor to the south, the kingdom of Kush, part of which is in present-day Sudan. Called Nubia by the Romans, perhaps from the Egyptian word for "gold," Kush is mentioned in Egyptian texts as early as the Old Kingdom. During the New Kingdom, the pharaohs colonized Nubia and appointed a viceroy to administer the Kushite kingdom, which included Abu Simbel (FIG. 3-22) and controlled the major trade route between Egypt and sub-Saharan Africa. But in the eighth century BCE, the Nubians conquered Egypt and ruled the land of the Nile as the 25th Dynasty.

TAHARQO Around 680 BCE, the Kushite pharaoh Taharqo (r. 690–664 BCE) constructed a temple at Kawa and placed a portrait of himself in it. Emulating traditional Egyptian types, the sculptor portrayed Taharqo as a sphinx (FIG. 3-37; compare FIG. 3-11) with the ears, mane, and body of a lion but with a human face and a headdress with two uraeus cobras. The king's name is inscribed on his chest, and his features are distinctly African, although, as in all pharaonic portraiture, they should be considered generic and idealized rather than a specific likeness.

1 in.

3-37 Taharqo as a sphinx, from temple T, Kawa, Sudan, 25th Dynasty, ca. 680 BCE. Granite, $1' 4'' \times 2' 4\frac{3}{4}''$. British Museum, London.

Nubian kings ruled Egypt during the 25th Dynasty and adopted traditional Egyptian artistic types, but the sculptor of the Taharqo sphinx reproduced the Kushite pharaoh's distinctly African features.

3-38 Temple of Horus, Edfu, Egypt, ca. 237–47 BCE.

The pylon temple at Edfu is more than a thousand years later than that at Karnak (FIG. 3-24), but it adheres to the same basic architectural scheme. Egyptian artistic forms tended to have very long lives.

After Alexander

Once formulated, Egyptian traditions tended to have very long lives, in architecture as in the other arts—even after Alexander the Great established Greek rule in the land of the Nile.

TEMPLE OF HORUS, EDFU The temple of Horus at Edfu (FIG. 3-38), built during the third, second, and first centuries BCE, after Alexander the Great's conquest of Egypt, still follows the basic pylon temple scheme architects worked out more than a thousand years before (compare the temple of Amen-Re at Karnak, FIG. 3-24). The great entrance pylon at Edfu is especially impressive. The broad sur-

face of its massive facade, with its sloping walls, is broken only by the doorway with its overshadowing *moldings* at the top and sides, deep channels to hold great flagstaffs, and sunken reliefs. The reliefs depict Horus and Hathor witnessing an oversized King Ptolemy XIII (r. 51–47 BCE) smiting undersized enemies. It is a striking monument to the persistence of Egyptian architectural and sculptural types.

Indeed, the exceptional longevity of formal traditions in Egypt is one of the marvels of the history of art. It testifies to the invention of an artistic style so satisfactory that it endured in Egypt for millennia. Everywhere else in the ancient Mediterranean world, stylistic change was the only common denominator.

EGYPT UNDER THE PHARAOHS

PREDYNASTIC AND EARLY DYNASTIC PERIODS, ca. 3500–2575 BCE

▌ The unification of Upper and Lower Egypt into a single kingdom under the rule of a divine pharaoh occurred around 3000–2920 BCE. The event was commemorated on the earliest preserved work of narrative art, the palette of King Narmer, which also established the basic principles of Egyptian representational art for 3,000 years.

▌ Imhotep, the first artist in history whose name is known, established the tradition of monumental stone architecture in Egypt in the funerary complex and Stepped Pyramid he built for King Djoser (r. 2630–2611 BCE) at Saqqara.

Palette of King Narmer,
ca. 3000–2920 BCE

OLD KINGDOM, ca. 2575–2134 BCE

▌ The Old Kingdom was the first golden age of Egyptian art and architecture, the time when three pharaohs of the Fourth Dynasty erected the Great Pyramids at Gizeh, the oldest of the Seven Wonders of the ancient world. The pyramids were emblems of the sun on whose rays the pharaohs ascended to the heavens after their death.

▌ Old Kingdom sculptors created seated and standing statuary types in which all movement was suppressed in order to express the eternal nature of pharaonic kingship. These types would dominate Egyptian art for 2,000 years.

Great Sphinx and Pyramids, Gizeh,
ca. 2550–2475 BCE

MIDDLE KINGDOM, ca. 2040–1640 BCE

▌ After an intermediate period of civil war, Mentuhotep II (r. 2050–1998 BCE) reestablished central rule and founded the Middle Kingdom.

▌ The major artistic innovation of this period was the rock-cut tomb in which both the facade and interior chambers were hewn out of the living rock. The fluted columns in Middle Kingdom tombs closely resemble the columns later used in Greek temples.

Tomb of Amenemhet, Beni Hasan,
ca. 1950–1900 BCE

NEW KINGDOM, ca. 1550–1070 BCE

▌ During the New Kingdom, Egypt extended its borders to the Euphrates River in the east and deep into Nubia in the south.

▌ The most significant architectural innovation of this period was the axially planned pylon temple incorporating an immense gateway, columnar courtyards, and a hypostyle hall with clerestory windows.

▌ Powerful pharaohs such as Hatshepsut (r. 1473–1458 BCE) and Ramses II (r. 1290–1224 BCE) erected gigantic temples in honor of their patron gods and, after their deaths, for their own worship.

▌ Akhenaton (r. 1353–1335 BCE) abandoned the traditional Egyptian religion in favor of Aton, the sun disk, and initiated a short-lived artistic revolution in which undulating curves and anecdotal content replaced the cubic forms and impassive stillness of earlier Egyptian art.

Akhenaton, Nefertiti, and three
daughters, ca. 1353–1335 BCE

FIRST MILLENNIUM BCE

▌ After the demise of the New Kingdom, Egypt's power in the ancient world declined and it came under the control of foreigners, such as the Kushite kings of Nubia and, after 332 BCE, Alexander the Great and his Greek successors. In 30 BCE, Egypt became a province of the Roman Empire.

▌ The traditional forms of Egyptian art and architecture lived on even under foreign rule—for example, in the pylon temple erected at Edfu in honor of Horus.

Temple of Horus, Edfu,
ca. 237–47 BCE

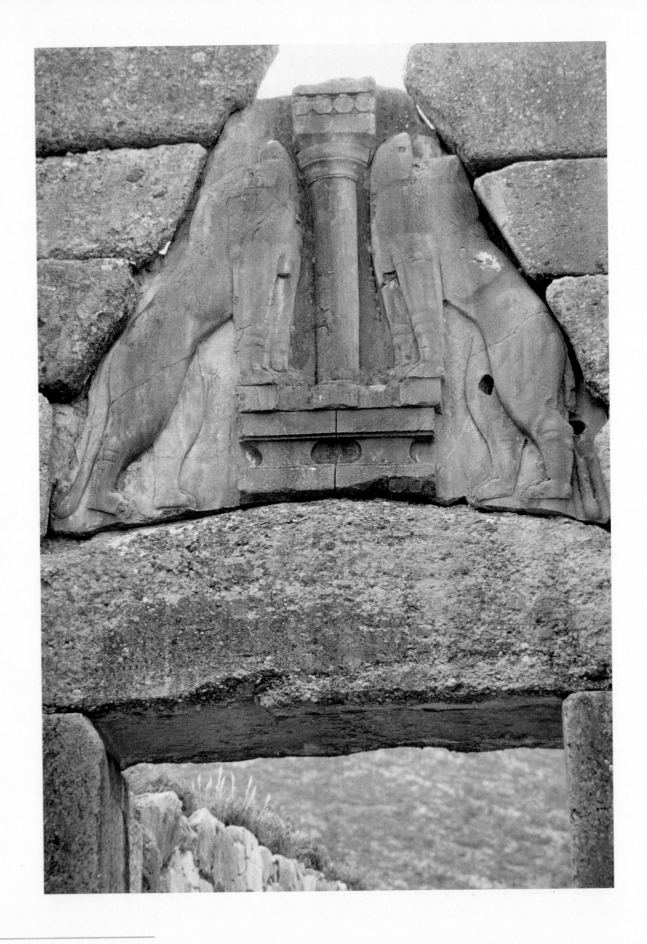

4-1 Relieving triangle with confronting lions, detail of Lion Gate (FIG. 4-19), Mycenae, Greece, ca. 1300–1250 BCE.

The gateway to the citadel of Mycenae, legendary home of King Agamemnon of Homer's *Iliad,* was built of such large stones that the later Greeks believed that giants, not mortals, erected it.

THE PREHISTORIC
AEGEAN

In the *Iliad,* Homer describes the might and splendor of the Greek armies poised before the walls of Troy.

> Clan after clan poured out from the ships and huts onto the plain . . . innumerable as the leaves and blossoms in their season . . . the Athenians . . . the men of Argos and Tiryns of the Great Walls . . . troops from the great stronghold of Mycenae, from wealthy Corinth . . . from Knossos . . . Phaistos . . . and the other troops that had their homes in Crete of the Hundred Towns.[1]

The Greeks had come from far and wide, from the mainland and the islands (MAP **4-1**), to seek revenge against Paris, the Trojan prince who had abducted Helen, wife of King Menelaus of Sparta. Composed around 750 BCE, the *Iliad* is the first great work of Greek literature. In fact, until about 1870, Homer's epic poem was generally regarded as pure fiction. Scholars discounted the bard as a historian, attributing the profusion of names and places in his writings to the rich abundance of his imagination. The prehistory of Greece remained shadowy and lost in an impenetrable world of myth.

TROY AND MYCENAE In the late 1800s, however, a wealthy German businessman turned archaeologist proved that scholars had done less than justice to the truth of Homer's account. Between 1870 and his death 20 years later, Heinrich Schliemann (whose methods have sometimes been harshly criticized) uncovered some of the very cities Homer named. In 1870, he began work at Hissarlik on the northwestern coast of Turkey, which a British archaeologist, Frank Calvert, had postulated was the site of Homer's Troy. Schliemann dug into a vast mound and found a number of fortified cities built on the remains of one another. One of them had been destroyed by fire in the 13th century BCE. This, scholars now generally agree, was the Troy of King Priam and his son Paris, the city Homer celebrated some 500 years later.

Schliemann continued his excavations at Mycenae on the Greek mainland, where, he believed, King Agamemnon, Menelaus's brother, had once ruled. Here his finds were even more startling. A massive fortress-palace with a monumental gateway (FIGS. **4-1** and 4-19); domed tombs beneath earthen mounds (FIGS. **4-20** and 4-21); quantities of gold jewelry, masks (FIG. 4-22), and cups; and inlaid bronze weapons

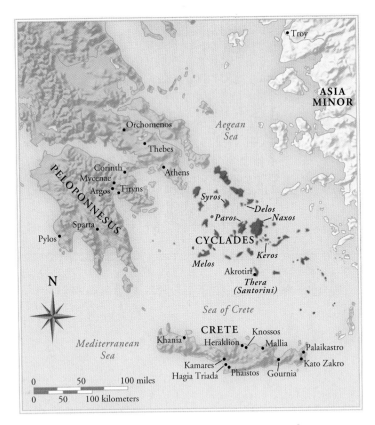

MAP 4-1 The prehistoric Aegean.

(FIG. 4-23) revealed a magnificent civilization far older than the famous vestiges of Classical Greece that had remained visible in Athens and elsewhere. Further discoveries proved that Mycenae had not been the only center of this fabulous civilization.

MINOAN CRETE Another legendary figure was King Minos of Knossos on the island of Crete. He had exacted from Athens a tribute of youths and maidens to be fed to the *Minotaur,* a creature half bull and half man housed in a vast labyrinth. Might this story, too, be based on fact? In 1900, an English archaeologist, Arthur Evans, began work at Knossos, where he uncovered a palace (FIGS. 4-4 and 4-5) that did indeed resemble a maze. Evans named its builders the Minoans, after their mythological king. Further evidence of the Minoans was soon uncovered at Phaistos, Hagia Triada, and other sites, including Gournia, which Harriet Boyd Hawes, an American archaeologist (and one of the first women of any nationality to direct a major excavation), explored between 1901 and 1904.

More recently, important Minoan remains have been excavated at many other locations on Crete, and contemporary sites have been discovered on other islands in the Aegean, most notably on Santorini (ancient Thera). Art historians now have many buildings, paintings, and, to a lesser extent, sculptures that attest to the wealth and sophistication of the people who lived in that once-obscure heroic age celebrated in later Greek mythology.

AEGEAN ARCHAEOLOGY TODAY Less glamorous than the palaces and art objects, but arguably more important for the understanding of Aegean society, are the many documents archaeologists have found written in scripts dubbed Linear A and Linear B. The progress made during the past several decades in deciphering these texts has provided a welcome corrective to the romanticism that characterized the work of Schliemann and Evans. Linear B can now be read as an early form of Greek, and scholars have begun to reconstruct Aegean civilization by referring to contemporaneous records and not just to Homer's heroic account. Archaeologists now also know that humans

inhabited Greece as far back as the late Paleolithic period and that village life was firmly established in Greece and on Crete in Neolithic times. But the heyday of the ancient Aegean was not until the second millennium BCE, well after the emergence of the river valley civilizations of Mesopotamia and Egypt (see Chapters 2 and 3).

The prehistoric Aegean has three geographic areas, and each has its own distinctive artistic identity. *Cycladic* art is the art of the Cycladic Islands (so named because they *circle* around Delos), as well as of the adjacent islands in the Aegean, excluding Crete. *Minoan* art encompasses the art of Crete. *Helladic* art is the art of the Greek mainland (*Hellas* in Greek). Scholars subdivide each area chronologically into early, middle, and late periods, with the art of the Late Helladic period designated Mycenaean after Agamemnon's great citadel of Mycenae.

CYCLADIC ART

Marble was abundantly available in the superb quarries of the Aegean Islands, especially on Naxos and Paros. The sculptors of the Early Cycladic period used that marble to produce statuettes (FIGS. 4-2 and 4-3) that collectors highly admire today (see "Archaeology, Art History, and the Art Market," page 69) because of their striking abstract forms, which call to mind the simple and sleek shapes of some modern sculptures (FIG. 24-20).

WOMAN FROM SYROS Most of the Cycladic sculptures, like many of their Stone Age predecessors in the Aegean, the Near East, and western Europe (FIG. 1-5), represent nude women with their arms folded across their abdomens. They have been found both in graves and in settlements and vary in height from a few inches to almost life-size. The statuette illustrated here (FIG. 4-2) is about a foot and a half tall—but only about a half inch thick—and comes from a grave on the island of Syros. The sculptor rendered the human body in a highly schematic manner. Large simple triangles dominate the form—the head, the body itself (which tapers from exceptionally broad shoulders to tiny feet), and the incised triangular pubis. The feet are too fragile to support the figurine. It must have been placed on its back in the grave—lying down, like the deceased. Whether the Syros statuette and the many other similar Cycladic figurines known

4-2 Figurine of a woman, from Syros (Cyclades), Greece, ca. 2500–2300 BCE. Marble, 1′ 6″ high. National Archaeological Museum, Athens.

Most Cycladic statuettes depict nude women. This one comes from a grave, but whether it represents the deceased is uncertain. The sculptor rendered the female body schematically as a series of large triangles.

1 in.

Archaeology, Art History, and the Art Market

One way the ancient world is fundamentally different from the world today is that ancient art is largely anonymous and undated. No equivalent exists in antiquity for the systematic signing and dating of artworks commonplace in the contemporary world. That is why the role of archaeology in the study of ancient art is so important. Only the scientific excavation of ancient monuments can establish their context. Exquisite and strikingly "modern" sculptures such as the marble Cycladic figurines illustrated in FIGS. 4-2 and 4-3 may be appreciated as masterpieces when displayed in splendid isolation in glass cases in museums or private homes. But to understand the role these or any other artworks played in ancient society—in many cases, even to determine the date and place of origin of an object—the art historian must know where the piece was uncovered. Only when the context of an artwork is known can one go beyond an appreciation of its formal qualities and begin to analyze its place in art history—and in the society that produced it.

The extraordinary popularity of Cycladic figurines in recent decades has had unfortunate consequences. Clandestine treasure hunters, eager to meet the insatiable demands of modern collectors, have plundered many sites and smuggled their finds out of Greece to sell to the highest bidder on the international art market. Entire prehistoric cemeteries and towns have been destroyed because of the high esteem in which these sculptures are now held. Two British scholars have calculated that only about 10 percent of the known Cycladic marble statuettes come from secure archaeological contexts. Many of the rest could be forgeries produced after World War II when developments in modern art fostered a new appreciation of these abstract renditions of human anatomy and created a boom in demand for "Cycladica" among collectors. For some categories of Cycladic sculptures—those of unusual type or size—not a single piece with a documented provenance exists. Those groups may be 20th-century inventions designed to fetch even higher prices due to their rarity. Consequently, most of the conclusions art historians have drawn about chronology, attribution to different workshops, range of types, and how the figurines were used are purely speculative. The importance of the information the original contexts would have provided cannot be overestimated. That information, however, can probably never be recovered.

4-3 Male lyre player, from Keros (Cyclades), Greece, ca. 2700–2500 BCE. Marble, 9″ high. National Archaeological Museum, Athens.

The meaning of all Cycladic figurines is elusive, but this seated musician may be playing for the deceased in the afterlife. The statuette displays the same simple geometric shapes and flat planes as FIG. 4-2.

today represent dead women or fertility figures or goddesses is still debated. In any case, the sculptors took pains to emphasize the breasts as well as the pubic area. In the Syros statuette, a slight swelling of the belly may suggest pregnancy. Traces of paint found on some of the Cycladic figurines indicate that at least parts of these sculptures were colored. The now almost featureless faces would have had painted eyes and mouths in addition to the sculpted noses. Red and blue necklaces and bracelets, as well as painted dots on the cheeks and necks, characterize a number of the surviving figurines.

LYRE PLAYER FROM KEROS Male figures also occur in the Cycladic repertoire. The most elaborate of these take the form of seated musicians, such as the lyre player (FIG. 4-3) from Keros. Wedged between the echoing shapes of chair and instrument, he may be playing for the deceased in the afterlife, although, again, the meaning of these statuettes remains elusive. The harpist reflects

the same preference for simple geometric shapes and large flat planes as the female figures. Still, the artist showed a keen interest in recording the elegant shape of what must have been a prized possession: the harp with a duck-bill or swan-head ornament at the apex of its sound box. (Animal-headed instruments are well documented in contemporary Mesopotamia [FIG. 2-10] and Egypt.)

In one instance, figurines of both a musician and a reclining woman were placed in a woman's grave. This suggests that the lyre players are not images of dead men, but it does not prove that the female figurines represent dead women. The man might be entertaining the deceased herself, not her image. Given the absence of written documents in Greece at this date, as everywhere else in prehistoric times, and the lack of information about the provenance of most finds, art historians cannot be sure of the meaning of the Cycladic sculptures. It is likely, in fact, that the same form took on different meanings in different contexts.

MINOAN ART

During the third millennium BCE, both on the Aegean Islands and on the Greek mainland, most settlements were small and consisted only of simple buildings. Only rarely were the dead buried with costly offerings such as the Cycladic statuettes just examined. In contrast, the construction of large palaces marked the opening centuries of the second millennium (the Middle Minoan period on Crete).

Architecture

The first, or Old Palace, period came to an abrupt end around 1700 BCE, when fire destroyed these grand structures, probably following an earthquake. Rebuilding began almost immediately, and the ensu-

ing Late Minoan (New Palace) period is the golden age of Crete, an era when the first great Western civilization emerged. The rebuilt palaces were large, comfortable, and handsome, with residential suites for the king and his family and courtyards for pageants, ceremonies, and games. They also had storerooms, offices, and shrines that permitted these huge complexes to serve as the key administrative, commercial, and religious centers of Minoan life. The principal palace sites on Crete are at Knossos, Phaistos, Mallia, Kato Zakro, and Khania. All of the complexes were laid out along similar lines. Their size and number, as well as the rich finds they have yielded, attest to the power and prosperity of the Minoans.

PALACE AT KNOSSOS The largest of the palaces, at Knossos (FIGS. **4-4** and **4-5**), was the legendary home of King Minos. Here,

4-4 Aerial view (looking northeast) of the palace at Knossos (Crete), Greece, ca. 1700–1400 BCE.

The Knossos palace is the largest on Crete and was the legendary home of King Minos. Its layout features a large central court, around which all the residential and administrative units were grouped.

4-5 Plan of the palace at Knossos (Crete), Greece, ca. 1700–1400 BCE.

The mazelike plan of the Knossos palace gave rise to the Greek myth of the Cretan labyrinth inhabited by the Minotaur, a half-man half-bull monster that the Athenian king Theseus killed.

Reconstruction

Earlier structures { Existing, Reconstruction }

1. West porch
2. Corridor of the procession
3. South propylon
4. Central court
5. "Theater area"
6. North-south corridor
7. Pillar hall
8. Magazines
9. Throne room
10. Palace shrine and lower verandas
11. Stepped porch
12. Grand staircase
13. Light well
14. East-west corridor
15. Hall of the Double Axes (principal reception room)
16. "Queen's Megaron"

the hero Theseus was said to have battled with the bull-man Minotaur. According to the myth, after defeating the monster, Theseus found his way out of the mazelike complex only with the aid of the king's daughter, Ariadne. She had given Theseus a spindle of thread to mark his path through the labyrinth and thus to find his way out safely again. In fact, the English word *labyrinth* derives from the intricate plan and scores of rooms of the Knossos palace. *Labrys* means "double ax," and it is a recurring motif in the Minoan palace, referring to sacrificial slaughter. The labyrinth was the "House of the Double Axes."

The Knossos palace was a rambling structure built against the upper slopes and across the top of a low hill that rises from a fertile plain (FIG. 4-4). All around the palace proper were mansions and villas of the Minoan elite. The great rectangular court (FIG. 4-5, no. 4), with the palace units grouped around it, had been leveled in the time of the old palace. The new layout suggests that the later palace was carefully planned, with the court serving as the major organizing element. A secondary organization of the palace plan involves two long corridors. On the west side of the court, a north-south corridor (FIG. 4-5, no. 6) separates official and ceremonial rooms from the storerooms (no. 8), where wine, grain, oil, and honey were stockpiled in large jars. On the east side of the court, a smaller east-west corridor (no. 14) separates the administrative areas (to the south) from the workrooms (to the north). At the northwest corner of the palace is a theaterlike area (no. 5) with steps on two sides that may have served as seats. This form is a possible forerunner of the later Greek theater (FIG. 5-71). Its purpose is unknown, but it is a feature paralleled in the Phaistos palace.

The Knossos palace was complex in elevation as well as plan. It had as many as three stories around the central court and even more on the south and east sides where the terrain sloped off sharply.

Interior light and air wells with staircases (FIG. 4-6) provided necessary illumination and ventilation. The Minoans also gave thought to issues such as drainage of rainwater. At Knossos, a remarkably efficient system of terracotta pipes underlies the enormous building.

The Cretan palaces were well constructed, with thick walls composed of rough, unshaped fieldstones embedded in clay. The builders used ashlar masonry at corners and around door and window openings. The painted wooden columns (which Evans restored in cement at Knossos) have distinctive capitals and shafts. The bulbous, cushionlike Minoan capitals resemble those of the later Greek Doric order (FIG. 5-14), but the column shafts—essentially stylized inverted tree trunks—taper from a wide top to a narrower base, the opposite of both Egyptian and later Greek columns.

Painting

Mural paintings liberally adorn the palace at Knossos, constituting one of its most striking features. The brightly painted walls and the red shafts and black capitals of the wooden columns provided an extraordinarily rich effect. The paintings depict many aspects of Minoan life (bull-leaping, processions, and ceremonies) and of nature (birds, animals, flowers, and marine life).

LA PARISIENNE From a ceremonial scene of uncertain significance comes the fragment (FIG. 4-7) dubbed *La Parisienne* (The Parisian Woman) on its discovery because of the elegant dress, elaborate coiffure, and full rouged lips of the young woman depicted. Some have argued that she is a priestess taking part in a religious ritual, but because the figure has no arms, it is most likely a statue of a goddess. Although the representation is still convention-bound (note especially the oversized frontal eye in the profile head), the charm and freshness of the mural are undeniable. Unlike the

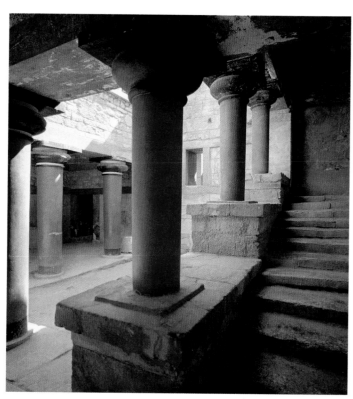

4-6 Stairwell in the residential quarter of the palace at Knossos (Crete), Greece, ca. 1700–1400 BCE.

The Knossos palace was complex in elevation as well as plan. It had at least three stories on all sides of the court. Minoan columns taper from top to bottom, the opposite of Egyptian and Greek columns.

4-7 Minoan woman or goddess (*La Parisienne*), from the palace at Knossos (Crete), Greece, ca. 1450–1400 BCE. Fragment of a fresco, 10″ high. Archaeological Museum, Herakleion.

Frescoes decorated the Knossos palace walls. This fragment depicts a woman or a goddess—perhaps a statue—with a large frontal eye in her profile head, as seen also in Near Eastern and Egyptian art.

1 in.

4-8 Bull-leaping, from the palace at Knossos (Crete), Greece, ca. 1450–1400 BCE. Fresco, 2′ 8″ high, including border. Archaeological Museum, Herakleion.

The subjects of the Knossos frescoes are often ceremonial scenes, like this one of bull-leaping. The women have fair skin and the man has dark skin, a common convention in ancient painting.

1 ft.

Egyptians, who painted in *fresco secco* (dry fresco), the Minoans coated the rough fabric of their rubble walls with a fine white lime plaster and used a true (wet) fresco method in which the pigments are mixed with water and become chemically bound to the plaster after it dries (see "Fresco Painting," Chapter 14, page 382). Consequently, the Minoan painters had to execute their work rapidly while the walls were still wet, in contrast to Egyptian practice.

BULL-LEAPING Another fresco (FIG. **4-8**) from the palace at Knossos depicts the Minoan ceremony of bull-leaping, in which young men grasped the horns of a bull and vaulted onto its back—a perilous and extremely difficult acrobatic maneuver. Only fragments of the full composition have been recovered (the dark patches are original; the rest is a modern restoration). The Minoan artist painted the young women (with fair skin) and the youth (with dark skin) according to the widely accepted ancient convention for distinguishing male and female. The painter brilliantly suggested the powerful charge of the bull by elongating the animal's shape and using sweeping lines to form a funnel of energy, beginning at the very narrow hindquarters of the bull and culminating in its large, sharp horns and galloping forelegs. The human figures also have stylized shapes, with typically Minoan pinched waists, and are highly animated. Although the profile pose with the full-view eye was a familiar convention in Egypt and Mesopotamia, the elegance of the Cretan figures, with their long, curly hair and proud and self-confident bearing, distinguishes them from all other early figure styles. In contrast to the angularity of the figures in Egyptian wall paintings, the curving lines the Minoan artist employed suggest the elasticity of living and moving beings.

THERA FRESCOES Much better preserved than the Knossos frescoes are those Greek archaeologists discovered in excavations begun in 1967 and still in progress at Akrotiri on the volcanic island of Santorini (ancient Thera) in the Cyclades, some 60 miles north of Crete. In the Late Cycladic period, Thera was artistically, and possibly also politically, within the Minoan orbit. The mural paintings from Akrotiri are invaluable additions to the fragmentary and frequently misrestored frescoes from Crete. The excellent condition of the Theran paintings is due to an enormous seismic explosion on Santorini that buried Akrotiri in volcanic pumice and ash, making it a kind of Pompeii of the prehistoric Aegean (see "The Theran Eruption and the Chronology of Aegean Art," page 73). The Akrotiri frescoes decorated the walls of houses, not the walls of a great palace such as that at Knossos, and therefore the number of painted walls from the site is especially impressive.

The almost perfectly preserved mural painting from Akrotiri known as the *Spring Fresco* (FIG. **4-9**) is one of the earliest examples of a pure landscape painting (compare FIG. **1-18**). The artist's aim, however, was not to render the rocky island terrain realistically but rather to capture the landscape's essence. The irrationally undulating and vividly colored rocks, the graceful lilies swaying in the cool island breezes, and the darting swallows express the vigor of growth, the delicacy of flowering, and the lightness of birdsong and flight. In the lyrical language of curving line, the artist celebrated the rhythms of spring. The *Spring Fresco* represents the polar opposite of the first efforts at mural painting in the caves of Paleolithic Europe (see Chapter 1), where animals (and occasionally humans) appeared as isolated figures without any indication of setting.

The Theran Eruption and the Chronology of Aegean Art

Today, ships bound for the beautiful Greek island of Santorini, with its picture-postcard white houses, churches, shops, and restaurants, weigh anchor in a bay beneath steep, crescent-shaped cliffs. Until about 20,000 BCE, however, ancient Thera had a roughly circular shape and gentler slopes. Then, suddenly, a volcanic eruption blew out the center of the island, leaving behind the moon-shaped main island and several lesser islands grouped around a bay that roughly corresponds to the shape of the gigantic ancient volcano. The volcano erupted again, thousands of years later, during the zenith of Aegean civilization.

In that eruption, the site of Akrotiri, which Greek excavators gradually are uncovering, was buried by a layer of pumice more than a yard deep in some areas and by an even larger volume of volcanic ash (*tephra*) that often exceeds five yards in depth, even after nearly 37 centuries of erosion. Tephra filled whole rooms, and boulders the volcano spewed forth pelted the walls of some houses. Closer to the volcano's cone, the tephra is almost 60 yards deep in places. In fact, the force of the eruption was so powerful that sea currents carried the pumice and wind blew the ash throughout the ancient Mediterranean, not only to Crete, Rhodes, and Cyprus but also as far away as Anatolia, Egypt, Syria, and Israel.

Until recently, most scholars embraced the theory formulated decades ago by Spyridon Marinatos, an eminent Greek archaeologist, that the otherwise unexplained demise of Minoan civilization on Crete around 1500 BCE was the by-product of the volcanic eruption on Thera. According to Marinatos, devastating famine followed the rain of ash that fell on Crete. But archaeologists now know that after the eruption, life went on in Crete, if not on Thera. At one Cretan site, the Minoans collected Theran pumice and deposited it in conical cups on a monumental stairway, possibly as a votive offering.

Teams of researchers, working closely in an impressive and most welcome interdisciplinary effort, have pinpointed 1628 BCE as the date of a major climatic event. They have studied tree rings at sites in Europe and in North America for evidence of retarded growth and have examined ice cores in Greenland for peak acidity layers. Both kinds of evidence testify to a significant disruption in weather patterns in that year. Most scholars now believe the cause of this disruption was the cataclysmic volcanic eruption on Thera. The discovery in 2006 of a datable olive tree in the Santorini tephra brought welcome confirmation for this theory.

The new 17th-century BCE date has profound consequences for the chronology of Aegean art. The Akrotiri frescoes (FIG. 4-9) must be around 150 years older than scholars thought when they were first discovered. The frescoes predate by many decades the Knossos palace murals (FIGS. 4-7 and 4-8).

4-9 Landscape with swallows (*Spring Fresco*), from room Delta 2, Akrotiri, Thera (Cyclades), Greece, ca. 1650 BCE. Fresco, 7′ 6″ high. National Archaeological Museum, Athens.

Aegean muralists painted in wet fresco, which required rapid execution. In this first known pure landscape, the Theran painter used vivid colors and undulating lines to capture the essence of springtime.

1 ft.

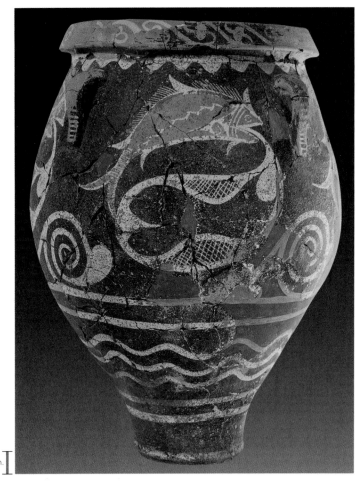

4-10 Kamares-ware jar, from Phaistos (Crete), Greece, ca. 1800–1700 BCE. 1′ 8″ high. Archaeological Museum, Herakleion.

Kamares vases have creamy white and reddish-brown decoration on a black background. This jar combines a fish (and a net?) with curvilinear abstract patterns including spirals and waves.

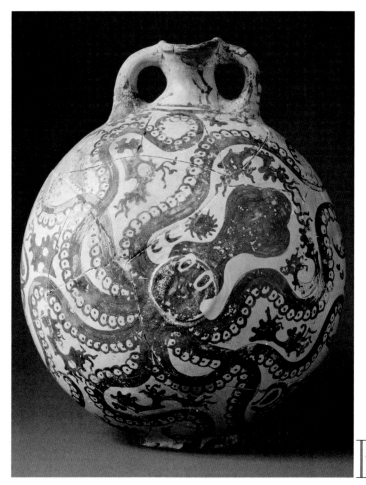

4-11 Marine Style octopus jar, from Palaikastro (Crete), Greece, ca. 1500 BCE. 11″ high. Archaeological Museum, Herakleion.

Marine Style vases have dark figures on a light ground. On this octopus jar the tentacles of the sea creature reach out over the curving surface of the vessel to fill the shape perfectly.

MINOAN POTTERY The love of nature manifested itself in Crete on the surfaces of painted vases even before the period of the new palaces. During the Middle Minoan period, Cretan potters fashioned sophisticated shapes using newly introduced potters' wheels, and decorated their vases in a distinctive and fully polychromatic style. These Kamares-ware vessels, named for the cave on the slope of Mount Ida where they were first discovered, have been found in quantity at Phaistos and Knossos and at sites throughout the Mediterranean and Near East. On the illustrated jar (FIG. **4-10**), as on other Kamares vases, the painter set creamy white and reddish-brown decoration against a rich black ground. The central motif is a great leaping fish and perhaps a fishnet surrounded by a host of curvilinear abstract patterns including waves and spirals. The swirling lines evoke life in the sea, and both the abstract and the natural forms beautifully complement the shape of the vessel.

The sea and the creatures that inhabit it also inspired the Late Minoan Marine Style octopus jar (FIG. **4-11**) from Palaikastro, which is contemporary with the new palaces at Knossos and elsewhere. The tentacles of the octopus reach out over the curving surfaces of the vessel, embracing the piece and emphasizing its volume. This is a masterful realization of the relationship between the vessel's decoration and its shape, always a problem for the vase painter. This later jar differs markedly from its Kamares-ware predecessor in color. Not only is the octopus vase more muted in tone, but the Late

Minoan artist also reversed the earlier scheme and placed dark silhouettes on a light ground. This dark-on-light format remained the norm for about a millennium in Greece, until about 530 BCE when, albeit in a very different form, light figures and a dark background emerged once again as the preferred manner (compare FIG. 5-22, *left* and *right*).

Sculpture

In contrast to Mesopotamia and Egypt, no temples or monumental statues of gods, kings, or monsters have been found in Minoan Crete. Large wooden images may once have existed—*La Parisienne* (FIG. 4-7) may depict one of them—but what remains of Minoan sculpture is uniformly small in scale.

SNAKE GODDESS One of the most striking finds at the palace at Knossos was the *faience* (low-fired opaque glasslike silicate) statuette popularly known as the *Snake Goddess* (FIG. 4-12). Reconstructed from many pieces, it is one of several similar figurines that some scholars believe may represent mortal attendants rather than a deity, although the prominently exposed breasts suggest that these figurines stand in the long line of prehistoric fertility images usually considered divinities. The Knossos woman holds snakes in her hands and also supports a leopardlike feline on her head. This implied power over the animal world also seems appropriate for a

4-12 *Snake Goddess,* from the palace at Knossos (Crete), Greece, ca. 1600 BCE. Faience, 1' 1½" high. Archaeological Museum, Herakleion.

This figurine may represent a priestess, but it is more likely a bare-breasted goddess. The snakes in her hands and the feline on her head imply that she has power over the animal world.

4-13 Young god(?), from Palaikastro (Crete), Greece, ca. 1500–1475 BCE. Ivory, gold, serpentine, and rock crystal, restored height 1' 7½". Archaeological Museum, Siteia.

This statuette, probably representing a young god, is a very early example of chryselephantine (gold and ivory) sculpture, a technique later used for the largest and costliest Greek cult statues.

deity. The frontality of the figure is reminiscent of Egyptian and Near Eastern statuary, but the costume, with its open bodice and flounced skirt, is distinctly Minoan. If the statuette represents a goddess, as seems likely, then it is yet another example of how human beings fashion their gods in their own image.

PALAIKASTRO YOUTH British excavations at Palaikastro between 1987 and 1990 yielded fragments of one of the most remarkable objects ever found on Crete. It is a statuette (FIG. **4-13**) nearly 20 inches tall, fashioned from hippopotamus-tusk ivory, gold, serpentine, and rock crystal. The figurine is a very early example of *chryselephantine* (gold and ivory) sculpture, a technique that the Greeks would later use for their largest and costliest cult images (FIG. 5-46). The ivory and gold were probably imported from Egypt, the source also of the pose with left foot advanced (FIG. 3-13), but the style and iconography are unmistakably Cretan. The work is the creation of a sculptor of extraordinary ability who delighted in rendering minute details of muscles and veins. The Palaikastro youth (his

coiffure, with shaved head save for a central braid, indicates his age) was displayed alone in a shrine and therefore seems to have been a god rather than a mortal. Archaeologists found the statuette in scattered and blackened fragments, suggesting fire following an act of vandalism in the 15th century BCE.

HARVESTERS VASE The finest surviving example of Minoan relief sculpture is the so-called *Harvesters Vase* (FIG. **4-14**) from Hagia Triada. Only the upper half of the egg-shaped body and neck of the vessel are preserved. Missing are the lower parts of the harvesters (or, as some think, sowers) and the ground on which they stand as well as the gold leaf that originally covered the relief figures. Formulaic scenes of sowing and harvesting were staples of Egyptian funerary art (FIG. 3-16), but the Minoan artist shunned static repetition in favor of a composition that bursts with the energy of its individually characterized figures. The relief shows a riotous crowd singing and shouting as they go to or return from the fields. The artist vividly captured the forward movement and lusty exuberance of the youths.

4-14 *Harvesters Vase,* from Hagia Triada (Crete), Greece, ca. 1500 BCE. Steatite, originally with gold leaf, greatest diameter 5". Archaeological Museum, Herakleion.

The relief sculptor of the singing harvesters on this small stone vase was one of the first artists in history to represent the underlying muscular and skeletal structure of the human body.

Although most of the figures conform to the age-old convention of combined profile and frontal views, the sculptor singled out one figure (FIG. **4-14,** *right*) from his companions. He shakes a rattle to beat time, and the artist depicted him in full profile with his lungs so inflated with air that his ribs show. This is one of the first instances in the history of art of a sculptor showing a keen interest in the underlying muscular and skeletal structure of the human body. The artist's painstaking study of human anatomy is a remarkable achievement, especially given the size of the *Harvesters Vase,* barely five inches at its greatest diameter. Equally noteworthy is how the sculptor recorded the tension and relaxation of facial muscles with astonishing exactitude, not just for this figure but for his three closest companions as well. This degree of animation of the human face is without precedent in ancient art.

MINOAN DECLINE Scholars dispute the circumstances ending the Minoan civilization, although they now widely believe that Mycenaeans had already moved onto Crete and established themselves at Knossos at the end of the New Palace period. From the palace at Knossos, these intruders appear to have ruled the island for at least a half century, perhaps much longer. Parts of the palace continued to be occupied until its final destruction around 1200 BCE, but its importance as a cultural center faded soon after 1400 BCE, as the focus of Aegean civilization shifted to the Greek mainland.

MYCENAEAN ART

The origins of the Mycenaean culture are still debated. The only certainty is the presence of these forerunners of the Greeks on the mainland about the time the old palaces were built on Crete—that is, about the beginning of the second millennium BCE. Doubtless, Cretan civilization influenced these people even then, and some believe that the mainland was a Minoan economic dependency for a long time. In any case, Mycenaean power developed on the mainland in the days of the new palaces on Crete, and by 1500 BCE a distinctive Mycenaean culture was flourishing in Greece. Several centuries later, Homer described Mycenae as "rich in gold." The dramatic discoveries of Schliemann and his successors have fully justified this characterization, even if today's archaeologists no longer view the Mycenaeans solely through the eyes of Homer.

4-15 Aerial view of the citadel at Tiryns, Greece, ca. 1400–1200 BCE.

In the *Iliad,* Homer called the fortified citadel of Tiryns the city "of the great walls." Its huge, roughly cut stone blocks are examples of Cyclopean masonry, named after the mythical one-eyed giants.

Architecture

The destruction of the Cretan palaces left the mainland culture supreme. Although this Late Helladic civilization has come to be called Mycenaean, Mycenae was but one of several large palace complexes. Archaeologists have also unearthed Mycenaean remains at Tiryns, Orchomenos, Pylos, and elsewhere, and Mycenaean fortification walls have even been found on the Acropolis of Athens. The best-preserved and most impressive Mycenaean remains are those of the fortified palaces at Tiryns and Mycenae. Both were built beginning about 1400 BCE and burned (along with all the others) between 1250 and 1200 BCE, when the Mycenaeans seem to have been overrun by northern invaders or to have fallen victim to internal warfare.

TIRYNS Homer knew the citadel of Tiryns (FIG. **4-15**), located about 10 miles from Mycenae, as Tiryns of the Great Walls. In the second century CE, when Pausanias, author of an invaluable guidebook to Greece, visited the long-abandoned site, he marveled at the towering fortifications and considered the walls of Tiryns as spectacular as the pyramids of Egypt. Indeed, the Greeks of the historical age believed mere humans could not have erected such edifices and instead attributed the construction of the great Mycenaean citadels to the mythical *Cyclopes*, a race of one-eyed giants. Historians still refer to the huge, roughly cut stone blocks forming the massive fortification walls of Tiryns and other Mycenaean sites as *Cyclopean masonry*.

The heavy walls of Tiryns and Mycenae contrast sharply with the open Cretan palaces (FIG. **4-4**) and clearly reveal their defensive character. Those of Tiryns average about 20 feet in thickness, and in one section they house a long gallery (FIG. **4-16**) covered by a corbeled vault (FIG. **4-17b**) similar to that constructed long before at Neolithic Newgrange (FIG. **1-19**). At Tiryns, the builders piled the large, irregular Cyclopean blocks in horizontal courses and then cantilevered them inward until the two walls met in a pointed arch. No mortar was used, and the vault is held in place only by the weight of the blocks (often several tons each), by the smaller stones used as wedges, and by the clay that fills some of the empty spaces. This primitive but effective vaulting scheme possesses an earthy monumentality. It is easy to see how a later

a

b

c

4-17
Three methods of spanning a passageway:
(a) post and lintel,
(b) corbeled arch,
(c) arch.

Post-and-lintel construction (**a**) was the norm in ancient Greece, but the Mycenaeans also used corbeled arches (**b**). The round arch (**c**), used already in the Near East, was popular in Rome.

4-16 Corbeled gallery in the walls of the citadel, Tiryns, Greece, ca. 1400–1200 BCE.

The walls of Tiryns contain a long corbel-vaulted gallery in which irregular Cyclopean blocks were piled in horizontal courses and then cantilevered inward until the two walls met in a pointed arch.

4-18 **Plan of the palace and southern part of the citadel, Tiryns, Greece, ca. 1400–1200 BCE.**

The king's reception and throne room, or megaron, was the main feature of Mycenaean palaces. Its plan, consisting of a hall with a columnar porch, is similar to that of early Greek temples (FIG. 5-6).

age came to believe that the uncouth Cyclopes were responsible for these massive but unsophisticated fortifications.

Would-be attackers at Tiryns were compelled to approach the palace (FIG. 4-18) within the walls via a long ramp that forced the (usually right-handed, as in FIG. 4-25) soldiers to expose their un-shielded sides to the Mycenaean defenders above. Then—if they got that far—they had to pass through a series of narrow gates that also could be defended easily. Inside, at Tiryns as elsewhere, the most important element in the palace plan was the *megaron*, or reception hall and throne room, of the king. The main room of the megaron had a throne against the right wall and a central hearth bordered by four Minoan-style wooden columns serving as supports for the roof. A vestibule with a columnar facade preceded the throne room. A variation of this plan later formed the core of some of the earliest Greek temple plans (FIG. 5-6), suggesting some architectural continuity between the Mycenaean age and historical Greece.

LION GATE, MYCENAE The severity of these fortress-palaces was relieved by frescoes, as in the Cretan palaces, and, at Agamemnon's Mycenae at least, by monumental architectural sculpture. The so-called Lion Gate (FIG. 4-19) is the outer gateway of the stronghold at Mycenae. It is protected on the left by a wall built on a natural rock outcropping and on the right by a projecting bastion of large blocks. Any approaching enemies would have had to enter this 20-foot-wide channel and face Mycenaean defenders above them on both sides. The gate itself consists of two great monoliths capped with a huge lintel (FIG. 4-17a). Above the lintel, the masonry courses form a *corbeled arch* (FIG. 4-17b), leaving an opening that lightens the weight the lintel carries. Filling this *relieving triangle* (FIG. 4-1) is a great limestone slab where two lions carved in high relief stand on the sides of a Minoan-type column. The whole design admirably matches its triangular space, harmonizing in dignity, strength, and scale with the mas-

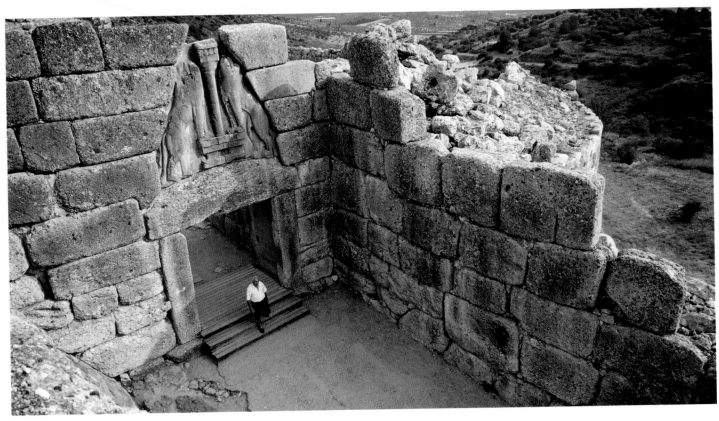

4-19 **Lion Gate, Mycenae, Greece, ca. 1300–1250 BCE. Limestone, relief panel 9′ 6″ high.**

The largest sculpture in the prehistoric Aegean is the relief of confronting lions (FIG. 4-1) that fills the relieving triangle of Mycenae's main gate. The gate itself consists of two great monoliths and a huge lintel.

4-20 Treasury of Atreus, Mycenae, Greece, ca. 1300–1250 BCE.

The best-preserved Mycenaean tholos tomb is named for Homer's King Atreus. An earthen mound covers the burial chamber, which is accessed through a doorway at the end of a long passageway.

sive stones that form the walls and gate. Similar groups appear in miniature on Cretan seals, but the idea of placing monstrous guardian figures at the entrances to palaces, tombs, and sacred places has its origin in the Near East and Egypt (FIGS. 2-18, 2-21, and 3-11). At Mycenae the animals' heads were fashioned separately and are lost. Some scholars have suggested that the "lions" were actually composite beasts in the Eastern tradition, possibly sphinxes.

TREASURY OF ATREUS The Lion Gate at Mycenae and the towering fortification wall circuit of which it formed a part were constructed a few generations before the presumed date of the Trojan War. At that time, wealthy Mycenaeans were laid to rest outside the citadel walls in beehive-shaped tombs covered by enormous earthen mounds. Nine are preserved at Mycenae and scores more at other sites. The best-preserved of these *tholos tombs* is Mycenae's so-called Treasury of Atreus (FIG. 4-20), which already in antiquity was mistakenly believed to be the repository of the treasure of Atreus, father of Agamemnon and Menelaus. Approached by a long passageway (*dromos*), the tomb chamber was entered through a doorway surmounted by a relieving triangle similar to that employed in the roughly contemporary Lion Gate. (As in the Lion Gate, the open triangle was originally covered. Both the doorway and the relieving triangle also once had engaged columns on each side, preserved in fragments today.) The *tholos* (FIG. 4-21) is composed of a series of

4-21 Vault of the tholos of the Treasury of Atreus, Mycenae, Greece, ca. 1300–1250 BCE.

The beehive-shaped tholos of the Treasury of Atreus is composed of corbeled courses of stone blocks laid on a circular base. The 43-foot-high dome was the largest in the world for almost 1,500 years.

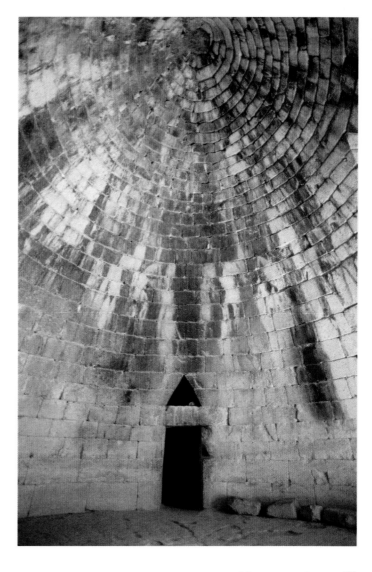

Mycenaean Art   **79**

stone corbeled courses laid on a circular base to form a lofty *dome*. The builders probably constructed the vault using rough-hewn blocks. After they set the stones in place, the masons had to finish the surfaces with great precision to make them conform to both the horizontal and vertical curves of the wall. The principle involved is no different from that of the corbeled gallery (FIG. 4-16) of Tiryns. But the problem of constructing a complete dome is much more complicated, and the execution of the vault in the Treasury of Atreus is far more sophisticated than that of the vaulted gallery at Tiryns. About 43 feet high, this was at the time the largest vaulted space without interior supports that had ever been built. The achievement was not surpassed until the Romans constructed the Pantheon (FIG. 7-51) almost 1,500 years later using a new technology—concrete construction—unknown to the Mycenaeans.

Metalwork, Sculpture, and Painting

The Treasury of Atreus had been thoroughly looted long before its modern rediscovery, but excavators have found spectacular grave goods elsewhere at Mycenae. Just inside the Lion Gate, Schliemann uncovered what archaeologists now designate as Grave Circle A. It predates the Lion Gate and the walls of Mycenae by some three centuries. Grave Circle A encloses six deep shafts that had served as tombs for kings and their families. The Mycenaeans laid their dead to rest on the floors of these shaft graves with masks covering their faces, recalling the Egyptian funerary practice. They buried women with their jewelry and men with their weapons and golden cups.

MASKS AND DAGGERS Among the most spectacular of Schliemann's finds is a gold mask (FIG. 4-22), one of several from the royal burial complex. The Mycenaean masks were made using the *repoussé* technique, that is, the goldsmiths hammered the shape from a single sheet of metal and pushed the features out from behind. The mask illustrated here has often been compared to Tutankhamen's gold mummy mask (FIG. 3-1). The treatment of the human face is, of course, more primitive in the Mycenaean mask. But this was one of the first attempts in Greece to render the human face at life-size, whereas Tutankhamen's mask stands in a long line of monumental Egyptian sculptures going back more than a millennium. It is not known whether the Mycenaean masks were intended as portraits, but the goldsmiths recorded different physical types with care. They portrayed youthful faces as well as mature ones. The illustrated example (FIG. 4-22), with its full beard, must depict a mature man, perhaps a king—although not Agamemnon, as Schliemann wished. If Agamemnon was a real king, he lived some 300 years after this mask was fashioned. Clearly the Mycenaeans were "rich in gold" long before Homer's heroes fought at Troy.

Also found in Grave Circle A were several magnificent bronze dagger blades inlaid with gold, silver, and *niello* (a black metallic alloy), again attesting to the wealth of the Mycenaean kings as well as to their warlike nature. The largest and most elaborate of the group is decorated on one side (FIG. 4-23) with a scene of four hunters attacking a lion that has struck down a fifth hunter, while two other lions flee. The other side shows lions attacking deer. The slim-waisted, long-haired figures are Minoan in style, but the artist borrowed the subject from the repertoire of the ancient Near East. It is likely that a Minoan metalworker made the dagger for a Mycenaean patron who admired Minoan art but whose taste in subject matter differed from that of his Cretan counterparts.

4-22 Funerary mask, from Grave Circle A, Mycenae, Greece, ca. 1600–1500 BCE. Beaten gold, 1′ high. National Archaeological Museum, Athens.

Homer described the Mycenaeans as "rich in gold." This beaten gold (repoussé) mask of a bearded man comes from a royal shaft grave. It is one of the first attempts at life-size sculpture in Greece.

1 in.

4-23 Inlaid dagger blade with lion hunt, from Grave Circle A, Mycenae, Greece, ca. 1600–1500 BCE. Bronze, inlaid with gold, silver, and niello, 9″ long. National Archaeological Museum, Athens.

The treasures buried with the Mycenaean kings attest to their wealth. The lion hunters on this bronze dagger are Minoan in style, but the metalworker borrowed the subject from the artistic repertoire of the Near East.

PLASTER SCULPTURE Large-scale figural art is very rare on the Greek mainland, as on Crete, other than the Minoan-style paintings that once adorned the walls of Mycenaean palaces. The triangular relief (FIG. 4-1) of the Lion Gate at Mycenae is exceptional, as is the painted plaster head (FIG. 4-24) of a woman, goddess, or, perhaps, sphinx found at Mycenae. The white flesh tone indicates that the head is female. The hair and eyes are dark blue, almost black, and the lips, ears, and headband are red. The artist decorated the cheeks and chin with red circles surrounded by a ring of red dots, recalling the facial paint or tattoos recorded on Early Cycladic figurines of women. Although the large staring eyes give the face a menacing, if not terrifying, expression appropriate for a guardian figure such as a sphinx, the closest parallels to this work in the prehistoric Aegean are terracotta images of goddesses. This head may therefore be a very early example of a monumental cult statue in Greece.

Were it not for this plaster head and a few other exceptional pieces, art historians might have concluded—wrongly—that the Mycenaeans had no monumental freestanding statuary—a reminder that it is

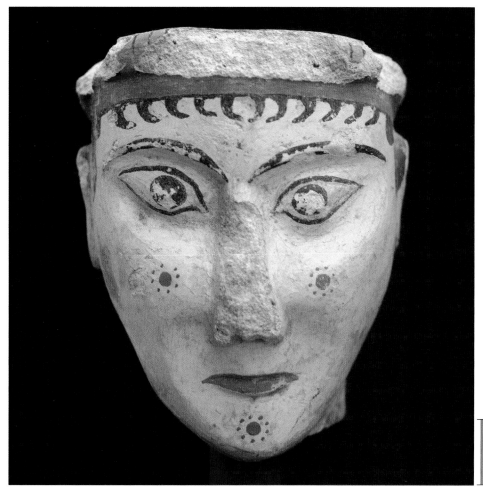

4-24 Female head, from Mycenae, Greece, ca. 1300–1250 BCE. Painted plaster, $6\frac{1}{2}$″ high. National Archaeological Museum, Athens.

This painted white plaster head of a woman with large staring eyes may be a very early example of a monumental statue of a goddess in Greece, but some scholars think it is the head of a sphinx.

4-25 *Warriors Vase,* from Mycenae, Greece, ca. 1200 BCE. 1′ 4″ high. National Archaeological Museum, Athens.

This krater, or mixing bowl, shows a woman bidding farewell to a column of heavily armed Mycenaean warriors depicted using both silhouette and outline and a combination of frontal and profile views.

always dangerous to generalize from the fragmentary remains of an ancient civilization. Nonetheless, life-size Aegean statuary must have been rare. After the collapse of Mycenaean civilization and for the next several hundred years, no attempts at monumental statuary are evident until, after the waning of the so-called Dark Ages, Greek sculptors were exposed to the great sculptural tradition of Egypt (see Chapter 5).

WARRIORS VASE An art form that did continue throughout the period after the downfall of the Mycenaean palaces was vase painting. One of the latest examples of Mycenaean painting is the *krater* (bowl for mixing wine and water) commonly called the *Warriors Vase* (FIG. **4-25**) after its prominent frieze of soldiers marching off to war. At the left a woman bids farewell to the column of heavily

armed warriors moving away from her. The painting on this vase reveals no setting and lacks the landscape elements that characterized earlier Minoan and Mycenaean art. All the soldiers also repeat the same pattern, a far cry from the variety and anecdotal detail of the lively procession of the Minoan *Harvesters Vase* (FIG. **4-14**).

This simplification of narrative has parallels in the increasingly schematic and abstract treatment of marine life on other painted vases. The octopus, for example, eventually became a stylized motif composed of concentric circles and spirals that are almost unrecognizable as a sea creature. By Homer's time, the heyday of Aegean civilization was but a distant memory, and the men and women of Crete and Mycenae—Minos and Ariadne, Agamemnon and Helen—had assumed the stature of heroes from a lost golden age.

THE PREHISTORIC AEGEAN

EARLY CYCLADIC ART, ca. 3000–2000 BCE

▌ Marble statuettes are the major surviving artworks of the Cycladic Islands during the third millennium BCE, but little is known about their function.

▌ Many of the Cycladic figurines were buried in graves and may represent the deceased, but others, for example, musicians, almost certainly do not. Whatever their meaning, these statuettes mark the beginning of the long history of marble sculpture in Greece.

Lyre player, Keros,
ca. 2700–2500 BCE

LATE MINOAN ART, ca. 1700–1200 BCE

▌ The so-called Old Palace period (ca. 2000–1700 BCE) on Crete saw the construction of the first palaces on the island, but the golden age of Crete was the Late Minoan period.

▌ The greatest Late Minoan palace was at Knossos. A vast multistory structure arranged around a central court, the Knossos palace was so complex in plan that it gave rise to the myth of the Minotaur in the labyrinth of King Minos.

▌ The largest art form in the Minoan world was fresco painting on walls, usually illustrating palace rituals like bull-leaping.

▌ Vase painting also flourished. Sea motifs, for example, the octopus, were popular subjects.

▌ Minoan sculpture was of small scale, consisting of statuettes of "snake goddesses" and reliefs on stone vases.

Bull-leaping fresco, Knossos,
ca. 1450–1400 BCE

Snake Goddess, Knossos,
ca. 1600 BCE

MYCENAEAN (LATE HELLADIC) ART, ca. 1700–1200 BCE

▌ The Mycenaeans, who with their Greek allies later waged war on Troy, were already by 1600–1500 BCE burying their kings in deep shaft graves with gold funerary masks and bronze daggers inlaid with gold and silver.

▌ By 1450 BCE, the Mycenaeans had occupied Crete, and between 1400 and 1200 BCE, they erected great citadels at Mycenae, Tiryns, and elsewhere with "Cyclopean" walls of huge, irregularly shaped stone blocks.

▌ Masters of corbel vaulting, the Mycenaeans also erected beehive-shaped tholos tombs like the so-called Treasury of Atreus, which had the largest dome in the pre-Roman world.

▌ The oldest preserved monumental sculptures in Greece, most notably Mycenae's Lion Gate, date to the end of the Mycenaean period.

Gold funerary mask, Mycenae,
ca. 1600–1500 BCE

Vault of the Treasury of Atreus,
Mycenae, ca. 1300–1250 BCE

5-1 The Persian king Darius III, detail of Philoxenos of Eretria, *Battle of Issus* (FIG. 5-70), Roman mosaic copy of a painting of ca. 310 BCE. Museo Archeologico Nazionale, Naples.

Greek painters were the first to employ foreshortening consistently, to model figures in color, and to depict reflections and shadows—practices that became standard in later painting in the Western world.

5

ANCIENT GREECE

Ancient Greek art occupies a special place in the history of art through the ages. Many of the cultural values of the Greeks, especially the exaltation of humanity as the "measure of all things," remain fundamental tenets of Western civilization. This humanistic worldview led the Greeks to create the concept of democracy (rule by the *demos,* the people) and to make seminal contributions in the fields of art, literature, and science. Ancient Greek ideas are so completely part of modern Western habits of mind that most people are scarcely aware that the concepts originated in Greece more than 2,500 years ago.

The Greeks, or *Hellenes,* as they called themselves, appear to have been the product of an intermingling of Aegean peoples and Indo-European invaders. They never formed a single nation but instead established independent city-states, or *poleis* (singular, *polis*). The Dorians of the north, who many believe brought an end to Mycenaean civilization, settled in the Peloponnesos (MAP **5-1**). The Ionians settled the western coast of Asia Minor (modern Turkey) and the islands of the Aegean Sea. The origin of the Ionians is disputed. Some say the northern invaders forced the Ionians out of Greece and that they then sailed eastward from Athens to their new homes. Others hold that the Ionians developed in Asia Minor between the 11th and 8th centuries BCE out of a mixed stock of settlers.

Whatever the origins of the various regional populations, in 776 BCE the separate Greek-speaking states held their first ceremonial games in common at Olympia. The later Greeks calculated their chronology from these first Olympic Games—the first *Olympiad.* From then on, despite their differences and rivalries, the Greeks regarded themselves as citizens of *Hellas* (the ancient name of Greece), distinct from the surrounding "barbarians" who did not speak Greek.

Even the gods of the Greeks (see "The Gods and Goddesses of Mount Olympus," page 87) differed in kind from those of neighboring civilizations. Unlike Egyptian and Mesopotamian deities, the Greek gods and goddesses differed from human beings only in that they were immortal. It has been said that the Greeks made their gods into humans and their humans into gods. The perfect individual became the Greek ideal—and the portrayal of beautiful humans became the focus of many of the greatest Greek artists.

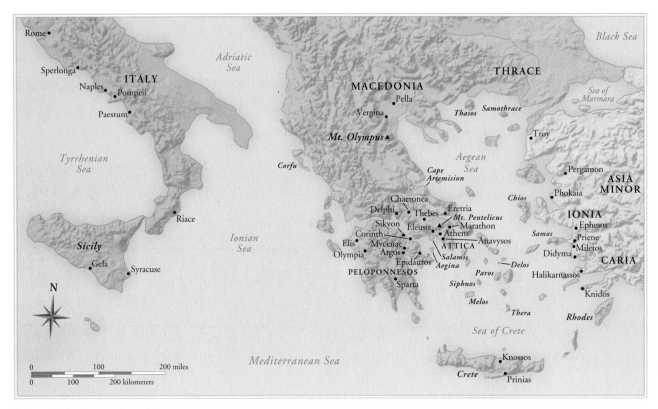

MAP 5-1 The Greek world.

Although the sculptures, paintings, and buildings discussed in this chapter were made and built all over Greece and in its many colonies abroad (MAP 5-1), Athens, the capital of Greece today, has justifiably become the symbol of ancient Greek culture. Athens is where the great plays of Aeschylus, Sophocles, and Euripides were first performed. And there, in the city's central square (*agora*), covered colonnades (*stoas*), and gymnasiums (*palaestras*), Socrates engaged his fellow citizens in philosophical argument, and Plato formulated his prescription for the ideal form of government in the *Republic*. Complementing the rich intellectual life of ancient Athens was a strong interest in physical exercise, which played a large role in education, as well as in daily life. The Athenian aim of achieving a balance of intellectual and physical discipline, an ideal of humanistic education, is well expressed in the familiar phrase "a sound mind in a sound body."

The distinctiveness and originality of Greek contributions to art, science, and politics should not, however, obscure the enormous debt the Greeks owed to the cultures of Egypt and the Near East. Scholars today increasingly recognize this debt, and the ancient Greeks themselves readily acknowledged borrowing ideas, motifs, conventions, and skills from those older civilizations. Nor should a high estimation of Greek art and culture blind anyone to the realities of Hellenic life and society. Even Athenian "democracy" was a political reality for only one segment of the demos. Slavery was regarded as natural, even beneficial, and was a universal institution among the Greeks. Greek women were in no way the equals of Greek men. Women normally remained secluded in their homes, emerging usually only for weddings, funerals, and religious festivals. They played little part in public or political life. Despite the fame of the poet Sappho, only a handful of female artists' names are known, and none of their works survive. Both the existence of slavery and the exclusion of women from public life are reflected in Greek art. On many occa-

sions freeborn men and women appear with their slaves in monumental sculpture. The *symposium* (a dinner party that only men and prostitutes attended) is a popular subject on painted vases.

Although the Greeks invented and passed on to future generations the concept and practice of democracy, most Greek states, even those constituted as democracies, were dominated by wellborn white males, and the most admired virtues were not wisdom and justice but statecraft and military valor. Greek men were educated in the values of Homer's heroes and in the athletic exercises of the palaestra. War among the city-states was chronic. Fighting among themselves, the Greeks eventually fell victim to the Macedonians and Romans.

GEOMETRIC AND ORIENTALIZING PERIODS

Disintegration of the Bronze Age social order accompanied the destruction of the Mycenaean palaces. The disappearance of powerful kings and their retinues led to the loss of the knowledge of how to cut masonry, to construct citadels and tombs, to paint frescoes, and to sculpt in stone. Even the arts of reading and writing were forgotten. Depopulation, poverty, and an almost total loss of contact with the outside world characterized the succeeding centuries, sometimes called the Dark Age of Greece. Only in the eighth century BCE did economic conditions improve and the population begin to grow again. This era was in its own way a heroic age, a time when the poleis of Classical Greece took shape; when the Greeks broke out of their isolation and once again began to trade with cities both in the east and the west; when Homer's epic poems, formerly memorized and passed down from bard to bard, were recorded in written form; and when the Olympic Games were established.

The Gods and Goddesses of Mount Olympus

The names of scores of Greek gods and goddesses were recorded as early as the eighth century BCE in Homer's epic tales of the war against Troy (*Iliad*) and of the adventures of the Greek hero Odysseus on his long and tortuous journey home (*Odyssey*). Even more are enumerated in the poems of Hesiod, especially his *Theogony* (*Genealogy of the Gods*) composed around 700 BCE.

The Greek deities most often represented in art are all ultimately the offspring of the two key elements of the Greek universe, Earth (*Gaia/Ge*; all names are given in their Greek and Latin, that is, Greek and Roman forms) and Heaven (*Ouranos/Uranus*). Earth and Heaven mated to produce 12 Titans, including Ocean (*Okeanos/Oceanus*) and his youngest brother *Kronos* (*Saturn*). Kronos castrated his father in order to rule in his place, married his sister *Rhea*, and then swallowed all his children as they were born, lest one of them seek in turn to usurp him. When *Zeus* (*Jupiter*) was born, Rhea deceived Kronos by feeding him a stone wrapped in clothes in place of the infant. After growing to manhood, Zeus forced Kronos to vomit up Zeus's siblings. Together they overthrew their father and the other Titans and ruled the world from their home on Mount Olympus, Greece's highest peak.

This cruel and bloody tale of the origin of the Greek gods has parallels in Near Eastern mythology and is clearly pre-Greek in origin, one of many Greek borrowings from the East. The Greek version of the creation myth, however, appears infrequently in painting and sculpture. Instead, the later 12 Olympian gods and goddesses, the chief deities of Greece, figure most prominently in art—not only in Greek, Etruscan, and Roman times but also in the Middle Ages, the Renaissance, and up to the present.

The 12 Olympian deities were

■ ***Zeus* (*Jupiter*)** King of the gods, Zeus ruled the sky and allotted the sea to his brother Poseidon and the Underworld to his other brother Hades. His weapon was the thunderbolt, and with it he led the other gods to victory over the giants, who had challenged the Olympians for control of the world. Jupiter was also the chief god of the Romans.

■ ***Hera* (*Juno*)** Wife and sister of Zeus, Hera was the goddess of marriage.

■ ***Poseidon* (*Neptune*)** Poseidon was one of the three sons of Kronos and Rhea and was lord of the sea. He controlled waves, storms, and earthquakes with his three-pronged pitchfork (*trident*).

■ ***Hestia* (*Vesta*)** Sister of Zeus, Poseidon, and Hera, Hestia was goddess of the hearth.

■ ***Demeter* (*Ceres*)** Third sister of Zeus, Demeter was the goddess of grain and agriculture. She taught humans how to sow and plow.

■ ***Ares* (*Mars*)** God of war, Ares was the son of Zeus and Hera and the lover of Aphrodite. Mars, father of the twin founders of Rome, Romulus and Remus, looms much larger in Roman mythology and religion than Ares does in Greek.

■ ***Athena* (*Minerva*)** Goddess of wisdom and warfare, Athena was a virgin (*parthenos* in Greek), born not from a woman's womb but from the head of her father, Zeus. She competed with Poseidon for the honor of becoming the patron deity of Athens. She won the contest and the city bears her name.

■ ***Hephaistos* (*Vulcan*)** God of fire and of metalworking, Hephaistos fashioned the armor Achilles wore in battle against Troy. He also provided Zeus his scepter and Poseidon his trident, and was the "surgeon" who split open Zeus's head when Athena was born. In some accounts, Hephaistos is the son of Hera without a male partner. In others, he is the son of Hera and Zeus. He was born lame and, uncharacteristically for a god, ugly. His wife Aphrodite was unfaithful to him.

■ ***Apollo* (*Apollo*)** God of light and music, and a great archer, Apollo was the son of Zeus with **Leto/Latona,** daughter of one of the Titans. His epithet *Phoibos* means "radiant," and the young, beautiful Apollo was sometimes identified with the sun (**Helios/Sol**).

■ ***Artemis* (*Diana*)** Sister of Apollo, Artemis was goddess of the hunt and of wild animals. As Apollo's twin, she was occasionally regarded as the moon (**Selene/Luna**).

■ ***Aphrodite* (*Venus*)** Daughter of Zeus and **Dione** (daughter of Okeanos and one of the *nymphs*—the goddesses of springs, caves, and woods), Aphrodite was the goddess of love and beauty. In one version of her myth, she was born from the foam (*aphros* in Greek) of the sea. She was the mother of Eros by Ares and of the Trojan hero Aeneas by Anchises.

■ ***Hermes* (*Mercury*)** Son of Zeus and another nymph, Hermes was the fleet-footed messenger of the gods and possessed winged sandals. He was also the guide of travelers, including the dead journeying to the Underworld. He carried the *caduceus,* a magical herald's rod, and wore a traveler's hat, often also shown with wings.

Other important Greek gods and goddesses were

■ *Hades* (*Pluto*) One of the children of Kronos who fought with his brothers against the Titans, Hades was equal in stature to the Olympians but never resided on Mount Olympus. Hades was the lord of the Underworld and god of the dead.

■ *Dionysos* (*Bacchus*) The son of Zeus and a mortal woman, Dionysos was the god of wine. In Roman times, an important mystery religion centered on Dionysos.

■ *Eros* (*Amor* or *Cupid*) The son of Aphrodite and Ares, Eros was the winged child-god of love. In early representations, he appears as an adolescent, but artists normally depicted him as an infant.

■ *Asklepios* (*Aesculapius*) The son of Apollo and a mortal woman, Asklepios was the Greek god of healing, whose serpent-entwined staff is the emblem of modern medicine.

Geometric Art

Also during the eighth century BCE, the human figure returned to Greek art—not in monumental statuary, which was exceedingly rare even in Bronze Age Greece, but in small bronze figurines and in paintings on ceramic pots.

DIPYLON KRATER One of the earliest examples of Greek figure painting is a huge krater (FIG. 5-2) that marked the grave of a man buried around 740 BCE in the Dipylon cemetery of Athens. At well over three feet tall, this vase is a considerable technical achievement and a testament both to the potter's skill and to the wealth and position of the deceased's family in the community. The bottom of the great vessel is open, perhaps to permit visitors to the grave to pour libations in honor of the dead, perhaps simply to provide a drain for rainwater, or both.

The artist covered much of the krater's surface with precisely painted abstract angular motifs in horizontal bands. Especially prominent is the *meander,* or key, pattern around the rim of the krater. Most early Greek painters decorated vases exclusively with abstract motifs. The nature of the ornament has led art historians to designate this formative period of Greek art as *Geometric.* The earliest examples of the Geometric style date to the ninth century BCE.

On this krater, the artist reserved the widest part of the vase for two bands of human figures and horse-drawn chariots rather than for geometric ornament. Befitting the vase's function as a grave marker, the scenes depict the mourning for a man laid out on his bier and the grand chariot procession in his honor. The painter filled every empty surface with circles and M-shaped designs, negating any sense that the mourners or soldiers inhabit open space. The human figures, animals, and furniture are as two-dimensional as the geometric shapes elsewhere on the vessel. For example, in the upper band, the shroud, raised to reveal the corpse, is an abstract checkerboard-like backdrop. The figures are silhouettes constructed of triangular (frontal) torsos with attached profile arms, legs, and heads (with a single large frontal eye in the center), following the age-old convention. To distinguish male from female, the painter added a penis growing out of one of the deceased's thighs. The mourning women, who tear their hair out in grief, have breasts emerging beneath their armpits. In both cases the artist's concern was specifying gender, not anatomical accuracy. Below, the warriors look like walking shields, and in the old conceptual manner, both wheels of the chariots are shown. The horses have the correct number of heads and legs but seem to share a common body, so that there is no sense of overlapping or depth. Despite the highly stylized and conventional manner of representation, this vessel marks a significant turning point in the history of Greek art. Not only was the human figure reintroduced into the painter's repertoire, but the art of storytelling also was revived.

HERAKLES AND NESSOS One of the most impressive surviving Geometric sculptures is a characteristically small solid-cast bronze group (FIG. 5-3) made up of two schematic figures locked in a hand-to-hand struggle. The man is a hero, probably Herakles (see "Herakles," page 106). His opponent is a *centaur* (a mythological beast that was part man, part horse), possibly Nessos, the centaur who had volunteered to carry the hero's bride across a river and then assaulted her. Whether or not the hero is Herakles and the centaur is Nessos, the mythological nature of the group is certain. The repertoire of the Geometric artist was not limited to scenes inspired by daily life (and death). Composite monsters were enormously popular in the ancient Near East and Egypt, and renewed contact with foreign cultures may have inspired the human-animal monsters of Geometric Greece. The centaur, however, is a purely Greek invention—and one that posed a problem for the artist, who, of course, had never seen such a creature. The Geometric artist conceived the centaur as a man in front and a horse in back, a rather unhappy and unconvincing configuration that results in the forelegs belonging to a different species from the hind legs. In this example, the sculptor rendered the figure of the hero and the human part of the centaur in a similar fashion. Both are bearded and wear helmets, but (contradictory to nature) the man is larger than the horse, probably to suggest that he will be the victor. Like other Geometric male figures, both painted and sculpted, this hero is nude, in contrast to the Near Eastern statuettes that might have inspired the Greek works. Here, at the very beginning of Greek figural art, one can recognize the Hellenic instinct for the natural beauty of the human figure. In fact, Greek athletes exercised without their clothes and even competed nude in the Olympic Games from very early times.

1 ft.

5-2 Geometric krater, from the Dipylon cemetery, Athens, Greece, ca. 740 BCE. 3′ 4½″ high. Metropolitan Museum of Art, New York.

Figure painting reappeared in Greece in the Geometric period, named for the abstract ornamentation on vessels like this krater, which features a mourning scene and procession in honor of the deceased.

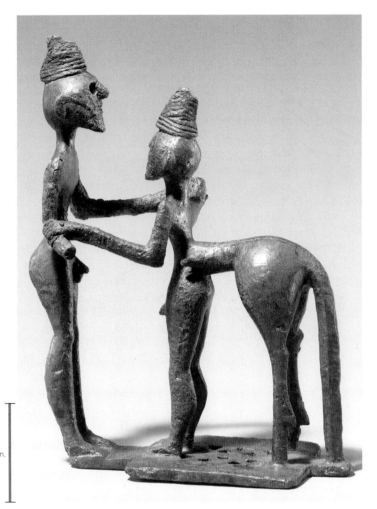

5-3 Hero and centaur (Herakles and Nessos?), from Olympia, Greece, ca. 750–730 BCE. Bronze, $4\frac{1}{2}''$ high. Metropolitan Museum of Art, New York (gift of J. Pierpont).

Sculpture of the Geometric period is small scale, and the figures have simple stylized shapes. This solid-cast bronze statuette depicts a hero battling a centaur—an early example of mythological narrative.

Orientalizing Art

During the 600s BCE, the pace and scope of Greek trade and colonization accelerated and Greek artists became exposed more than ever before to Eastern artworks, especially small portable objects such as Syrian ivory carvings. The closer contact had a profound effect on the development of Greek art. Indeed, so many motifs borrowed from or inspired by Egyptian and Near Eastern art entered the Greek pictorial vocabulary at this time that art historians have dubbed the seventh century BCE the *Orientalizing* period.

MANTIKLOS APOLLO One of the masterworks of the early seventh century BCE is the *Mantiklos Apollo* (FIG. **5-4**), a small bronze statuette dedicated to Apollo at Thebes by an otherwise unknown man named Mantiklos. With characteristic pride in the ability to write, the sculptor (or another) scratched into the thighs of the figure a message from the dedicator to the deity: "Mantiklos dedicated me as a tithe to the far-shooting Lord of the Silver Bow; you, Phoibos [Apollo], might give some pleasing favor in return." Because the Greeks conceived their gods in human form, it is uncertain whether the figure represents the youthful Apollo or Mantiklos

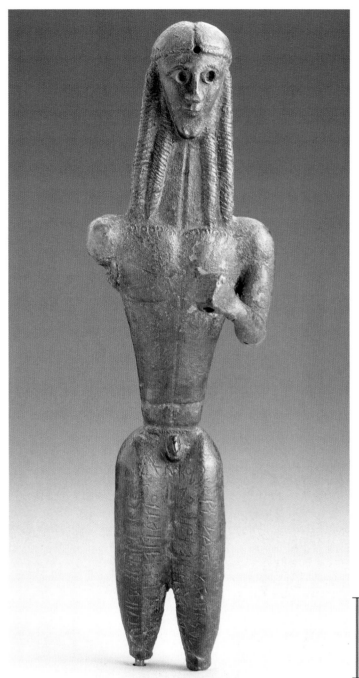

5-4 *Mantiklos Apollo,* statuette of a youth dedicated by Mantiklos to Apollo, from Thebes, Greece, ca. 700–680 BCE. Bronze, 8″ high. Museum of Fine Arts, Boston.

Mantiklos dedicated this statuette to Apollo, and it probably represents the god. The treatment of the body reveals the interest seventh-century BCE Greek artists had in reproducing details of human anatomy.

(or neither). But if the left hand at one time held a bow, then the statuette is certainly an image of the deity. In any case, the purpose of the votive offering is clear. Equally apparent is the increased interest Greek artists at this time had in reproducing details of human anatomy, such as the long hair framing the unnaturally elongated neck, and the pectoral and abdominal muscles, which define the stylized triangular torso. The triangular face has eye sockets that were once inlaid, and the head may have had a separately fashioned helmet on it.

Greek Vase Painting

The techniques Greek ceramists used to shape and decorate fine vases required great skill, which they acquired over many years as apprentices in the workshops of master potters. During the Archaic and Classical periods, when the art of vase painting was at its zenith in Greece, both potters and painters frequently signed their work. These signatures reveal the pride of the artists.

The signatures also might have functioned as "brand names" for a large export market. The products of the workshops in Corinth and Athens in particular were highly prized and have been found all over the Mediterranean world. The Corinthian Orientalizing amphora shown here (FIG. 5-5) was found on Rhodes, an island at the opposite side of the Aegean from mainland Corinth (MAP 5-1). The Etruscans of central Italy (MAP 6-1) were especially good customers. Athenian vases were staples in Etruscan tombs, and all but one of the illustrated examples (FIGS. 5-20 to 5-24, 5-59, and 5-60) came from an Etruscan site. Other painted Athenian pots have been found as far away as France, Russia, and the Sudan.

The first step in manufacturing a Greek vase was to remove any impurities found in the natural clay and then to knead it, like dough, to remove air bubbles and make it flexible. The Greeks used dozens of different kinds and shapes of pots, and most were produced in several parts. Potters formed the vessel's body by placing the clay on a rotating horizontal wheel. While an apprentice turned the wheel by hand, the potter pulled up the clay with the fingers until the desired shape was achieved. The handles were shaped separately and attached to the vase body by applying *slip* (liquefied clay) to the joints.

Then a specialist, the painter, was called in, although many potters decorated their own work. (Today most people tend to regard painters as more elevated artists than potters, but in Greece the potters owned the shops and employed the painters.) Art historians customarily refer to the "pigment" the painter applied to the clay surface as *glaze,* but the black areas on Greek pots are neither pigment nor glaze but a slip of finely sifted clay that originally was of the same rich red-orange color as the clay of the pot. In the three-phase firing process Greek potters used, the first (*oxidizing*) phase turned both pot and slip red. During the second (*reducing*) phase, the potter shut off the oxygen supply into the kiln, and both pot and slip turned black. In the final (*reoxidizing*) phase, the pot's coarser material reabsorbed oxygen and became red again, whereas the smoother, silica-laden slip did not and remained black. After long experiment, Greek potters developed a velvety jet-black "glaze" of this kind, produced in kilns heated to temperatures as high as 950° Celsius (about 1,742° Fahrenheit).

The firing process was the same whether the painter worked in black-figure or in red-figure. In fact, sometimes Greek artists employed both manners on the same vase (FIG. 5-22).

5-5 Corinthian black-figure amphora with animal friezes, from Rhodes, Greece, ca. 625–600 BCE. 1′ 2″ high. British Museum, London.

The Corinthians invented the black-figure technique of vase painting in which artists painted black silhouettes and then incised linear details within the forms. This early example features Orientalizing animals.

ORIENTALIZING AMPHORA An elaborate Corinthian *amphora* (FIG. 5-5), or two-handled storage jar, typifies the new Greek fascination with the Orient. In a series of registers recalling the organization of Geometric painted vases, animals such as the native boar appear beside exotic lions and panthers and composite creatures inspired by Eastern monsters such as the sphinx and lamassu. In this instance, the painter prominently displayed a *siren* (part bird, part woman) on the amphora's neck. The wide appeal of such vases was not due solely to their Orientalizing animal friezes. They owed their popularity also to a new ceramic technique the Corinthians invented. Art historians call this type of vase decoration *black-figure painting* (see "Greek Vase Painting," above). The black-figure painter first put down black silhouettes on the clay surface of the vessel, as in Geometric times, but then used a sharp pointed instrument to incise linear details within the forms, usually adding highlights in white or purplish-red over the black figures before firing the vase. The combination of the weighty black silhouettes with the delicate detailing and the bright polychrome overlay proved to be irresistible, and Athenian painters soon copied the technique the Corinthians pioneered.

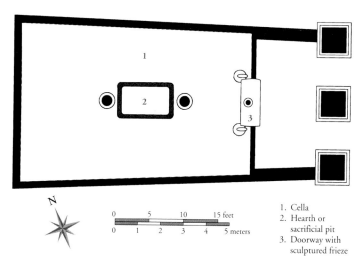

5-6 Plan of Temple A, Prinias, Greece, ca. 625 BCE.

1. Cella
2. Hearth or sacrificial pit
3. Doorway with sculptured frieze

The first Greek stone temples, like this one at Prinias, were similar in plan to the megarons of Mycenaean palaces, with a porch and a main room with two columns flanking a hearth or sacrificial pit.

TEMPLE A, PRINIAS The foundation of the Greek trading colony of Naukratis in Egypt (MAP 3-1) before 630 BCE brought the Greeks into direct contact with the monumental stone architecture of the Egyptians. Not long after that, construction began in Greece of the first stone buildings since the fall of the Mycenaean kingdoms. At Prinias on Crete, for example, the Greeks built a stone temple, called Temple A (FIG. 5-6), around 625 BCE to honor an unknown deity. Although the inspiration for the structure may have come from the East, the form resembles that of a typical Mycenaean megaron, such as that at Tiryns (FIG. 4-18), with two interior columns flanking a hearth or sacrificial pit. The facade consisted of three great piers. The roof was probably flat. Temple A at Prinias is the earliest known example of a Greek temple with sculptured decoration. Above the doorway was a huge limestone lintel with a relief frieze of Orientalizing panthers with frontal heads—the same motif as that on the contemporary Corinthian black-figure amphora (FIG. 5-5), underscoring the stylistic unity of Greek art at this time.

LADY OF AUXERRE Probably also originally from Crete is a limestone statuette of a goddess or maiden (*kore;* plural, *korai*) popularly known as the *Lady of Auxerre* (FIG. 5-7) after the French town that is her oldest recorded location. As with the figure Mantiklos dedicated (FIG. 5-4), it is uncertain whether the young woman is a mortal or a deity. She is clothed, as are all Greek goddesses and women of this period, but she does not wear a headdress, as a goddess probably would. Moreover, the placement of the right hand across the chest is probably a gesture of prayer, also indicating that this is a kore. The style is much more naturalistic than in Geometric times, but the love of abstract shapes can still be seen. Note, for example, the triangular flat-topped head framed by long strands of hair that form triangles complementary to the shape of the face, and the decoration of the long skirt with its incised concentric squares, once brightly painted, as were all Greek stone statues. The modern notion that Greco-Roman statuary was pure white is mistaken. The Greeks did not, however, color their statues garishly. The flesh was left in the natural color of the stone, which was waxed and polished, while eyes, lips, hair, and drapery were painted in *encaustic* (see "Iaia of Cyzicus and the Art of Encaustic Painting," Chapter 7, page 195). In this technique, the painter mixed the pigment with hot wax and applied the tinted wax to the statue to produce a durable coloration.

5-7 *Lady of Auxerre,* ca. 650–625 BCE. Limestone, 2' 1½" high. Louvre, Paris.

Probably from Crete, this kore (maiden) typifies the so-called Daedalic style of the seventh century BCE with its triangular face and hair and lingering Geometric fondness for abstract pattern.

ARCHAIC PERIOD

The *Lady of Auxerre* is the masterpiece of the style that art historians usually refer to as *Daedalic,* after the legendary artist Daedalus, whose name means "the skillful one." In addition to having been a great sculptor, Daedalus was said to have built the labyrinth (FIG. 4-5) in Crete to house the Minotaur and also to have designed a temple at Memphis in Egypt (MAP 3-1). The historical Greeks attributed to him almost all the great achievements in early sculpture and architecture before the names of artists and architects were recorded. The story that Daedalus worked in Egypt reflects the enormous impact of Egyptian art and architecture on the Greeks of the aptly named Orientalizing age of the seventh century, as well as on their offspring in the succeeding *Archaic* period of the sixth century BCE.

Statuary

According to one Greek writer, Daedalus used the same compositional patterns for his statues as the Egyptians used for theirs, and the first truly monumental stone statues of the Greeks follow very closely the canonical Egyptian format.

NEW YORK KOUROS One of the earliest examples (FIG. **5-8**) of life-size statuary in Greece is the marble *kouros* ("youth"; plural, *kouroi*) now in New York. The Greek kouros emulates the stance of

5-8 Kouros, ca. 600 BCE. Marble, 6' ½" high. Metropolitan Museum of Art, New York.

The sculptors of the earliest life-size statues of kouroi (young men) adopted the Egyptian pose for standing figures (FIG. 3-13), but the kouroi are nude and liberated from the original block of stone.

Egyptian statues (FIG. 3-13). In both Egypt and Greece, the figure is rigidly frontal with the left foot advanced slightly. The arms are held beside the body, and the fists are clenched with the thumbs forward. The New York kouros, like most Egyptian statues, was also a funerary statue. It stood over a grave in the countryside somewhere near Athens. Statues like this one replaced the huge vases (FIG. 5-2) of Geometric times as the preferred form of grave marker in the sixth century BCE. The Greeks also used kouroi as votive offerings in sanctuaries. The kouros type, because of its generic quality, could be employed in several different contexts.

Despite the adherence to Egyptian prototypes, Greek kouros statues differ from their models in two important ways. First, the Greek sculptors liberated them from their original stone block. The Egyptian obsession with permanence was alien to the Greeks, who were preoccupied with finding ways to represent motion rather than stability in their sculpted figures. Second, the kouroi are nude, and in the absence of identifying attributes, they, like the bronze statuette (FIG. 5-4) Mantiklos dedicated, are formally indistinguishable from Greek images of deities with their perfect bodies exposed for all to see.

The New York kouros shares many traits with the *Mantiklos Apollo* and other Orientalizing works such as the *Lady of Auxerre* (FIG. 5-7), especially the triangular shape of head and hair and the flatness of the face—the hallmarks of the Daedalic style. Eyes, nose, and mouth all sit on the front of the head, and the ears on the sides. The long hair forms a flat backdrop behind the head. The placement of the various anatomical parts is the result of the sculptor's having drawn these features on four independent sides of the marble block, following the same workshop procedure used in Egypt for millennia. The New York kouros also has the slim waist of earlier Greek statues and exhibits the same love of pattern. The pointed arch of the rib cage, for example, echoes the **V**-shaped ridge of the hips, which suggests but does not accurately reproduce the rounded flesh and muscle of the human body.

CALF BEARER A generation later than the New York kouros is the statue (FIG. **5-9**) of a *moschophoros*, or calf bearer, found in fragments on the Athenian Acropolis. Its inscribed base (not visible in the photograph) states that a man named Rhonbos dedicated the statue. Rhonbos is almost certainly the calf bearer himself, bringing an offering to Athena in thanksgiving for his prosperity. He stands in the left-foot-forward manner of the kouroi, but he has a beard and therefore is no longer a youth. He wears a thin cloak (once painted to set it off from the otherwise nude body). No one dressed this way in ancient Athens. The sculptor adhered to the artistic convention of male nudity and attributed to the calf bearer the noble perfection that nudity suggests while also indicating that this mature gentleman is clothed, as any respectable citizen would be in this context. The Archaic sculptor's love of pattern may be seen once again in the handling of the difficult problem of representing man and animal together. The calf's legs and the moschophoros's arms form a bold **X** that unites the two bodies both physically and formally.

The calf bearer's face differs markedly from those of earlier Greek statues (and those of Egypt and the Near East) in one notable way. The man smiles—or at least seems to. From this time on, Archaic Greek statues always smile, even in the most inappropriate contexts (see, for example, FIG. 5-28, where a dying warrior with an arrow piercing his chest grins broadly at the spectator). This so-called *Archaic smile* has been variously interpreted, but it is not to be taken literally. Rather, the smile seems to be the Archaic sculptor's way of indicating that the person portrayed is alive. By adopting this

1 ft.

convention, the Greek artist signaled a very different intention from any Egyptian counterpart.

ANAVYSOS KOUROS Sometime around 530 BCE a young man named Kroisos died a hero's death in battle, and his family erected a kouros statue (FIG. 5-10) over his grave at Anavysos, not far from Athens. Fortunately, some of the paint is preserved, giving a better sense of the statue's original appearance. The inscribed base invites visitors to "stay and mourn at the tomb of dead Kroisos, whom raging Ares destroyed one day as he fought in the foremost ranks." The statue, with its distinctive Archaic smile, is no more a portrait of a specific youth than is the New York kouros. But two generations later, without rejecting the Egyptian stance, the Greek sculptor rendered the human body in a far more naturalistic manner. The head is no longer too large for the body, and the face is more rounded, with swelling cheeks replacing the flat planes of the earlier work. The long hair does not form a stiff backdrop to the head but falls naturally over the back. Rounded hips replace the V-shaped ridges of the New York kouros.

5-9 Calf bearer, dedicated by Rhonbos on the Acropolis, Athens, Greece, ca. 560 BCE. Marble, restored height 5′ 5″; fragment 3′ 11½″ high. Acropolis Museum, Athens.

This statue of a bearded man bringing a calf to sacrifice in thanksgiving to Athena is one of the first to employ the so-called Archaic smile, the Archaic Greek sculptor's way of indicating a person is alive.

5-10 Kroisos, from Anavysos, Greece, ca. 530 BCE. Marble, 6′ 4″ high. National Archaeological Museum, Athens.

This later kouros stood over the grave of Kroisos, a young man who died in battle. The statue displays increased naturalism in its proportions and more rounded modeling of face, torso, and limbs.

PEPLOS KORE A stylistic "sister" to the Anavysos kouros is the statue of a woman traditionally known as the *Peplos Kore* (FIG. 5-11) because until recently scholars thought this kore wore a peplos. A *peplos* is a simple, long, woolen belted garment. Careful examination of the statue has revealed, however, that she wears four different garments, one of which only goddesses wore. The attribute the goddess once held in her left hand would immediately have identified her. Whoever she is, the contrast with the *Lady of Auxerre* (FIG. 5-7) is striking. Although in both cases the drapery conceals the entire body save for head, arms, and feet, the sixth-century BCE sculptor rendered the soft female form much more naturally. This softer treatment of the flesh also sharply differentiates later korai from contemporary kouroi, which have hard, muscular bodies.

Traces of paint are preserved on the *Peplos Kore*. Like the Anavysos kouros, this Athenian statue was buried for more than two millennia. The earthen "grave" protected the painted surface from the destructive effects of exposure to the atmosphere and to bad weather. The *Peplos Kore*—along with the calf bearer (FIG. 5-9) and many other statues—had been knocked over by the Persians during their sack of the Acropolis in 480 BCE (see page 104). Shortly thereafter, the Athenians buried all the damaged Archaic sculptures. Before that time, they stood as votive offerings in Athena's sanctuary.

KORE IN IONIAN DRESS By the late sixth century BCE, the light linen Ionian *chiton*, worn in conjunction with a heavier *himation* (mantle), was the garment of choice for fashionable women. Archaic

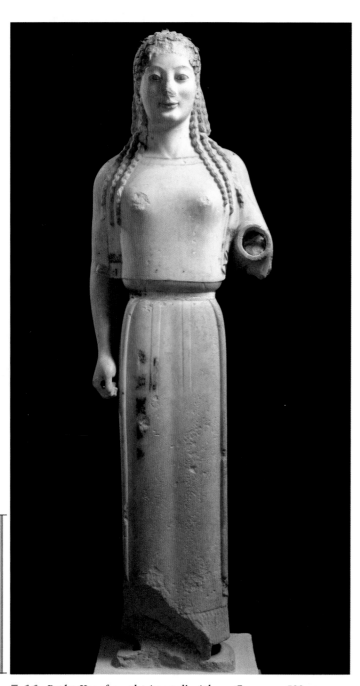

5-11 *Peplos Kore,* from the Acropolis, Athens, Greece, ca. 530 BCE. Marble, 4′ high. Acropolis Museum, Athens.

Unlike men, women are always clothed in Archaic statuary. This kore is a votive statue of a goddess wearing four garments. She once held her identifying attribute in her missing left hand.

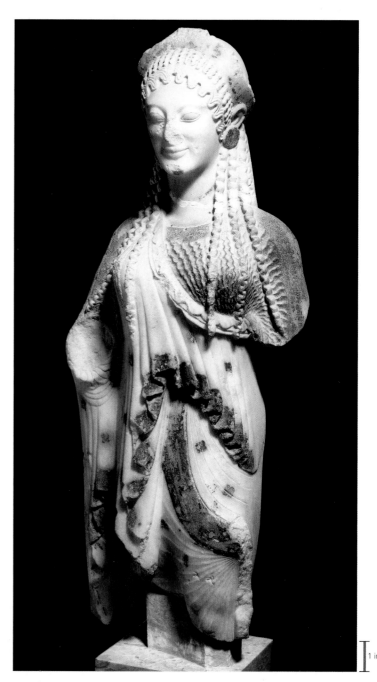

5-12 Kore, from the Acropolis, Athens, Greece, ca. 520–510 BCE. Marble, 1′ 9″ high. Acropolis Museum, Athens.

Archaic sculptors delighted in rendering the intricate asymmetrical patterns created by the cascading folds of garments like the Ionian chiton and himation worn by this smiling Acropolis kore.

Greek Temple Plans

The core of an ancient Greek temple plan (FIG. 5-13) was the *naos*, or *cella*, a room with no windows that usually housed the cult statue of the deity. It was preceded by a *pronaos*, or porch, often with two columns between the *antae*, or extended walls (columns *in antis*). A smaller second room might be placed behind the cella (FIG. 5-16), but in its canonical form, the Greek temple had a porch at the rear (*opisthodomos*) set against the blank back wall of the cella. The purpose was not functional but decorative, satisfying the Greek passion for balance and symmetry. A colonnade could be placed across the front of the temple (*prostyle*; FIG. 5-52), across both front and back (*amphiprostyle*; FIG. 5-55), or, more commonly, all around the cella and its porch(es) to form a *peristyle*, as in FIG. 5-13 (compare FIG. 5-15). Single (*peripteral*) colonnades were the norm, but double (*dipteral*) colonnades were features of especially elaborate temples (FIG. 5-75).

5-13 Plan of a typical Greek peripteral temple.

The basic form of the canonical Greek temple derives from that of the megaron of a Mycenaean palace (FIG. 4-18), but Greek temples housed statues of deities and most were surrounded by columns.

sculptors delighted in rendering the intricate patterns created by the cascading folds of thin, soft material. In another Acropolis kore (FIG. 5-12), the asymmetry of the folds greatly relieves the stiff frontality of the body and makes the figure appear much more lifelike than contemporary kouroi. The sculptor achieved added variety by showing the kore grasping part of her chiton in her left hand (unfortunately broken off) to lift it off the ground in order to take a step forward. This is the equivalent of the advanced left foot of the kouroi and became standard for statues of korai. Despite the varied surface treatment of brightly colored garments on the korai, the kore postures are as fixed as those of their male counterparts.

Architecture and Architectural Sculpture

Many of the earliest Greek temples do not survive because they were built of wood and mud brick. Pausanias noted in his second-century CE guidebook to Greece that in the even-then-ancient Temple of Hera at Olympia, one oak column was still in place. (Stone columns had replaced the others.) Archaic and later Greek temples, however, were constructed of more permanent materials—limestone, in many cases, and, where it was available, marble, which was more impressive and durable (and more expensive). In Greece proper, if not in its western colonies, marble was readily at hand. Bluish-white marble came from Hymettus, just east of Athens. Glittering white marble particularly adapted for carving was brought from Pentelicus, northeast of the city, and from the Aegean Islands, especially Paros.

Already in the Orientalizing seventh century BCE, the Greeks had built at Prinias a stone temple (FIG. 5-6) embellished with stone sculptures, but the Cretan temple resembled the megaron of a Mycenaean palace more than anything Greek traders had seen in their travels overseas. In the Archaic age of the sixth century, with the model of Egyptian columnar halls such as that at Karnak (FIG. 3-25) before them, Greek architects began to build the columnar stone temples that became more influential on the later history of architecture in the Western world than any other building type ever devised.

Greek temples differed in function from most later religious shrines. The altar lay outside the temple—at the east end, facing the rising sun—and the Greeks gathered outside, not inside, the building to worship. The temple proper housed the so-called *cult statue* of

the deity, the grandest of all votive offerings. Both in its early and mature manifestations, the Greek temple was the house of the god or goddess, not of his or her followers.

TEMPLE PLANS In basic plan (see "Greek Temple Plans," above, and FIG. 5-13), the Greek temple still discloses a close affinity with the Mycenaean megaron (FIG. 4-18), and, even in its most elaborate form, it retains the latter structure's basic simplicity. In all cases, the remarkable order, compactness, and symmetry of the Greek scheme strike the eye first, reflecting the Greeks' sense of proportion and their effort to achieve ideal forms in terms of regular numerical relationships and geometric rules. Whether the plan is simple or more complex, no fundamental change occurs in the nature of the units or of their grouping. Classical Greek architecture, like classical music, has a simple core theme with a series of complex, but always quite intelligible, variations developed from it.

The Greeks' insistence on proportional order guided their experiments with the proportions of temple plans. The earliest temples tended to be long and narrow, with the proportion of the ends to the sides roughly expressible as 1:3. From the sixth century BCE on, plans approached but rarely had a proportion of exactly 1:2. Classical temples tended to be a little longer than twice their width. To the Greek mind, proportion in architecture and sculpture was much the same as harmony in music, reflecting and embodying the cosmic order.

TEMPLE ORNAMENTATION Figural sculpture played a major role in the exterior program of the Greek temple from early times, partly to embellish the god's shrine, partly to tell something about the deity symbolized within, and partly to serve as a votive offering. But the building itself, with its finely carved capitals and moldings, also was conceived as sculpture, abstract in form and possessing the power of sculpture to evoke human responses. The commanding importance of the sculptured temple, its inspiring function in public life, was emphasized in its elevated site, often on a hill above the city (*acropolis* means "high city").

Sculptural ornament was concentrated on the upper part of the building, in the frieze and pediments (see "Doric and Ionic Orders," page 96). Architectural sculpture, like freestanding statuary, was painted (FIG. 5-27, *right*) and usually was placed only in the building parts that had no structural function. This is true particularly of the

Doric and Ionic Orders

Architectural historians describe the elevation (FIG. 5-14) of a Greek temple in terms of the platform, the colonnade, and the superstructure (*entablature*). In the Archaic period, two basic systems evolved for articulating the three units. These are the so-called *orders* of Greek architecture. The orders are differentiated both in the nature of the details and in the relative proportions of the parts. The names of the orders derive from the Greek regions where they were most commonly employed. The *Doric*, formulated on the mainland, remained the preferred manner there and in the western colonies of the Greeks. The *Ionic* was the order of choice in the Aegean Islands and on the western coast of Asia Minor. The geographical distinctions are by no means absolute. The Ionic order, for example, was often used in Athens (where, according to some, the Athenians considered themselves Ionians who never migrated).

In both orders, the columns rest on the *stylobate*, the uppermost course of the platform. Metal clamps held together the stone blocks in each horizontal course, and metal dowels joined vertically the blocks of different courses. The columns have two or three parts, depending on the order: the *shaft*, which is marked with vertical channels (*flutes*); the *capital*; and, in the Ionic order, the *base*. Greek column shafts, in contrast to their Minoan and Mycenaean forebears, taper gradually from bottom to top. They usually are composed of separate *drums* joined by metal dowels to prevent turning as well as shifting, although instances of *monolithic* (single-piece) columns are known. The capital has two elements. The lower part (the *echinus*) varies with the order. In the Doric, it is convex and cushionlike, similar to the echinus of Minoan (FIG. 4-6) and Mycenaean (FIG. 4-1) capitals. In the Ionic, it is small and supports a bolster ending in scroll-like spirals (the *volutes*). The upper element, present in both orders, is a flat, square block (the *abacus*) that provides the immediate support for the entablature.

The entablature has three parts: the *architrave*, the main weight-bearing and weight-distributing element; the *frieze*; and the *cornice*, a molded horizontal projection that together with two sloping (*raking*) cornices forms a triangle that enframes the *pediment*. In the Ionic order, the architrave is usually subdivided into three horizontal bands. In the Doric order, the frieze is subdivided into *triglyphs* and *metopes*, whereas in the Ionic the frieze is left open to provide a continuous field for relief sculpture.

The Doric order is massive in appearance, its sturdy columns firmly planted on the stylobate. Compared with the weighty and severe Doric, the Ionic order seems light, airy, and much more decorative. Its columns are more slender and rise from molded bases. The most obvious differences between the two orders are, of course, in the capitals—the Doric, severely plain, and the Ionic, highly ornamental.

DORIC ORDER

IONIC ORDER

5-14 Elevations of the Doric and Ionic orders.

The major differences between the Doric and Ionic orders are the form of the capitals and the treatment of the frieze. The Doric frieze is divided into triglyphs and metopes.

5-15 Temple of Hera I ("Basilica"), Paestum, Italy, ca. 550 BCE.

The peristyle of this huge early Doric temple consists of heavy, closely spaced, cigar-shaped columns with bulky, pancakelike capitals, characteristic features of Archaic Greek architecture.

Doric order (FIG. **5-14,** *left*), where decorative sculpture appears only in the metope and pediment "voids." Ionic (FIG. **5-14,** *right*) builders, less severe in this respect as well, were willing to decorate the entire frieze and sometimes even the lower column drums. Occasionally, they replaced their columns with female figures (*caryatids;* FIGS. **5-18** and **5-54**). Capitals, decorative moldings, and other architectural elements were also painted. By painting parts of the building, the designer could bring out more clearly the relationships of the structural parts and soften the stone's glitter at specific points, as well as provide a background to set off the figures.

Although the Greeks used color for emphasis and to relieve what might have seemed too bare a simplicity, Greek architecture primarily depended on clarity and balance. To the Greeks, it was unthinkable to use surfaces in the way the Egyptians used their gigantic columns—as fields for complicated ornamentation (FIG. **3-25**). The history of Greek temple architecture is the history of Greek architects' unflagging efforts to find the most satisfactory (that is, what they believed were perfect) proportions for each part of the building and for the structure as a whole.

BASILICA, PAESTUM The prime example of early Greek efforts at Doric temple design is not in Greece but in Italy, south of Naples, at Paestum (Greek Poseidonia). The huge (80 × 170 feet) Archaic temple (FIG. **5-15**) erected there around 550 BCE retains its entire peripteral colonnade, but most of the entablature, including the frieze, pediment, and all of the roof, has vanished. Called the "Basilica" after the Roman columnar hall building type (see Chapter 10) that early investigators felt it resembled, the structure was actually a temple of Hera. Scholars refer to it as the Temple of Hera I to distinguish it from its later neighbor, the Temple of Hera II (FIG. **5-30**). The misnomer is partly due to the building's plan (FIG. **5-16**), which differs from that of most other Greek temples. The unusual feature, found only in early Archaic temples, is the central row of columns that divides the cella into two aisles. Placing columns underneath the *ridgepole* (the timber beam running the length of the building below the peak of the gabled roof) might seem the logical way to provide interior support for the roof structure, but it resulted in several disadvantages. Among these was that this interior arrangement allowed no place for a central statue of the deity to whom the temple was

5-16 Plan of the Temple of Hera I, Paestum, Italy, ca. 550 BCE.

1. Cella with central row of columns
2. Pronaos with three columns in antis

The Hera temple's plan also reveals its early date. The temple has an odd number of columns on the facade and a single row of columns in the cella, leaving no place for a central cult statue.

dedicated. Also, the peripteral colonnade, in order to correspond with the interior, required an odd number of columns (nine in this case) across the building's facade. At Paestum, the builders also set three columns in antis instead of the standard two, which in turn ruled out a central doorway for viewing the statue. (Some scholars have suggested, however, that this design was well suited for two statues, perhaps of Zeus and Hera.) The architect nonetheless achieved a simple 1:2 ratio of facade and flank columns by erecting 18 columns on each side of the temple.

Another early aspect of the Paestum temple is the shape of its heavy, closely spaced columns (FIG. **5-15**) with their large, bulky, pancakelike Doric capitals, which seem compressed by the overbearing weight of the entablature. The columns have a pronounced swelling (*entasis*) at the middle of the shafts, giving them a profile akin to that of a cigar. If the temple's immense roof were preserved, the columns would seem even more compressed, squatting beneath

5-17 West pediment from the Temple of Artemis, Corfu, Greece, ca. 600–580 BCE. Limestone, greatest height 9′ 4″. Archaeological Museum, Corfu.

The hideous Medusa and two panthers at the center of this early pediment serve as temple guardians. To either side, and much smaller, are scenes from the Trojan War and the battle of gods and giants.

what must have been a high and massive entablature. The columns and capitals thus express in a vivid manner their weight-bearing function. One structural reason, perhaps, for the heaviness of the design and the narrowness of the spans between the columns might be that the Archaic builders were afraid thinner and more widely spaced columns would result in the superstructure's collapse. In later Doric temples (FIGS. 5-25, 5-30, and 5-44), the builders placed the columns farther apart and refined the forms. The shafts became more slender, the entasis subtler, the capitals smaller, and the entablature lighter. Greek architects sought the ideal proportional relationship among the parts of their buildings. The sculptors of Archaic kouroi and korai grappled with similar problems. Architecture and sculpture developed in a parallel manner in the sixth century BCE.

TEMPLE OF ARTEMIS, CORFU Architects and sculptors were also frequently called on to work together, as at Corfu (ancient Corcyra), where the Greeks constructed a great Doric temple dedicated to Artemis in the sixth century BCE. Corfu, an island off the western coast of Greece, was an important stop on the trade route between the mainland and the Greek settlements in Italy (MAP 5-1). Prosperity made possible the erection of one of the earliest stone peripteral temples in Greece, one also lavishly embellished with sculpture. Reliefs (unfortunately very fragmentary today) decorated the metopes, and huge high-relief sculptures (more than nine feet high at the center) filled both pediments. The pediments appear to have been decorated in an identical manner. The west pediment (FIG. 5-17) is better preserved.

Designing figural decoration for a pediment was never an easy task for the Greek sculptor because of the pediment's awkward triangular shape. The central figures had to be of great size. In contrast, as the pediment tapered toward the corners, the available area became increasingly cramped. At the center of the Corfu pediment is the *gorgon* Medusa, a demon with a woman's body and a bird's wings. Medusa also had a hideous face and snake hair, and anyone who gazed at her turned into stone. The sculptor depicted her in the conventional Archaic bent-leg, bent-arm, pinwheel-like posture that signifies running or, for a winged creature, flying. To her left and right are two great felines. Together they serve as temple guardians, repulsing all enemies from the sanctuary of the goddess. Similar panthers

stood sentinel on the lintel of the seventh-century BCE temple at Prinias. The Corfu felines are in the tradition of the guardian lions of the citadel gate (FIG. 4-1) at Mycenae and the beasts that stood guard at the entrances to Near Eastern palaces (FIGS. 2-18 and 2-21). The triad of Medusa and the felines recalls as well Mesopotamian heraldic human-and-animal compositions (FIG. 2-10). The Corfu figures are, in short, still further examples of the Orientalizing manner in early Greek sculpture.

Between Medusa and the two felines are two smaller figures—the human Chrysaor at her left and the winged horse Pegasus at her right (only the rear legs are preserved next to Medusa's right foot). Chrysaor and Pegasus were Medusa's children. According to legend, they sprang from her head when the Greek hero Perseus severed it with his sword. Their presence here on either side of the living Medusa is therefore a chronological impossibility. The Archaic artist had less interest in telling a coherent story than in identifying the central figure by depicting her offspring. Narration was, however, the purpose of the much smaller groups situated in the pediment corners. To the viewer's right is Zeus, brandishing his thunderbolt and slaying a kneeling giant. In the extreme corner (not preserved) was probably a dead giant. The *gigantomachy* (battle of gods and giants) was a popular theme in Greek art from Archaic through Hellenistic times and was a metaphor for the triumph of reason and order over chaos. In the pediment's left corner is one of the Trojan War's climactic events: Achilles' son Neoptolemos kills the enthroned King Priam. The fallen figure to the left of this group may be a dead Trojan.

The master responsible for the Corfu pediments was a pioneer, and the composition shows all the signs of experimentation. The lack of narrative unity and the figures' extraordinary diversity of scale eventually gave way to pedimental designs with freestanding figures in place of reliefs all acting out a single event and appearing the same size. But the Corfu designer already had shown the way, by realizing, for example, that the area beneath the raking cornice could be filled with gods and heroes of similar size if a combination of standing, leaning, kneeling, seated, and prostrate figures were employed in the composition. The Corfu master also discovered that animals could be very useful space fillers because, unlike humans, they have one end taller than the other.

5-18 Reconstruction drawing of the Siphnian Treasury, Delphi, Greece, ca. 530 BCE (John Burge).

Treasuries were storehouses in sanctuaries for a city's votive offerings. The Ionic treasury the Siphnians erected at Delphi featured caryatids in the porch, and sculptures in the pediment and frieze.

Doric columns in the porch and sculptured metopes in the frieze. The Siphnians equally characteristically employed the Ionic order for their Delphic treasury. Wealth from the island's gold and silver mines made the luxurious building possible. In the porch, where one would expect to find fluted Ionic columns, far more elaborate *caryatids* were employed instead. Caryatids are rare, even in Ionic architecture, but they are unknown in Doric architecture, where they would have been discordant elements in that much more severe order. The Siphnian statue-columns resemble contemporary korai dressed in Ionian chitons and himations (FIG. 5-12).

Another Ionic feature of the Siphnian Treasury is the continuous sculptured frieze on all four sides of the building. The north frieze represents the popular theme of the gigantomachy, but the rendition is much more detailed than that in the corner of the Corfu pediment. In the section reproduced here (FIG. 5-19), Apollo and Artemis pursue a fleeing giant at the right, while behind them one of the lions pulling a goddess's chariot attacks a giant and bites into his midsection. Paint originally enlivened the crowded composition, and painted labels identified the various protagonists. Some figures had metal weapons. The effect must have been dazzling. On one of the shields the sculptor inscribed his name (unfortunately lost), a clear indication of pride in accomplishment.

SIPHNIAN TREASURY, DELPHI The sixth century BCE also saw the erection of grandiose Ionic temples on the Aegean Islands and the west coast of Asia Minor. The gem of Archaic Ionic architecture and architectural sculpture, however, is not a temple but a treasury erected by the city of Siphnos in the Sanctuary of Apollo at Delphi. It can be reliably reconstructed (FIG. 5-18) based on the surviving fragments now on display in the Delphi museum. Greek *treasuries* were small buildings set up for the safe storage of votive offerings. At Delphi many poleis expressed their civic pride by erecting these templelike but nonperipteral structures. Athens built one with

5-19 Gigantomachy, detail of the north frieze of the Siphnian Treasury, Delphi, Greece, ca. 530 BCE. Marble, 2′ 1″ high. Archaeological Museum, Delphi.

Greek friezes were brightly painted. As in contemporaneous vase painting, the Siphnian frieze also had painted labels identifying the various gods and giants. Some of the figures held metal weapons.

Vase Painting

Labeled figures and artists' signatures also appear on Archaic painted vases. By the mid-sixth century BCE, the Athenians, having learned the black-figure technique from the Corinthians (FIG. 5-5), had taken over the export market for fine painted ceramics.

FRANÇOIS VASE The masterpiece of early Athenian black-figure painting is the *François Vase* (FIG. **5-20**), named for the excavator who uncovered it in an Etruscan tomb at Chiusi. The vase is a new kind of krater with volute-shaped handles, probably inspired by costly metal prototypes. It was signed by both its painter ("KLEITIAS painted me") and potter ("ERGOTIMOS made me"), whose signatures each appear twice among the more than 200 figures in six registers. Labels abound, naming humans and animals alike, even some inanimate objects. The painter devoted only one of the bands to the Orientalizing repertoire of animals and sphinxes. The rest constitute a selective encyclopedia of Greek mythology, focusing on the exploits of Peleus and his son Achilles, the great hero of Homer's *Iliad,* and of Theseus, the legendary king of Athens.

1 ft.

In the detail shown here (FIG. 5-20, *bottom*), Lapiths (a northern Greek tribe) and centaurs battle (*centauromachy*) after a wedding celebration where the man-beasts, who were invited guests, got drunk and attempted to abduct the Lapith maidens and young boys. Theseus, also on the guest list, was prominent among the centaurs' Greek adversaries. Kleitias did not fill the space between his figures with decorative ornament, as did his Geometric predecessors (FIG. 5-2). But his heroes still conform to the age-old composite type (profile heads with frontal eyes, frontal torsos, and profile legs and arms). His centaurs, however, are much more believable than their Geometric counterparts (FIG. 5-3). The man-horse combination is top/bottom rather than front/back. The lower (horse) portion has four legs of uniform type, and the upper part of the monster is fully human. In characteristic fashion, Kleitias painted the animal section of the centaur in strict profile, whereas the human head and torso are a composite of frontal and profile views. (He used a consistent profile for the more adventurous detail of the collapsed centaur at the right.)

EXEKIAS The acknowledged master of the black-figure technique was an Athenian named EXEKIAS, whose vases were not only widely exported but copied as well. Perhaps his greatest work is an amphora (FIG. **5-21**), found in an Etruscan tomb at Vulci, that Exekias signed as both painter and potter. Unlike Kleitias, Exekias did not divide the surface of the vase into a series of horizontal bands. Instead, he placed figures of monumental stature in a single large framed panel. At the left is Achilles, fully armed. He plays a dice game with his comrade Ajax. From the lips of Achilles comes the word *tesara* (four). Ajax calls out *tria* (three). Although Ajax has taken off his helmet, both men hold their spears, and their shields are close at hand. Each man is ready for action at a moment's notice. This depiction of "the calm before the storm" is the antithesis of the Archaic preference for dramatic action. The gravity and tension that will characterize much Classical Greek art of the next century, but that are absent in Archaic art, already may be seen in this vase.

Exekias had no equal as a black-figure painter. This is evident in such details as the extraordinarily intricate engraving of the patterns on the heroes' cloaks (highlighted with delicate touches of white) and in the brilliant composition. The arch formed by the backs of the two warriors echoes the shape of the rounded shoulders of the amphora. The shape of the vessel (compare FIG. 5-22) is echoed again in the void between the heads and spears of Achilles and Ajax. Exekias also used the spears to lead the viewer's eyes toward the thrown dice, where the heroes' eyes are fixed. Of course, those eyes

1 in.

5-20 KLEITIAS and ERGOTIMOS, *François Vase* (Athenian black-figure volute krater), from Chiusi, Italy, ca. 570 BCE. General view (*top*) and detail of centauromachy on other side of vase (*bottom*). 2′ 2″ high. Museo Archeologico, Florence.

Found in an Etruscan tomb, this huge krater is signed by both the painter and the potter and has more than 200 mythological figures presented in registers, as on Geometric and Orientalizing vases.

5-21 Exekias, Achilles and Ajax playing a dice game (detail from an Athenian black-figure amphora), from Vulci, Italy, ca. 540–530 BCE. Whole vessel 2′ high; detail 8½″ high. Musei Vaticani, Rome.

The dramatic tension, adjustment of figures' poses to the vase's shape, and intricacy of the engraved patterns of the cloaks are hallmarks of Exekias, the greatest master of black-figure painting.

do not really look down at the table but stare out from the profile heads in the old manner. For all his brilliance, Exekias was still wedded to many of the old conventions. True innovation in figure drawing would have to await the invention of a new ceramic painting technique of greater versatility than black-figure, with its dark silhouettes and incised details.

BILINGUAL PAINTING The birth of this new technique came around 530 BCE from an artist known as the ANDOKIDES PAINTER, that is, the anonymous painter who decorated the vases signed by the potter Andokides. The differences between the two techniques can best be studied on a series of experimental vases with the same composition painted on both sides, once in black-figure and once in the new technique, *red-figure*. Such vases, nicknamed *bilingual vases*, were produced for only a short time. An especially interesting example is an amphora (FIG. **5-22**) by the Andokides Painter that features copies of the Achilles and Ajax panel by Exekias, his teacher.

In neither black-figure nor red-figure did the Andokides Painter capture the intensity of the model, and the treatment of details is decidedly inferior. Yet the new red-figure technique had obvious advantages over the old black-figure treatment. Red-figure is the opposite of black-figure. What was previously black became red, and vice versa. The artist employed the same black glaze but instead of using it to create the silhouettes of figures, the painter outlined the figures and then colored the background black. The artist reserved the red clay for the figures themselves. Interior details were then drawn with a soft brush in place of a stiff metal graver, giving the painter much greater flexibility. The artist could vary the thickness of the lines and even build up the glaze to give relief to curly hair or dilute it to create brown shades, thereby expanding the chromatic range of the Greek vase painter's craft. The Andokides Painter—many think he was the potter Andokides himself—did not yet appreciate the full potential of his invention. But he created a technique that, in the hands of other, more skilled artists, helped revolutionize the art of drawing.

5-22 ANDOKIDES PAINTER, Achilles and Ajax playing a dice game (Athenian bilingual amphora), from Orvieto, Italy, ca. 525–520 BCE. Black-figure side (*left*) and red-figure side (*right*). 1′ 9″ high. Museum of Fine Arts, Boston.

Around 530 BCE, the Andokides Painter invented the red-figure technique. Some of his early vases are "bilingual"—that is, the same scene appears on both sides, one in black-figure and one in red-figure.

5-23 Euphronios, Herakles wrestling Antaios (detail of an Athenian red-figure calyx krater), from Cerveteri, Italy, ca. 510 BCE. Whole vessel 1′ 7″ high; detail 7¾″ high. Louvre, Paris.

Euphronios rejected the age-old composite view for his depiction of Herakles and the giant Antaios and instead attempted to reproduce how the human body is seen from a particular viewpoint.

EUPHRONIOS One of these younger and more adventurous painters was EUPHRONIOS, whose krater depicting the struggle between Herakles and Antaios (FIG. **5-23**) reveals the exciting possibilities of the new red-figure technique. Antaios was a Libyan giant, a son of Earth, and he derived his power from contact with the ground. To defeat him, Herakles had to lift him into the air and strangle him while no part of the giant's body touched the earth. In the scene on the krater, the two wrestle on the ground, and Antaios still possesses enormous strength. Nonetheless, Herakles has the upper hand. The giant's face is a mask of pain. His eyes roll and his teeth are bared. His right arm is paralyzed, with the fingers limp.

Euphronios used diluted glaze to show Antaios's unkempt golden brown hair—intentionally contrasted with the neat coiffure and carefully trimmed beard of the emotionless Greek hero. The artist also used thinned glaze to delineate the muscles of both figures. But rendering human anatomy convincingly was not his only interest. Euphronios also wished to show that his figures occupy space. He deliberately rejected the conventional composite posture for the human figure, which communicates so well the specific parts of the human body, and attempted instead to reproduce how a particular human body is *seen*. He presented, for example, not only Antaios's torso but also his right thigh from the front. The lower leg disappears behind the giant, and one glimpses only part of the right foot. The viewer must mentally make the connection between the upper leg and the foot. The red-figure painter did not create a two-dimensional panel filled with figures in stereotypical postures, as his Archaic and pre-Greek predecessors always did. His panel is a window onto a mythological world with protagonists moving in three-dimensional space—a revolutionary new conception of what a picture was supposed to be.

EUTHYMIDES A preoccupation with the art of drawing per se may be seen in a remarkable amphora (FIG. **5-24**) painted by EUTHYMIDES, a rival of Euphronios. The subject is appropriate for a wine storage jar—three tipsy revelers. But the theme was little more than an excuse for the artist to experiment with the representation of unusual positions of the human form. It is no coincidence that the bodies do not overlap, for each is an independent figure study. Euthymides cast aside the conventional frontal and profile composite views. Instead, he painted torsos that are not two-dimensional surface patterns but are *foreshortened*, that is, drawn in a three-quarter view. Most noteworthy is the central figure, who is shown from the rear with a twisting spinal column and buttocks in three-quarter view. Earlier artists had no interest in attempting such postures because they not only are incomplete but also do not show the "main"

side of the human body. But for Euthymides the challenge of drawing the figure from such an unusual viewpoint was a reward in itself. With understandable pride he proclaimed his achievement by adding to the formulaic signature "Euthymides painted me" the phrase "as never Euphronios [could do!]"

5-24 Euthymides, Three revelers (Athenian red-figure amphora), from Vulci, Italy, ca. 510 BCE. 2′ high. Staatliche Antikensammlungen, Munich.

Euthymides chose this theme as an excuse to represent bodies in unusual positions, including a foreshortened three-quarter view from the rear. He claimed to have surpassed Euphronios as a draftsman.

5-25 Temple of Aphaia, Aegina, Greece, ca. 500–490 BCE.

In this refined early-fifth-century BCE Doric design (compare FIG. 5-15), the columns are more slender and widely spaced, and there are only 6 columns on the facade and 12 on the flanks.

5-26 Model of the Temple of Aphaia, Aegina, Greece, ca. 500–490 BCE, showing internal elevation. Glyptothek, Munich.

Later Doric architects also modified the plan of their temples (compare FIG. 5-16). The Aegina temple's cella has two colonnades of two stories each (originally with a statue of the deity between them).

Aegina and the Transition to the Classical Period

The years just before and after 500 BCE were also a time of dynamic transition in architecture and architectural sculpture. Some of the changes were evolutionary in nature, others revolutionary. Both kinds are evident in the Temple at Aegina dedicated to Aphaia, a local goddess.

TEMPLE OF APHAIA, AEGINA The temple (FIG. 5-25) sits on a prominent ridge with dramatic views out to the sea. The colonnade is 45 × 95 feet and consists of 6 Doric columns on the facade and 12 on the flanks. This is a much more compact structure than the impressive but ungainly Archaic Temple of Hera I (FIG. 5-15) at Paestum, even though the ratio of width to length is similar. Doric architects had learned a great deal in the half century that elapsed between construction of the two temples. The columns

of the Aegina temple are more widely spaced and more slender. The capitals create a smooth transition from the vertical shafts below to the horizontal architrave above. Gone are the Archaic flattened echinuses and bulging shafts of the Paestum columns. The Aegina architect also refined the internal elevation (FIG. 5-26) and plan (FIG. 5-27, *left*). In place of a single row of columns down the center of the cella is a double colonnade—and each row has two stories. This arrangement allowed a statue to be placed on the central axis and also gave worshipers gathered in front of the building an unobstructed view through the pair of columns in the pronaos.

Both pediments featured painted life-size statuary (FIG. 5-27, *right*) in place of the high reliefs characteristic of Archaic temple pediments. The theme of both statuary groups was the battle of Greeks and Trojans, but the sculptors depicted different episodes. The compositions were nonetheless almost identical, with Athena at the center of the bloody combat. She is larger than all the other figures because she is superhuman, but all the mortal heroes are the

5-27 Plan (*left*) and GUILLAUME-ABEL BLOUET's 1828 restored view of the facade (*right*) of the Temple of Aphaia, Aegina, Greece, ca. 500–490 BCE.

The restored view suggests how colorful Greek temples were. The designer solved the problem of composing figures in a pediment by using the whole range of body postures from upright to prostrate.

5-28 Dying warrior, from the west pediment of the Temple of Aphaia, Aegina, Greece, ca. 490 BCE. Marble, 5′ 2½″ long. Glyptothek, Munich.

The statues of the west pediment of the early-fifth-century BCE temple at Aegina exhibit Archaic features. This fallen warrior still has a rigidly frontal torso and an Archaic smile on his face.

5-29 Dying warrior, from the east pediment of the Temple of Aphaia, Aegina, Greece, ca. 480 BCE. Marble, 6′ 1″ long. Glyptothek, Munich.

The eastern dying warrior already belongs to the Classical era. His posture is more natural, and he exhibits a new self-consciousness. Concerned with his own pain, he does not face the viewer.

same size, regardless of the statue's position in the pediment. Unlike the experimental design at Corfu (FIG. **5-17**), the Aegina pediments feature a unified theme and consistent scale. The designer was able to keep the size of the figures constant by using the whole range of body postures from upright (Athena) to leaning, falling, kneeling, and lying (Greeks and Trojans).

The sculptures of the Aegina pediments were probably set in place when the temple was completed around 490 BCE. Many scholars believe the statues at the eastern end were damaged and replaced with a new group a decade or two later, although some think both groups were installed after 480 BCE. Whatever the precise dates of the sculptures, it is very instructive to compare the eastern and western figures. The west pediment's dying warrior (FIG. **5-28**) was still conceived in the Archaic mode. His torso is rigidly frontal, and he looks out directly at the spectator—with his face set in an Archaic smile in spite of the bronze arrow that punctures his chest. He is like a mannequin in a store window whose arms and legs have been arranged by someone else for effective display. There is no sense whatsoever of a thinking and feeling human being.

The comparable figure (FIG. **5-29**) in the east pediment is radically different. His posture is more natural and more complex, with the torso placed at an angle to the viewer. (He is on a par with the painted figures of Euphronios, FIG. **5-23**.) Moreover, he reacts to his wound as a flesh-and-blood human would. He knows that death is inevitable, but he still struggles to rise once again, using his shield for support. And he does not look out at the spectator. He is concerned with his pain, not with the viewer. No more than a decade separates the two statues, but they belong to different eras. The eastern warrior is not a creation of the Archaic world, when sculptors imposed anatomical patterns (and smiles) on statues from without. This statue belongs to the Classical world, where statues move as humans move and

possess the self-consciousness of real men and women. This was a radical change in the conception of what a statue was meant to be. In sculpture, as in painting, the Classical revolution had occurred.

EARLY AND HIGH CLASSICAL PERIODS

Art historians mark the beginning of the Classical* age from a historical event: the defeat of the Persian invaders of Greece by the allied Hellenic city-states. Shortly after the Persians occupied and sacked Athens in 480 BCE, the Greeks won a decisive naval victory over the Persians at Salamis. It had been a difficult war, and at times it had seemed as though Asia would swallow up Greece, and the Persian king Xerxes (see Chapter 2) would rule over all. When the Persians destroyed the Greek city Miletos in 494 BCE, they killed the male inhabitants and sold the women and children into slavery. The narrow escape of the Greeks from domination by Asian "barbarians" nurtured a sense of Hellenic identity so strong that from then on the history of European civilization would be distinct from the civilization of Asia, even though they continued to interact. Typical of the time were the views of the great dramatist Aeschylus, who celebrated, in his *Oresteia* trilogy, the triumph of reason and law over barbarous crimes, blood feuds, and mad vengeance. Himself a veteran of the epic battle of Marathon, Aeschylus repudiated in majestic verse all the slavish and inhuman traits of nature that the Greeks at that time of crisis associated with the Persians.

*Note: In *Art through the Ages*, the adjective "Classical," with uppercase C, refers specifically to the Classical period of ancient Greece, 480–323 BCE. Lowercase "classical" refers to Greco-Roman antiquity in general, that is, the period treated in Chapters 5, 6, and 7.

5-30 Temple of Hera II, Paestum, Italy, ca. 460 BCE.

The second Hera temple at Paestum was modeled on Libon's Temple of Zeus at Olympia. The Paestum temple reflects the Olympia design, but the later building lacks the pedimental sculpture of its model.

Architecture and Architectural Sculpture

The decades following the removal of the Persian threat are universally considered the high point of Greek civilization. This is the era of the dramatists Sophocles and Euripides, as well as Aeschylus; the historian Herodotus; the statesman Pericles; the philosopher Socrates; and many of the most famous Greek architects, sculptors, and painters.

TEMPLE OF ZEUS, OLYMPIA The first great monument of Classical art and architecture is the Temple of Zeus at Olympia, site of the Olympic Games. The temple was begun about 470 BCE and was probably completed by 457 BCE. The architect was Libon of Elis. Today the structure is in ruins, its picturesque tumbled column drums an eloquent reminder of the effect of the passage of time on even the grandest monuments humans have built. A good idea of its original appearance can be gleaned, however, from a slightly later Doric temple modeled closely on the Olympian shrine of Zeus—the second Temple of Hera (FIG. 5-30) at Paestum. The plans and elevations of both temples follow the pattern of the Temple of Aphaia (FIGS. 5-26 and 5-27) at Aegina: an even number of columns (six) on the short ends, two columns in antis, and two rows of columns in two stories inside the cella. But the Temple of Zeus was more lavishly decorated than even the Aphaia temple. Statues filled both pediments, and the six metopes over the doorway in the pronaos and the matching six of the opisthodomos were adorned with reliefs.

The subject of the Temple of Zeus's east pediment (FIG. 5-31) had deep local significance: the chariot race between Pelops (from whom the Peloponnesos takes its name) and King Oinomaos. The story is a sinister one. Oinomaos had one daughter, Hippodameia, and it was foretold that he would die if she married. Consequently, Oinomaos challenged any suitor who wished to make Hippodameia his bride to a chariot race from Olympia to Corinth. If the suitor won, he also won the hand of the king's daughter. But if he lost, he was killed. The outcome of each race was predetermined, because Oinomaos possessed the divine horses of his father Ares. To ensure his victory when all others had failed, Pelops resorted to bribing the king's groom, Myrtilos, to rig the royal chariot so that it would collapse during the race. Oinomaos was killed and Pelops won his bride, but he drowned Myrtilos rather than pay his debt to him. Before he died, Myrtilos brought a curse on Pelops and his descendants. This curse led to the murder of Pelops's son Atreus and to events that figure prominently in some of the greatest Greek tragedies of the Classical era, Aeschylus's three plays known collectively as the *Oresteia:* the sacrifice by Atreus's son Agamemnon of his daughter Iphigeneia; the slaying of Agamemnon by Aegisthus, lover of Agamemnon's wife Clytaemnestra; and the murder of Aegisthus and Clytaemnestra by Orestes, the son of Agamemnon and Clytaemnestra.

Indeed, the pedimental statues (FIG. 5-31), which faced toward the starting point of all Olympic chariot races, are posed as actors on a stage—Zeus in the center, Oinomaos and his wife on one side, Pelops and Hippodameia on the other, and their respective chariots to each side. All are quiet. The horrible events known to every

1 ft.

5-31 East pediment from the Temple of Zeus, Olympia, Greece, ca. 470–456 BCE. Marble, 87′ wide. Archaeological Museum, Olympia.

The east pediment of the Zeus temple depicts the chariot race between Pelops and Oinomaos, which began at Olympia. The actors in the pediment faced the starting point of Olympic chariot races.

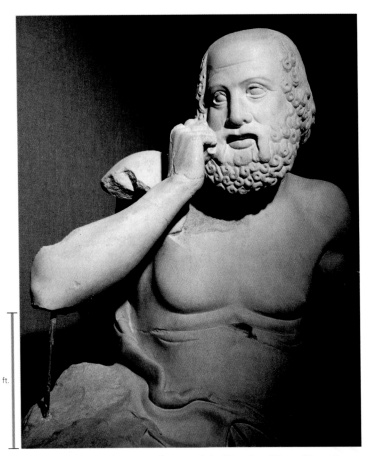

5-32 Seer, from the east pediment of the Temple of Zeus, Olympia, Greece, ca. 470–456 BCE. Marble, full figure 4′ 6″ high; detail 3′ 2½″ high. Archaeological Museum, Olympia.

The balding seer in the Olympia east pediment is a rare depiction of old age in Classical sculpture. He has a shocked expression because he foresees the tragic outcome of the chariot race.

spectator have yet to occur. Only one man reacts—a seer who knows the future (FIG. 5-32). He is a remarkable figure. Unlike the gods, heroes, and noble youths and maidens who are the almost exclusive subjects of Archaic and Classical Greek statuary, this seer is a rare depiction of old age. He has a balding, wrinkled head and sagging musculature—and a shocked expression on his face. This is a true show of emotion, unlike the stereotypical Archaic smile, without precedent in earlier Greek sculpture and not a regular feature of Greek art until the Hellenistic age.

The metopes of the Zeus temple are also thematically connected with the site, for they depict the 12 labors of Herakles (see "Herakles, Greatest of Greek Heroes," right), the legendary founder of the Olympic Games. In the metope illustrated here (FIG. 5-33), Herakles holds up the sky (with the aid of the goddess Athena—and a cushion) in place of Atlas, who had undertaken the dangerous journey to fetch the golden apples of the Hesperides for the hero. The load soon will be transferred back to Atlas (at the right, still holding the apples), but now each of the very high relief figures in the metope stands quietly with the same serene dignity as the statues in the Olympia pediment. In both attitude and dress (simple Doric peplos for the women), all the Olympia figures display a severity that contrasts sharply with the smiling and elaborately clad figures of the Late Archaic period. Many art historians call this Early Classical phase of Greek art the *Severe Style*.

Herakles, Greatest of Greek Heroes

Greek heroes were a class of mortals of intermediate status between ordinary humans and the immortal gods. Most often the children of gods, some were great warriors, such as those who fought at Troy and were celebrated in Homer's epic poems. Others pursued one fabulous adventure after another, ridding the world of monsters and generally benefiting humankind. Many heroes were worshiped after their deaths, and the greatest of them were honored with shrines, especially in the cities with which they were most closely associated.

The greatest Greek hero was *Herakles* (the Roman *Hercules*), born in Thebes and the son of Zeus and Alkmene, a mortal woman. Zeus's jealous wife Hera hated Herakles and sent two serpents to attack him in his cradle, but the infant strangled them. Later, Hera caused the hero to go mad and to kill his wife and children. As punishment he was condemned to perform 12 great labors. In the first, he defeated the legendary lion of Nemea and ever after wore its pelt. The lion's skin and his weapon, a club, are Herakles' distinctive attributes (FIG. 5-66). His last task was to obtain the golden apples Gaia gave to Hera at her marriage (FIG. 5-33). They grew from a tree in the garden of the Hesperides at the western edge of the ocean, where a dragon guarded them. After completion of the 12 seemingly impossible tasks, Herakles was awarded immortality. Athena, who had watched over him carefully throughout his life and assisted him in performing the labors, introduced him into the realm of the gods on Mount Olympus. According to legend, it was Herakles who established the Olympic Games.

5-33 Athena, Herakles, and Atlas with the apples of the Hesperides, metope from the Temple of Zeus, Olympia, Greece, ca. 470–456 BCE. Marble, 5′ 3″ high. Archaeological Museum, Olympia.

Herakles founded the Olympic Games, and his 12 labors were the subjects of the 12 Doric metopes of the Zeus temple. This one shows the hero holding up the world (with Athena's aid) for Atlas.

Statuary

Early Classical sculptors were also the first to break away from the rigid and unnatural Egyptian-inspired pose of the Archaic kouroi. This change is evident in the postures of the Olympia figures, but it occurred even earlier in independent statuary.

KRITIOS BOY Although it is well under life-size, the marble statue known as the *Kritios Boy* (FIG. 5-34)—so titled because it was once thought the sculptor Kritios carved it—is one of the most important works of Greek sculpture. Never before had a sculptor been concerned with portraying how a human being (as opposed to a stone image) actually stands. Real people do not stand in the stiff-legged pose of the kouroi and korai or their Egyptian predecessors. Humans shift their weight and the position of the main body parts around the vertical but flexible axis of the spine. When humans move, the body's elastic musculoskeletal structure dictates a harmonious, smooth motion of all its elements. The sculptor of the *Kritios*

Boy was among the first to grasp this fact and to represent it in statuary. The youth has a slight dip to the right hip, indicating the shifting of weight onto his left leg. His right leg is bent, at ease. The head also turns slightly to the right and tilts, breaking the unwritten rule of frontality dictating the form of virtually all earlier statues. This weight shift, which art historians describe as *contrapposto* (counterbalance), separates Classical from Archaic Greek statuary.

RIACE WARRIOR The innovations of the *Kritios Boy* were carried even further in the bronze statue (FIG. 5-35) of a warrior found in the sea near Riace at the "toe" of the Italian "boot." It is one of a pair of statues divers accidentally discovered in the cargo of a ship that sank in antiquity on its way from Greece probably to Rome, where Greek sculpture was much admired. Known as the Riace Bronzes, they had to undergo several years of cleaning and restoration after nearly two millennia of submersion in salt water, but they are nearly intact. The statue shown here lacks only its shield, spear, and helmet. It is a masterpiece of hollow-casting (see "Hollow-Casting Life-Size Bronze

5-34 *Kritios Boy,* from the Acropolis, Athens, Greece, ca. 480 BCE. Marble, 3′ 10″ high. Acropolis Museum, Athens.

This is the first statue to show how a person naturally stands. The sculptor depicted the shifting of weight from one leg to the other (contrapposto). The head turns slightly, and the Archaic smile is gone.

1 ft.

5-35 Warrior, from the sea off Riace, Italy, ca. 460–450 BCE. Bronze, 6′ 6″ high. Museo Archeologico Nazionale, Reggio Calabria.

The bronze Riace warrior statue has inlaid eyes, silver teeth and eyelashes, and copper lips and nipples (FIG. I-17). The contrapposto is more pronounced than in the *Kritios Boy* (FIG. 5-34).

1 ft.

Hollow-Casting Life-Size Bronze Statues

Monumental bronze statues such as the Riace warrior (FIG. 5-35), the Delphi charioteer (FIG. 5-37), and the Artemision god (FIG. 5-38) required great technical skill to produce. They could not be manufactured using a single simple mold, as were small-scale Geometric and Archaic figures (FIGS. 5-3 and 5-4). Weight, cost, and the tendency of large masses of bronze to distort when cooling made life-size castings in solid bronze impractical, if not impossible. Instead, large statues were hollow-cast by the *cire perdue* (*lost-wax*) method. The lost-wax process entailed several steps and had to be repeated many times, because monumental statues were typically cast in parts—head, arms, hands, torso, and so forth.

First, the sculptor fashioned a full-size clay model of the intended statue. Then a clay master mold was made around the model and removed in sections. When dry, the various pieces of the master mold were reassembled for each separate body part. Next, a layer of beeswax was applied to the inside of each mold. When the wax cooled, the mold was removed, and the sculptor was left with a hollow wax model in the shape of the original clay model. The artist could then correct or refine details—for example, engrave fingernails on the wax hands or individual locks of hair on the head.

In the next stage, a final clay mold (*investment*) was applied to the exterior of the wax model, and a liquid clay core was poured inside the hollow wax. Metal pins (*chaplets*) were driven through the new mold to connect the investment with the clay core (FIG. 5-36a). Then the wax was melted out ("lost") and molten bronze poured into the mold in its place (FIG. 5-36b). When the bronze hardened and assumed the shape of the wax model, the investment and as much of the core as possible were removed, and the casting process was complete. Finally, the individually cast pieces were fitted together and soldered, surface imperfections smoothed, eyes inlaid, teeth and eyelashes added, attributes such as spears and wreaths provided, and so forth. Bronze statues were costly to make and highly prized.

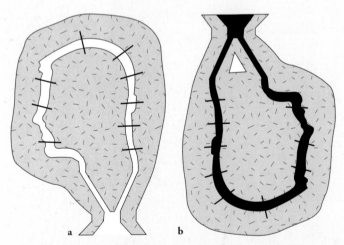

5-36 Two stages of the lost-wax method of bronze casting (after Sean A. Hemingway).

Drawing *a* shows a clay mold (investment), wax model, and clay core connected by chaplets. Drawing *b* shows the wax melted out and the molten bronze poured into the mold to form the cast bronze head.

5-37 Charioteer, from a group dedicated by Polyzalos of Gela in the sanctuary of Apollo, Delphi, Greece, ca. 475 BCE. Bronze, 5′ 11″ high. Archaeological Museum, Delphi.

The charioteer is almost all that remains of a large bronze group that also included a chariot, a team of horses, and a groom, requiring hundreds of individually cast pieces soldered together.

1 ft.

Statues," page 108), and FIG. 5-36), with inlaid eyes, silver teeth and eyelashes, and copper lips and nipples (FIG. I-17). The weight shift is more pronounced than in the *Kritios Boy*. The warrior's head turns more forcefully to the right, his shoulders tilt, his hips swing more markedly, and his arms have been freed from the body. Natural motion in space has replaced Archaic frontality and rigidity.

CHARIOTEER OF DELPHI The high technical quality of the Riace warrior is equaled in another bronze statue set up a decade or two earlier to commemorate the victory of the tyrant Polyzalos of Gela (Sicily) in a chariot race at Delphi. The statue (FIG. 5-37) is almost all that remains of a large group composed of Polyzalos's driver, the chariot, the team of horses, and a young groom. The charioteer stands in an almost Archaic pose, but the turn of the head and feet in opposite directions as well as a slight twist at the waist are in keeping with the Severe Style. The moment chosen for depiction is not during the frenetic race but after, when the driver quietly and modestly holds his horses still in the winner's circle. He grasps the reins in his outstretched right hand (the lower left arm, cast separately, is missing), and he wears the standard charioteer's garment,

girdled high and held in at the shoulders and the back to keep it from flapping. The folds emphasize both the verticality and calm of the figure and recall the flutes of a Greek column. A band inlaid with silver, tied around the head, confines the hair. Delicate bronze lashes shade the eyes made of glass paste.

ARTEMISION ZEUS The male human form in motion is, in contrast, the subject of another Early Classical bronze statue (FIG. 5-38), which, like the Riace warrior, divers found in an ancient shipwreck, this time off the coast of Greece itself at Cape Artemision. The bearded god once hurled a weapon held in his right hand, probably a thunderbolt, in which case he is Zeus. A less likely suggestion is that this is Poseidon with his trident. The pose could be employed equally well for a javelin thrower. Both arms are boldly extended, and the right heel is raised off the ground, underscoring the lightness and stability of hollow-cast monumental statues.

MYRON, *DISKOBOLOS* A bronze statue similar to the Artemision Zeus was the renowned *Diskobolos* (*Discus Thrower*) by the Early Classical master MYRON. The original is lost. Only marble copies (FIG. 5-39) survive, made in Roman times, when demand so

5-38 Zeus (or Poseidon?), from the sea off Cape Artemision, Greece, ca. 460–450 BCE. Bronze, 6′ 10″ high. National Archaeological Museum, Athens.

In this Early Classical statue of Zeus hurling a thunderbolt, both arms are boldly extended and the right heel is raised off the ground, underscoring the lightness and stability of hollow-cast bronze statues.

5-39 MYRON, *Diskobolos* (*Discus Thrower*). Roman marble copy of a bronze original of ca. 450 BCE, 5′ 1″ high. Museo Nazionale Romano–Palazzo Massimo alle Terme.

This marble copy of Myron's lost bronze statue captures how the sculptor froze the action of discus throwing and arranged the nude athlete's body and limbs so that they formed two intersecting arcs.

Early and High Classical Periods **109**

Polykleitos's Prescription
for the Perfect Statue

One of the most influential philosophers of the ancient world was Pythagoras of Samos, who lived during the latter part of the sixth century BCE. A famous geometric theorem still bears his name. Pythagoras also is said to have discovered that harmonic chords in music are produced on the strings of a lyre at regular intervals that may be expressed as ratios of whole numbers—2:1, 3:2, 4:3. He and his followers, the Pythagoreans, believed more generally that underlying harmonic proportions could be found in all of nature, determining the form of the cosmos as well as of things on earth, and that beauty resided in harmonious numerical ratios.

By this reasoning, a perfect statue would be one constructed according to an all-encompassing mathematical formula. In the midfifth century BCE, the sculptor Polykleitos of Argos set out to make just such a statue (FIG. 5-40). He recorded the principles he followed and the proportions he used in a treatise titled the *Canon* (that is, the standard of perfection). His treatise is unfortunately lost, but Galen, a physician who lived during the second century CE, summarized the sculptor's philosophy as follows:

> [Beauty arises from] the commensurability [*symmetria*] of the parts, such as that of finger to finger, and of all the fingers to the palm and the wrist, and of these to the forearm, and of the forearm to the upper arm, and, in fact, of everything to everything else, just as it is written in the *Canon* of Polykleitos. . . . Polykleitos supported his treatise [by making] a statue according to the tenets of his treatise, and called the statue, like the work, the *Canon*.*

This is why Pliny the Elder, writing in the first century CE, maintained that Polykleitos "alone of men is deemed to have rendered art itself [that is, the theoretical basis of art] in a work of art."[†]

Polykleitos's belief that a successful statue resulted from the precise application of abstract principles is reflected in an anecdote (probably a later invention) told by the Roman historian Aelian:

> Polykleitos made two statues at the same time, one which would be pleasing to the crowd and the other according to the principles of his art. In accordance with the opinion of each person who came into his workshop, he altered something and changed its form, submitting to the advice of each. Then he put both statues on display. The one was marvelled at by everyone, and the other was laughed at. Thereupon Polykleitos said, "But the one that you find fault with, you made yourselves; while the one that you marvel at, I made."[‡]

5-40 POLYKLEITOS, *Doryphoros* (*Spear Bearer*). Roman marble copy from Pompeii, Italy, after a bronze original of ca. 450–440 BCE, 6′ 11″ high. Museo Archeologico Nazionale, Naples.

Polykleitos sought to portray the perfect man and to impose order on human movement. He achieved his goals by employing harmonic proportions and a system of cross balance for all parts of the body.

1 ft.

*Galen, *De placitis Hippocratis et Platonis*, 5. Translated by J. J. Pollitt, *The Art of Ancient Greece: Sources and Documents* (New York: Cambridge University Press, 1990), 76.
†Pliny the Elder, *Natural History*, 34.55. Translated by Pollitt, 75.
‡Aelian, *Varia historia*, 14.8. Translated by Pollitt, 79.

far exceeded the supply of Greek statues that a veritable industry was born to meet the call for Greek statuary to display in public places and private villas alike. The copies usually were made in less costly marble. The change in medium resulted in a different surface appearance. In most cases, the copyist also had to add an intrusive tree trunk to support the great weight of the stone statue and struts between arms and body to strengthen weak points. The copies rarely approach the quality of the originals, and the Roman sculptors sometimes took liberties with their models to conform to their own tastes and needs. Occasionally, for example, a mirror image of the

original was created for a specific setting. Nevertheless, the copies are indispensable today. Without them it would be impossible to reconstruct the history of Greek sculpture after the Archaic period.

Myron's *Diskobolos* is a vigorous action statue, like the Artemision Zeus, but it is composed in an almost Archaic manner, with profile limbs and a nearly frontal chest, suggesting the tension of a coiled spring. Like the arm of a pendulum clock, the right arm of the *Diskobolos* has reached the apex of its arc but has not yet begun to swing down again. Myron froze the action and arranged the body and limbs to form two intersecting arcs (one from the discus to the left hand, one from the head to the right knee), creating the impression of a tightly stretched bow a moment before the string is released. This tension is not, however, mirrored in the athlete's face, which remains expressionless. Once again, as in the warrior statue (FIG. 5-29) from the Aegina temple's east pediment, the head is turned away from the spectator. In contrast to Archaic athlete statues, the Classical *Diskobolos* does not perform for the spectator but concentrates on the task at hand.

POLYKLEITOS, *DORYPHOROS* One of the most frequently copied Greek statues was the *Doryphoros* (*Spear Bearer*) by the sculptor POLYKLEITOS, whose work epitomizes the intellectual rigor of Classical art. The best marble replica (FIG. 5-40) stood in a palaestra at Pompeii, where it served as a model for Roman athletes. The *Doryphoros* was the embodiment of Polykleitos's vision of the ideal statue of a nude male athlete or warrior. In fact, the sculptor made it as a demonstration piece to accompany a treatise on the subject. *Spear Bearer* is a modern descriptive title for the statue. The name Polykleitos assigned to it was *Canon* (see "Polykleitos's Prescription for the Perfect Statue," page 110).

The *Doryphoros* is the culmination of the evolution in Greek statuary from the Archaic kouros to the *Kritios Boy* to the Riace warrior. The contrapposto is more pronounced than ever before in a standing statue, but Polykleitos was not content with simply rendering a figure that stood naturally. His aim was to impose order on human movement, to make it "beautiful," to "perfect" it. He achieved this through a system of cross balance. What appears at first to be a casually natural pose is, in fact, the result of an extremely complex and subtle organization of the figure's various parts. Note, for instance, how the statue's straight-hanging arm echoes the rigid supporting leg, providing the figure's right side with the columnar stability needed to anchor the left side's dynamically flexed limbs. If read anatomically, however, the tensed and relaxed limbs may be seen to oppose each other diagonally—the right arm and the left leg are relaxed, and the tensed supporting leg opposes the flexed arm, which held a spear. In like manner, the head turns to the right while the hips twist slightly to the left. And although the *Doryphoros* seems to take a step forward, the figure does not move. This dynamic asymmetrical balance, this motion while at rest, and the resulting harmony of opposites are the essence of the Polykleitan style.

The Athenian Acropolis

While Polykleitos was formulating his *Canon* in Argos, the Athenians, under the leadership of Pericles, were at work on one of the most ambitious building projects ever undertaken, the reconstruction of the Acropolis after the Persian sack of 480 BCE. Athens, despite the damage it suffered at the hands of the army of Xerxes, emerged from the war with enormous power and prestige. The Athenian commander Themistocles had decisively defeated the Persian navy off the island of Salamis, southwest of Athens, and forced it to retreat to Asia.

In 478 BCE, in the aftermath of the Persians' expulsion from the Aegean, the Greeks formed an alliance for mutual protection against any renewed threat from the east. The new confederacy came to be known as the Delian League, because its headquarters were on the sacred island of Delos, midway between the Greek mainland and the coast of Asia Minor. Although at the outset each league member had an equal vote, Athens was "first among equals," providing the allied fleet commander and determining which cities were to furnish ships and which were instead to pay an annual tribute to the treasury at Delos. Continued fighting against the Persians kept the alliance intact, but Athens gradually assumed a dominant role. In 454 BCE the Delian treasury was transferred to Athens, ostensibly for security rea-

sons. Pericles, who was only in his teens when the Persians laid waste to the Acropolis, was by midcentury the recognized leader of the Athenians, and he succeeded in converting the alliance into an Athenian empire. Tribute continued to be paid, but the surplus reserves were not expended for the common good of the allied Greek states. Instead, Pericles expropriated the money to pay the enormous cost of executing his grand plan to embellish the Acropolis of Athens.

The reaction of the allies—in reality the subjects of Athens—was predictable. Plutarch, who wrote a biography of Pericles in the early second century CE, indicated the wrath the Greek victims of Athenian tyranny felt by recording the protest voiced against Pericles' decision even in the Athenian assembly. Greece, Pericles' enemies said, had been dealt "a terrible, wanton insult" when Athens used the funds contributed out of necessity for a common war effort to "gild and embellish itself with images and extravagant temples, like some pretentious woman decked out with precious stones."[1] The source of funds for the Acropolis building program is important to keep in mind when examining those great and universally admired buildings erected in accordance with Pericles' vision of his polis reborn from the ashes of the Persian sack. They are not the glorious fruits of Athenian democracy but are instead the by-products of tyranny and the abuse of power. Too often art and architectural historians do not ask how a monument was financed. The answer can be very revealing—and very embarrassing.

PORTRAIT OF PERICLES A number of Roman copies are preserved of a famous portrait statue of Pericles by KRESILAS, who was born on Crete but who worked in Athens. The bronze portrait was set up on the Acropolis, probably immediately after the leader's death in 429 BCE, and depicted Pericles in heroic nudity. The statue must have resembled the Riace warrior (FIG. 5-35). The copies, in marble, reproduce the head only, sometimes in the form of a *herm* (a bust on a square pillar, FIG. 5-41), a popular format in Roman times

5-41 KRESILAS, Pericles. Roman marble herm copy of a bronze original of ca. 429 BCE. Full herm 6′ high; detail 4′ 6½″ high. Musei Vaticani, Rome.

In his portrait of Pericles, Kresilas was said to have made a noble man appear even nobler. Classical Greek portraits were not likenesses but idealized images in which humans appeared godlike.

for abbreviated copies of famous statues. The herm is inscribed "Pericles, son of Xanthippos, the Athenian," leaving no doubt as to the identification. Pericles wears the helmet of a *strategos* (general), the position he was elected to 15 times. The Athenian leader was said to have had an abnormally elongated skull, and Kresilas recorded this feature (while also concealing it) by providing a glimpse through the helmet's eye slots of the hair at the top of the head. This, together with the unblemished features of Pericles' Classically aloof face and, no doubt, his body's perfect physique, led Pliny to assert that Kresilas had the ability to make noble men appear even more noble in their portraits. This praise was apt because the Pericles herm is not a portrait at all in the modern sense of a record of actual features. Pliny referred to Kresilas's "portrait" as "the Olympian Pericles," for in this image Pericles appeared almost godlike.[2]

PERICLEAN ACROPOLIS The centerpiece of the Periclean building program on the Acropolis (FIG. **5-42**) was the Parthenon (FIG. **5-43**, no. 1), or the Temple of Athena Parthenos, erected in the remarkably short period between 447 and 438 BCE. (Work on the great temple's ambitious sculptural ornamentation continued until 432 BCE.) As soon as the Parthenon was completed, construction commenced on a grand new gateway to the Acropolis from the west (the only accessible side of the natural plateau), the Propylaia (FIG. 5-43, no. 2). Begun in 437 BCE, it was left unfinished in 431 at the outbreak of the Peloponnesian War between Athens and Sparta. Two later temples, the Erechtheion (FIG. 5-43, no. 4) and the Temple of Athena Nike (FIG. 5-43, no. 5), built after Pericles died, were probably also part of the original design. The greatest Athenian architects and sculptors of the Classical period focused their attention on the construction and decoration of these four buildings.

That these fifth-century BCE buildings exist at all today is something of a miracle. In the Middle Ages, the Parthenon, for example, was converted into a Byzantine and later a Roman Catholic church and then, after the Ottoman conquest of Greece, into a mosque. Each time the building was remodeled for a different religion, it was modified structurally. The Christians early on removed the colossal statue of Athena inside. The churches had a great curved *apse* at the east end

housing the altar, and the mosque had a *minaret* (tower used to call Muslims to prayer). In 1687 the Venetians besieged the Acropolis, which at that time was in Turkish hands. Venetian weaponry scored a direct hit on the ammunition depot the Turks had installed in part of the Parthenon. The resultant explosion blew out the building's center. To make matters worse, the Venetians subsequently tried to remove some of the statues from the Parthenon's pediments. In more than one case, they dropped statues, which then smashed on the ground. From 1801 to 1803, Lord Elgin brought most of the surviving sculptures to England. For the past two centuries they have been on exhibit in the British Museum (FIGS. 5-47 to 5-50), although Greece has appealed many times for the return of the "Elgin Marbles." Today, a uniquely modern blight threatens the Parthenon and the other buildings of the Periclean age. The corrosive emissions of factories and automobiles are decomposing the ancient marbles. A major campaign has been under way for decades to protect the columns and walls from further deterioration. What little original sculpture remained in place when modern restoration began, the Greeks transferred to the Acropolis Museum's climate-controlled rooms.

PARTHENON: ARCHITECTURE Despite the ravages of time and humanity, most of the Parthenon's peripteral colonnade (FIG. **5-44**) is still standing (or has been reerected), and art historians know a great deal about the building and its sculptural program. The architects were IKTINOS and KALLIKRATES. The statue of Athena (FIG. 5-46) in the cella was the work of PHIDIAS, who was also the overseer of the temple's sculptural decoration. In fact, Plutarch claimed that Phidias was in charge of the entire Acropolis project.

Just as the contemporary *Doryphoros* (FIG. 5-40) may be seen as the culmination of nearly two centuries of searching for the ideal proportions of the various human body parts, so, too, the Parthenon may be viewed as the ideal solution to the Greek architect's quest for perfect proportions in Doric temple design. Its well-spaced columns, with their slender shafts, and the capitals, with their straight-sided conical echinuses, are the ultimate refinement of the bulging and squat Doric columns and compressed capitals of the Archaic Hera temple at Paestum (FIG. 5-15). The Parthenon architects and Poly-

5-42 Aerial view of the Acropolis looking southeast, Athens, Greece.

Under the leadership of Pericles, the Athenians undertook the costly project of reconstructing the Acropolis after the Persian sack of 480 BCE. The funds came from the Delian League treasury.

5-43 Restored view of the Acropolis, Athens, Greece (John Burge). (1) **Parthenon,** (2) **Propylaia,** (3) **pinakotheke,** (4) **Erechtheion,** (5) **Temple of Athena Nike.**

Of the four main fifth-century BCE buildings on the Acropolis, the first to be erected was the Parthenon, followed by the Propylaia, the Erechtheion, and the Temple of Athena Nike.

kleitos were kindred spirits in their belief that beautiful proportions resulted from strict adherence to harmonious numerical ratios, whether in a temple more than 200 feet long or a life-size statue of a nude man. For the Parthenon, the controlling ratio for the *symmetria* of the parts may be expressed algebraically as $x = 2y + 1$. Thus, for example, the temple's short ends have 8 columns and the long sides have 17, because $17 = (2 \times 8) + 1$. The stylobate's ratio of length to width is 9:4, because $9 = (2 \times 4) + 1$. This ratio also characterizes the cella's proportion of length to width, the distance between the centers of two adjacent column drums (the *interaxial*) in proportion to the columns' diameter, and so forth.

The Parthenon's harmonious design and the mathematical precision of the sizes of its constituent elements tend to obscure the fact that this temple, as actually constructed, is quite irregular in shape. Throughout the building are pronounced deviations from the strictly horizontal and vertical lines assumed to be the basis of all Greek post-and-lintel structures. The stylobate, for example, curves upward at the center on the sides and both facades, forming a kind of shallow dome, and this curvature is carried up into the entablature. Moreover, the peristyle columns lean inward slightly. Those at the corners have a diagonal inclination and are also about two inches thicker than the rest. If their lines continued, they would meet about 1.5 miles above the temple. These deviations from the norm meant that virtually every Parthenon block and drum had to be carved according to the special set of specifications dictated by its unique place in the structure. This was obviously a daunting task, and a reason must have existed for these so-called refinements in the Parthenon. Some modern observers note, for example, how the curving of horizontal lines and the tilting of vertical ones create a dynamic balance in the building—a kind of architectural contrapposto—and give it a greater sense of life. The oldest recorded explanation, however, may be the most likely. Vitruvius, a Roman architect of the late first century BCE who claimed to have had access to Iktinos's treatise on the Parthenon—again note the kinship with the *Canon* of Polykleitos—maintained that the builders made these adjustments to compensate for optical illusions. Vitruvius noted, for example, that if a stylobate is laid out on a level surface, it will appear to sag at the center, and that the corner columns of a building should be thicker because they are surrounded by light and would otherwise appear thinner than their neighbors.

The Parthenon is "irregular" in other ways as well. One of the ironies of this most famous of all Doric temples is that it is "contaminated" by Ionic elements (FIG. 5-45). Although the cella had a two-story Doric colonnade, the back room (which housed the goddess's treasury and the tribute collected from the Delian League) had four

5-44 IKTINOS and KALLIKRATES, Parthenon (Temple of Athena Parthenos, looking southeast), Acropolis, Athens, Greece, 447–438 BCE.

The architects of the Parthenon believed that perfect beauty could be achieved by using harmonic proportions. The ratio for larger and smaller parts was $x = 2y + 1$ (for example, a plan of 17 × 8 columns).

5-45 Plan of the Parthenon, Acropolis, Athens, Greece, with diagram of the sculptural program (after Andrew Stewart), 447–432 BCE.

The Parthenon was lavishly decorated under the direction of Phidias. Statues filled both pediments, and figural reliefs adorned all 92 metopes. There was also an inner 524-foot sculptured Ionic frieze.

in turn, dictated the width of the facade—eight columns at a time when six columns were the norm.

Athena was fully armed with shield, spear, and helmet, and she held Nike (the winged female personification of Victory) in her extended right hand. No one doubts that this Nike referred to the victory of 479 BCE. The memory of the Persian sack of the Acropolis was still vivid, and the Athenians were intensely conscious that by driving back the Persians, they were saving their civilization from the eastern "barbarians" who had committed atrocities at Miletos. In fact, the *Athena Parthenos* had multiple allusions to the Persian defeat. On the thick soles of Athena's sandals was a representation of a centauromachy. The exterior of her shield was emblazoned with high reliefs depicting the battle of Greeks and Amazons (*Amazonomachy*), in which Theseus drove the Amazons out of Athens. And Phidias painted a gigantomachy on the shield's interior. Each of these mythological contests was a metaphor for the triumph of order over chaos, of civilization over barbarism, and of Athens over Persia.

PARTHENON: METOPES Phidias took up these same themes again in the Parthenon's Doric metopes (FIG. 5-45). The best-preserved metopes—although the paint on these and all the other Parthenon marbles long ago disappeared—are those of the south side, which depicted the battle of Lapiths and centaurs, a combat in which Theseus of Athens played a major role. On one extraordinary slab (FIG. 5-47), a triumphant centaur rises up on its hind legs, exulting over the crumpled body of the Greek it has defeated. The relief is so high that parts are fully in the round. Some have broken off. The sculptor knew how to distinguish the vibrant, powerful form of the living beast from the lifeless corpse on the ground. In other metopes the Greeks have the upper

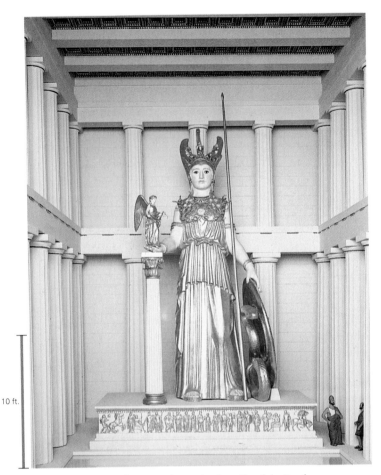

5-46 PHIDIAS, *Athena Parthenos*, in the cella of the Parthenon, Acropolis, Athens, Greece, ca. 438 BCE. Model of the lost chryselephantine statue. Royal Ontario Museum, Toronto.

Inside the cella of the Parthenon was Phidias's 38-foot-tall gold-and-ivory statue of Athena Parthenos (the Virgin), fully armed and holding Nike (Victory) in her extended right hand.

tall and slender Ionic columns as sole supports for the superstructure. And whereas the temple's exterior had a canonical Doric frieze, the inner frieze that ran around the top of the cella wall was Ionic. Perhaps this fusion of Doric and Ionic elements reflects the Athenians' belief that the Ionians of the Aegean Islands and Asia Minor were descended from Athenian settlers and were therefore their kin. Or it may be Pericles' and Iktinos's way of suggesting that Athens was the leader of *all* the Greeks. In any case, a mix of Doric and Ionic features characterizes the fifth-century BCE buildings of the Acropolis as a whole.

ATHENA PARTHENOS The costly decision to incorporate two sculptured friezes in the Parthenon's design is symptomatic. This Pentelic-marble temple was more lavishly adorned than any Greek temple before it, Doric or Ionic. Every one of the 92 Doric metopes was decorated with relief sculpture. So, too, was every inch of the 524-foot-long Ionic frieze. The two pediments were filled with dozens of larger-than-life-size statues. And inside was the most expensive item of all—Phidias's gold-and-ivory (*chryselephantine*) statue of *Athena Parthenos*, the Virgin. Art historians know a great deal about Phidias's lost statue from descriptions by Greek and Latin authors and from Roman copies. A model (FIG. 5-46) gives a good idea of its appearance and setting. Athena stood 38 feet tall, and to a large extent the Parthenon was designed around her. To accommodate the statue's huge size, the cella had to be wider than usual. This,

5-47 Lapith versus centaur, metope from the south side of the Parthenon, Acropolis, Athens, Greece, ca. 447–438 BCE. Marble, 4′ 8″ high. British Museum, London.

The Parthenon's centauromachy metopes allude to the Greek defeat of the Persians. The sculptor of this metope knew how to distinguish the vibrant living centaur from the lifeless Greek corpse.

hand, but the full set suggests that the battle was a difficult one against a dangerous enemy and that losses as well as victories occurred. The same was true of the war against the Persians.

PARTHENON: PEDIMENTS The subjects of the two pediments were especially appropriate for a temple that celebrated Athena—and the Athenians. The east pediment depicted the birth of the goddess. At the west was the contest between Athena and Poseidon to determine which one would become the city's patron deity. Athena won, giving her name to the polis and its citizens. It is significant that in the story and in the pediment the Athenians are the judges of the relative merits of the two gods. The choice of theme reflects the same arrogance that led to the Athenians' use of Delian League funds to adorn the Acropolis.

The center of the east pediment was damaged when the apse was added to the Parthenon at the time of its conversion into a church. What remains are the spectators to the left and the right who witnessed Athena's birth on Mount Olympus. At the far left (FIG. 5-48) are the head and arms of Helios (the Sun) and his chariot horses rising from the pediment floor. Next to them is a powerful male figure usually identified as Dionysos or possibly Herakles, who entered the realm of the gods on completion of his 12 labors. At the right (FIG.

5-49) are three goddesses, probably Hestia, Dione, and Aphrodite, and either Selene (the Moon) or Nyx (Night) and more horses, this time sinking below the pediment's floor. Here, Phidias, who designed the composition even if his assistants executed it, discovered an entirely new way to deal with the awkward triangular frame of the pediment. Its bottom line is the horizon line, and charioteers and their horses move through it effortlessly. The individual figures, even the animals, are brilliantly characterized. The horses of the Sun, at the beginning of the day, are energetic. Those of the Moon or Night, having labored until dawn, are weary. The reclining figures fill the space beneath the raking cornice beautifully. Dionysos/Herakles and Aphrodite in the lap of her mother Dione are monumental Olympian presences yet totally relaxed organic forms. The sculptors fully understood not only the surface appearance of human anatomy, both male and female, but also the mechanics of how muscles and bones make the body move. The Phidian school also mastered the rendition of clothed forms. In the Dione-Aphrodite group, the thin and heavy folds of the garments alternately reveal and conceal the main and lesser body masses while swirling in a compositional tide that subtly unifies the two figures. The articulation and integration of the bodies produce a wonderful variation of surface and play of light and shade.

5-48 Helios and his horses, and Dionysos (Herakles?), from the east pediment of the Parthenon, Acropolis, Athens, Greece, ca. 438–432 BCE. Marble, greatest height 4′ 3″. British Museum, London.

The east pediment of the Parthenon depicts the birth of Athena. At the left, the horses of Helios (the Sun) emerge from the pediment's floor, suggesting the sun rising above the horizon at dawn.

5-49 Three goddesses (Hestia, Dione, and Aphrodite?), from the east pediment of the Parthenon, Acropolis, Athens, Greece, ca. 438–432 BCE. Marble, greatest height 4′ 5″. British Museum, London.

The statues of Hestia, Dione, and Aphrodite conform perfectly to the sloping right side of the east pediment. The thin and heavy folds of the garments alternately reveal and conceal the body forms.

PARTHENON: IONIC FRIEZE In many ways the most remarkable part of the Parthenon's sculptural program is the inner Ionic frieze (FIG. 5-50). Scholars still debate its subject, but most agree that it represents the Panathenaic Festival procession that took place every four years in Athens. If this identification is correct, the Athenians judged themselves fit for inclusion in the temple's sculptural decoration. It is another example of the extraordinarily high opinion the Athenians had of their own worth.

The procession began at the Dipylon Gate, passed through the agora (central square), and ended on the Acropolis, where the Athenians placed a new peplos on an ancient wooden statue of Athena. That statue (probably similar in general appearance to the *Lady of Auxerre*, FIG. 5-7) was housed in the Archaic temple the Persians razed in 480 BCE. The statue had been removed from the Acropolis before the Persian attack for security reasons, and eventually it was installed in the Erechtheion (FIG. 5-53, no. 1). On the Parthenon frieze the procession begins on the west, that is, at the temple's rear, the side facing the gateway to the Acropolis. It then proceeds in parallel lines down the long north and south sides of the building and ends at the center of the east frieze, over the doorway to the cella housing Phidias's statue of Athena. It is noteworthy that the upper part of the frieze is in higher relief than the lower part so that the more distant and more shaded upper zone is as legible from the ground as the lower part of the frieze. This is another instance of the architects' taking optical effects into consideration.

The frieze vividly communicates the procession's acceleration and deceleration. At the outset, on the west side, marshals gather and youths mount their horses. On the north (FIG. 5-50, *top*) and south, the momentum picks up as the cavalcade moves from the lower town to the Acropolis, accompanied by chariots, musicians, jar carriers, and animals destined for sacrifice. On the east, seated gods and goddesses (FIG. 5-50, *center*), the invited guests, watch the procession slow almost to a halt (FIG. 5-50, *bottom*) as it nears its goal at the shrine of Athena's ancient wooden idol. Most remarkable of all is the role assigned to the Olympian deities. They do not take part in the festival or determine its outcome but are merely spectators. Aphrodite, in fact, extends her left arm to draw her son Eros's attention to the Athenians, just as today a parent at a parade would point out important people to a child. And the Athenian people *were* important—

5-50 Details of the Panathenaic Festival procession frieze, from the Parthenon, Acropolis, Athens, Greece, ca. 447–438 BCE. Marble, 3′ 6″ high. Horsemen of north frieze (*top*), British Museum, London; seated gods and goddesses (Poseidon, Apollo, and Artemis) of east frieze (*center*), Acropolis Museum, Athens; and elders and maidens of east frieze (*bottom*), Louvre, Paris.

The Parthenon's Ionic frieze represents the procession of citizens on horseback and on foot that took place every four years under the watchful eyes of the gods. The temple celebrated the Athenians as much as Athena.

Mnesikles disguised the change of ground level by splitting the Propylaia into eastern and western sections. Each facade resembles a Doric temple but with a wider space between the central columns.

western sections (FIG. 5-43, no. 2), each one resembling a Doric temple facade. Practical considerations dictated that the space between the central pair of columns on each side be enlarged. This was the path the chariots and animals of the Panathenaic Festival procession took, and they required a wide ramped causeway. To either side of the central ramp were stairs for pedestrian traffic. Inside, tall, slender Ionic columns supported the split-level roof. Once again an Athenian architect mixed the two orders on the Acropolis. But as with the Parthenon, he used the Doric order for the stately exterior and the Ionic only for the interior.

Mnesikles' full plan for the Propylaia was never executed because of a change in the fortunes of Athens after the outbreak of the Peloponnesian War in 431 BCE. Of the side wings that were part of the original project, only the northwest one (FIG. 5-43, no. 3) was completed. That wing is of special importance in the history of art. In Roman times it housed a *pinakotheke* (picture gallery). In it were displayed paintings on wooden panels by some of the major artists of the fifth century BCE. It is uncertain whether this was the wing's original function. If it was, the Propylaia's pinakotheke is the first recorded structure built for the specific purpose of displaying paintings, and it is the forerunner of modern museums.

ERECHTHEION In 421 BCE work finally began on the temple that was to replace the Archaic Athena temple the Persians had destroyed. The new structure, the Erechtheion (FIGS. 5-52 and

self-important, some might say. They were the masters of an empire, and in Pericles' famous funeral oration he painted a picture of Athens that elevated its citizens almost to the stature of gods. The Parthenon celebrated the greatness of Athens and the Athenians as much as it honored Athena.

PROPYLAIA Even before all the sculpture was in place on the Parthenon, work began on a new monumental entrance to the Acropolis, the Propylaia (FIG. 5-51). The architect entrusted with this important commission was MNESIKLES. The site was a difficult one, on a steep slope, but Mnesikles succeeded in disguising the change in ground level by splitting the building into eastern and

5-52 Erechtheion (looking northwest), Acropolis, Athens, Greece, ca. 421–405 BCE.

The Erechtheion is in many ways the antithesis of the Doric Parthenon directly across from it. An Ionic temple, it has some of the finest decorative details of any ancient Greek building.

1. Shrine housing wooden image of Athena
2. Athena's olive tree
3. Poseidon's trident mark
4. Ruins of Archaic temple

N

5-53 Plan of the Erechtheion, Acropolis, Athens, Greece, ca. 421–405 BCE.

The asymmetrical form of the Erechtheion is unique for a Greek temple. It reflects the need to incorporate preexisting shrines into the plan, including those of the kings Erechtheus and Kekrops.

5-54 Caryatid from the south porch of the Erechtheion, Acropolis, Athens, Greece, ca. 421–405 BCE. Marble, 7′ 7″ high. British Museum, London.

The south porch of the Erechtheion features caryatids, updated Classical versions with contrapposto stances of the Archaic caryatids of the porch of the Siphnian Treasury (FIG. 5-18) at Delphi.

1 ft.

5-53), built to the north of the old temple's remains, was, however, to be a multiple shrine. It honored Athena and housed the ancient wooden image of the goddess that was the goal of the Panathenaic Festival procession. But it also incorporated shrines to a host of other gods and demigods who loomed large in the city's legendary past. Among these were Erechtheus, an early king of Athens, during whose reign the ancient wooden idol of Athena was said to have fallen from the heavens, and Kekrops, another king of Athens, who served as judge of the contest between Athena and Poseidon. In fact, the site chosen for the new temple was the very spot where that contest occurred. Poseidon had staked his claim to Athens by striking the Acropolis rock with his trident and producing a salt-water spring. The imprint of his trident remained for Athenians of the historical period to see. Nearby, Athena had miraculously caused an olive tree to grow. This tree still stood as a constant reminder of her victory over Poseidon.

The asymmetrical plan (FIG. 5-53) of the Ionic Erechtheion is unique for a Greek temple and the antithesis of the simple and harmoniously balanced plan of the Doric Parthenon across the way. Its irregular form reflected the need to incorporate the tomb of Kekrops and other preexisting shrines, the trident mark, and the olive tree into a single complex. The unknown architect responsible for the building also had to struggle with the problem of uneven terrain. The area could not be made level by terracing because that would disturb the ancient sacred sites. As a result, the Erechtheion has four sides of very different character, and each side rests on a different ground level.

Perhaps to compensate for the awkward character of the building as a whole, the architect took great care with the Erechtheion's decorative details. The frieze, for example, was given special treat-

ment. The stone chosen was the dark-blue limestone of Eleusis to contrast with the white Pentelic marble of the walls and columns and the marble relief figures attached to the dark frieze. But the temple's most striking and famous feature is its south porch, where cary-

5-55 KALLIKRATES, Temple of Athena Nike (looking southwest), Acropolis, Athens, Greece, ca. 427–424 BCE.

The Ionic temple at the entrance to the Acropolis is an unusual amphiprostyle building. It celebrated Athena as bringer of victory, and one of the friezes depicts the Persian defeat at Marathon.

atids (FIG. 5-54) replaced Ionic columns, as they did a century earlier on the Ionic Siphnian Treasury (FIG. 5-18) at Delphi. The Delphi caryatids resemble Archaic korai, and their Classical counterparts equally characteristically look like Phidian-era statues. Although they exhibit the weight shift that was standard for the fifth century BCE, the role of the caryatids as architectural supports for the unusual flat roof is underscored by the vertical flutelike drapery folds concealing their stiff, weight-bearing legs. The Classical architect-sculptor successfully balanced the dual and contradictory functions of these female statue-columns. The figures have enough rigidity to suggest the structural column and just the degree of flexibility needed to suggest the living body.

TEMPLE OF ATHENA NIKE Another Ionic building on the Athenian Acropolis is the little Temple of Athena Nike (FIG. 5-55), designed by Kallikrates, who worked with Iktinos on the Parthenon (and perhaps was responsible for the Ionic elements of that Doric temple). The temple is amphiprostyle with four columns on both the east and west facades. It stands on what used to be a Mycenaean bastion near the Propylaia and greets all visitors entering Athena's great sanctuary. As on the Parthenon, reference was made here to the victory over the Persians—and not just in the temple's name. Part of its frieze was devoted to a representation of the decisive battle at Marathon that turned the tide against the Persians—a human event, as in the Parthenon's Panathenaic Festival procession frieze. But now the sculptors chronicled a specific occasion, not a recurring event involving anonymous citizens.

Around the building, at the bastion's edge, was a *parapet* decorated with exquisite reliefs. The theme of the balustrade matched that of the temple proper—victory. Nike's image was repeated dozens of times, always in different attitudes, sometimes erecting trophies bedecked with Persian spoils and sometimes bringing for-

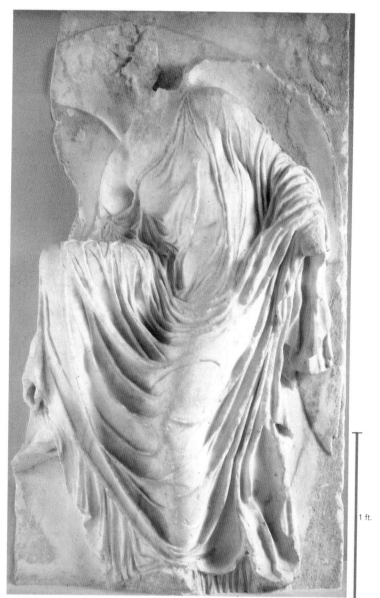

1 ft.

5-56 Nike adjusting her sandal, from the south side of the parapet of the Temple of Athena Nike, Acropolis, Athens, Greece, ca. 410 BCE. Marble, 3′ 6″ high. Acropolis Museum, Athens.

The image of winged Victory was repeated dozens of times on the parapet around the Athena Nike temple. Here, the sculptor carved a figure whose garments appear almost transparent.

ward sacrificial bulls to Athena. One relief (FIG. 5-56) shows Nike adjusting her sandal—an awkward posture that the sculptor rendered elegant and graceful. Here, the artist carried the style of the Parthenon pediments (FIG. 5-49) even further and created a figure whose garments cling so tightly to the body that they seem almost transparent, as if drenched with water. The sculptor was, however, interested in much more than revealing the supple beauty of the young female body. The drapery folds form intricate linear patterns unrelated to the body's anatomical structure and have a life of their own as abstract designs.

HEGESO STELE Although the decoration of the great building projects on the Acropolis must have occupied most of the finest sculptors of Athens in the second half of the fifth century BCE, other

The Hegeso Stele

In Geometric times, huge painted vases (FIG. 5-2) marked the graves of wealthy Athenians. In the Archaic period, kouroi (FIGS. 5-8 and 5-10) and, to a lesser extent, korai were placed over Greek burials, as were grave stelae ornamented with relief depictions of the deceased. The grave stele (FIG. 5-57) of Hegeso is in this tradition. It was erected at the end of the fifth or beginning of the fourth century BCE to commemorate the death of Hegeso, daughter of Proxenos. Both names are inscribed on the cornice of the pediment that crowns the stele. Antae at left and right complete the architectural framework.

Hegeso is the well-dressed woman seated on an elegant chair (with footstool). She examines a piece of jewelry (once rendered in paint, not now visible) selected from a box a servant girl brings to her. The maid's simple unbelted chiton contrasts sharply with the more elaborate attire of her mistress. The garments of both women reveal the body forms beneath them. The faces are serene, without a trace of sadness. Indeed, both mistress and maid are shown in a characteristic shared moment out of daily life. Only the epitaph reveals that Hegeso is the one who has departed.

The simplicity of the scene on the Hegeso stele is deceptive, however. This is not merely a bittersweet scene of tranquil domestic life before an untimely death. The setting itself is significant—the secluded women's quarters of a Greek house, from which Hegeso rarely would have emerged. Contemporary grave stelae of men regularly show them in the public domain, as warriors. And the servant girl is not so much the faithful companion of the deceased in life as she is Hegeso's possession, like the jewelry box. The slave girl may look solicitously at her mistress, but Hegeso has eyes only for her ornaments. Both slave and jewelry attest to the wealth of Hegeso's father, unseen but prominently cited in the epitaph. (It is noteworthy that the mother's name is not mentioned.) Indeed, even the jewelry box carries a deeper significance, for it probably represents the dowry Proxenos would have provided to his daughter's husband when she left her father's home to enter her husband's home. In the patriarchal society of ancient Greece, the dominant position of men is manifest even when only women are depicted.

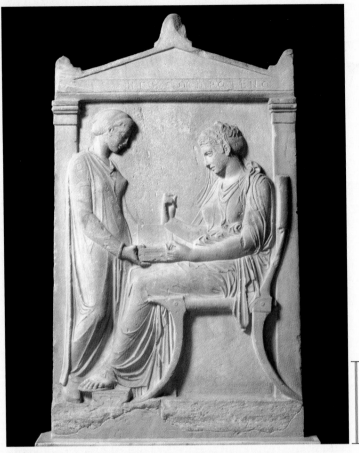

5-57 Grave stele of Hegeso, from the Dipylon cemetery, Athens, Greece, ca. 400 BCE. Marble, 5′ 2″ high. National Archaeological Museum, Athens.

On her tombstone, Hegeso examines jewelry from a box her servant girl holds. Mistress and maid share a serene moment of daily life. Only the epitaph reveals that Hegeso is the one who died.

commissions were available in the city, notably in the Dipylon cemetery. There, around 400 BCE, a beautiful and touching grave stele (FIG. 5-57) in the style of the Temple of Athena Nike parapet reliefs was set up in memory of a woman named Hegeso. Its subject—a young woman in her home, attended by her maid (see "The Hegeso Stele," above)—and its composition have close parallels in contemporary vase painting.

Painting

In the Classical period, some of the most renowned artists were the painters of monumental wooden panels displayed in public buildings, both secular and religious. Such works are by nature perishable, and all of the great panels of the masters are unfortunately lost. Nonetheless, one can get some idea of the polychrome nature of those panel paintings by studying Greek vases, especially those painted using the *white-ground* technique, which takes its name from the chalky-white clay slip used to provide a background for the painted figures. Experiments with white-ground painting date back to the Andokides Painter, but the method became popular only toward the middle of the fifth century BCE.

ACHILLES PAINTER One of the masters of white-ground painting was the so-called ACHILLES PAINTER, who decorated the *lekythos* (flask containing perfumed oil) in FIG. 5-58. White-ground is essentially a variation of the red-figure technique. First the painter covered the pot with a slip of very fine white clay, then applied black glaze to outline the figures and colored them with diluted brown, purple, red, and white. Other colors—for example, the yellow chosen for the garments of both figures on the Achilles Painter's lekythos—also could be employed, but these had to be applied after firing because the Greeks did not know how to make them withstand the heat of the kiln. Despite the obvious attractions of the technique, the impermanence of the expanded range of colors discouraged white-ground painting on everyday vessels, such as drinking cups and kraters. In fact, artists explored the full polychrome possibilities of the white-ground technique almost exclusively on lekythoi, which were commonly placed in Greek graves as offerings to the deceased. For vessels designed for short-term use, the fragile nature of white-ground painting was of little concern.

The Achilles Painter's lekythos is decorated with a scene appropriate for its funerary purpose. A youthful warrior takes leave of his

5-58 ACHILLES PAINTER, Warrior taking leave of his wife (Athenian white-ground lekythos), from Eretria, Greece, ca. 440 BCE. 1′ 5″ high. National Archaeological Museum, Athens.

White-ground painters applied the colors after firing because most colored glazes could not withstand the kiln's heat. The Achilles Painter here displayed his mastery at drawing an eye in profile.

wife. The red scarf, mirror, and jug hanging on the wall behind the woman indicate that the setting is the interior of their home. The motif of the seated woman is strikingly similar to that of Hegeso on her grave stele (FIG. 5-57), but here the woman is the survivor. It is her husband, preparing to go to war with helmet, shield, and spear, who will depart, never to return. On his shield is a large painted eye, roughly life-size. Greek shields often were decorated with devices such as the horrific face of snake-haired Medusa, intended to ward off evil spirits and frighten the enemy. This eye undoubtedly was meant to recall this tradition, but it was little more than an excuse for the Achilles Painter to display superior drawing skills. Since the

5-59 NIOBID PAINTER, Artemis and Apollo slaying the children of Niobe (Athenian red-figure calyx krater), from Orvieto, Italy, ca. 450 BCE. 1′ 9″ high. Louvre, Paris.

The placement of figures on different levels in a landscape on this red-figure krater depicting the massacre of Niobe's children reflects the compositions of the lost panel paintings of Polygnotos of Thasos.

late sixth century BCE, Greek painters had abandoned the Archaic habit of placing frontal eyes on profile faces and attempted to render the eyes in profile. The Achilles Painter's mastery of this difficult problem in foreshortening is on exhibit here.

POLYGNOTOS The leading painter of the first half of the fifth century BCE was Polygnotos of Thasos, whose works adorned important buildings both in Athens and Delphi. One of these was the pinakotheke of Mnesikles' Propylaia, but the most famous was a portico in the Athenian marketplace that came to be called the Stoa Poikile (Painted Stoa). Descriptions of Polygnotos's paintings make clear that he introduced a revolutionary compositional style. Before Polygnotos, figures stood on a common ground line at the bottom of the picture plane, whether they appeared in horizontal bands or single panels. Polygnotos placed his figures on different levels, staggered in tiers in the manner of Ashurbanipal's lion-hunt relief (FIG. 2-23) of two centuries before. He also incorporated landscape elements into his paintings, making his pictures true "windows onto the world" and not simply surface designs peopled with foreshortened figures. Polygnotos's abandonment of a single ground line was as momentous a break from the past as Early Classical Greek sculptors' rejection of frontality in statuary.

NIOBID PAINTER Polygnotos's influence is evident on a red-figure krater (FIG. 5-59) painted around the middle of the fifth century BCE by the NIOBID PAINTER—so named because one side of the krater depicts the massacre of the Niobids, the children of Niobe. Niobe, who had at least a dozen children, had boasted that she was superior to the goddess Leto, who had only two offspring, Apollo

5-60 PHIALE PAINTER, Hermes bringing the infant Dionysos to Papposilenos (Athenian white-ground calyx krater), from Vulci, Italy, ca. 440–435 BCE. 1′ 2″ high. Musei Vaticani, Rome.

In the Phiale Painter's white-ground representation of Hermes and the infant Dionysos at Nysa, the use of diluted brown to color and shade the rocks may also reflect the work of Polygnotos.

and Artemis. To punish Niobe's *hubris* (arrogance) and teach the lesson that no mortal could be superior to a god or goddess, Leto sent her two children to slay all of Niobe's many sons and daughters. On the Niobid Painter's krater, the horrible slaughter occurs in a schematic landscape setting of rocks and trees. The figures are disposed on several levels, and they actively interact with their setting. One slain son, for example, not only has fallen upon a rocky outcropping but is partially hidden by it. The Niobid Painter also drew the son's face in a three-quarter view, something that not even Euphronios and Euthymides had attempted.

PHIALE PAINTER Further insight into the appearance of monumental panel painting of the fifth century BCE comes from a white-ground krater (FIG. 5-60) by the so-called PHIALE PAINTER. The subject is Hermes handing over his half brother, the infant Dionysos, to Papposilenos ("grandpa-satyr"). The other figures represent the nymphs in the shady glens of Nysa, where Zeus had sent Dionysos, one of his numerous natural sons, to be raised, safe from the possible wrath of his wife Hera. Unlike the decorators of funerary lekythoi, the Phiale Painter used for this krater only colors that could survive the heat of a Greek kiln—reds, brown, purple, and a special snowy white reserved for the flesh of the nymphs and for such details as the hair, beard, and shaggy body of Papposilenos. The use of diluted brown wash to color and shade the rocks may reflect the coloration of Polygnotos's landscapes. This vase and the Niobid krater together provide a shadowy idea of the character and magnificence of Polygnotos's great paintings.

TOMB OF THE DIVER, PAESTUM Although all of the panel paintings of the masters disappeared long ago, some Greek mural paintings are preserved today. An early example is in the so-called Tomb of the Diver at Paestum. The four walls of this small, coffinlike tomb are decorated with banquet scenes such as appear

5-61 Youth diving, painted ceiling of the Tomb of the Diver, Paestum, Italy, ca. 480 BCE. 3′ 4″ high. Museo Archeologico Nazionale, Paestum.

This tomb in Italy is a rare example of Classical mural painting. The diving scene most likely symbolizes the deceased's plunge into the Underworld. The trees resemble those on the Niobid krater (FIG. 5-59).

regularly on Greek vases. On the tomb's ceiling (FIG. 5-61), a youth dives from a stone platform into a body of water. The scene most likely symbolizes the plunge from this life into the next. Trees resembling those on the Niobid krater are included within the decorative frame.

LATE CLASSICAL PERIOD

The Peloponnesian War, which began in 431 BCE, ended in 404 BCE with the complete defeat of a plague-weakened Athens. The victor, Sparta, and then Thebes undertook the leadership of Greece, both unsuccessfully. In the middle of the fourth century BCE, a threat from without caused the rival Greek states to put aside their animosities and unite for their common defense, as they had earlier against the Persians. But at the battle of Chaeronea in 338 BCE, the Greek cities suffered a devastating loss and had to relinquish their independence to the Macedonian king, Philip II. Philip was assassinated in 336, and his son, Alexander III, better known simply as Alexander the Great, succeeded him. In the decade before his death in 323 BCE, Alexander led a powerful army on an extraordinary campaign that overthrew the Persian Empire (the ultimate revenge for the Persian invasion of Greece in the early fifth century BCE), wrested control of Egypt, and even reached India.

Sculpture

The fourth century BCE was thus a time of political upheaval in Greece, and the chaos had a profound impact on the psyche of the Greeks and on the art they produced. In the fifth century BCE, Greeks had generally believed that rational human beings could impose order on their environment, create "perfect" statues such as the *Canon* of Polykleitos, and discover the "correct" mathematical formulas for constructing temples such as the Parthenon. The Parthenon frieze celebrated the Athenians as a community of citizens with shared values. The Peloponnesian War and the unceasing strife of the fourth century BCE brought an end to the serene idealism of the previous century. Disillusionment and alienation followed. Greek thought and Greek art began to focus more on the individual and on the real world of appearances rather than on the community and the ideal world of perfect beings and perfect buildings.

PRAXITELES The new approach to art is immediately apparent in the work of PRAXITELES, one of the great masters of the fourth century BCE. Praxiteles did not reject the themes favored by the sculptors of the High Classical period. His Olympian gods and goddesses retained their superhuman beauty, but in his hands they lost some of their solemn grandeur and took on a worldly sensuousness. Nowhere is this new humanizing spirit plainer than in the statue of Aphrodite (FIG. 5-62) that Praxiteles sold to the Knidians after another city had rejected it. The lost original, carved from Parian marble, is known only through copies of Roman date, but Pliny considered it "superior to all the works, not only of Praxiteles, but indeed in the whole world." It made Knidos famous, and many people sailed there just to see the statue in its round temple (compare FIG. 5-72), where "it was possible to view the image of the goddess from every side." According to Pliny, some visitors were "overcome with love for the statue."[3]

The *Aphrodite of Knidos* caused such a sensation in its time because Praxiteles took the unprecedented step of representing the goddess of love completely nude. Female nudity was rare in earlier Greek art and had been confined almost exclusively to paintings on vases designed for household use. The women so depicted also tended to be courtesans or slave girls, not noblewomen or goddesses, and no one had dared place a statue of an unclothed goddess in a

temple. Moreover, Praxiteles' Aphrodite is not a cold and remote image. In fact, the goddess engages in a trivial act out of everyday life. She has removed her garment, draped it over a large *hydria* (water pitcher), and is about to step into the bath.

Although shocking in its day, the *Aphrodite of Knidos* is not openly erotic (the goddess modestly shields her pelvis with her right hand), but she is quite sensuous. Lucian wrote in the second century CE that she had a "welcoming look" and a "slight smile" and that Praxiteles was renowned for his ability to transform marble into soft and radiant flesh. Lucian mentioned, for example, the "dewy quality of Aphrodite's eyes."[4] Unfortunately, the rather mechanical Roman copies do not capture the quality of Praxiteles' modeling of the stone.

Those qualities are evident, however, in a statue once thought to be by the hand of the master himself but now generally considered either a copy of the highest quality or an original work by a son or grandson of Praxiteles. Found in the Temple of Hera at Olympia, the

1 ft.

5-62 PRAXITELES, *Aphrodite of Knidos.* Roman marble copy of an original of ca. 350–340 BCE, 6′ 8″ high. Musei Vaticani, Rome.

The first nude statue of a goddess caused a sensation in the fourth century BCE. But Praxiteles was also famous for his ability to transform marble into soft and radiant flesh. His Aphrodite had "dewy eyes."

5-63 PRAXITELES(?), Hermes and the infant Dionysos, from the Temple of Hera, Olympia, Greece. Copy of a statue by Praxiteles of ca. 340 BCE or an original work of ca. 330–270 BCE by a son or grandson. Marble, 7' 1" high. Archaeological Museum, Olympia.

Praxiteles humanized the Olympian deities. This Hermes is as sensuous as the sculptor's Aphrodite. The god gazes dreamily into space while he dangles grapes as temptation for the infant god of wine.

followers. But other sculptors pursued very different interests. One of these was SKOPAS OF PAROS, and although his work reflects the general trend toward the humanization of the Greek gods and heroes, his hallmark was intense emotionalism. None of Skopas's statues survives, but a grave stele (FIG. 5-64) found near the Ilissos River in Athens exhibits the psychological tension for which the master's works were famous. The stele was originally set into an architectural frame similar to that of the earlier Hegeso stele (FIG. 5-57). A comparison between the two works is very telling. In the Ilissos stele, the relief is much higher, with parts of the figures carved fully in the round. But the major difference is the pronounced change in mood, which reflects the innovations of Skopas. The later work makes a clear distinction between the living and the dead, and depicts overt mourning. The deceased is a young hunter who has the large, deeply set eyes and fleshy overhanging brows that characterized Skopas's sculpted figures. At his feet a small boy, either his servant or perhaps a younger brother, sobs openly. The hunter's dog also droops its head in sorrow. Beside the youth, an old man, undoubtedly his father, leans on a walking stick and, in a gesture reminiscent of that of the Olympia seer (FIG. 5-32), ponders the irony of fate that has taken the life of his powerful son and preserved him in

statue of Hermes and the infant Dionysos (FIG. 5-63) brings to the realm of monumental statuary the theme the Phiale Painter had chosen for a white-ground krater (FIG. 5-60) a century earlier. Hermes has stopped to rest in a forest on his journey to Nysa to entrust the upbringing of Dionysos to Papposilenos and the nymphs. Hermes leans on a tree trunk (here it is an integral part of the composition and not a copyist's addition), and his slender body forms a sinuous, shallow S-curve that is the hallmark of many of Praxiteles' statues. He looks off dreamily into space while he dangles a bunch of grapes (now missing) as a temptation for the infant, who is to become the Greek god of the vine. This is the kind of tender and very human interaction between an adult and a child that is common in real life but that had been absent from Greek statuary before the fourth century BCE.

The quality of the carving is superb. The modeling is deliberately smooth and subtle, producing soft shadows that follow the planes as they flow almost imperceptibly one into another. The delicacy of the marble facial features stands in sharp contrast to the metallic precision of Polykleitos's bronze *Doryphoros* (FIG. 5-40). Even the *Spear Bearer*'s locks of hair were subjected to the fifth-century sculptor's laws of symmetry and do not violate the skull's perfect curve. A comparison of these two statues reveals how broad was the change in artistic attitude and intent from the fifth to the fourth century BCE. In the statues of Praxiteles, the deities of Mount Olympus still possess a beauty mortals can aspire to, although not achieve, but they are no longer remote. Praxiteles' gods have stepped off their fifth-century pedestals and entered the fourth-century BCE world of human experience.

SKOPAS In the Archaic period and throughout most of the Early and High Classical periods, Greek sculptors generally shared common goals, but in the Late Classical period of the fourth century BCE, distinctive individual styles emerged. The dreamy, beautiful divinities of Praxiteles had enormous appeal, and the master had many

5-64 Grave stele of a young hunter, found near the Ilissos River, Athens, Greece, ca. 340–330 BCE. Marble, 5' 6" high. National Archaeological Museum, Athens.

The emotional intensity of this stele representing an old man mourning the loss of his son and the figures' large, deeply set eyes with fleshy overhanging brows reflect the style of Skopas of Paros.

scrape his left arm. At the same time, he will shift his weight and reverse the positions of his legs. Lysippos also began to break down the dominance of the frontal view in statuary and encouraged the observer to look at his athlete from multiple angles. Because Lysippos represented the athlete with his right arm boldly thrust forward, the figure breaks out of the shallow rectangular box that defined the boundaries of earlier statues. To comprehend the action, the observer must move to the side and view Lysippos's work at a three-quarter angle or in full profile.

To grasp the full meaning of another work of Lysippos, a colossal statue (FIG. 5-66) depicting a weary Herakles, the viewer must walk around it. Once again, the original is lost. The most impressive of the surviving marble copies is nearly twice life-size and was exhibited in the Baths of Caracalla in Rome. Like the marble copy of Polykleitos's *Doryphoros* (FIG. 5-40) from the Roman palaestra at

his frail old age. Most remarkable of all, the hunter himself looks out at the viewer, inviting sympathy and creating an emotional bridge between the spectator and the artwork inconceivable in the art of the High Classical period.

LYSIPPOS The third great Late Classical sculptor, LYSIPPOS OF SIKYON, won such renown that Alexander the Great selected him to create his official portrait. (Alexander could afford to employ the best. The Macedonian kingdom enjoyed vast wealth. King Philip hired the leading thinker of his age, Aristotle, as the young Alexander's tutor.) Lysippos introduced a new canon of proportions in which the bodies were more slender than those of Polykleitos—whose own canon continued to exert enormous influence—and the heads roughly one-eighth the height of the body rather than one-seventh, as in the previous century. The new proportions are apparent in one of Lysippos's most famous works, a bronze statue of an *apoxyomenos* (an athlete scraping oil from his body after exercising), known, as usual, only from Roman copies in marble (FIG. 5-65). A comparison with Polykleitos's *Doryphoros* (FIG. 5-40) reveals more than a change in physique. A nervous energy, lacking in the balanced form of the *Doryphoros*, runs through Lysippos's *Apoxyomenos*. The *strigil* (scraper) is about to reach the end of the right arm, and at any moment the athlete will switch it to the other hand so that he can

5-66 LYSIPPOS, Weary Herakles (*Farnese Herakles*). Roman marble copy from Rome, Italy, signed by GLYKON OF ATHENS, of a bronze original of ca. 320 BCE, 10′ 5″ high. Museo Archeologico Nazionale, Naples.

Lysippos's portrayal of Herakles after the hero obtained the golden apples of the Hesperides ironically shows the mythological strong man as so weary that he must lean on his club for support.

Pompeii, Lysippos's muscle-bound Greek hero provided inspiration for Romans who came to the baths to exercise. (The copyist, GLYKON OF ATHENS, signed the statue. Lysippos's name is not mentioned, but the educated Roman public did not need a label to identify the famous work.) In the hands of Lysippos, however, the exaggerated muscular development of Herakles is poignantly ironic, for the sculptor depicted the strong man as so weary that he must lean on his club for support. Without that prop, Herakles would topple over. Lysippos and other fourth-century BCE artists rejected stability and balance as worthy goals for statuary.

Herakles holds the golden apples of the Hesperides in his right hand behind his back—unseen unless the viewer walks around the statue. Lysippos's subject is thus the same as that of the metope (FIG. 5-33) of the Early Classical Temple of Zeus at Olympia, but the fourth-century BCE Herakles is no longer serene. Instead of expressing joy, or at least satisfaction, at having completed one of the impossible 12 labors, he is almost dejected. Exhausted by his physical efforts, he can think only of his pain and weariness, not of the reward of immortality that awaits him. Lysippos's portrayal of Herakles in this statue is an eloquent testimony to Late Classical sculptors' interest in humanizing the great gods and heroes of the Greeks. In this respect, despite their divergent styles, Praxiteles, Skopas, and Lysippos followed a common path.

Alexander the Great and Macedonian Court Art

Alexander the Great's favorite book was the *Iliad*, and his own life was very much like an epic saga, full of heroic battles, exotic places, and unceasing drama. Alexander was a man of singular character, an inspired leader with boundless energy and an almost foolhardy courage. He personally led his army into battle on the back of Bucephalus, the wild and mighty steed only he could tame and ride (FIG. 5-70).

ALEXANDER'S PORTRAITS Ancient sources reveal that Alexander believed only Lysippos had captured his essence in a portrait, and that is why only he was authorized to sculpt the king's image. Lysippos's most famous portrait of the Macedonian king was a full-length heroically nude bronze statue of Alexander holding a lance and turning his head toward the sky. Plutarch reported that an epigram inscribed on the base stated that the statue depicted Alexander gazing at Zeus and proclaiming, "I place the earth under my sway. You, O Zeus, keep Olympus." Plutarch further stated that the portrait had "leonine" hair and a "melting glance."[5] The Lysippan original is lost, and because Alexander was portrayed so many times for centuries after his death, it is very difficult to determine which of the many surviving images is most faithful to the fourth-century BCE portrait. A leading candidate is a third-century BCE marble head (FIG. 5-67) from Pella, the capital of Macedonia and Alexander's birthplace. It has the sharp turn of the head and thick mane of hair that were key ingredients of Lysippos's portrait. The sculptor's treatment of the features also is consistent with the style of the later fourth century BCE. The deep-set eyes and parted lips recall the manner of Skopas, and the delicate handling of the flesh brings to mind the faces of Praxitelean statues. Although not a copy, this head very likely approximates the young king's official portrait and provides insight into Alexander's personality as well as the art of Lysippos.

PELLA MOSAICS Alexander's palace has not been excavated, but the sumptuousness of life at the Macedonian court is evident from the costly objects found in Macedonian graves and from the abundance of mosaics (see "Mosaics," Chapter 8, page 223)

1 in.

5-67 Head of Alexander the Great, from Pella, Greece, third century BCE. Marble, 1′ high. Archaeological Museum, Pella.

Lysippos was the official portrait sculptor of Alexander the Great. This third-century BCE sculpture has the sharp turn of the head and thick mane of hair of Lysippos's statue of Alexander with a lance.

1 ft.

5-68 GNOSIS, Stag hunt, from Pella, Greece, ca. 300 BCE. Pebble mosaic, figural panel 10′ 2″ high. Archaeological Museum, Pella.

The floor mosaics at the Macedonian capital of Pella are of the early type made with pebbles of various natural colors. This stag hunt by Gnosis bears the earliest known signature of a mosaicist.

uncovered at Pella in the homes of the wealthy. The Pella mosaics are *pebble mosaics*. The floors consist of small stones of various colors collected from beaches and riverbanks and set into a thick coat of cement. The finest pebble mosaic yet to come to light has a stag hunt (FIG. 5-68) as its *emblema* (central framed panel), bordered in turn by an intricate floral pattern and a stylized wave motif (not shown in the illustration). The artist signed his work in the same manner as proud Greek vase painters and potters did: "GNOSIS made it." This is the earliest mosaicist's signature known, and its prominence in the design undoubtedly attests to the artist's reputation. The house owner wanted guests to know that Gnosis himself, and not an imitator, created this floor.

The Pella stag hunt, with its light figures against a dark ground, has much in common with red-figure painting. In the pebble mosaic, however, thin strips of lead or terracotta define most of the contour lines and some of the interior details. Subtle gradations of yellow, brown, and red, as well as black, white, and gray pebbles suggest the interior volumes. The musculature of the hunters, and even their billowing cloaks and the animals' bodies, are modeled by shading. Such use of light and dark to suggest volume is rarely seen on Greek painted vases, although examples do exist. Monumental painters, however, commonly used shading. The Greek term for shading was *skiagraphia* (literally, "shadow painting"), and it was said to have been invented by an Athenian painter of the fifth century BCE named Apollodoros. Gnosis's emblema, with its sparse landscape setting, probably reflects contemporaneous panel painting.

HADES AND PERSEPHONE Recent excavations at Vergina have provided valuable additional information about Macedonian art and about Greek mural painting. One of the most important finds is a painted tomb with a representation of Hades, lord of the Underworld, abducting Persephone, the daughter of Demeter, the goddess of grain. The mural (FIG. 5-69) is remarkable for its intense drama and for the painter's use of foreshortening and shading. Hades holds the terrified seminude Persephone in his left arm and steers his racing chariot with his right as Persephone's garments and hair blow in the wind. The artist depicted the heads of both figures and even the chariot's wheels in three-quarter views. The chariot, in fact, seems to be bursting into the viewer's space. Especially noteworthy is the way the painter used short dark brush strokes to

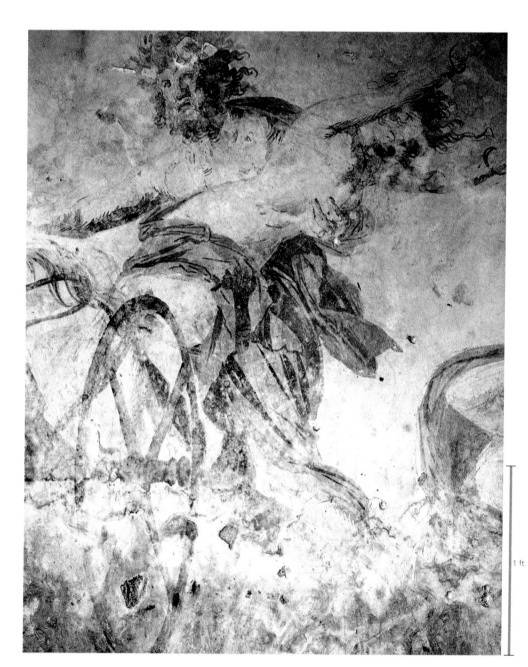

5-69 Hades abducting Persephone, detail of a wall painting in tomb 1, Vergina, Greece, mid-fourth century BCE. 3′ 3$\frac{1}{2}$″ high.

The intense drama, three-quarter views, and shading in this representation of the lord of the Underworld kidnapping Demeter's daughter are characteristics of mural painting at the time of Alexander.

1 ft.

5-70 PHILOXENOS OF ERETRIA, *Battle of Issus*, ca. 310 BCE. Roman copy (*Alexander Mosaic*) from the House of the Faun, Pompeii, Italy, late second or early first century BCE. Tessera mosaic, 8′ 10″ × 16′ 9″. Museo Archeologico Nazionale, Naples.

Philoxenos's *Battle of Issus* (see also FIG. 5-1) was considered one of the greatest paintings of antiquity. In it he captured the psychological intensity of the confrontation between the two kings.

suggest shading on the under side of Hades' right arm, on Persephone's torso, and elsewhere. Although fragmentary, the Vergina mural is a precious document of the almost totally lost art of monumental painting in ancient Greece.

BATTLE OF ISSUS Further insight into developments in painting at the time of Alexander comes from a large mosaic that decorated the floor of one room of a lavishly appointed Roman house at Pompeii. In the *Alexander Mosaic* (FIG. 5-70), as it is usually called, the mosaicist employed *tesserae* (tiny stones or pieces of glass cut to the desired size and shape) instead of pebbles (see "Mosaics," Chapter 8, page 223). The subject is a great battle between the armies of Alexander the Great and the Persian king Darius III, probably the battle of Issus in southeastern Turkey, when Darius fled the battlefield in his chariot in humiliating defeat. The mosaic dates to the late second or early first century BCE. It is widely believed to be a reasonably faithful copy of *Battle of Issus*, a famous panel painting of ca. 310 BCE made by PHILOXENOS OF ERETRIA for King Cassander, one of Alexander's successors. Some scholars have proposed, however, that the mosaic is a copy of a painting by one of the few Greek female artists whose name is known, Helen of Egypt.

Battle of Issus is notable for the artist's technical mastery of problems that had long fascinated Greek painters. Even Euthymides would have marveled at the fourth-century BCE painter's depiction of the rearing horse (FIG. 5-1) seen in a three-quarter rear view below Darius. The subtle modulation of the horse's rump through shading in browns and yellows is much more accomplished than the comparable attempts at shading in the Pella mosaic (FIG. 5-68) or the Vergina mural (FIG. 5-69). Other details are even more impres-

sive. The Persian to the right of the rearing horse has fallen to the ground and raises, backward, a dropped Macedonian shield to protect himself from being trampled. Philoxenos recorded the reflection of the man's terrified face on the polished surface of the shield. Everywhere in the scene, men, animals, and weapons cast shadows on the ground. The interest of Greek painters in the reflection of insubstantial light on a shiny surface, and in the absence of light (shadows), was far removed from earlier painters' preoccupation with the clear presentation of weighty figures seen against a blank background. The Greek painter here truly opened a window into a world filled not only with figures, trees, and sky but also with light. This Classical Greek notion of what a painting should be characterizes most of the history of art in the Western world from the Renaissance on.

Most impressive about *Battle of Issus*, however, is the psychological intensity of the drama unfolding before the viewer's eyes. Alexander is on horseback leading his army into battle, recklessly one might say, without even a helmet to protect him. He drives his spear through one of Darius's trusted "Immortals," who were sworn to guard the king's life, while the Persian's horse collapses beneath him. The Macedonian king is only a few yards away from Darius, and Alexander directs his gaze at the Persian king, not at the man impaled on his now-useless spear. Darius has called for retreat. In fact, his charioteer is already whipping the horses and speeding the king to safety. Before he escapes, Darius looks back at Alexander and in a pathetic gesture reaches out toward his brash foe. But victory has slipped from his hands. Pliny said Philoxenos's painting of the battle between Alexander and Darius was "inferior to none."[6] It is easy to see why he reached that conclusion.

The Greeks always situated their theaters on hillsides, which supported the cavea of stone seats overlooking the circular orchestra. The Epidauros theater is the finest in Greece. It accommodated 12,000 spectators.

Architecture

In architecture, as in sculpture and painting, the Late Classical period was a time of innovation and experimentation.

THEATER OF EPIDAUROS In ancient Greece, plays were not performed repeatedly over months or years as they are today but only during sacred festivals. Greek drama was closely associated with religious rites and was not pure entertainment. At Athens in the fifth century BCE, for example, the great tragedies of Aeschylus, Sophocles, and Euripides were performed at the Dionysos festival in the theater dedicated to the god on the southern slope of the Acropolis. The finest theater in Greece, however, constructed shortly after Alexander the Great was born, is located at Epidauros in the Peloponnesos. The architect was POLYKLEITOS THE YOUNGER, possibly a nephew of the great fifth-century sculptor. His theater (FIG. 5-71) is still used for performances of ancient Greek dramas.

The precursor of the formal Greek theater was a place where ancient rites, songs, and dances were performed. This circular piece of earth with a hard, level surface later became the orchestra of the theater. *Orchestra* literally means "dancing place." The actors and the chorus performed there, and at Epidauros an altar to Dionysos stood at the center of the circle. The spectators sat on a slope overlooking the orchestra—the *theatron*, or "place for seeing." When the Greek theater took architectural shape, the auditorium (*cavea*, Latin for "hollow place, cavity") was always situated on a hillside. The cavea at Epidauros, composed of wedge-shaped sections (*cunei*, singular *cuneus*) of stone benches separated by stairs, is somewhat greater than a semicircle in plan. The auditorium is 387 feet in diameter, and its 55 rows of seats accommodated about 12,000 spectators. They entered the theater via a passageway between the seating area and the scene building (*skene*), which housed dressing rooms for the actors and also formed a backdrop for the plays. The design is simple but perfectly suited to its function. Even in antiquity the Epidauros theater won renown for the harmony of its proportions. Although spectators sitting in some of the seats would have had a poor view of the skene, all had unobstructed views of the orchestra. Because of the open-air cavea's excellent acoustics, everyone could hear the actors and chorus.

CORINTHIAN CAPITALS The theater at Epidauros is situated some 500 yards southeast of the sanctuary of Asklepios, and Polykleitos the Younger worked there as well. He was the architect of the *tholos,* the circular shrine that probably housed the sacred snakes of the healing god. That building lies in ruins today, its architectural fragments removed to the local museum, but an approximate idea of its original appearance can be gleaned from the somewhat earlier and partially reconstructed tholos (FIG. 5-72) at Delphi that THEODOROS OF PHOKAIA designed. Both tholoi had an exterior colonnade of Doric columns. Inside, however, the columns had

5-72 THEODOROS OF PHOKAIA, Tholos, Delphi, Greece, ca. 375 BCE.

Theodoros of Phokaia's tholos at Delphi, although in ruins, is the best-preserved example of a round temple of the Classical period. It had Doric columns on the exterior and Corinthian columns inside.

The Corinthian Capital

The Corinthian capital (FIG. 5-73) is more ornate than either the Doric or Ionic (FIG. 5-14). It consists of a double row of acanthus leaves, from which tendrils and flowers emerge, wrapped around a bell-shaped echinus. Although this capital often is cited as the distinguishing feature of the Corinthian order, in strict terms no such order exists. Architects simply substituted the new capital type for the volute capital in the Ionic order.

The sculptor Kallimachos invented the Corinthian capital during the second half of the fifth century BCE. Vitruvius recorded the circumstances that supposedly led to its creation:

A maiden who was a citizen of Corinth . . . died. After her funeral, her nurse collected the goblets in which the maiden had taken delight while she was alive, and after putting them together in a basket, she took them to the grave monument and put them on top of it. In order that they should remain in place for a long time, she covered them with a tile. Now it happened that this basket was placed over the root of an acanthus. As time went on the acanthus root, pressed down in the middle by the weight, sent forth, when it was about springtime, leaves and stalks; its stalks growing up along the sides of the basket and being pressed out from the angles because of the weight of the tile, were forced to form volute-like curves at their extremities. At this point, Kallimachos happened to be going by and noticed the basket with this gentle growth of leaves around it. Delighted with the order and the novelty of the form, he made columns using it as his model and established a canon of proportions for it.*

Kallimachos worked on the Acropolis in Pericles' great building program. Many scholars believe that a Corinthian column supported the outstretched right hand of Phidias's *Athena Parthenos* (FIG. 5-46) because some of the Roman copies of the lost statue include a Corinthian column. In any case, the earliest preserved Corinthian capital dates to the time of Kallimachos. The new type was rarely used before the mid-fourth century BCE, however, and did not become popular until Hellenistic and especially Roman times. Later architects favored the Corinthian capital because of its ornate character and because it eliminated certain problems of both the Doric and Ionic orders.

The Ionic capital, unlike the Doric, has two distinct profiles—the front and back (with the volutes) and the sides. The volutes always faced outward on a Greek temple, but architects met with a vexing problem at the corners of their buildings, which had two adjacent "fronts." They solved the problem by placing volutes on both outer faces of the corner capitals (as on the Erechtheion, FIG. 5-52, and the Temple of Athena Nike, FIG. 5-55), but the solution was an awkward one.

Doric design rules also presented problems for Greek architects at the corners of buildings. The Doric frieze was organized according to three supposedly inflexible rules:

▌ A triglyph must be exactly over the center of each column.

▌ A triglyph must be over the center of each *intercolumniation* (the space between two columns).

▌ Triglyphs at the corners of the frieze must meet so that no space is left over.

These rules are contradictory, however. If the corner triglyphs must meet, then they cannot be placed over the center of the corner column (FIGS. 5-25, 5-30, and 5-44).

The Corinthian capital eliminated both problems. Because the capital's four sides have a similar appearance, corner Corinthian capitals do not have to be modified, as do corner Ionic capitals. And because the Ionic frieze is used for the Corinthian "order," architects do not have to contend with metopes or triglyphs.

5-73 POLYKLEITOS THE YOUNGER, Corinthian capital, from the tholos, Epidauros, Greece, ca. 350 BCE. Archaeological Museum, Epidauros.

Corinthian capitals, invented in the fifth century BCE by the sculptor Kallimachos, are more ornate than Doric and Ionic capitals. They feature a double row of acanthus leaves with tendrils and flowers.

*Vitruvius, *De architectura*, 4.1.8–10. Translated by J. J. Pollitt, *The Art of Ancient Greece: Sources and Documents* (New York: Cambridge University Press, 1990), 193–194.

Corinthian capitals (FIG. **5-73**; see "The Corinthian Capital," above), an invention of the second half of the fifth century BCE.

Consistent with the extremely conservative nature of Greek temple design, architects did not readily embrace the Corinthian capital. Until the second century BCE, Corinthian capitals were employed, as at Delphi and Epidauros, only for the interiors of sacred buildings. The earliest instance of a Corinthian capital on the exterior of a Greek building is the Choragic Monument of Lysikrates

(FIG. **5-74**), which is not really a building at all. Lysikrates had sponsored a chorus in a theatrical contest in 334 BCE, and after he won, he erected a monument to commemorate his victory. The monument consists of a cylindrical drum resembling a tholos on a rectangular base. Engaged Corinthian columns adorn the drum of Lysikrates' monument, and a huge Corinthian capital sits atop the roof. The freestanding capital once supported the victor's trophy, a bronze *tripod* (a deep bowl on a tall three-legged stand).

HELLENISTIC PERIOD

Alexander the Great's conquest of the Near East and Egypt (where the Macedonian king was buried) ushered in a new cultural age that historians and art historians alike call *Hellenistic*. The Hellenistic period opened with the death of Alexander in 323 BCE and lasted nearly three centuries, until the double suicide of Queen Cleopatra of Egypt and her Roman consort Mark Antony in 30 BCE after their decisive defeat at the battle of Actium by Antony's rival Augustus. That year, Augustus made Egypt a province of the Roman Empire.

The cultural centers of the Hellenistic period were the court cities of the Greek kings who succeeded Alexander and divided his far-flung empire among themselves. Chief among them were Antioch in Syria, Alexandria in Egypt, and Pergamon in Asia Minor. An international culture united the Hellenistic world, and its language was Greek. Hellenistic kings became enormously rich on the spoils of the East, priding themselves on their libraries, art collections, scientific enterprises, and skills as critics and connoisseurs, as well as on the learned men they could assemble at their courts. The world of the small, austere, and heroic city-state passed away, as did the power and prestige of its center, Athens. A cosmopolitan ("citizen of the world," in Greek) civilization, much like today's, replaced it.

Architecture

The greater variety, complexity, and sophistication of Hellenistic culture called for an architecture on an imperial scale and of wide diversity, something far beyond the requirements of the Classical polis, even beyond that of Athens at the height of its power. Building activity shifted from the old centers on the Greek mainland to the opulent cities of the Hellenistic monarchs in the East.

TEMPLE OF APOLLO, DIDYMA Great scale, a theatrical element of surprise, and a willingness to break the rules of canonical temple design characterize one of the most ambitious temple projects of the Hellenistic period, the Temple of Apollo at Didyma. The Hellenistic temple was built to replace the Archaic temple at the site the Persians had burned down in 494 BCE when they sacked nearby Miletos. Construction began in 313 BCE according to the design of two architects who were natives of the area, PAIONIOS OF EPHESOS and DAPHNIS OF MILETOS. So vast was the undertaking, however, that work on the temple continued off and on for more than 500 years—and still the project was never completed.

The temple was dipteral in plan (FIG. **5-75**, *left*) and had an unusually broad facade of 10 huge Ionic columns almost 65 feet tall. The sides had 21 columns, consistent with the Classical formula for

Dipteral colonnade

Inner shrine

Courtyard

Oracular room

0 25 50 75 100 feet
0 5 10 20 30 meters

5-75 PAIONIOS OF EPHESOS and DAPHNIS OF MILETOS, Temple of Apollo, Didyma, Turkey, begun 313 BCE. Plan (*left*) and aerial view (*right*).

This unusual Hellenistic temple was hypaethral (open to the sky) and featured a double peripteral (dipteral) colonnade with a smaller temple inside the interior courtyard of the larger temple.

5-76 Restored view of the city of Priene, Turkey, fourth century BCE and later (John Burge).

Despite its irregular terrain, Priene had a strict grid plan conforming to the principles of Hippodamos of Miletos, whom Aristotle singled out as the father of rational city planning.

perfect proportions used for the Parthenon—21 = (2 × 10) + 1—but nothing else about the design is Classical. One anomaly immediately apparent to anyone who approached the building was that it had no pediment and no roof—it was *hypaethral*, or open to the sky. Also, the grand doorway to what should be the temple's cella was elevated nearly five feet off the ground so that it could not be entered. The explanation for these peculiarities is that the doorway served rather as a kind of stage where the oracle of Apollo could be announced to those assembled in front of the temple. The unroofed dipteral colonnade was really only an elaborate frame for a central courtyard (FIG. **5-75,** *right*) with a small prostyle shrine containing a statue of Apollo. Entrance to the interior court was through two smaller doorways to the left and right of the great portal and down two narrow vaulted tunnels that could accommodate only a single file of people. From these dark and mysterious lateral passageways, worshipers emerged into the clear light of the courtyard, which also had a sacred spring and laurel trees in honor of Apollo. Opposite Apollo's inner temple, a stairway some 50 feet wide rose majestically toward three portals leading into the oracular room that also opened onto the front of the temple. This complex spatial planning marked a sharp departure from Classical Greek architecture, which stressed a building's exterior almost as a work of sculpture and left its interior relatively undeveloped.

HIPPODAMOS OF MILETOS When the Persians were finally expelled from Asia Minor in 479 BCE, the Greek cities there were in near ruin. Reconstruction of Miletos began after 466 BCE according to a plan laid out by Hippodamos of Miletos, whom Aristotle singled out as the father of rational city planning. Hippodamos imposed a strict grid plan on the site, regardless of the terrain, so that all streets met at right angles. Such *orthogonal plans* actually predate Hippodamos, not only in Archaic Greece and Etruscan Italy but also in the ancient Near East and Egypt. But Hippodamos was so famous that his name has ever since been synonymous with such urban plans. The so-called *Hippodamian plan* also designated separate quarters for public, private, and religious functions. A "Hippodamian city" was logically as well as regularly planned. This desire to impose order on nature and to assign a proper place in the whole to each of the city's constituent parts was very much in keeping with the philosophical tenets of the fifth century BCE. Hippodamos's formula for the ideal city was another manifestation of the same outlook that produced Polykleitos's *Canon* and Iktinos's Parthenon.

PRIENE Hippodamian planning was still the norm in Late Classical and Hellenistic Greece. The city of Priene (FIG. **5-76**), also in Asia Minor, was laid out during the fourth century BCE. It had fewer than 5,000 inhabitants (Hippodamos thought 10,000 was the ideal number). Situated on sloping ground, many of its narrow north-south streets were little more than long stairways. Uniformly sized city blocks, the standard planning unit, were nonetheless imposed on the irregular terrain. More than one unit was reserved for major structures such as the Temple of Athena and the theater. The central agora was allotted six blocks.

STOA OF ATTALOS, ATHENS Priene's agora was bordered by *stoas.* These covered colonnades, or *porticos,* which often housed shops and civic offices, were ideal vehicles for shaping urban spaces, and they were staples of Hellenistic cities. Even the agora of Athens, an ancient city notable for its haphazard, unplanned development, was eventually framed to the east and south by stoas placed at right angles to one another. These new porticos joined the famous Painted Stoa (see page 121), where the Hellenistic philosopher Zeno and his successors taught. The *Stoic* school of Greek philosophy took its name from that building.

The finest of the new Athenian stoas was the Stoa of Attalos II (FIG. **5-77**), a gift to the city by a grateful alumnus, the king of Pergamon, who had studied at Athens in his youth. The stoa was meticulously reconstructed under the direction of the American School of Classical Studies at Athens and today has a second life as a museum housing more than seven decades of finds from the Athenian agora, as well as the offices of the American excavation team. The stoa has two stories, each with 21 shops opening onto the colonnade. The facade columns are Doric on the ground level and Ionic on the second story. The mixing of the two orders on a single facade had occurred even in the Late Classical period. But it became increasingly common in the Hellenistic period, when architects showed greatly diminished respect for the old rules of Greek architecture, and a desire for variety and decorative effects often prevailed. Practical considerations also governed the form of the Stoa of Attalos. The columns are far more widely spaced than in Greek temple architecture, to allow for easy access. And the builders left the lower third of every Doric column shaft unfluted to guard against damage from constant traffic.

5-77 Stoa of Attalos II, Agora, Athens, Greece, ca. 150 BCE (with the Acropolis in the background).

The Stoa of Attalos II in the Athenian agora has been meticulously restored. Greek stoas were covered colonnades that housed shops and civic offices. They were also ideal vehicles for shaping urban spaces.

Pergamon

Pergamon, the kingdom of Attalos II (r. 159–138 BCE), was one of those born in the early third century BCE after the breakup of Alexander's empire. Founded by Philetairos, the Pergamene kingdom embraced almost all of western and southern Asia Minor. Upon the death in 133 BCE of its last king, Attalos III (r. 138–133 BCE), Pergamon was bequeathed to Rome, which by then was the greatest power in the Mediterranean world. The Attalids enjoyed immense wealth, and much of it was expended on embellishing their capital city, especially its acropolis. Located there were the royal palace, an arsenal and barracks, a great library and theater, an agora, and the sacred precincts of Athena and Zeus.

ALTAR OF ZEUS, PERGAMON The Altar of Zeus at Pergamon, erected about 175 BCE, is the most famous Hellenistic sculptural ensemble. The monument's west front (FIG. 5-78) has been reconstructed in Berlin. The altar proper was on an elevated platform and framed by an Ionic stoalike colonnade with projecting wings on either side of a broad central staircase. All around the altar platform was a sculpted frieze almost 400 feet long, populated by about a hundred larger-than-life-size figures. The subject is the battle of Zeus and the gods against the giants. It is the most extensive representation Greek artists ever attempted of that epic conflict for control of the world. A similar subject appeared on the shield of Phidias's *Athena Parthenos* and on some of the Parthenon metopes, where the Athenians wished to draw a parallel between the defeat of the giants and the defeat of the Persians. In the third century BCE, King Attalos I (r. 241–197 BCE) had successfully turned back an invasion of the Gauls in Asia Minor. The gigantomachy of the Altar of Zeus alluded to that Pergamene victory over those barbarians.

5-78 Reconstructed west front of the Altar of Zeus, Pergamon, Turkey, ca. 175 BCE. Staatliche Museen, Berlin.

The gigantomachy frieze of Pergamon's monumental Altar of Zeus is almost 400 feet long. The battle of gods and giants alluded to the victory of King Attalos I over the Gauls of Asia Minor.

5-79 Athena battling Alkyoneos, detail of the gigantomachy frieze, from the Altar of Zeus, Pergamon, Turkey, ca. 175 BCE. Marble, 7′ 6″ high. Staatliche Museen, Berlin.

The tumultuous battle scenes of the Pergamon altar have an emotional power unparalleled in earlier Greek art. Violent movement, swirling draperies, and vivid depictions of suffering fill the frieze.

A deliberate connection was also made with Athens, whose earlier defeat of the Persians was by then legendary, and with the Parthenon, which already was recognized as a Classical monument—in both senses of the word. The figure of Athena (FIG. **5-79**), for example, is a variation of the Athena from the Parthenon's east pediment. While Ge, the earth goddess and mother of all the giants, emerges from the ground and looks on with horror, Athena grabs the hair of the giant Alkyoneos as Nike flies in to crown her. Zeus himself (not illustrated) was based on the Poseidon of the west pediment. But the Pergamene frieze is not a dry series of borrowed motifs. On the contrary, its tumultuous narrative has an emotional intensity that has no parallel in earlier sculpture. The battle rages everywhere, even up and down the very steps one must ascend to reach Zeus's altar (FIG. 5-78). Violent movement, swirling draperies, and vivid depictions of death and suffering are the norm. Wounded figures writhe in pain, and their faces reveal their anguish. When Zeus hurls his thunderbolt, one can almost hear the thunderclap. Deep carving creates dark shadows. The figures project from the background like bursts of light. These features have been justly termed "baroque" and reappear in 17th-century European sculpture (see Chapter 19). One can hardly imagine a greater contrast than between the Pergamene gigantomachy frieze and that of the Archaic Siphnian Treasury (FIG. 5-19) at Delphi.

DYING GAULS On the Altar of Zeus, sculptors presented the victory of Attalos I over the Gauls in mythological disguise. An earlier Pergamene statuary group explicitly represented the defeat of the barbarians. Roman copies of some of these figures survive. The sculptor carefully studied and reproduced the distinctive features of the foreign Gauls, most notably their long, bushy hair and mustaches and the *torques* (neck bands) they frequently wore. The Pergamene victors were apparently not included in the group. The viewer saw only their foes and their noble and moving response to defeat.

In what was probably the centerpiece of the Attalid group, a heroic Gallic chieftain (FIG. **5-80**) defiantly drives a sword into his own chest just below the collarbone, preferring suicide to surrender. He already has taken the life of his wife, who, if captured, would have been sold as a slave. In the best Lysippan tradition, the group can be fully appreci-

5-80 EPIGONOS(?), Gallic chieftain killing himself and his wife. Roman marble copy of a bronze original of ca. 230–220 BCE, 6′ 11″ high. Museo Nazionale Romano–Palazzo Altemps, Rome.

The defeat of the Gauls was also the subject of Pergamene statuary groups. The centerpiece of one group was a Gallic chieftain committing suicide after taking his wife's life. He preferred death to surrender.

5-81 Epigonos(?), Dying Gaul. Roman marble copy of a bronze original of ca. 230–220 BCE, 3' $\frac{1}{2}$" high. Museo Capitolino, Rome.

The Gauls in the Pergamene victory groups were shown as barbarians with bushy hair, mustaches, and neck bands, but they were also portrayed as noble foes who fought to the end.

1 ft.

ated only by walking around it. From one side, the observer sees the Gaul's intensely expressive face, from another his powerful torso, and from a third the woman's limp and almost lifeless body. The man's twisting posture, the almost theatrical gestures, and the emotional intensity of the suicidal act are hallmarks of the Pergamene baroque style and have close parallels in the later frieze of Zeus's altar.

The third Gaul from this group is a trumpeter (FIG. 5-81) who collapses upon his large oval shield as blood pours from the gash in his chest. He stares at the ground with a pained expression. The Hellenistic figure recalls the dying warrior (FIG. 5-29) from the east pediment of the Temple of Aphaia at Aegina, but the pathos and drama of the suffering Gaul are far more pronounced. As in the suicide group and the gigantomachy frieze, the sculptor rendered the male musculature in an exaggerated manner. Note the tautness of the chest and the bulging veins of the left leg—implying that the unseen Attalid hero who has struck down this noble and savage foe must have been an extraordinary warrior. If this figure is the *tubicen* (trumpeter) Pliny mentioned as the work of the Pergamene master EPIGONOS, then Epigonos may be the sculptor of the entire group and the creator of the dynamic Hellenistic baroque style.

Sculpture

In different ways, Praxiteles, Skopas, and Lysippos had already taken bold steps in redefining the nature of Greek statuary. But Hellenistic sculptors went still further, both in terms of style and in expanding the range of subjects considered suitable for monumental sculpture.

NIKE OF SAMOTHRACE One of the masterpieces of Hellenistic baroque sculpture was set up in the Sanctuary of the Great Gods on the island of Samothrace. The *Nike of Samothrace* (FIG. 5-82) has just alighted on the prow of a Greek warship. Her missing right arm was once raised high to crown the naval victor, just as Nike placed a wreath on Athena on the Altar of Zeus (FIG. 5-79). But the Pergamene

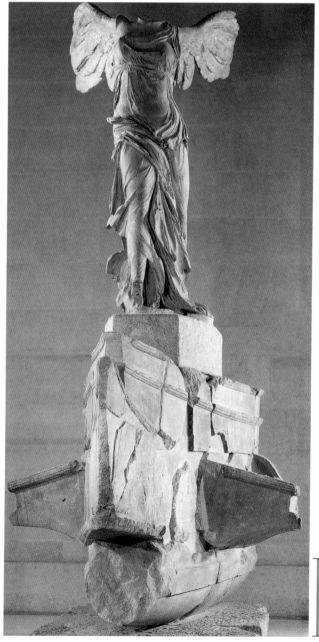

5-82 Nike alighting on a warship (*Nike of Samothrace*), from Samothrace, Greece, ca. 190 BCE. Marble, figure 8' 1" high. Louvre, Paris.

Victory has just landed on a prow to crown a victor at sea. Her wings still beat, and the wind sweeps her drapery. The placement of the statue in a fountain of splashing water heightened the dramatic visual effect.

1 ft.

relief figure seems calm by comparison. The Samothracian Nike's wings still beat, and the wind sweeps her drapery. Her himation bunches in thick folds around her right leg, and her chiton is pulled tightly across her abdomen and left leg.

The statue's setting amplified its theatrical effect. The war galley was displayed in the upper basin of a two-tiered fountain. In the lower basin were large boulders. The fountain's flowing water created the illusion of rushing waves dashing up against the prow of the ship. The statue's reflection in the shimmering water below accentuated the sense of lightness and movement. The sound of splashing water added an aural dimension to the visual drama. Art and nature were here combined in one of the most successful sculptures ever fashioned. In the *Nike of Samothrace* and other works in the Hellenistic baroque manner, sculptors resoundingly rejected the Polykleitan conception of a statue as an ideally proportioned, self-contained entity on a bare pedestal. The Hellenistic statues interact with their environment and appear as living, breathing, and intensely emotive human (or divine) presences.

VENUS DE MILO In the Hellenistic period, sculptors regularly followed Praxiteles' lead in undressing Aphrodite, but they also openly explored the eroticism of the nude female form. The famous *Venus de Milo* (FIG. 5-83) is a larger-than-life-size marble statue of Aphrodite found on Melos together with its inscribed base (now lost) signed by the sculptor, ALEXANDROS OF ANTIOCH-ON-THE-MEANDER. In this statue, the goddess of love is more modestly draped than the *Aphrodite of Knidos* (FIG. 5-62) but is more overtly sexual. Her left hand (separately preserved) holds the apple Paris awarded her when he judged her the most beautiful goddess of all. Her right hand may have lightly grasped the edge of her drapery near the left hip in a half-hearted attempt to keep it from slipping farther down her body. The

5-83 ALEXANDROS OF ANTIOCH-ON-THE-MEANDER, Aphrodite (*Venus de Milo*), from Melos, Greece, ca. 150–125 BCE. Marble, 6′ 7″ high. Louvre, Paris.

Displaying the eroticism of many Hellenistic statues, this Aphrodite is more overtly sexual than the Knidian Aphrodite (FIG. 5-62). The goddess has a slipping garment to tease the spectator.

5-84 Sleeping satyr (*Barberini Faun*), from Rome, Italy, ca. 230–200 BCE. Marble, 7′ 1″ high. Glyptothek, Munich.

In this statue of a restlessly sleeping, drunken satyr, a Hellenistic sculptor portrayed a semihuman in a suspended state of consciousness—the antithesis of the Classical ideals of rationality and discipline.

sculptor intentionally designed the work to tease the spectator, imbuing his partially draped Aphrodite with a sexuality absent from Praxiteles' entirely nude image of the goddess.

BARBERINI FAUN Archaic statues smile at their viewers, and even when Classical statues look away from the viewer they are always awake and alert. Hellenistic sculptors often portrayed sleep. The suspension of consciousness and the entrance into the fantasy world of dreams—the antithesis of the Classical ideals of rationality and discipline—had great appeal for them. This newfound interest can be seen in a statue of a drunken, restlessly sleeping *satyr* (a semi-human follower of Dionysos) known as the *Barberini Faun* (FIG. 5-84) after the Italian cardinal who once owned it. The statue was found in Rome in the 17th century and restored (not entirely accurately) by Gianlorenzo Bernini, the great Italian Baroque sculptor (see Chapter 19). Bernini no doubt felt that this dynamic statue in the Pergamene manner was the work of a kindred spirit. The satyr has consumed too much wine and has thrown down his panther skin on a convenient rock and then fallen into a disturbed, intoxicated sleep. His brows are furrowed, and one can almost hear him snore.

Eroticism also comes to the fore in this statue. Although men had been represented naked in Greek art for hundreds of years, Archaic kouroi and Classical athletes and gods do not exude sexuality. Sensuality surfaced in the works of Praxiteles and his followers in the fourth century BCE. But the dreamy and supremely beautiful Hermes playfully dangling grapes before the infant Dionysos (FIG. 5-63) has nothing of the blatant sexuality of the *Barberini Faun*, whose wantonly spread legs focus attention on his genitals. Homosexuality was common in the man's world of ancient Greece. It is not surprising that when Hellenistic sculptors began to explore the sexuality of the human body, they turned their attention to both men and women.

DEFEATED BOXER Although Hellenistic sculptors tackled an expanded range of subjects, they did not abandon such traditional themes as the Greek athlete. But they often rendered the old subjects in novel ways. This is certainly true of the magnificent bronze statue (FIG. 5-85) of a seated boxer, a Hellenistic original found in Rome and perhaps at one time part of a group. The boxer is not a victorious young athlete with a perfect face and body but a heavily battered, defeated veteran whose upward gaze may have been directed at the man who had just beaten him. Too many punches from powerful hands wrapped in leather thongs—Greek boxers did not use the modern sport's cushioned gloves—have distorted the boxer's face. His nose is broken, as are his teeth. He has smashed, "cauliflower" ears. Inlaid copper blood drips from the cuts on his forehead, nose, and cheeks. How radically different is this rendition of a powerful bearded man from that of the noble warrior from Riace (FIGS. 5-35 and I-17) of the Early Classical period. The Hellenistic sculptor appealed not to the intellect but to the emotions when striving to evoke compassion for the pounded hulk of a once-mighty fighter.

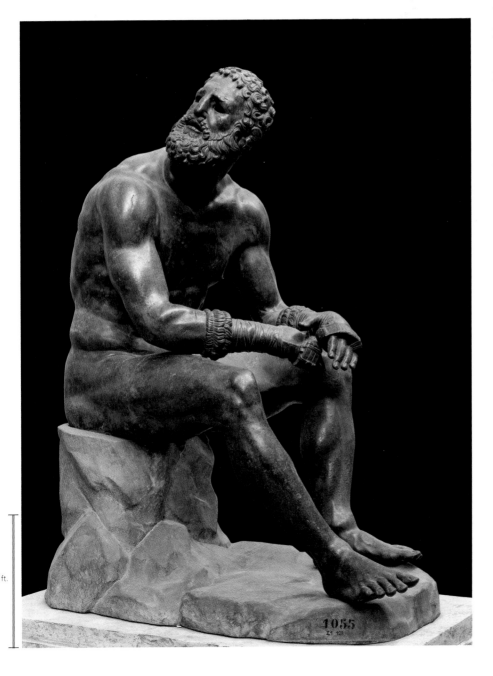

1 ft.

5-85 Seated boxer, from Rome, Italy, ca. 100–50 BCE. Bronze, 4′ 2″ high. Museo Nazionale Romano–Palazzo Massimo alle Terme, Rome.

Even when Hellenistic artists treated traditional themes, they approached them in novel ways. This bronze statue represents an older, defeated boxer with a broken nose and battered ears.

5-86 Old market woman, ca. 150–100 BCE. Marble, $4' \frac{1}{2}''$ high. Metropolitan Museum of Art, New York.

Consistent with the realism of much Hellenistic art, many statues portrayed old men and women from the lowest rungs of society. They were never considered suitable subjects in earlier Greek statuary.

OLD MARKET WOMAN The realistic bent of much of Hellenistic sculpture—the very opposite of the Classical period's idealism—is evident above all in a series of statues of old men and women from the lowest rungs of the social order. Shepherds, fishermen, and drunken beggars are common—the kinds of people pictured earlier on red-figure vases but never before thought worthy of monumental statuary. One of the finest preserved statues of this type depicts a haggard old woman (FIG. **5-86**) bringing chickens and a basket of fruits and vegetables to sell in the market. Her face is wrinkled, her body bent with age, and her spirit broken by a lifetime of poverty. She carries on because she must, not because she derives any pleasure from life. No one knows the purpose of these statues, but they attest to an interest in social realism absent in earlier Greek statuary.

Statues of the aged and the ugly are, of course, the polar opposites of the images of the young and the beautiful that dominated Greek art until the Hellenistic age, but they are consistent with the period's changed character. The Hellenistic world was a cosmopolitan place, and the highborn could not help but encounter the poor and a growing number of foreigners (non-Greek "barbarians") on a daily basis. Hellenistic art reflects this different social climate in the depiction of a much wider variety of physical types, including different ethnic types. The sensitive portrayal of Gallic warriors with their

5-87 POLYEUKTOS, Demosthenes. Roman marble copy of a bronze original of ca. 280 BCE, $6' 7\frac{1}{2}''$ high. Ny Carlsberg Glyptotek, Copenhagen.

One of the earliest Hellenistic portraits, frequently copied, was Polyeuktos's representation of the great orator Demosthenes as a frail man who possessed great courage and moral conviction.

shaggy hair, strange mustaches, and golden torques (FIG. **5-80** and **5-81**) has already been noted. Africans, Scythians, and others, formerly only the occasional subject of vase painters, also entered the realm of monumental sculpture in Hellenistic art.

DEMOSTHENES These sculptures of foreigners and the urban poor, however realistic, are not portraits. Rather, they are sensitive studies of physical types. But the growing interest in the individual beginning in the Late Classical period did lead in the Hellenistic era to the production of true likenesses of specific persons. In fact, one of the

5-88 Athanadoros, Hagesandros, and Polydoros of Rhodes, Laocoön and his sons, from Rome, Italy, early first century CE. Marble, 7′ 10½″ high. Musei Vaticani, Rome.

Hellenistic style lived on in Rome. Although stylistically akin to Pergamene sculpture, this statue of sea serpents attacking Laocoön and his two sons matches the account given only in the *Aeneid*.

great achievements of Hellenistic artists was the redefinition of portraiture. In the Classical period, Kresilas was admired for having made the noble Pericles appear even nobler in his portrait (FIG. 5-41). But in Hellenistic times sculptors sought not only to record the actual appearance of their subjects in bronze and stone but also to capture the essence of their personalities in likenesses that were at once accurate and moving.

One of the earliest of these, perhaps the finest of the Hellenistic age and frequently copied in Roman times, was a bronze portrait statue of Demosthenes (FIG. 5-87) by POLYEUKTOS. The original was set up in the Athenian agora in 280 BCE, 42 years after the great orator's death. Demosthenes was a frail man and in his youth even suffered from a speech impediment, but he had enormous courage and great moral conviction. A veteran of the disastrous battle against Philip II at Chaeronea, he repeatedly tried to rally opposition to Macedonian imperialism, both before and after Alexander's death. In the end, when it was clear the Macedonians would capture him, he took his own life by drinking poison.

Polyeuktos rejected Kresilas's and Lysippos's notions of the purpose of portraiture and did not attempt to portray a supremely confident leader with a magnificent physique. His Demosthenes has an aged and slightly stooped body. The orator clasps his hands nervously in front of him as he looks downward, deep in thought. His face is lined, his hair is receding, and his expression is one of great sadness. Whatever physical discomfort Demosthenes felt is here joined by an inner pain, his deep sorrow over the tragic demise of democracy at the hands of the Macedonian conquerors.

Hellenistic Art under Roman Patronage

In the opening years of the second century BCE, the Roman general Flaminius defeated the Macedonian army and declared the old poleis of Classical Greece free once again. The city-states never regained their former glory, however. Greece became a Roman province in 146 BCE. When, 60 years later, Athens sided with King Mithridates VI of Pontus (r. 120–63 BCE) in his war against Rome, the general Sulla crushed the Athenians. Thereafter, Athens retained some of its earlier prestige as a center of culture and learning, but politically it was just another city in the ever-expanding Roman Empire. Nonetheless, Greek artists continued to be in great demand, both to furnish the Romans with an endless stream of copies of Classical and Hellenistic masterpieces and to create new statues *à la grecque* (in the Greek style) for Roman patrons.

LAOCOÖN   One such work is the famous group (FIG. 5-88) of the Trojan priest Laocoön and his sons, which was unearthed in Rome in

1506 in the presence of the great Italian Renaissance artist Michelangelo. The marble group, long believed an original of the second century BCE, was found in the remains of the palace of the emperor Titus (r. 79–81 CE), exactly where Pliny had seen it more than 14 centuries before. Pliny attributed the statue to three sculptors—ATHANADOROS, HAGESANDROS, and POLYDOROS OF RHODES—whom most art historians now think worked in the early first century CE. They probably based their group on a Hellenistic masterpiece depicting Laocoön and only one son. Their variation on the original added the son at Laocoön's left (note the greater compositional integration of the two other figures) to conform with the Roman poet Vergil's account in the *Aeneid*. Vergil vividly described the strangling of Laocoön and his *two* sons by sea serpents while sacrificing at an altar. The gods who favored the Greeks in the war against Troy had sent the serpents to punish Laocoön, who had tried to warn his compatriots about the danger of bringing the Greeks' wooden horse within the walls of their city.

In Vergil's graphic account, Laocoön suffered in terrible agony, and the sculptors communicated the torment of the priest and his sons in a spectacular fashion in the marble group. The three Trojans writhe in pain as they struggle to free themselves from the death grip of the serpents. One bites into Laocoön's left hip as the priest lets out a ferocious cry. The serpent-entwined figures recall the suffering giants of the great frieze of the Altar of Zeus at Pergamon, and Laocoön himself is strikingly similar to Alkyoneos (FIG. 5-79), Athena's opponent. In fact, many scholars believe that a Pergamene statuary group of the second century BCE was the inspiration for the three Rhodian sculptors.

SPERLONGA That the work seen by Pliny and displayed in the Vatican Museums today was made for Romans rather than Greeks was confirmed in 1957 by the discovery of fragments of several Hellenistic-style groups illustrating scenes from Homer's *Odyssey*. These fragments were found in a grotto that served as the picturesque summer banquet hall of the seaside villa of the Roman emperor Tiberius (r. 14–37 CE) at Sperlonga, some 60 miles south of Rome. One of these groups—depicting the monster Scylla attacking Odysseus's ship—is signed by the same three sculptors Pliny cited as the creators of the Laocoön group. Another of the groups, installed around a central pool in the grotto, depicted the blinding of the Cyclops Polyphemos by Odysseus and his comrades, an incident also set in a cave in the Homeric epic. The head of Odysseus (FIG. 5-89) from this theatrical group is one of the finest sculptures of antiquity. The hero's cap can barely contain his swirling locks of hair. Even Odysseus's beard seems to be swept up in the emotional intensity of the moment. The parted lips and the deep shadows produced by sharp undercutting add drama to the head, which complemented Odysseus's agitated body.

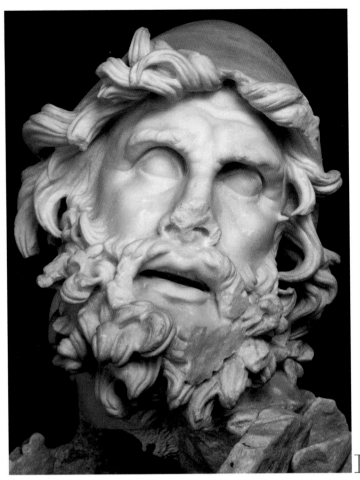

1 in.

5-89 ATHANADOROS, HAGESANDROS, and POLYDOROS OF RHODES, head of Odysseus, from Sperlonga, Italy, early first century CE. Marble, 2′ 1¼″ high. Museo Archeologico, Sperlonga.

This emotionally charged depiction of Odysseus was part of a mythological statuary group that the Laocoön sculptors made for a grotto at the emperor Tiberius's seaside villa at Sperlonga.

At Tiberius's villa in Sperlonga and in Titus's palace in Rome, the baroque school of Hellenistic sculpture lived on long after Greece ceased to be a political force. When Rome inherited the Pergamene kingdom from the last of the Attalids in 133 BCE, it also became heir to the Greek artistic legacy, and what Rome adopted from Greece it in turn passed on to the medieval and modern worlds. If Greece was peculiarly the inventor of the European spirit, Rome surely was its propagator and amplifier.

ANCIENT GREECE

GEOMETRIC AND ORIENTALIZING ART, ca. 900–600 BCE

▌ Homer lived during the eighth century BCE, the era when the city-states of Classical Greece took shape, the Olympic Games were founded (776 BCE), and the Greeks began to trade with their neighbors to both east and west.

▌ Also at this time, the human figure returned to Greek art in the form of bronze statuettes and simple silhouettes amid other abstract motifs on Geometric vases.

▌ Increasing contact with the civilizations of the Near East precipitated the so-called Orientalizing phase (ca. 700–600 BCE) of Greek art, when Eastern monsters began to appear on black-figure vases.

Dipylon krater, Athens,
ca. 740 BCE

ARCHAIC ART, ca. 600–480 BCE

▌ Around 600 BCE, the first life-size stone statues appeared in Greece. The earliest kouroi emulated the frontal poses of Egyptian statues, but artists depicted the young men nude, the way Greek athletes competed at Olympia.

▌ During the course of the sixth century BCE, Greek sculptors refined the proportions and added "Archaic smiles" to the faces of their statues to make them seem more lifelike.

▌ The Archaic age also saw the erection of the first stone temples with peripteral colonnades and the codification of the Doric and Ionic orders.

▌ The Andokides Painter invented red-figure vase painting around 530 BCE. Euphronios and Euthymides rejected the age-old composite view for the human figure and experimented with foreshortening.

Kroisos, kouros from Anavysos,
ca. 530 BCE

EARLY AND HIGH CLASSICAL ART, ca. 480–400 BCE

▌ The Classical period opened with the Persian sack of the Athenian Acropolis in 480 BCE and the Greek victory a year later. The fifth century BCE was the golden age of Greece, when Aeschylus, Sophocles, and Euripides wrote their plays, and Herodotus, the "father of history," lived.

▌ During the Early Classical period (480–450 BCE), sculptors revolutionized statuary by introducing contrapposto (weight shift) to their figures.

▌ In the High Classical period (450–400 BCE), Polykleitos developed a canon of proportions for the perfect statue. Iktinos and Kallikrates similarly applied mathematical formulas to temple design in the belief that beauty resulted from the use of harmonic numbers.

▌ Under the patronage of Pericles and the artistic directorship of Phidias, the Athenians rebuilt the Acropolis after 447 BCE. The Parthenon, Phidias's *Athena Parthenos,* and the works of Polykleitos have defined what it means to be "Classical" ever since.

Parthenon, Acropolis, Athens,
447–438 BCE

LATE CLASSICAL ART, ca. 400–323 BCE

▌ In the aftermath of the Peloponnesian War, which ended in 404 BCE, Greek artists, while still adhering to the philosophy that humanity was the "measure of all things," began to focus more on the real world of appearances than on the ideal world of perfect beings.

▌ Late Classical sculptors humanized the remote deities, athletes, and heroes of the fifth century BCE. Praxiteles, for example, caused a sensation when he portrayed Aphrodite undressed. Lysippos depicted Herakles as a strong man so weary that he needed to lean on his club for support.

▌ In architecture, the ornate Corinthian capital became increasingly popular, breaking the monopoly of the Doric and Ionic orders.

▌ The period closed with Alexander the Great, who transformed the Mediterranean world politically and ushered in a new artistic age as well.

Praxiteles, *Aphrodite of Knidos,*
ca. 350–340 BCE

HELLENISTIC ART, ca. 323–30 BCE

▌ The Hellenistic age extends from the death of Alexander until the death of Cleopatra, when Egypt became a province of the Roman Empire. The great cultural centers of the era were no longer the city-states of Archaic and Classical Greece but royal capitals such as Alexandria in Egypt and Pergamon in Asia Minor.

▌ In art, both architects and sculptors broke most of the rules of Classical design. At Didyma, for example, a temple to Apollo was erected that had no roof and contained a smaller temple within it.

▌ Hellenistic sculptors explored new subjects—Gauls with strange mustaches and necklaces, impoverished old women—and treated traditional subjects in new ways—athletes with battered bodies and faces, openly erotic goddesses. Artists delighted in depicting violent movement and unbridled emotion.

Altar of Zeus, Pergamon,
ca. 175 BCE

6-1 Double-flute player, detail of a mural painting in the Tomb of the Leopards, Tarquinia, Italy, ca. 480–470 BCE. Detail 3′ 3½″ high.

Although Etruscan art owes an obvious stylistic debt to Greek art, painted murals in monumental tombs such as the Tomb of the Leopards at Tarquinia are unknown in Greece at the same time.

1 ft.

6

THE ETRUSCANS

"The Etruscans, as everyone knows, were the people who occupied the middle of Italy in early Roman days, and whom the Romans, in their usual neighborly fashion, wiped out entirely." So opens D. H. Lawrence's witty and sensitive *Etruscan Places* (1929), one of the earliest modern essays to value Etruscan art highly and treat it as much more than a debased form of the art of the contemporaneous city-states of Greece and southern Italy. ("Most people despise everything B.C. that isn't Greek, for the good reason that it ought to be Greek if it isn't," Lawrence quipped.) Today it is no longer necessary to argue the importance and originality of Etruscan art. Deeply influenced by, yet different from, Greek art, Etruscan sculpture, painting, and architecture not only provided the models for early Roman art and architecture but also had an impact on the art of the Greek colonies in Italy.

The heartland of the Etruscans was the territory between the Arno and Tiber rivers of central Italy (MAP **6-1**). The lush green hills still bear their name—Tuscany, the land of the people the Romans called Tusci, the region centered on Florence, birthplace of Renaissance art. So do the blue waters that splash against the western coastline of the Italian peninsula, for the Greeks referred to the Etruscans as Tyrrhenians and gave that name to the sea off Tuscany. The origin of the Tusci—the enduring "mystery of the Etruscans"—is not clear at all, however. Their language, although written in a Greek-derived script and extant in inscriptions that are still in large part obscure, is unrelated to the Indo-European linguistic family. Ancient authors, as fascinated by the puzzle as modern scholars are, generally felt that the Etruscans emigrated from the east. Herodotus, the fifth-century BCE Greek historian, specifically declared they came from Lydia in Asia Minor and that King Tyrsenos was their leader—hence their Greek name. But Dionysius of Halicarnassus, writing at the end of the first century BCE, maintained the Tusci were native Italians. And some modern researchers have theorized the Etruscans came into Italy from the north.

All these theories are current today, and no doubt some truth exists in each one. The Etruscan people of historical times were very likely the result of a gradual fusion of native and immigrant populations. This mixing of peoples occurred in the early first millennium BCE. At that time the Etruscans emerged as a people with a culture related to but distinct from those of other Italic peoples and from the civilizations of Greece and the Orient.

MAP 6-1 Italy in Etruscan times.

mies gave way to prosperous cities engaged in international commerce. Elite families could afford to acquire foreign goods, and Etruscan aristocrats quickly developed a taste for luxury objects incorporating Eastern motifs. To satisfy the demand, local artisans, inspired by imported goods, produced magnificent objects for both homes and tombs. As in Greece at the same time, the locally produced Orientalizing artifacts cannot be mistaken for their foreign models.

REGOLINI-GALASSI TOMB About 650–640 BCE, a wealthy Etruscan family stocked the so-called Regolini-Galassi Tomb (named for its excavators) at Cerveteri with bronze cauldrons and gold jewelry of Etruscan manufacture and Orientalizing style. The most spectacular of the many luxurious objects in the family tomb is a golden *fibula* (clasp or safety pin; FIG. 6-2) of unique shape used to fasten a woman's gown at the shoulder. The giant fibula is in the Italic tradition, but the five lions that stride across the gold surface are motifs originating in the Orient. The technique, also emulating Eastern imports, is masterful, combining *repoussé* (hammered relief) and *granulation* (the fusing of tiny metal balls, or granules, to a metal surface). The Regolini-Galassi fibula equals or exceeds in quality anything that might have served as a model.

During the eighth and seventh centuries BCE, the Etruscans, as highly skilled seafarers, enriched themselves through trade abroad. By the sixth century, they controlled most of northern and central Italy from such strongholds as Tarquinia (ancient Tarquinii), Cerveteri (Caere), Vulci, and Veii. But these cities never united to form a state, so it is inaccurate to speak of an Etruscan "nation" or "kingdom," only of Etruria, the territory the Etruscans occupied. Their cities coexisted, flourishing or fading independently. Any semblance of unity among them was based primarily on common linguistic ties and religious beliefs and practices. This lack of political cohesion eventually made the Etruscans relatively easy prey for the Romans.

EARLY ETRUSCAN ART

Although recognizing the distinctive character of Etruscan painting, sculpture, and architecture, art historians still usually divide the history of Etruscan art into periods mirroring those of Greek art. The seventh century BCE is the Orientalizing period of Etruscan art (followed by Archaic, Classical, and Hellenistic periods).

Orientalizing Art

During the seventh century BCE, the Etruscans successfully mined iron, tin, copper, and silver, creating great mineral wealth that transformed Etruscan society. Villages with agriculturally based econo-

1 in.

6-2 Fibula with Orientalizing lions, from the Regolini-Galassi Tomb, Cerveteri, Italy, ca. 650–640 BCE. Gold, 1′ 1½″ high. Musei Vaticani, Rome.

This huge gold pin found with other Orientalizing jewelry in a Cerveteri tomb combines repoussé and granulation and is the work of an Etruscan artist, but the lions are Near Eastern motifs.

The jewelry from the Regolini-Galassi Tomb also includes a golden *pectoral* that covered a deceased woman's chest, and two gold circlets that may be earrings, although they are large enough to be bracelets. A taste for this kind of ostentatious display is frequently the hallmark of newly acquired wealth, and this was certainly the case in seventh-century BCE Etruria.

Archaic Art and Architecture

Etruscan artists looking eastward for inspiration were also greatly impressed by the art and architecture of Greece. But however eager they may have been to emulate Greek works, the distinctive Etruscan temperament always manifested itself. The vast majority of Archaic Etruscan artworks depart markedly from their prototypes.

ETRUSCAN TEMPLES The design of Etruscan temples superficially owes much to Greece, but the differences far outweigh the similarities. Because of the materials Etruscan architects employed, usually only the foundations of Etruscan temples have survived. These are nonetheless sufficient to reveal the plans of the edifices. Supplementing the archaeological record is the Roman architect Vitruvius's treatise on architecture written near the end of the first century BCE. In it, Vitruvius provided an invaluable chapter on Etruscan temple design.

Archaeologists have constructed a model (FIG. 6-3) of a typical Archaic Etruscan temple based on Vitruvius's account. The sixth-century BCE Etruscan temple resembled contemporary Greek stone gable-roofed temples (see Chapter 5), but it had wooden columns and a terracotta-tiled wooden roof, and its walls were of sun-dried brick. Entrance was possible only via a narrow staircase at the center of the front of the temple, which sat on a high podium, the only part of the building made of stone. Columns, often three times a man's height or more, also were restricted to the front of the building, creating a deep porch that occupied roughly half the podium and setting off one side of the structure as the main side. In contrast, the front and rear of Greek temples were indistinguishable, and builders placed steps and columns on all sides (FIG. 5-13). The Etruscan

Etruscan Counterparts of Greco-Roman Gods and Heroes

Etruscan	*Greek*	*Roman*
Tinia	Zeus	Jupiter
Uni	Hera	Juno
Menrva	Athena	Minerva
Apulu	Apollo	Apollo
Artumes	Artemis	Diana
Hercle	Herakles	Hercules

temple was not intended to be viewed as a sculptural mass from the outside and from all directions, as Greek temples were. Instead it functioned primarily as an ornate home for grand statues of Etruscan gods. It was a place of shelter, protected by the wide overhang of its roof.

Etruscan temples differed in other ways from those of Greece. Etruscan (or Tuscan) columns resembled Greek Doric columns (FIG. 5-14, *left*), but *Tuscan columns* were made of wood, were unfluted, and had bases. Because of the lightness of the superstructure they had to support, Tuscan columns were, as a rule, much more widely spaced than Greek columns. Unlike their Greek counterparts, Etruscan temples frequently had three cellas—one for each of their chief gods, Tinia, Uni, and Menrva (see "Etruscan Counterparts of Greco-Roman Gods and Heroes," above). And pedimental statuary was exceedingly rare in Etruria. The Etruscans normally placed life-size narrative statuary—in terracotta instead of stone—on the peaks of their temple roofs.

6-3 Model of a typical sixth-century BCE Etruscan temple as described by Vitruvius. Istituto di Etruscologia e di Antichità Italiche, Università di Roma, Rome.

Etruscan temples resembled Greek temples but had widely spaced unfluted wooden columns only at the front, walls of sun-dried mud brick, and a narrow staircase at the center of the facade.

Etruscan Artists in Rome

In 616 BCE, according to the traditional chronology, Tarquinius Priscus of Tarquinia became Rome's first Etruscan king. He ruled for almost 40 years. His grandson, Tarquinius Superbus ("the Arrogant"), was Rome's last king. Outraged by his tyrannical behavior, the Romans drove him out in 509 BCE. Before his expulsion, however, Tarquinius Superbus embarked on a grand program to embellish the city he ruled.

The king's most ambitious undertaking was the erection of a magnificent temple on the Capitoline Hill for the joint worship of Jupiter, Juno, and Minerva. For this great commission, he summoned architects, sculptors, and workers from all over Etruria. Rome's first great religious shrine was Etruscan in patronage, in manufacture, and in form. The architect's name is unknown, but several sources preserve the identity of the Etruscan sculptor brought in to adorn the temple. His name was Vulca of Veii, and he may also have made a statue of the god Apulu (FIG. 6-4) for his native city. Pliny the Elder described his works as "the finest images of deities of that era . . . more admired than gold."* The Romans entrusted Vulca with making the statue of Jupiter that stood in the central cella of the Capitoline temple's three cellas. He also fashioned the enormous terracotta statuary group of Jupiter in a four-horse chariot, which was mounted on the roof at the highest point directly over the center of the temple facade. The fame of Vulca's red-faced (painted terracotta) portrayal of Jupiter was so great that Roman generals would paint their faces red in emulation of his Jupiter when they paraded in triumph through Rome after a battlefield victory. (The model of a three-cella Etruscan temple in FIG. 6-3 also gives an approximate idea of the appearance of the Capitoline Jupiter temple and of Vulca's roof statue.)

Vulca is the only Etruscan artist any ancient writer names, but the signatures of other Etruscan artists appear on preserved artworks. One of these is Novios Plautios (FIG. 6-13), who also worked in Rome, although a few centuries later. By then the Etruscan kings

6-4 Apulu (Apollo), from the roof of the Portonaccio temple, Veii, Italy, ca. 510–500 BCE. Painted terracotta, 5′ 11″ high. Museo Nazionale di Villa Giulia, Rome.

The Veii Apulu was part of a statuary group depicting a Greek myth. Distinctly Etruscan, however, are the god's vigorous motion and gesticulating arms and the placement of the statue on a temple roof.

1 ft.

of Rome were a distant memory, and the Romans had captured Veii and annexed its territory.

*Pliny, *Natural History*, 35.157.

APULU OF VEII The finest of these rooftop statues to survive today is the life-size image of Apulu (FIG. **6-4**), which displays the energy and excitement that characterize Archaic Etruscan art in general. The statue comes from a temple in the Portonaccio sanctuary at Veii. It is but one of a group of at least four painted terracotta figures that adorned the top of the temple roof and depicted one of the 12 labors of Herakles/Hercles (see "Herakles," Chapter 5, page 106). The god confronts Hercle for possession of the Ceryneian hind, a wondrous beast with golden horns that was sacred to Apulu's sister Artumes. The bright paint and the rippling folds of Apulu's garment call to mind the Archaic korai of the Acropolis in Ionian garb (FIG. 5-12). But Apulu's vigorous striding motion, gesticulating arms, fan-like calf muscles, and animated face are distinctly Etruscan. Some scholars have attributed the Apulu statue to VULCA OF VEII, the most

famous Etruscan sculptor of the time (see "Etruscan Artists in Rome," above). The statue's discovery in 1916 was instrumental in prompting a reevaluation of the originality of Etruscan art.

CERVETERI SARCOPHAGUS Although life-size terracotta statuary was known in Greece, this medium was especially favored in Etruria. Another Archaic Etruscan terracotta masterwork is the sarcophagus (FIG. **6-5**) from a Cerveteri tomb in the form of a husband and wife reclining on a banquet couch. The sarcophagus, which was once brightly painted, was cast in four sections and is of monumental size, but it contained only the ashes of the deceased. Cremation was the most common means of disposing of the dead in Italy at this time. This kind of funerary monument had no parallel at this date in Greece, where there were no monumental tombs that

The "Audacity" of Etruscan Women

At the instigation of the emperor Augustus at the end of the first century BCE, Titus Livy wrote a history of Rome from its legendary founding in 753 BCE to his own day. In the first book of his great work, Livy recounted the tale of Tullia, daughter of Servius Tullius, an Etruscan king of Rome in the sixth century BCE. The princess had married the less ambitious of two brothers of the royal Tarquinius family, while her sister had married the bolder of the two princes. Together, Tullia and her brother-in-law, Tarquinius Superbus, arranged for the murder of their spouses. They then married each other and plotted the overthrow and death of Tullia's father. After the king's murder, Tullia ostentatiously drove her carriage over her father's corpse, spraying herself with his blood. (The Roman road where the evil deed occurred is still called the Street of Infamy.) Livy, though condemning Tullia's actions, placed them in the context of the famous "audacity" of Etruscan women.

The independent spirit and relative freedom women enjoyed in Etruscan society similarly horrified (and threatened) other Greco-Roman male authors. The stories the fourth-century BCE Greek historian Theopompus heard about the debauchery of Etruscan women appalled him. They epitomized immorality for Theopompus, but much of what he reported is untrue. Etruscan women did not, for example, exercise naked alongside Etruscan men. But archaeological evidence confirms the accuracy of at least one of his "slurs": Etruscan women did attend banquets and recline with their husbands on a common couch (FIGS. 6-5 and 6-9). Aristotle also remarked on this custom. It was so foreign to the Greeks that it both shocked and frightened them. Only men, boys, slave girls, and prostitutes attended Greek symposiums. The wives remained at home, excluded from most aspects of public life. In Etruscan Italy, in striking contrast to contemporaneous Greece, women also regularly attended sporting events with men. This, too, is well documented in Etruscan paintings and reliefs.

Etruscan inscriptions also reflect the higher status of women in Etruria as compared with Greece. They often give the names of both the father and mother of the person commemorated (for example, the inscribed portrait of Aule Metele, FIG. 6-16), a practice unheard of in Greece (witness the grave stele of "Hegeso, daughter of Proxenos," FIG. 5-57). Etruscan women, moreover, retained their own names and could legally own property independently of their husbands. The frequent use of inscriptions on Etruscan mirrors and other toiletry items (FIG. 6-13) buried with women seems to attest to a high degree of female literacy as well.

6-5 Sarcophagus with reclining couple, from Cerveteri, Italy, ca. 520 BCE. Painted terracotta, 3′ 9½″ × 6′ 7″. Museo Nazionale di Villa Giulia, Rome.

Sarcophagi in the form of a husband and wife on a dining couch have no parallels in Greece. The artist's focus on the upper half of the figures and the emphatic gestures are Etruscan hallmarks.

1 ft.

could house large sarcophagi. The Greeks buried their dead in simple graves marked by a stele or a statue. Moreover, although banquets were common subjects on Greek vases (which, by the late sixth century BCE, the Etruscans imported in great quantities and regularly deposited in their tombs), only men dined at Greek symposiums. The image of a husband and wife sharing the same banquet couch is uniquely Etruscan (see "The 'Audacity' of Etruscan Women," above).

The man and woman on the Cerveteri sarcophagus are as animated as the Veii Apulu (FIG. 6-4), even though they are at rest. They are the antithesis of the stiff and formal figures encountered in Egyptian tomb sculptures (compare FIG. 3-13). Also typically Etruscan, and in striking contrast to contemporaneous Greek statues with their emphasis on proportion and balance, is the manner in which the Cerveteri sculptor rendered the upper and lower parts of each body. The legs were only summarily modeled, and the transition to

6-6 Tumuli in the Banditaccia necropolis, Cerveteri, Italy, seventh to second centuries BCE.

In the Banditaccia necropolis (city of the dead) at Cerveteri, the Etruscans buried several generations of families in multi-chambered rock-cut underground tombs covered by great earthen mounds (tumuli).

the torso at the waist is unnatural. The Etruscan artist's interest focused on the upper half of the figures, especially on the vibrant faces and gesticulating arms. Gestures are still an important ingredient of Italian conversation today, and the Cerveteri banqueters and the Veii Apulu speak to the viewer in a way that Greek statues of similar date, with their closed contours and calm demeanor, never do.

BANDITACCIA NECROPOLIS The exact findspot of the Cerveteri sarcophagus is not known, but the kind of tomb that housed such sarcophagi is well documented. The typical tomb in Cerveteri's Banditaccia necropolis (FIG. 6-6) took the form of a mound, or *tumulus*, not unlike the Mycenaean Treasury of Atreus (FIG. 4-20). But whereas the Mycenaean tholos tomb was constructed of masonry blocks and then covered by an earthen mound, each Etruscan tumulus covered one or more subterranean multichambered tombs cut out of the dark local limestone called tufa. These burial mounds sometimes reached colossal size, with diameters in excess of 130 feet. They were arranged in cemeteries in an orderly manner along a network of streets, producing the effect of veritable "cities of the dead" (the literal meaning of the Greek word *necropolis*), and were always located some distance from the cities of the living.

The underground tomb chambers cut into the rock resembled the houses of the living. In the plan (FIG. 6-7) of the Tomb of the Shields and Chairs, for example, the central entrance and the smaller chambers opening onto a large central space mirror the axial sequence of rooms in Etruscan dwellings of the time. The effect of a domestic interior was enhanced by the beds and grand armchairs with curved backs and footstools (clearly visible on the plan), as well as the ceiling beams, framed doorways, and even windows that the sculptors cut out of the rock. The technique recalls that of rock-cut Egyptian tombs (FIG. 3-19) and highlights the very different values of the Etruscans and the Greeks. The Etruscans' temples no longer stand because they constructed them of wood and mud brick, but their grand subterranean tombs are as permanent as the bedrock itself. The Greeks employed stone for the shrines of their gods but only rarely built monumental tombs for their dead.

6-7 Plan of the Tomb of the Shields and Chairs, Cerveteri, Italy, second half of the sixth century BCE.

In plan, the subterranean tombs of Cerveteri resemble the houses of the living. Sculptors enhanced the effect of a domestic interior by carving beds, chairs, doors, and ceiling beams out of the bedrock.

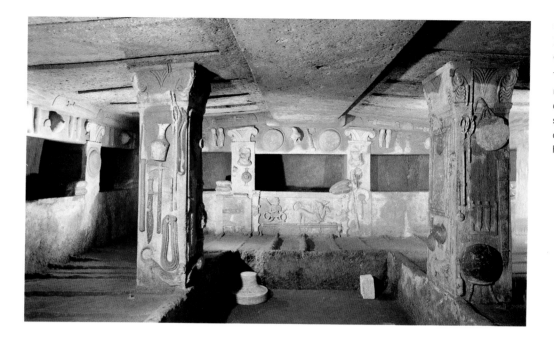

The Tomb of the Reliefs takes its name from the painted stucco reliefs covering its walls and piers. The stools, mirrors, drinking cups, and other items are reminders of the houses of the living.

TOMB OF THE RELIEFS The most elaborate of the Cerveteri tombs, in decoration if not in plan, is the so-called Tomb of the Reliefs (FIG. **6-8**). Like the much earlier Tomb of the Shields and Chairs, it accommodated several generations of a single family. The walls and piers of this tomb were, as usual, gouged out of the tufa bedrock, but in this instance painted stucco reliefs covered the stone. The stools, mirrors, drinking cups, pitchers, and knives effectively suggest a domestic context, underscoring the connection between Etruscan houses of the dead and those of the living. Other reliefs, such as the helmet and shields over the main funerary couch (the pillows are also shallow reliefs), are signs of the elite status of this Cerveteri family. The three-headed dog Cerberus, guardian of the gate to the Underworld, beneath the same couch is a reference to the passage from this life to the next.

TARQUINIA Large underground burial chambers hewn out of the natural rock were also the norm at Tarquinia. Earthen mounds may once have covered the Tarquinia tombs too, but the tumuli are no longer preserved. In contrast to Cerveteri, the subterranean rooms at Tarquinia do not have carvings imitating the appearance of Etruscan houses. In some cases, however, paintings decorate the walls. Painted tombs are statistically rare, the privilege of only the wealthiest Etruscan families. Nevertheless, archaeologists have discovered many paintings at Tarquinia by using periscopes to explore tomb interiors from the surface before considering time-consuming and costly excavation. Consequently, art historians have an almost unbroken record of monumental painting in Etruria from Archaic to Hellenistic times.

TOMB OF THE LEOPARDS A characteristic example dating to the early fifth century BCE is the Tomb of the Leopards (FIG. **6-9**), named for the beasts that guard the interior of the painted chamber from their perch within the pediment of the rear wall. They

6-9 Interior of the Tomb of the Leopards, Tarquinia, Italy, ca. 480–470 BCE.

Mural paintings adorn many of the underground tombs at Tarquinia. In this tomb, banqueting couples, servants, and musicians celebrate the joys of the good life. The men have dark skin, the women fair skin.

6-10 Diving and fishing, detail of a mural painting in the Tomb of Hunting and Fishing, Tarquinia, Italy, ca. 530–520 BCE. Detail, 5′ 6½″ high.

Scenes of young men enjoying the pleasures of nature cover the walls of this Tarquinian tomb. The Etruscan diving scene predates a similar landscape painting (FIG. 5-61) in a Greek tomb at Paestum.

are reminiscent of the panthers on each side of Medusa in the pediment (FIG. 5-17) of the Temple of Artemis at Corfu. But mythological figures, whether Greek or Etruscan, are uncommon in Tarquinian murals, and the Tomb of the Leopards has none. Instead, banqueting couples (the men with dark skin, the women with light skin, in conformity with the age-old convention) adorn the walls—painted versions of the terracotta sarcophagus (FIG. 6-5) from Cerveteri. Pitcher- and cup-bearers serve the guests, and musicians entertain them. The banquet takes place in the open air or perhaps in a tent set up for the occasion. In characteristic Etruscan fashion, the banqueters, servants, and entertainers all make exaggerated gestures with unnaturally enlarged hands (FIG. 6-1). The man on the couch at the far right on the rear wall holds up an egg, the symbol of regeneration. The tone is joyful. The painting is a celebration of life, food, wine, music, and dance, rather than a somber contemplation of death.

In stylistic terms, the Etruscan figures are comparable to those on sixth-century Greek vases before Late Archaic painters became preoccupied with the problem of foreshortening. Etruscan painters may be considered somewhat backward in this respect, but in other ways they seem to have outpaced their counterparts in Greece, especially in their interest in rendering nature. In the Tomb of the Leopards, the landscape is but a few trees and shrubs placed between the

entertainers (and leopards) and behind the banquet couches. But elsewhere the natural environment was the chief interest of Tarquinian painters.

TOMB OF HUNTING AND FISHING Scenes of Etruscans enjoying the pleasures of nature decorate all the walls of the main chamber of the aptly named Tomb of Hunting and Fishing at Tarquinia. In the detail reproduced here (FIG. 6-10), a youth dives off a rocky promontory, while others fish from a boat and birds fill the sky all around. On another wall, youthful hunters aim their slingshots at the brightly painted birds. The scenes of hunting and fishing recall the paintings in Egyptian tombs (FIGS. 3-15 and 3-28) and may indicate knowledge of that Eastern funerary tradition. The multicolored rocks resemble those of the Theran *Spring Fresco* (FIG. 4-9), but art historians know of nothing similar in contemporaneous Greek art save the Tomb of the Diver (FIG. 5-61) at Paestum. That exceptional Greek work, however, is from a tomb in Italy dated about a half century later than the Tarquinian tomb. In fact, the Paestum composition probably emulated older Etruscan designs, undermining the now-outdated judgment of art historians that Etruscan art was merely derivative and that Etruscan artists never set the standard for Greek artists.

An Etruscan sculptor cast this bronze statue of the she-wolf that nursed the infants Romulus and Remus, founders of Rome. The animal has a tense, gaunt body and an unforgettable psychic intensity.

1 ft.

LATER ETRUSCAN ART

The fifth century BCE was a golden age in Greece but not in Etruria. In 509 BCE the Romans expelled the last of their Etruscan kings, Tarquinius Superbus (see "Etruscan Artists in Rome," page 146), replacing the monarchy with a republican form of government. In 474 BCE an alliance of Cumaean Greeks and Hieron I of Syracuse (Sicily) defeated the Etruscan fleet off Cumae, effectively ending Etruscan dominance of the seas—and with it Etruscan prosperity.

Classical Art

These events had important consequences in the world of art and architecture. The number of Etruscan tombs, for example, decreased sharply, and the quality of the furnishings declined markedly. No longer were tombs filled with golden jewelry and imported Greek vases or decorated with mural paintings of the first rank. But art did not cease in Etruria. Indeed, in specialties in which Etruscan artists excelled, especially the casting of statues in bronze and terracotta,

they continued to produce impressive works, even though fewer in number.

CAPITOLINE WOLF The best-known of these later Etruscan statues—one of the most memorable portrayals of an animal in the history of world art—is the *Capitoline Wolf* (FIG. **6-11**). The statue is a somewhat larger than life-size hollow-cast bronze portrayal of the she-wolf that, according to legend, nursed Romulus and Remus after they were abandoned as infants. When the twins grew to adulthood, they quarreled, and Romulus killed his brother. On April 21, 753 BCE, Romulus founded Rome and became the city's king. The statue of the she-wolf seems to have been made, however, for the new Roman Republic after the expulsion of Tarquinius Superbus. The appropriately defiant image became the new government's totem and has remained the emblem of Rome to this day.

The *Capitoline Wolf,* however, is not a work of Roman art, which had not yet developed a distinct identity, but rather is the product of an Etruscan workshop. (The suckling infants are 15th-century additions.) The vitality accorded the human figure in Etruscan art is here concentrated in the tense, watchful animal body of the she-wolf, with her spare flanks, gaunt ribs, and taut, powerful legs. The lowered neck and head, alert ears, glaring eyes, and ferocious muzzle capture the psychic intensity of the fierce and protective beast as danger approaches. Not even the great animal reliefs of Assyria (FIG. **2-23**) match this profound characterization of animal temperament.

CHIMERA OF AREZZO Another masterpiece of Etruscan bronze-casting is the *Chimera of Arezzo* (FIG. **6-12**), which dates about a century later than the *Capitoline Wolf.* The *chimera* is a monster of Greek invention with a lion's head and body and a serpent's tail (restored in this case). A second head, that of a goat, grows out of the lion's left side. The goat's neck bears the wound the Greek hero Bellerophon inflicted when he hunted

6-12 *Chimera of Arezzo,* from Arezzo, Italy, first half of fourth century BCE. Bronze, 2′ 7½″ high. Museo Archeologico Nazionale, Florence.

The chimera was a composite monster slain by the Greek hero Bellerophon. In this Etruscan statue, the artist depicted the wounded beast poised to attack and growling ferociously.

1 ft.

6-13 Novios Plautios, *Ficoroni Cista,* from Palestrina, Italy, late fourth century BCE. Bronze, 2′ 6″ high. Museo Nazionale di Villa Giulia, Rome.

Novios Plautios made this container for a woman's toiletry articles in Rome and engraved it with the myth of the Argonauts. The composition is probably an adaptation of a Greek painting.

1 in.

and slew the composite beast. As rendered by the Etruscan sculptor, the chimera, although injured and bleeding, is far from defeated. Like the earlier she-wolf statue, the bronze chimera has muscles that are stretched tightly over its rib cage. The monster prepares to attack, and a ferocious cry emanates from its open jaws. Some scholars have postulated that the statue was part of a group that originally included Bellerophon, but the chimera could just as well have stood alone. The menacing gaze upward toward an unseen adversary need not have been answered. In this respect, too, the chimera is in the tradition of the *Capitoline Wolf.*

Etruscan Art and the Rise of Rome

At about the time the *Chimera of Arezzo* was fashioned, Rome began to appropriate Etruscan territory. Veii fell to the Romans in 396 BCE, after a terrible 10-year siege. Peace was concluded with Tarquinia in 351, but by the beginning of the next century, Rome had annexed Tarquinia too, and in 273 BCE the Romans conquered Cerveteri.

FICORONI CISTA Rome's growing power in central Italy is indicated indirectly by the engraved inscription on the *Ficoroni Cista* (FIG. 6-13). Etruscan artists began to produce such *cistae* (cylindrical containers for a woman's toiletry articles), made of sheet bronze with cast handles and feet and elaborately engraved bodies, in large numbers in the fourth century BCE. Along with engraved bronze mirrors, they were popular gifts for both the living and the dead. The center of the Etruscan bronze cista industry was Palestrina (ancient Praeneste), where the *Ficoroni Cista* was found. The inscription on the handle states that Dindia Macolnia, a local noblewoman, gave the bronze container to her daughter and that the artist was Novios Plautios. According to the inscription, his workshop was not in Palestrina but in Rome, which by this date was becoming an important Italian cultural as well as political center.

The engraved frieze of the *Ficoroni Cista* depicts an episode from the Greek story of the expedition of the Argonauts in search of the Golden Fleece. Scholars generally agree that the composition is an adaptation of a lost Greek panel painting, perhaps one then on display in Rome—additional testimony to the burgeoning wealth and prestige of the city Etruscan kings once ruled. The Greek source for Novios Plautios's engraving is evident in the figures seen entirely from behind or in three-quarter view, and in the placement of the protagonists on several levels in the Polygnotan manner (FIG. 5-59).

PORTA MARZIA, PERUGIA In the third century BCE, the Etruscan city of Perugia (ancient Perusia) formed an alliance with Rome and was spared the destruction that Veii, Cerveteri, and other Etruscan towns suffered. Portions of Perugia's ancient walls are still standing, as are some of its gates. One of these, the so-called Porta Marzia (Gate of Mars), was dismantled during the Renaissance, but the upper part of the gate (FIG. 6-14) is preserved, embedded in a later wall. The archway is formed by a series of trapezoidal stone *voussoirs* held in place by the weight of the blocks pressing against one another (FIG. 4-17c). Earlier architects built arches in Greece as well as in Mesopotamia (FIG. 2-24), but in Italy, first under the Etruscans and later under the Romans, *arcuated* (arch-shaped) gateways and freestanding ("triumphal") arches became a major architectural type.

The use of Hellenic-inspired *pilasters* (flat columns) to frame the rounded opening of the Porta Marzia typifies the Etruscan adaptation of Greek motifs. Arches bracketed by engaged columns or

The arch has a long history in ancient architecture, but it was most commonly used in Etruscan and Roman buildings. Often Greek pilasters or engaged columns frame an arcuated opening.

pilasters have a long and distinguished history in Roman and later times. In the Porta Marzia, sculpted half-figures of Jupiter and his sons Castor and Pollux and their steeds look out from between the fluted pilasters. The divine twins had appeared miraculously on a battlefield in 484 BCE to turn the tide in favor of the Romans. The presence of these three deities at the apex of the Porta Marzia may reflect the new Roman practice of erecting triumphal arches with gilded bronze statues on top.

SARCOPHAGUS OF LARS PULENA In Hellenistic Etruria, the counterparts of the magnificent Archaic terracotta sarcophagus (FIG. 6-5) from Cerveteri were made of local stone. The leading production center was Tarquinia, where an Etruscan sculptor fashioned the sarcophagus of Lars Pulena (FIG. 6-15) early in the second century BCE. The scene sculpted on the front of the coffin shows the deceased in the Underworld between two *charuns* (Etruscan death demons) swinging hammers. It signifies that Lars Pulena has successfully made the

6-15 Sarcophagus of Lars Pulena, from Tarquinia, Italy, early second century BCE. Tufa, 6′ 6″ long. Museo Archeologico Nazionale, Tarquinia.

Images of the deceased on late Etruscan sarcophagi are much more somber than those on Archaic examples (FIG. 6-5), but Lars Pulena proudly displays a list of his life's achievements on an open scroll.

1 ft.

Later Etruscan Art   **153**

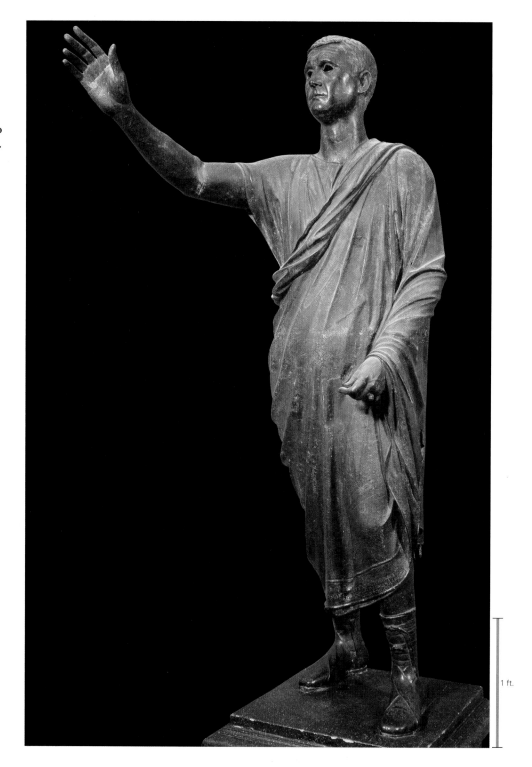

6-16 Aule Metele (*Arringatore*), from Cortona, near Lake Trasimeno, Italy, early first century BCE. Bronze, 5′ 7″ high. Museo Archeologico Nazionale, Florence.

Inscribed in Etruscan, this bronze statue of an orator is Etruscan in name only. Aule Metele wears the short toga and high boots of a Roman magistrate, and the style of the portrait is also Roman.

1 ft.

journey to the afterlife. Above, the deceased is shown in a reclining position, but he is not at a festive banquet, and his wife is not present. His somber expression contrasts sharply with the smiling, confident faces of the Archaic era when Etruria enjoyed its greatest prosperity. Similar heads—realistic but generic types, not true portraits—are found on all later Etruscan sarcophagi and in tomb paintings. They are symptomatic of the economic and political decline of the once-mighty Etruscan city-states. Nonetheless, Lars Pulena is a proud man. He wears a wreath around his neck and displays a partially unfurled scroll inscribed with the record of his life's accomplishments.

AULE METELE An even later Etruscan portrait is the statue (FIG. **6-16**) of the magistrate Aule Metele raising his arm to address an assembly—hence his modern nickname *Arringatore* (*Orator*).

This life-size statue proves that Etruscan artists continued to be experts at bronze-casting long after the heyday of Etruscan prosperity. The *Arringatore* was most likely produced at about the time the Romans achieved total hegemony over the Etruscans. The so-called Social War of the early first century BCE ended in 89 BCE with the conferring of Roman citizenship on all of Italy's inhabitants. In fact, Aule Metele—his Etruscan name and his father's and mother's names are inscribed on the hem of his garment—wears the short toga and high laced boots of a Roman magistrate. His head, with its close-cropped hair and signs of age in the face, resembles portraits produced in Rome at the time. This orator is Etruscan in name only. If the origin of the Etruscans remains debatable, the question of their demise has a ready answer. Aule Metele and his compatriots became Romans, and Etruscan art became Roman art.

THE ETRUSCANS

ORIENTALIZING ART, ca. 700–600 BCE

▌ During the early first millennium BCE, the Etruscans emerged as a people with a culture distinct from those of other Italic peoples and the Greeks.

▌ In the seventh century BCE, the Etruscans traded metals from their mines for foreign goods and began to produce jewelry and other luxury objects decorated with motifs modeled on those found on imports from the Near East.

Regolini-Galassi fibula, Cerveteri, ca. 650–640 BCE

ARCHAIC ART, ca. 600–480 BCE

▌ The sixth century BCE was the apex of Etruscan power in Italy. Etruscan kings even ruled Rome until 509 BCE.

▌ The Etruscans admired Greek art and architecture but did not copy Greek works. Etruscan temples were made of wood and mud brick instead of stone and had columns and stairs only at the front. Terracotta statuary decorated the roof.

A typical sixth-century BCE Etruscan temple

▌ Most surviving Etruscan artworks come from underground tomb chambers. At Cerveteri, great earthen mounds (tumuli) covered tombs with interiors sculptured to imitate the houses of the living.

▌ At Tarquinia, painters covered the tomb walls with monumental frescoes, usually depicting funerary banquets attended by both men and women.

Tomb of the Leopards, Tarquinia, ca. 480–470 BCE

CLASSICAL AND HELLENISTIC ART, ca. 480–489 BCE

▌ The Greek defeat of the Etruscan fleet off Cumae in 474 BCE ended Etruscan domination of the sea and marked the beginning of Etruria's decline. Rome destroyed Veii in 396 BCE and conquered Cerveteri in 273 BCE. All of Italy became Romanized by 89 BCE.

▌ A very different, more somber, mood pervades Etruscan art during the fifth through first centuries BCE, as seen, for example, in the sarcophagus of Lars Pulena.

Sarcophagus of Lars Pulena, early second century BCE

▌ Later Etruscan architecture is noteworthy for the widespread use of the stone arch, often framed with Greek pilasters or columns, as on the Porta Marzia at Perugia.

Porta Marzia, Perugia, second century BCE

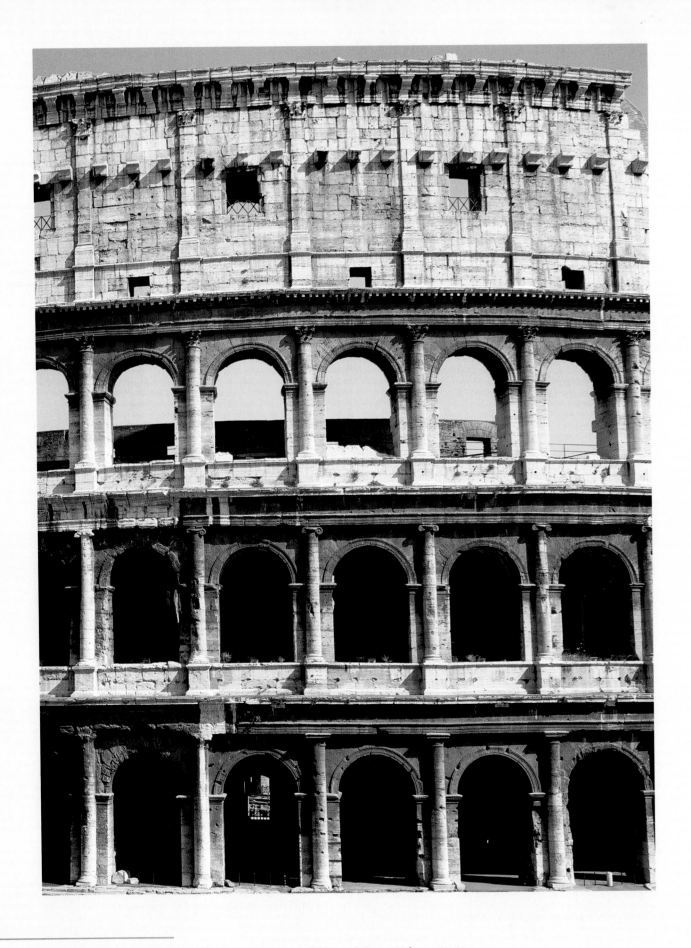

7-1 Detail of the facade of the Colosseum (Flavian Amphitheater), Rome, Italy, ca. 70–80 CE.

Rome's most famous landmark (FIG. 7-36) is a prime example of Roman eclecticism. The architect mixed Greek columns and Roman arches on the facade, which masked a skeleton of concrete vaults.

THE ROMAN EMPIRE

With the rise and triumph of Rome, a single government ruled, for the first time in history, from the Strait of Gibraltar to the Nile, from the Tigris and Euphrates to the Rhine, Danube, Thames and beyond (MAP **7-1**). Within the Roman Empire's borders lived millions of people of numerous races, religions, tongues, and cultures: Britons and Gauls, Greeks and Egyptians, Africans and Syrians, Jews and Christians, to name but a few. Of all the ancient civilizations, the Roman most closely approximated today's world in its multicultural character.

Roman monuments of art and architecture, spread throughout the vast territory the Romans governed, are the most conspicuous and numerous of all the remains of ancient civilization. In Europe, the Middle East, and Africa today, Roman temples and basilicas have an afterlife as churches. The powerful concrete vaults of ancient Roman buildings form the cores of modern houses, stores, restaurants, factories, and museums. Bullfights, sports events, operas, and rock concerts are staged in Roman amphitheaters. Ships dock in what were once Roman ports, and Western Europe's highway system still closely follows the routes of Roman roads.

Ancient Rome also lives on in the Western world in concepts of law and government, in languages, in the calendar—even in the coins used daily. Roman art speaks in a language almost every Western viewer can readily understand. Its diversity and eclecticism foreshadowed the modern world. The Roman use of art, especially portraits and narrative reliefs, to manipulate public opinion is similar to the carefully crafted imagery of contemporary political campaigns. And the Roman mastery of concrete construction began an architectural revolution still felt today.

The center of the far-flung Roman Empire was the city on the Tiber River that, according to legend, Romulus and his twin brother Remus founded on April 21, 753 BCE. Their Rome consisted only of small huts clustered together on the Palatine Hill (FIG. **7-2,** no. 3) overlooking what was then uninhabited marshland. In the Archaic period, Rome was essentially an Etruscan city, both politically and culturally. Its greatest shrine, the Temple of Jupiter Optimus Maximus (Best and Greatest) on the Capitoline Hill, was built by an Etruscan king, designed by an Etruscan architect, made of wood and mud brick in the Etruscan manner, and decorated with terracotta statuary created by an Etruscan sculptor (see "Etruscan Artists in Rome," Chapter 6, page 146).

Map 7-1 The Roman Empire at the death of Trajan in 117 CE.

7-2 Model of the city of Rome during the early fourth century CE. Museo della Civiltà Romana, Rome.
(1) Temple of Portunus,
(2) Circus Maximus,
(3) Palatine Hill, (4) Temple of Jupiter Capitolinus,
(5) Pantheon, (6) Column of Trajan, (7) Forum of Trajan,
(8) Markets of Trajan,
(9) Forum of Julius Caesar,
(10) Forum of Augustus,
(11) Forum Romanum,
(12) Basilica Nova, (13) Arch of Titus, (14) Temple of Venus and Roma, (15) Arch of Constantine, (16) Colossus of Nero, (17) Colosseum.

By the time of Constantine, the city of Rome was densely packed with temples, forums, triumphal arches, theaters, baths, racetracks, aqueducts, markets, private homes, and apartment houses.

An Outline of Roman History

MONARCHY (753–509 BCE)
Latin and Etruscan kings ruled Rome from the city's founding by Romulus and Remus until the revolt against Tarquinius Superbus (exact dates of rule unreliable).

REPUBLIC (509–27 BCE)
The Roman Republic lasted from the expulsion of Tarquinius Superbus until the bestowing of the title of Augustus on Octavian, the grandnephew of Julius Caesar and victor over Mark Antony in the civil war that ended the Republic. Some major figures were

- Marcellus, b. 268(?), d. 208 BCE, consul
- Marius, b. 157, d. 86 BCE, consul
- Sulla, b. 138, d. 79 BCE, consul and dictator
- Pompey, b. 106, d. 48 BCE, consul
- Julius Caesar, b. 100, d. 44 BCE, consul and dictator
- Mark Antony, b. 83, d. 30 BCE, consul

EARLY EMPIRE (27 BCE–96 CE)
The Early Empire began with the rule of Augustus and his Julio-Claudian successors and continued until the end of the Flavian dynasty. Selected emperors and their dates of rule (with names of the most influential empresses in parentheses) were

- Augustus (Livia), r. 27 BCE–14 CE
- Tiberius, r. 14–37
- Caligula, r. 37–41
- Claudius (Agrippina the Younger), r. 41–54
- Nero, r. 54–68
- Vespasian, r. 69–79

- Titus, r. 79–81
- Domitian, r. 81–96

HIGH EMPIRE (96–192 CE)
The High Empire began with the rule of Nerva and the Spanish emperors, Trajan and Hadrian, and ended with the last emperor of the Antonine dynasty. The emperors (and empresses) of this period were

- Nerva, r. 96–98
- Trajan (Plotina), r. 98–117
- Hadrian (Sabina), r. 117–138
- Antoninus Pius (Faustina the Elder), r. 138–161
- Marcus Aurelius (Faustina the Younger), r. 161–180
- Lucius Verus, coemperor with Marcus Aurelius, r. 161–169
- Commodus, r. 180–192

LATE EMPIRE (193–337 CE)
The Late Empire began with the Severan dynasty and included the so-called soldier emperors of the third century, the tetrarchs, and Constantine, the first Christian emperor. Selected emperors (and empresses) were

- Septimius Severus (Julia Domna), r. 193–211
- Caracalla (Plautilla), r. 211–217
- Severus Alexander, r. 222–235
- Trajan Decius, r. 249–251
- Trebonianus Gallus, r. 251–253
- Diocletian, r. 284–305
- Constantine I, r. 306–337

REPUBLIC

In 509 BCE the Romans overthrew Tarquinius Superbus, the last of Rome's Etruscan kings, and established a constitutional government (see "An Outline of Roman History," above). The new Roman Republic vested power mainly in a *senate* (literally, "a council of elders," *senior* citizens) and in two elected *consuls*. Under extraordinary circumstances, a *dictator* could be appointed for a specified time and a specific purpose, such as commanding the army during a crisis. All leaders came originally from among the wealthy landowners, or *patricians,* but later also from the *plebeian* class of small farmers, merchants, and freed slaves.

Before long, the descendants of Romulus conquered Rome's neighbors one by one: the Etruscans and the Gauls to the north, the Samnites and the Greek colonists to the south. Even the Carthaginians of North Africa, who under Hannibal's dynamic leadership had annihilated some of Rome's legions and almost brought down the Republic, fell before the mighty Roman armies.

Architecture

The year 211 BCE was a turning point both for Rome and for Roman art. Breaking with precedent, Marcellus, conqueror of the fabulously wealthy Sicilian Greek city of Syracuse, brought back to Rome not only the usual spoils of war—captured arms and armor, gold and silver coins, and the like—but also the city's artistic patrimony. Thus began, in the words of the historian Livy, "the craze for works of

Greek art."[1] Exposure to Greek sculpture and painting and to the splendid marble temples of the Greek gods increased as the Romans expanded their conquests beyond Italy. Greece became a Roman province in 146 BCE, and in 133 BCE the last Attalid king of Pergamon willed his kingdom to Rome (see Chapter 5). Nevertheless, although the Romans developed a virtually insatiable taste for Greek "antiques," the Etruscan basis of Roman art and architecture was never forgotten. The buildings and statues of the Roman Republic are highly eclectic, drawing on both Greek and Etruscan traditions.

TEMPLE OF PORTUNUS, ROME Eclecticism is the primary characteristic of the Republican temple on the east bank of the Tiber popularly known as the Temple of Fortuna Virilis (FIGS. 7-2, no. 1, and 7-3). It is actually a temple dedicated to Portunus, the Roman god of harbors. Its plan follows the Etruscan pattern with a high podium and a flight of steps only at the front. Freestanding columns are confined to the deep porch. But the structure is built of stone (local tufa and travertine), overlaid originally with stucco in imitation of Greek marble. The columns are not Tuscan but Ionic, complete with flutes and bases, and there is a matching Ionic frieze (see "Doric and Ionic Orders," Chapter 5, page 96). Moreover, in an effort to approximate a peripteral Greek temple yet maintain the basic Etruscan plan, the architect added a series of engaged Ionic half columns to the sides and back of the cella. The result was a *pseudoperipteral* temple. Although the design combines Etruscan and Greek elements, the resultant mix is uniquely Roman.

7-3 Temple of Portunus (Temple of "Fortuna Virilis"), Rome, Italy, ca. 75 BCE.

Republican temples combine Etruscan plans and Greek elevations. This pseudoperipteral stone temple employs the Ionic order, but it has a staircase and freestanding columns only at the front.

7-4 Temple of Vesta(?), Tivoli, Italy, early first century BCE.

The round, or tholos, temple type is unknown in Etruria. The models for the Tivoli temple's builders were in Greece (FIG. 5-72), but the Roman building has a frontal orientation and a concrete cella.

TEMPLE OF VESTA, TIVOLI The Romans' admiration for the Greek temples they encountered in their conquests also led to the importation into Republican Italy of a temple type unknown in Etruscan architecture—the round, or tholos, temple. At Tivoli (ancient Tibur), on a dramatic site overlooking a deep gorge, a Republican architect erected such a Greek-inspired temple (FIG. 7-4) early in the first century BCE. The temple is circular in plan—standard for shrines of Vesta—and has travertine Corinthian columns. The frieze is carved with garlands held up by oxen heads, also in emulation of Greek models. But the high podium can be reached only via a narrow stairway leading to the cella door. This arrangement introduced an axial alignment not found in Greek tholoi (FIG. 5-72), where, as in Greek rectangular temples, steps continue all around the structure. Also in contrast with the Greeks, the Roman builders constructed the cella wall not with masonry blocks but with a new material of recent invention: concrete (see "Roman Concrete Construction," page 161).

SANCTUARY OF FORTUNA, PALESTRINA The most impressive and innovative use of concrete during the Republic was in the Sanctuary of Fortuna Primigenia (FIG. 7-5), the goddess of good fortune, at Palestrina (ancient Praeneste, formerly an Etruscan city). The great complex was constructed in the late second century BCE. Spread out over several terraces leading up the hillside to a tho-

7-5 Restored view of the Sanctuary of Fortuna Primigenia, Palestrina, Italy, late second century BCE (John Burge).

Fortuna's hillside sanctuary at Palestrina was made possible by the use of concrete barrel vaults for terraces, ramps, shops, and porticos spread out over several levels. A tholos temple crowned the complex.

Roman Concrete Construction

The history of Roman architecture would be very different had the Romans been content to use the same building materials as the Greeks, Etruscans, and other ancient peoples. Instead, the Romans developed concrete construction, which revolutionized architectural design. Roman *concrete* was made from a changing recipe of lime mortar, volcanic sand, water, and small stones (*caementa,* from which the English word *cement* derives). Builders placed the mixture in wooden frames and left it to dry. When the concrete hardened completely, they removed the wooden molds, leaving behind a solid mass of great strength, though rough in appearance. The Romans often covered the rough concrete with stucco or with marble *revetment* (facing). Despite this lengthy procedure, concrete walls were much less costly to construct than walls of imported Greek marble or even local tufa and travertine.

The advantages of concrete go well beyond cost, however. It is possible to fashion concrete shapes that masonry construction cannot achieve, especially huge vaulted and domed rooms without internal supports. Concrete enabled Roman builders to think of architecture in revolutionary ways. Roman concrete became a vehicle for shaping architectural space.

The most common types of Roman concrete vaults and domes are

▌ *Barrel Vaults* Also called the *tunnel vault,* the *barrel vault* (FIG. 7-6*a*) is an extension of a simple arch, creating a semicylindrical ceiling over parallel walls. Pre-Roman builders constructed barrel vaults using traditional ashlar masonry (FIG. 2-24), but those earlier vaults were less stable than concrete barrel vaults. If even a single block of a cut-stone vault comes loose, the whole vault may collapse. Also, masonry barrel vaults can be illuminated only by light entering at either end of the tunnel. Using concrete, Roman builders could place windows at any point in a barrel vault, because once the concrete hardens, it forms a seamless sheet of "artificial stone" in which the openings do not lessen the vault's structural integrity. Whether made of stone or concrete, barrel vaults

require *buttressing* (lateral support) of the walls below the vaults to counteract their downward and outward *thrust.*

▌ *Groin Vaults* A *groin* or *cross vault* (FIG. 7-6*b*) is formed by the intersection at right angles of two barrel vaults of equal size. Besides appearing lighter than the barrel vault, the groin vault needs less buttressing. The barrel vault's thrust is concentrated along the entire length of the supporting wall. The groin vault's thrust, however, is concentrated along the *groins,* the lines at the juncture of the two barrel vaults. Buttressing is needed only at the points where the groins meet the vault's vertical supports, usually *piers.* The system leaves the area between the supports open, permitting light to enter. Groin vaults, like barrel vaults, can be built using stone blocks—but with the same structural limitations when compared with concrete vaulting.

When a series of groin vaults covers an interior hall (FIG. 7-6*c;* compare FIG. 7-46), the open lateral arches of the vaults form the equivalent of a *clerestory* of a traditional timber-roofed structure (for example, FIG. 8-10). Such a *fenestrated* (with openings or windows) sequence of groin vaults has a major advantage over wooden clerestories. Concrete vaults are relatively fireproof, always an important consideration given that fires were common occurrences (see "Timber Roofs and Stone Vaults," Chapter 12, page 313).

▌ *Hemispherical Domes* The largest domed space in the ancient world for more than a millennium was the corbeled, beehive-shaped tholos (FIG. 4-21) of the Treasury of Atreus at Mycenae. The Romans were able to surpass the Mycenaeans by using concrete to construct hemispherical *domes* (FIG. 7-6*d*), which usually rested on concrete cylindrical *drums.* If a barrel vault is described as a round arch extended in a line, then a hemispherical dome may be described as a round arch rotated around the full circumference of a circle. Masonry domes, like masonry vaults, cannot accommodate windows without threatening their stability. Concrete domes can be opened up even at their apex with a circular *oculus* ("eye"), allowing much-needed light to reach the vast spaces beneath (FIGS. 7-35 and 7-51).

7-6 Roman concrete construction. (a) barrel vault, (b) groin vault, (c) fenestrated sequence of groin vaults, (d) hemispherical dome with oculus (John Burge).

Concrete domes and vaults of varying designs enabled Roman builders to revolutionize the history of architecture by shaping interior spaces in novel ways.

los at the peak of an ascending triangle, the layout reflects the new Republican familiarity with the terraced sanctuaries of the Hellenistic East. The means of construction, however, was distinctly Roman. The builders used concrete barrel vaults (FIG. 7-6*a*) of enormous strength to support the imposing terraces and to cover the great ramps leading to the grand central staircase, as well as to give shape

to the shops selling food, souvenirs, and the like, aligned on two consecutive levels. In this way, the Romans transformed the entire hillside, subjecting nature itself to human will and rational order. The Palestrina sanctuary is emblematic of the growing dominance of Rome in the Mediterranean world. By the end of the second century BCE, Romulus's village of huts belonged to the legendary past.

Sculpture

Nearly all the builders of Republican temples and sanctuaries were men from old and distinguished families. Often they were victorious generals who used the spoils of war to finance public works. These aristocratic patricians were fiercely proud of their lineage. They kept likenesses (*imagines*) of their ancestors in wooden cupboards in their homes and paraded them at the funerals of prominent relatives. Portraiture was one way the patrician class celebrated its elevated position in society. The case of Marius, a renowned Republican general who lacked a long and distinguished genealogy, underscores the importance of ancestral imagines in elite circles. Marius's patrician colleagues in the Senate ridiculed him as a man who had no portraits in his home.

VERISM The subjects of these portraits were almost exclusively men (and to a lesser extent women) of advanced age, for generally only elders held power in the Republic. These patricians did not ask sculptors to make them appear nobler than they were, as Kresilas portrayed Pericles (FIG. 5-41). Instead, they requested brutally realistic images with distinctive features, in the tradition of the treasured household *imagines*. One of the most striking of these so-called *veristic* (superrealistic) portraits is the head (FIG. 7-7) of an unidentified patrician from Osimo. The sculptor painstakingly recorded each rise and fall, each bulge and fold, of the facial surface, like a mapmaker who did not want to miss the slightest detail of surface change. Scholars debate whether such portraits were truly blunt records of actual features or exaggerated types designed to make a statement about personality: serious, experienced, determined, loyal to family and state—virtues that were much admired during the Republic.

7-8 Portrait of a Roman general, from the Sanctuary of Hercules, Tivoli, Italy, ca. 75–50 BCE. Marble, 6′ 2″ high. Museo Nazionale Romano–Palazzo Massimo alle Terme, Rome.

The sculptor based this life-size portrait of a general on idealized Greek statues of heroes and athletes, but the man's head is a veristic likeness. The eclectic combination is typical of Republican art.

TIVOLI GENERAL The Osimo head also illustrates that the Romans believed the head alone was enough to constitute a portrait. The Greeks, in contrast, believed the head and body were inseparable parts of an integral whole, so their portraits were always full length (FIG. 5-87). In fact, in Republican portraiture, veristic heads were often—although incongruously—placed on bodies to which they could not possibly belong. Such is the case in the curious and discordant portrait of a general (FIG. 7-8) found at Tivoli. The *cuirass* (leather breastplate) at his side, which serves as a prop for the heavy marble statue, is the emblem of his rank. But the general does not appear as he would in life. Although he has a typically stern and lined Republican head, it sits atop a powerful, youthful, almost nude body. The sculptor modeled the portrait on the statues of Greek athletes and heroes the Romans admired so much and often copied (see Chapter 5). The incorporation of references to Greek art in these portrait statues evoked the notion of patrician cultural superiority and elevated the person portrayed to heroic status.

NONELITE PORTRAITURE In stark contrast to this elite tradition of publicly displaying portraits, slaves and former slaves could not possess *any* family portraits, because under Roman law, their parents and grandparents were not people but property. Freed slaves, however, often ordered portrait reliefs (FIGS. 7-9 and 7-10) for their tombs to commemorate their new status as Roman citizens (see "Art for Former Slaves," page 163).

7-7 Head of an old man, from Osimo, mid-first century BCE. Marble, life-size. Palazzo del Municipio, Osimo.

Veristic (superrealistic) portraits of old men from distinguished families were the norm during the Republic. The sculptor of this head painstakingly recorded every detail of the elderly man's face.

Art for Former Slaves

Historians and art historians alike tend to focus on the lives and monuments of famous individuals, but some of the most interesting remains of ancient Roman civilization are the artworks commissioned by ordinary people, especially former slaves, or *freedmen* and *freedwomen*. Slavery was common in the Roman world. Indeed, researchers estimate that Italy at the end of the Republic had some two million slaves, or roughly one slave for every three citizens. The very rich might own hundreds of slaves, but slaves could be found in all but the poorest households. The practice was so much a part of Roman society that even slaves often became slave owners when their former masters freed them. Some gained freedom in return for meritorious service. Others were only freed in their masters' wills. Most slaves died as slaves in service to their original or new owners.

The most noteworthy artworks that Roman freedmen and freedwomen commissioned are the stone reliefs that regularly adorned their tomb facades. One of these reliefs (FIG. 7-9) depicts three people, all named Gessius. At the left is Gessia Fausta, at the right Gessius Primus. Both are the freed slaves of Publius Gessius, the freeborn citizen in the center, shown wearing a general's cuirass and portrayed in the standard Republican veristic fashion (FIGS. 7-7 and 7-8). As slaves this couple had no legal standing. They were the property of Publius Gessius. After they were freed, however, they became people by law. These stern frontal portraits proclaim their new status as legal members of Roman society—and, by including him in the relief, their gratitude to Publius Gessius for granting them that status.

As was the custom, the two former slaves bear their patron's name, but whether they are sister and brother, wife and husband, or unrelated is unclear. The inscriptions on the relief explicitly state that the monument was paid for with funds provided by the will of Gessius Primus and that the work was directed by Gessia Fausta, the only survivor of the three. The relief thus depicts the living and the dead side by side, indistinguishable except by the accompanying message. This theme is common in Roman art and affirms that death does not break bonds formed in life.

More rarely, freed slaves commissioned tomb reliefs that were narrative in character. A relief (FIG. 7-10) from Amiternum depicts the honorary funeral cortege, complete with musicians, professional female mourners who pull their hair in a display of feigned grief, and the deceased's wife and children. The deceased is laid out on a bier with a canopy as a backdrop, much like the figures on Greek Geometric vases (FIG. 5-2). Surprisingly, however, the dead man here props himself up as if still alive, surveying his own funeral. This may be an effigy, like the reclining figures on the lids of Etruscan sarcophagi (FIGS. 6-5 and 6-15), rather than the deceased himself.

Compositionally, the relief is also unexpected. Mourners and musicians stand on floating ground lines, as if on flying carpets. They are not to be viewed as suspended in space, however, but as situated behind the front row of pallbearers and musicians. This sculptor, in striking contrast to the (usually Greek) artists the patrician aristocracy employed, had little regard for the rules of Classical art. The Amiternum artist studiously avoided overlapping and placed the figures wherever they fit, so long as they were clearly visible. This approach to making pictures was characteristic of pre-Classical art, but it had been out of favor for several centuries. There are no similar compositions in the art of the consuls and senators of the Roman Republic. In ancient Rome's cosmopolitan world, as today, stylistic tastes often were tied to a person's political and social status.

7-9 Funerary relief with portraits of the Gessii, from Rome(?), Italy, ca. 30 BCE. Marble, 2′ 1½″ high. Museum of Fine Arts, Boston.

Roman freedmen often placed reliefs depicting themselves and their former owners on the facades of their tombs. The portraits and inscriptions celebrated their freedom and new status as citizens.

7-10 Relief with funerary procession, from Amiternum, Italy, second half of first century BCE. Limestone, 2′ 2″ high. Museo Nazionale d'Abruzzo, L'Aquila.

This depiction of a procession of mourners and musicians in honor of a dead freedman has figures standing on floating ground lines. The sculptor ignored the rules of Classical art that elite patrons favored.

Republic **163**

7-11 Denarius with portrait of Julius Caesar, 44 BCE. Silver, diameter ¾″. American Numismatic Society, New York.

Julius Caesar was the first to place his own portrait on the Roman coinage during his lifetime. This denarius, issued just before his assassination, shows the dictator with a deeply lined face and neck.

JULIUS CAESAR Beginning early in the first century BCE, the Roman desire to vaunt distinguished ancestry led to the placement of portraits of illustrious forebears on Republican coins. These ancestral portraits supplanted the earlier Roman tradition (based on Greek convention) of using images of divinities on coins. No Roman, however, dared to place his own likeness on a coin until 44 BCE, when Julius Caesar, shortly before his assassination on the Ides of March, issued coins featuring his portrait and his newly acquired title, *dictator perpetuo* (dictator for life). The *denarius* (the standard Roman silver coin, from which the word *penny* ultimately derives) illustrated here (FIG. **7-11**) records Caesar's aging face and receding hairline in conformity with the Republican veristic tradition. But placing the likeness of a living person on a coin violated all the norms of Republican propriety. Henceforth, Roman coins, which circulated throughout the vast territories under Roman control, would be used to mold public opinion in favor of the ruler by announcing his achievements—both real and fictional.

POMPEII AND THE CITIES OF VESUVIUS

On August 24, 79 CE, Mount Vesuvius, a long-dormant volcano, suddenly erupted (see "An Eyewitness Account of the Eruption of Mount Vesuvius," page 165). Many prosperous towns around the Bay of Naples (the ancient Greek city of Neapolis), among them Pompeii, were buried in a single day. This event was a catastrophe for the inhabitants of the Vesuvian cities but became a boon for archaeologists and art historians. When researchers first explored the buried cities in the 18th century, the ruins had been undisturbed for nearly 1,700 years. The Vesuvian sites permit a reconstruction of the art and life of Roman towns of the Late Republic and Early Empire to a degree impossible anywhere else.

The Oscans, one of the many Italic tribes that occupied Italy during the peak of Etruscan culture, were the first to settle at Pompeii. Toward the end of the fifth century BCE, the Samnites, another Italic people, took over the town. Under the influence of their Greek neighbors, the Samnites greatly expanded the original settlement and gave monumental shape to the city center. Pompeii fought with other Italian cities on the losing side against Rome in the so-called Social War that ended in 89 BCE, and in 80 BCE Sulla founded a new Roman colony on the site, with Latin as its official language. The colony's population had grown to between 10,000 and 20,000 when, in February 62 CE, an earthquake shook the city, causing extensive damage. When Mount Vesuvius erupted 17 years later, repairs were still in progress.

Architecture

Walking through Pompeii today is an unforgettable experience. The streets, with their heavy flagstone pavements and sidewalks, are still there, as are the stepping stones that enabled pedestrians to cross the streets without having to step in puddles. Ingeniously, the city planners placed these stones in such a way that vehicle wheels could straddle them, enabling supplies to be brought directly to the shops, taverns, and bakeries. Tourists still can visit the impressive concrete-vaulted rooms of Pompeii's public baths, sit in the seats of its theater and amphitheater, enter the painted bedrooms and statue-filled gardens of private homes, even walk among the tombs outside the city's walls. Pompeii has been called the living city of the dead for good reason.

7-12 Aerial view of the forum (looking northeast), Pompeii, Italy, second century BCE and later. (1) forum, (2) Temple of Jupiter (Capitolium), (3) basilica.

The center of Roman civic life was the forum. At Pompeii, colonnades frame a rectangular plaza with the Capitolium at the northern end. At the southwestern corner is the basilica, Pompeii's law court.

An Eyewitness Account of the Eruption
of Mount Vesuvius

Pliny the Elder, whose *Natural History* is one of the most important sources for the history of Greek art, was among those who tried to rescue others from danger when Mount Vesuvius erupted. He was overcome by fumes the volcano spewed forth, and died. His nephew, Pliny the Younger, a government official under the emperor Trajan, left an account of the eruption and his uncle's death:

> [The volcanic cloud's] general appearance can best be expressed as being like a pine . . . for it rose to a great height on a sort of trunk and then split off into branches. . . . Sometimes it looked white, sometimes blotched and dirty, according to the amount of soil and ashes it carried with it. . . . The buildings were now shaking with

violent shocks, and seemed to be swaying to and fro as if they were torn from their foundations. Outside, on the other hand, there was the danger of falling pumice-stones, even though these were light and porous. . . . Elsewhere there was daylight, [but around Vesuvius, people] were still in darkness, blacker and denser than any night that ever was. . . . When daylight returned on the 26th—two days after the last day [my uncle] had been seen—his body was found intact and uninjured, still fully clothed and looking more like sleep than death.*

*Betty Radice, trans., *Pliny the Younger: Letters and Panegyricus,* vol. 1 (Cambridge, Mass.: Harvard University Press, 1969), 427–433.

FORUM The center of civic life in any Roman town was its *forum,* or public square, usually located at the city's geographic center at the intersection of the main north-south street, the *cardo,* and the main east-west avenue, the *decumanus* (FIG. 7-42). The forum, however, generally was closed to all but pedestrian traffic. Pompeii's forum (FIG. 7-12) lies in the southwest corner of the expanded Roman city but at the heart of the original town. The forum probably took on monumental form in the second century BCE when the Samnites, inspired by Hellenistic architecture, erected two-story colonnades on three sides of the long and narrow plaza. At the north end they constructed a temple of Jupiter (FIG. 7-12, no. 2). When Pompeii became a Roman colony in 80 BCE, the Romans converted the temple into a *Capitolium*—a triple shrine of Jupiter, Juno, and Minerva, the chief Roman gods. The temple is of standard Republican type, constructed of tufa covered with fine white stucco and combining an Etruscan plan with Corinthian columns. It faces into the civic square, dominating the area. This arrangement contrasts with the siting of Greek temples (FIGS. 5-42 and 5-43), which stood in isolation and could be approached and viewed from all sides, like colossal statues on giant stepped pedestals. The Roman forum, like the Etrusco-Roman temple, has a chief side, a focus of attention.

The area within the porticos of the forum at Pompeii was empty, except for statues portraying local dignitaries and, later, Roman emperors. This is where the citizens conducted daily commerce and held festivities. All around the square, behind the colonnades, were secular and religious structures, including the town's administrative offices. Most noteworthy is the *basilica* (FIG. 7-12, no. 3) at the southwest corner, the earliest well-preserved building of its kind. Constructed during the late second century BCE, the basilica housed the law court of Pompeii and also was used for other official purposes. In plan it resembles the forum itself: long and narrow, with two stories of internal columns dividing the space into a central *nave* and flanking *aisles.* This scheme had a long afterlife in architectural history and will be familiar to anyone who has ever entered a church.

AMPHITHEATER Shortly after the Romans took control of Pompeii, two of the town's wealthiest officials, Quinctius Valgus and Marcus Porcius, used their own funds to erect a large amphitheater (FIG. 7-13) at the southeastern end of town. It is the earliest amphitheater known and could seat some 20,000 spectators—more

than the entire population of the town even a century and a half after its construction. The donors would have enjoyed choice reserved seats in the new entertainment center. In fact, seating was assigned by rank, both civic and military, so that the Roman social hierarchy was on display at every event.

The word *amphitheater* means "double theater," and Roman amphitheaters closely resemble two Greek theaters put together. Greek theaters were situated on natural hillsides (FIG. 5-71), but supporting an amphitheater's continuous elliptical *cavea* (seating area) required building an artificial mountain. Only concrete, unknown to the Greeks, could meet that requirement. In the Pompeii amphitheater, a series of shallow concrete barrel vaults forms a giant retaining wall that holds up the earthen mound and stone seats. Barrel vaults

7-13 Aerial view of the amphitheater, Pompeii, Italy, ca. 70 BCE.

Pompeii's amphitheater is the oldest known. It is also an early example of Roman concrete technology. In the arena, bloody gladiatorial combats and wild animal hunts were staged for 20,000 spectators.

7-14 Brawl in the Pompeii amphitheater, wall painting from House I,3,23, Pompeii, Italy, ca. 60–79 CE. Fresco, 5′ 7″ × 6′ 1″. Museo Archeologico Nazionale, Naples.

This mural painting records a brawl that broke out in the Pompeii amphitheater in 59 CE. The painter included the cloth awning that could be rolled down to shield the audience from the sun and rain.

7-15 Atrium of the House of the Vettii, Pompeii, Italy, second century BCE, rebuilt 62–79 CE.

Roman townhouses had a central atrium with an impluvium to collect rainwater. Cubicula (bedrooms) opened onto the atrium, and in Hellenized houses such as this one, builders added a peristyle garden at the rear.

running all the way through the mountain of earth form the tunnels leading to the *arena*, the central area where bloody gladiatorial combats and wild animal hunts (see "Spectacles in the Colosseum," page 180) occurred. (*Arena* is Latin for "sand," which soaked up the blood of the wounded and killed.) The Roman amphitheater stands in sharp contrast, both architecturally and functionally, to the Greek theater, home of refined performances of comedies and tragedies.

A painting (FIG. **7-14**) on the wall of a Pompeian house records an unfortunate incident that occurred in the amphitheater. A brawl broke out between the Pompeians and their neighbors, the Nucerians, during a gladiatorial contest in 59 CE. The fighting left many seriously wounded and led to the closing of the amphitheater for a decade. The painting shows the cloth awning (*velarium*) that could be rolled down from the top of the cavea to shield spectators from sun and rain. It also features the distinctive external double staircases (not visible in FIG. **7-13**) that enabled large numbers of people to enter and exit the cavea in an orderly fashion.

HOUSE OF THE VETTII The evidence from Pompeii regarding Roman domestic architecture (see "The Roman House," page 167) is unparalleled anywhere else and is the most precious by-product of the catastrophic volcanic eruption of 79 CE. One of the best-preserved houses at Pompeii, partially rebuilt, is the House of the Vettii, an old Pompeian house remodeled and repainted after the 62 CE earthquake. A photograph (FIG. **7-15**) taken in the *fauces* (foyer; see FIG. **7-16**) shows the *impluvium* in the center of the *atrium*, the opening in the roof above, and, in the background, the *peristyle* garden with its marble tables and splendid mural paintings dating to the last years of the Vesuvian city. At that time, two brothers, Aulus Vettius Restitutus and Aulus Vettius Conviva, probably freedmen who had made their fortune as merchants, owned the house. Their wealth enabled them to purchase and furnish the kind of fashionable townhouse that in an earlier era only patricians could have acquired.

Painting

The houses and villas around Mount Vesuvius have yielded a treasure trove of mural paintings, the most complete record of the changing fashions in interior decoration found anywhere in the ancient world. The sheer quantity of these paintings tells a great deal about both the prosperity and the tastes of the times. How many homes today, even of the very wealthy, have custom-painted murals in nearly every room? Roman wall paintings were true frescoes (see "Fresco Painting," Chapter 14, page 382), with the colors applied while the plaster was still damp. The process was painstaking. First the painter had to prepare the wall by applying the plaster (mixed with marble dust if the patron could afford it) in several layers with a smooth trowel. Only then could painting begin. Finally, when the surface dried, the painter polished the wall to achieve a marblelike finish.

In the early years of exploration at Pompeii and nearby Herculaneum, excavators focused almost exclusively on the figural panels that formed part of the overall mural designs, especially those depicting Greek heroes and famous myths. Workers cut the panels out of the walls and transferred them to the Naples Archaeological Museum. In time, more enlightened archaeologists halted the practice of cutting pieces out of the walls and began to give serious attention to the mural designs as a whole. Toward the end of the 19th century, August Mau, a German art historian, divided the various mural painting schemes into four so-called Pompeian Styles. Mau's classification system, although later refined and modified in detail, still serves as the basis for the study of Roman painting.

The Roman House

The Roman house was more than just a place to live. It played an important role in Roman societal rituals. In the Roman world, individuals were frequently bound to others in a patron-client relationship whereby a wealthier, better-educated, and more powerful *patronus* would protect the interests of a *cliens*, sometimes large numbers of them. The standing of a patron in Roman society often was measured by clientele size. Being seen in public accompanied by a crowd of clients was a badge of honor. In this system, a plebeian might be bound to a patrician, a freed slave to a former owner, or even one patrician to another. Regardless of rank, all clients were obligated to support their patron in political campaigns and to perform specific services on request, as well as to call on and salute the patron at the patron's home.

A client calling on a patron would enter the typical Roman *domus* (private house) through a narrow *fauces* (the "jaws" of the house), which led to a large central reception area, the *atrium*. The rooms flanking the fauces could open onto the atrium, as in FIG. 7-16, or onto the street, in which case they were rented out as shops. The roof over the atrium was partially open to the sky, not only to admit light but also to channel rainwater into a basin (*impluvium*) below. The water could be stored in cisterns for household use. Opening onto the atrium was a series of small bedrooms called *cubicula* (cubicles). At the back were two recessed areas (*alae*, wings) and the patron's *tablinum* or "home office," a dining room (*triclinium*), a kitchen, and sometimes a small garden.

Endless variations of the same basic plan exist, dictated by an owner's personal tastes and means, the size and shape of the lot purchased, and so forth, but all Roman houses of this type were inward-looking in nature. The design shut off the street's noise and dust, and all internal activity focused on the brightly illuminated atrium at the center of the residence. This basic module (only the front half of the typical house in FIG. 7-16) resembles the plan of the typical Etruscan house as reflected in the Tomb of the Shields and Chairs (FIG. 6-7) and other tombs at Cerveteri. Thus, few scholars doubt that the early Roman house, like the early Roman temple, grew out of the Etruscan tradition.

During the second century BCE, when Roman architects were beginning to construct stone temples with Greek columns, the Roman house also took on Greek airs. Builders added a *peristyle* garden behind the Etruscan-style house, providing a second internal source of illumination as well as a pleasant setting for meals served in a summer triclinium. The axial symmetry of the plan meant that on entering the fauces of the house, a visitor could be greeted by a vista through the atrium directly into the peristyle garden (as in FIG. 7-15), which often boasted a fountain or pool, marble statuary, mural paintings, and mosaic floors.

While such private houses were typical of Pompeii and other Italian towns, they were very rare in large cities such as Rome, where the masses lived instead in multistory apartment houses (FIG. 7-54).

7-16 Restored view and plan of a typical Roman house of the Late Republic and Early Empire (John Burge). (1) fauces, (2) atrium, (3) impluvium, (4) cubiculum, (5) ala, (6) tablinum, (7) triclinium, (8) peristyle.

Older Roman houses closely followed Etruscan models and had atriums and small gardens, but during the Late Republic and Early Empire, Roman builders added peristyles with Greek columns.

7-17 First Style wall painting in the fauces of the Samnite House, Herculaneum, Italy, late second century BCE.

In First Style murals, the decorator's aim was to imitate costly marble panels using painted stucco relief. The style is Greek in origin and another example of the Hellenization of Republican architecture.

FIRST STYLE The *First Style* is also called the Masonry Style because the decorator's aim was to imitate costly marble panels using painted stucco relief. The fauces (FIG. 7-17) of the Samnite House at Herculaneum greets the visitor with a stunning illusion of walls constructed, or at least faced, with marbles imported from quarries all over the Mediterranean. This approach to wall decoration is comparable to the modern practice, employed in private libraries and corporate meeting rooms alike, of using cheaper manufactured materials to approximate the look and shape of genuine wood paneling. The practice is not, however, uniquely Pompeian or Roman. First Style walls are well documented in the Greek world from the late fourth century BCE on. The use of the First Style in Republican houses is yet another example of the Hellenization of Roman architecture.

SECOND STYLE The First Style never went completely out of fashion, but after 80 BCE a new approach to mural design became more popular. The *Second Style* is in most respects the antithesis of the First Style. Some scholars have argued that the Second Style also has precedents in Greece, but most believe it is a Roman invention. Certainly, the Second Style evolved in Italy and was popular until around 15 BCE, when Roman painters introduced the Third Style. Second Style painters did not aim to create the illusion of an elegant marble wall, as First Style painters sought to do. Rather, they wanted to dissolve a room's confining walls and replace them with the illusion of an imaginary three-dimensional world.

VILLA OF THE MYSTERIES An early example of the new style is the room (FIG. 7-18) that gives its name to the Villa of the Mysteries at Pompeii. Many scholars believe this chamber was used to celebrate, in private, the rites of the Greek god Dionysos (Roman Bacchus). Dionysos was the focus of an unofficial mystery religion popular among women in Italy at this time. The precise nature of the Dionysiac rites is unknown, but the figural cycle in the Villa of the Mysteries, illustrating mortals (all female save for one boy) interacting with mythological figures, probably provides some evidence for the cult's initiation rites. In these rites young women, emulating Ariadne, daughter of King Minos (see Chapter 4), united in marriage with Dionysos.

The backdrop for the nearly life-size figures is a series of painted panels imitating marble revetment, just as in the First Style but without the modeling in relief. In front of this marble wall (but actually on the same two-dimensional surface), the painter created the illusion of a shallow ledge on which the human and divine actors move around the room. Especially striking is the way some of the figures interact across the corners of the room. For example, a seminude winged woman at the far right of the rear wall lashes out with her whip across the space of the room at a kneeling woman with a bare back (the initiate and bride-to-be of Dionysos) on the left end of the right wall. Nothing comparable to this room existed in Hellenistic Greece. Despite the presence of Dionysos, satyrs, and other figures from Greek mythology, this is a Roman design.

VILLA AT BOSCOREALE In the early Second Style Dionysiac mystery frieze, the spatial illusionism is confined to the painted platform that projects into the room. But in mature Second Style designs, Roman painters created a three-dimensional setting that also extends beyond the wall. An example is a cubiculum (FIG. 7-19) from the Villa of Publius Fannius Synistor at Boscoreale, near Pompeii, decorated between 50 and 40 BCE. The excavators removed the frescoes soon after their discovery, and today they are part of a reconstructed Roman bedroom in the Metropolitan Museum of Art. All around the room the Second Style painter opened up the walls with vistas of Italian towns, marble temples, and colonnaded courtyards. Painted doors and gates invite the viewer to walk through the wall into the magnificent world the painter created.

Although the Boscoreale painter was inconsistent in applying it, this Roman artist, like many others around the Bay of Naples, demonstrated a knowledge of single-point *linear perspective*, often incorrectly said to be an innovation of Italian Renaissance artists (see "Renaissance Perspectival Systems," Chapter 16, page 425). In this kind of perspective, all the receding lines in a composition converge on a single point along the painting's central axis to show depth and distance. Ancient writers noted that Greek painters of the fifth century BCE first used linear perspective for the design of Athenian stage sets (hence its Greek name, *skenographia*, "scene painting"). In the Boscoreale cubiculum, the painter most successfully employed the device in the far corners, where a low gate leads to a

7-18 Dionysiac mystery frieze, Second Style wall paintings in room 5 of the Villa of the Mysteries, Pompeii, Italy, ca. 60–50 BCE. Fresco, frieze 5′ 4″ high.

Second Style painters created the illusion of an imaginary three-dimensional world on the walls of Roman houses. The figures in this room are acting out the initiation rites of the Dionysiac mysteries.

7-19 Second Style wall paintings (general view, *left*, and detail of tholos, *right*) from cubiculum M of the Villa of Publius Fannius Synistor, Boscoreale, Italy, ca. 50–40 BCE. Fresco, 8′ 9″ high. Metropolitan Museum of Art, New York.

In this Second Style bedroom, the painter opened up the walls with vistas of towns, temples, and colonnaded courtyards. The convincing illusionism is due in part to the use of linear perspective.

7-20 Gardenscape, Second Style wall paintings, from the Villa of Livia, Primaporta, Italy, ca. 30–20 BCE. Fresco, 6′ 7″ high. Museo Nazionale Romano–Palazzo Massimo alle Terme, Rome.

The ultimate example of a Second Style "picture-window" wall is Livia's gardenscape. To suggest recession, the painter used atmospheric perspective, intentionally blurring the most distant forms.

peristyle framing a tholos temple (FIG. **7-19**, *right*). Linear perspective was a favored tool of Second Style painters seeking to transform the usually windowless walls of Roman houses into "picture-window" vistas that expanded the apparent space of the rooms.

VILLA OF LIVIA, PRIMAPORTA The ultimate example of a Second Style picture-window mural (FIG. **7-20**) comes from the Villa of Livia, wife of the emperor Augustus, at Primaporta, just north of Rome. There, imperial painters decorated all the walls of a vaulted room with lush gardenscapes. The only architectural element is the flimsy fence of the garden itself. To suggest recession, the painter mastered another kind of perspective, *atmospheric perspective*, indicating depth by the increasingly blurred appearance of objects in the distance. At Livia's villa, the artist precisely painted the fence, trees, and birds in the foreground, whereas the details of the dense foliage in the background are indistinct. Among the wall paintings examined so far, only the landscape fresco (FIG. **4-9**) from Thera offers a similar wraparound view of nature. But the Aegean fresco's white sky and red, yellow, and blue rock formations do not create a successful illusion of a world filled with air and light just a few steps away.

7-21 Detail of a Third Style wall painting, from cubiculum 15 of the Villa of Agrippa Postumus, Boscotrecase, Italy, ca. 10 BCE. Fresco, 7′ 8″ high. Metropolitan Museum of Art, New York.

In the Third Style, Roman painters decorated walls with delicate linear fantasies sketched on predominantly monochromatic backgrounds. Here, a tiny floating landscape on a black ground is the central motif.

THIRD STYLE The Primaporta gardenscape is the polar opposite of First Style designs, which reinforce, rather than deny, the heavy presence of confining walls. But tastes changed rapidly in the Roman world, as in society today. Not long after Livia had her villa painted, Roman patrons began to favor mural designs that reasserted the primacy of the wall surface. In the *Third Style* of Pompeian painting, artists no longer attempted to replace the walls with three-dimensional worlds of their own creation. Nor did they seek to imitate the appearance of the marble walls of Hellenistic kings. Instead they decorated walls with delicate linear fantasies sketched on predominantly *monochromatic* (one-color) backgrounds.

VILLA AT BOSCOTRECASE One of the earliest examples of the new style is a cubiculum (FIG. **7-21**) in the Villa of Agrippa Postumus at Boscotrecase. The villa was probably painted just before 10 BCE. Nowhere did the artist use illusionistic painting to penetrate the wall. In place of the stately columns of the Second Style are insubstantial and impossibly thin *colonnettes* supporting featherweight canopies barely reminiscent of pediments. In the center of this delicate and elegant architectural frame is a tiny floating landscape painted directly on the jet black ground. It is hard to imagine a sharper contrast with the panoramic gardenscape at Livia's villa. On other Third Style walls, landscapes and mythological scenes appear in frames, like modern canvas paintings hung on walls. Never could these framed panels be mistaken for windows opening onto a world beyond the room.

FOURTH STYLE In the *Fourth Style*, however, a taste for illusionism returned once again. This style became popular in the 50s CE, and it was the preferred manner of mural decoration at Pompeii when the eruption of Vesuvius buried the town in volcanic ash in 79. Some examples of the new style, such as room 78 (FIG. **7-22**) in the emperor Nero's Golden House in Rome (see page 179), display a kinship with the Third Style. All the walls are an austere creamy white. In some areas the artist painted sea creatures, birds, and other motifs directly on the monochromatic background, much like the landscape in the Boscotrecase villa (FIG. **7-21**). Landscapes appear here too—as framed paintings in the center of each large white subdivision of the wall. Views through the wall are also part of the design, but the Fourth Style architectural vistas are irrational fantasies. The viewer looks out not on cityscapes or round temples set in peristyles but at fragments of buildings—columns supporting half-pediments, double stories of columns supporting nothing at all—painted on the same white ground as the rest of the wall. In the Fourth Style, architecture became just another motif in the painter's ornamental repertoire.

7-22 Fourth Style wall paintings in room 78 of the Domus Aurea (Golden House) of Nero, Rome, Italy, 64–68 CE.

The creamy white walls of this room in Nero's Golden House display a kinship with the Third Style, but views through the wall revealing irrational architectural vistas characterize the new Fourth Style.

7-23 Fourth Style wall paintings in the Ixion Room (triclinium P) of the House of the Vettii, Pompeii, Italy, ca. 70–79 CE.

Late Fourth Style murals are often garishly colored, crowded, and confused compositions with a mixture of architectural views, framed mythological panel paintings, and First and Third Style motifs.

IXION ROOM In the latest Fourth Style designs, Pompeian painters rejected the quiet elegance of the Third Style and early Fourth Style in favor of crowded and confused compositions and sometimes garish color combinations. The Ixion Room (FIG. 7-23) of the House of the Vettii at Pompeii was decorated in this manner just before the eruption of Mount Vesuvius. The room served as a triclinium in the house the Vettius brothers remodeled after the earthquake. It opened onto the peristyle seen in the background of FIG. 7-15.

The decor of the Ixion Room serves as a synopsis of all the previous styles, another instance of the eclecticism noted earlier as characteristic of Roman art in general. The lowest zone, for example, is one of the most successful imitations anywhere of costly multicolored imported marbles, despite the fact that the painter created the illusion without recourse to relief, as in the First Style. The large white panels in the corners of the room, with their delicate floral frames and floating central motifs, would fit naturally into the most elegant Third Style design. Unmistakably Fourth Style, however, are the fragmentary architectural vistas of the central and upper zones of the walls. They are unrelated to one another, do not constitute a unified cityscape beyond the wall, and incorporate figures that would tumble into the room if they took a single step forward.

The Ixion Room takes its name from the mythological panel painting at the center of the rear wall (FIG. 7-23). Ixion had attempted to seduce Hera, and Zeus punished him by binding him to a perpetually spinning wheel. The panels on the two side walls also have Greek myths as subjects. The Ixion Room may be likened to a small private art gallery with paintings decorating the walls, as in many modern homes. Scholars long have believed that these and the many other mythological paintings on Third and Fourth Style walls were based on lost Greek panels. They attest to the Romans' continuing admiration for Greek artworks three centuries after Marcellus brought the treasures of Syracuse to Rome. But few, if any, of these mythological paintings can be described as true copies of "Old Masters," as are the many Roman replicas of famous Greek statues that have been found throughout the Roman world, including Pompeii (FIG. 5-40).

WALL MOSAICS Mythological figures were on occasion also the subject of Roman mosaics. In the ancient world, mosaics were usually confined to floors (as was the Pompeian *Alexander Mosaic*, FIG. 5-70), where the tesserae formed a durable as well as decorative surface. In Roman times, however, mosaics also decorated walls and even ceilings, foreshadowing the extensive use of wall and vault mosaics in the Middle Ages (see "Mosaics," Chapter 8, page 223). The mosaic shown in FIG. 7-24 adorns a wall in the House of Neptune and Amphitrite at Herculaneum. The statuesque figures of the sea god and his wife preside over the running water of the fountain in the courtyard in front of them where the home's owners and guests enjoyed outdoor dining in warm weather.

PRIVATE PORTRAITS The subjects chosen for Roman wall paintings and mosaics were diverse. Although mythological themes were immensely popular, Romans commissioned a vast range of other subjects. As noted, landscape paintings frequently appear on Second, Third, and Fourth Style walls. Paintings and mosaics depicting scenes from history include the *Alexander Mosaic* (FIG. 5-70) and

7-24 Neptune and Amphitrite, wall mosaic in the summer triclinium of the House of Neptune and Amphitrite, Herculaneum, Italy, ca. 62–79 CE.

In the ancient world, mosaics were usually confined to floors, but this example depicting Neptune and Amphitrite decorates the wall of a private house. The sea deities fittingly overlook an elaborate fountain.

7-25 Portrait of a husband and wife, wall painting from House VII,2,6, Pompeii, Italy, ca. 70–79 CE. Fresco, 1′ 11″ × 1′ 8½″. Museo Archeologico Nazionale, Naples.

This husband and wife wished to present themselves to their guests as thoughtful and well-read. The portraits are individualized likenesses, but the poses and attributes they hold are standard types.

the mural painting (FIG. 7-14) of the brawl in the amphitheater of Pompeii. Given the Roman custom of keeping *imagines* of illustrious ancestors in atriums, it is not surprising that painted portraits also appear in Pompeian houses. The portrait of a husband and wife illustrated here (FIG. 7-25) originally formed part of a Fourth Style wall of an *exedra*, or recessed area, opening onto the atrium of a Pompeian house. The man holds a scroll and the woman a *stylus* (writing instrument) and a wax writing tablet, standard attributes in Roman marriage portraits. They suggest the fine education of those depicted—even if, as was sometimes true, the individuals were uneducated or even illiterate. Such portraits were thus the Roman equivalent of modern wedding photographs of the bride and groom posing in rented formal garments that they never wore before or afterward (see "Role Playing in Roman Portraiture," page 174). In contrast, the heads are not standard types but sensitive studies of the couple's individual faces. This is another instance of a realistic portrait placed on a conventional figure type (compare FIG. 7-8), a recurring phenomenon in Roman portraiture.

STILL-LIFE PAINTING The Roman interest in recording the unique appearance of individual people extended to everyday objects. This explains the frequent inclusion of *still-life* paintings (representations of inanimate objects, artfully arranged) in the mural schemes of the Second, Third, and Fourth Styles. A still life with peaches and a carafe (FIG. 7-26), a detail of a painted wall from Herculaneum, demonstrates that Roman painters sought to create illusionistic effects when depicting small objects as well as buildings and landscapes. The artist paid as much attention to shadows and highlights on the fruit, the stem and leaves, and the glass jar as to the objects themselves. Art historians have not found evidence of paintings comparable to these Roman studies of food and other inanimate objects until the Dutch still lifes of the 17th and 18th centuries (FIGS. 20-22 and 20-23).

7-26 Still life with peaches, detail of a Fourth Style wall painting, from Herculaneum, Italy, ca. 62–79 CE. Fresco, 1′ 2″ × 1′ 1½″. Museo Archeologico Nazionale, Naples.

The Roman interest in illusionism explains the popularity of still-life paintings. This painter paid scrupulous attention to the play of light and shadow on different shapes and textures.

Role Playing in Roman Portraiture

In every town throughout the vast Roman Empire, portraits of the emperors and empresses and their families were on display—in forums, basilicas, baths, and markets; in front of temples; atop triumphal arches—anywhere a statue could be placed. The rulers' heads varied little from Britain to Syria. All were replicas of official images, either imported or scrupulously copied by local artists. But the Roman sculptors placed the portrait heads on many types of bodies. The type chosen depended on the position the person held in Roman society or the various fictitious guises members of the imperial family assumed. Portraits of Augustus, for example, show him not only as armed general (FIG. 7-27) but also as recipient of the civic crown for saving the lives of fellow citizens (FIG. I-9). Other statues show him as veiled priest, toga-clad magistrate, traveling commander on horseback, heroically nude warrior, and various Roman gods, including Jupiter, Apollo, and Mercury.

Such role playing was not confined to emperors and princes but extended to their wives, daughters, sisters, and mothers. Portraits of Livia (FIG. 7-28) depict her as many goddesses, including Ceres, Juno, Venus, and Vesta. She also appears as the personification of Health, Justice, and Piety. In fact, it was common for imperial women to appear on Roman coins as goddesses or as embodiments of feminine virtue. Faustina the Younger, for example, the wife of Marcus Aurelius and mother of 13 children, appears as Venus and Fecundity, among many other roles. Julia Domna (FIG. 7-63), Septimius Severus's wife, is Juno, Venus, Peace, or Victory in some portraits.

Ordinary citizens also engaged in role playing. Some assumed literary pretensions, as did a husband and wife (FIG. 7-25) in their Pompeian home. Others equated themselves with Greek heroes (FIG. 7-60) or Roman deities (FIG. 7-61) on their coffins. The common people followed the lead of the emperors and empresses.

7-27 Portrait of Augustus as general, from Primaporta, Italy, early-first-century CE copy of a bronze original of ca. 20 BCE. Marble, 6′ 8″ high. Musei Vaticani, Rome.

Augustus's idealized portraits were modeled on Classical Greek statues (FIG. 5-40) and depict him as a never-aging son of a god. This portrait presents the emperor in armor in his role as general.

EARLY EMPIRE

The murder of Julius Caesar on the Ides of March, 44 BCE, plunged the Roman world into a bloody civil war. The fighting lasted until 31 BCE when Octavian (better known as Augustus), Caesar's grand-nephew and adopted son, crushed the naval forces of Mark Antony and Queen Cleopatra of Egypt at Actium in northwestern Greece. Antony and Cleopatra committed suicide, and in 30 BCE, Egypt, once the wealthiest and most powerful kingdom of the ancient world, became another province in the ever-expanding Roman Empire.

Historians mark the passage from the Roman Republic to the Roman Empire from the day in 27 BCE when the Senate conferred the majestic title of Augustus (r. 27 BCE–14 CE) on Octavian. The Empire was ostensibly a continuation of the Republic, with the same constitutional offices, but in fact Augustus, whom the Senate recognized as *princeps* (first citizen), occupied all the key positions. He was consul and *imperator* (commander in chief; root of the word *emperor*) and even, after 12 BCE, *pontifex maximus* (chief priest of the state religion). These offices gave Augustus control of all aspects of Roman public life.

PAX ROMANA With powerful armies keeping order on the Empire's frontiers and no opposition at home, Augustus brought peace and prosperity to a war-weary Mediterranean world. Known in his own day as the *Pax Augusta* (Augustan Peace), the peace Augustus established prevailed for two centuries. It came to be called simply the *Pax Romana*. During this time the emperors commissioned a huge number of public works throughout the Empire: roads, bridges, theaters, amphitheaters, and bathing complexes, all on an unprecedented scale. The erection of imperial portrait statues and monuments covered with reliefs recounting the rulers' great

1 in.

deeds reminded people everywhere of the source of this beneficence. These portraits and reliefs often presented a picture of the emperors and their achievements that bore little resemblance to historical fact. Their purpose, however, was not to provide an objective record but to mold public opinion. The Roman emperors and the artists they employed have had few equals in the effective use of art and architecture for propagandistic ends.

Augustus and the Julio-Claudians

When Augustus vanquished Antony and Cleopatra at Actium and became undisputed master of the Mediterranean world, he was not yet 32 years old. The rule by elders that had characterized the Roman Republic for nearly a half millennium came to an abrupt end. Suddenly, Roman portraitists were called on to produce images of a *youthful* head of state. But Augustus was not merely young. Caesar had been made a god after his death, and Augustus, though never claiming to be a god himself, widely advertised himself as the son of a god. His portraits were designed to present the image of a godlike leader who miraculously never aged. Although Augustus lived until 14 CE, even official portraits made near the end of his life show him as a handsome youth (FIG. I-9). Such fictional portraits might seem ridiculous today, when the media circulate pictures of world leaders as they truly appear, but in antiquity few people had actually seen the emperor. His official image was all most knew. It therefore could be manipulated at will.

AUGUSTUS AS IMPERATOR The portraits of Augustus depict him in his many different roles in the Roman state (see "Role Playing in Roman Portraiture," page 174), but the models for many of them were Classical Greek statues. The portrait (FIG. 7-27) of the emperor found at his wife Livia's villa (FIG. 7-20) at Primaporta portrays Augustus as general, standing in the pose of Polykleitos's *Doryphoros* (FIG. 5-40) but with his right arm raised to address his troops in the manner of the orator Aule Metele (FIG. 6-16). Augustus's head, although portraying a recognizable individual, also emulates the idealized head of the Polykleitan spear bearer in its overall shape, the sharp ridges of the brows, and the tight cap of layered hair. Augustus is not a nude athlete, however, and the details of the statue carry political messages. The reliefs on the cuirass advertise an important diplomatic victory—the return of the Roman military standards the Parthians had captured from a Republican general—and the Cupid at Augustus's feet alludes to his divine descent. (Caesar's family, the Julians, traced their ancestry back to Venus. Cupid was the goddess's son.)

LIVIA A marble portrait (FIG. 7-28) of Livia shows that the imperial women of the Augustan age shared the emperor's eternal youthfulness. Although she sports the latest Roman coiffure, with the hair rolled over the forehead and knotted at the nape of the neck, Livia's blemish-free skin and sharply defined features derive from images of Classical Greek goddesses. Livia outlived Augustus by 15 years, dying at age 87. In her portraits, the coiffure changed with the introduction of each new fashion, but her face remained ever young, befitting her exalted position in the Roman state.

7-29 Ara Pacis Augustae (Altar of Augustan Peace; looking northeast), Rome, Italy, 13–9 BCE.

Augustus sought to present his new order as a Golden Age equaling that of Athens under Pericles. The Ara Pacis celebrates the emperor's most important achievement, the establishment of peace.

7-30 Female personification (Tellus?), panel from the east facade of the Ara Pacis Augustae, Rome, Italy, 13–9 BCE. Marble, 5′ 3″ high.

This female personification with two babies on her lap epitomizes the fruits of the Pax Augusta. All around her the bountiful earth is in bloom, and animals of different species live together peacefully.

1 ft.

ARA PACIS AUGUSTAE On Livia's birthday in 9 BCE, Augustus dedicated the Ara Pacis Augustae (Altar of Augustan Peace; FIG. 7-29), the monument celebrating his most significant achievement, the establishment of peace. Figural reliefs and acanthus tendrils adorn the altar's marble precinct walls. Four panels on the east and west ends depict carefully selected mythological subjects, including (at the right in FIG. 7-29) a relief of Aeneas making a sacrifice. Aeneas was the son of Venus and one of Augustus's forefathers. The connection between the emperor and Aeneas was a key element of Augustus's political ideology for his new Golden Age. It is no coincidence that Vergil wrote the *Aeneid* during the rule of Augustus. The epic poem glorified the young emperor by celebrating the founder of the Julian line.

A second panel (FIG. 7-30), on the other end of the altar enclosure, depicts a seated matron with two lively babies on her lap. Her identity is uncertain. She is usually called Tellus (Mother Earth), although some scholars have named her Pax (Peace), Ceres (goddess of grain), or even Venus. Whoever she is, she epitomizes the fruits of the Pax Augusta. All around her the bountiful earth is in bloom, and animals of different species live peacefully side by side. Personifications of refreshing breezes (note their windblown drapery) flank her. One

rides a bird, the other a sea creature. Earth, sky, and water are all elements of this picture of peace and fertility in the Augustan cosmos.

Processions of the imperial family (FIG. 7-31) and other important dignitaries appear on the long north and south sides of the Ara Pacis. These parallel friezes were clearly inspired to some degree by the Panathenaic procession frieze (FIG. 5-50, *bottom*) of the Parthenon. Augustus sought to present his new order as a Golden Age equaling that of Athens under Pericles in the mid-fifth century BCE. The emulation of Classical models thus made a political statement as well as an artistic one.

Even so, the Roman procession is very different in character from that on the Greek frieze. On the Parthenon, anonymous figures act out an event that recurred every four years. The frieze stands for *all* Panathenaic Festival processions. The Ara Pacis depicts a specific event—possibly the inaugural ceremony of 13 BCE when work on the altar began—and recognizable contemporary figures. Among those

7-31 Procession of the imperial family, detail of the south frieze of the Ara Pacis Augustae, Rome, Italy, 13–9 BCE. Marble, 5′ 3″ high.

Although inspired by the Panathenaic procession frieze (FIG. **5-50**) of the Parthenon, the Ara Pacis friezes depict recognizable individuals, including children. Augustus promoted marriage and child-bearing.

Luna). Prior to the opening of these quarries in the second half of the first century BCE, marble had to be imported at great cost from abroad, and the Romans used it sparingly. The ready availability of Italian marble under Augustus made possible the emperor's famous boast that he found Rome a city of brick and transformed it into a city of marble.

The extensive use of Carrara marble for public monuments (including the Ara Pacis) must be seen as part of Augustus's larger program to make his city the equal of Periclean Athens. In fact, the Forum of Augustus incorporated several explicit references to Classical Athens and to the Acropolis in particular, most notably copies of the caryatids (FIG. **5-54**) of the Erechtheion in the upper story of the porticos. The forum also evoked Roman history. The porticos contained dozens of portrait statues, including images of all the major figures of the Julian family going back to Aeneas. Augustus's forum became a kind of public atrium filled with *imagines*. His family history thus became part of the Roman state's official history.

portrayed are children, who restlessly tug on their elders' garments and talk to one another when they should be quiet on a solemn occasion—in short, children who act like children and not like miniature adults, as they frequently do in the history of art. Their presence lends a great deal of charm to the procession, but that is not why children were included on the Ara Pacis when they had never before appeared on any Greek or Roman state monument. Augustus was concerned about a decline in the birthrate among the Roman nobility, and he enacted a series of laws designed to promote marriage, marital fidelity, and raising children. The portrayal of men with their families on the Altar of Peace served as a moral exemplar. Once again, the emperor used art to further his political and social agendas.

FORUM OF AUGUSTUS Augustus's most ambitious project in the capital was the construction of a new forum (FIG. **7-2**, no. 10) next to Julius Caesar's forum (FIG. **7-2**, no. 9), which Augustus completed. Both forums featured white marble from Carrara (ancient

NÎMES The Forum of Augustus is in ruins today, but many scholars believe some workers on that project also erected the so-called Maison Carrée (Square House; FIG. **7-32**) at Nîmes (ancient

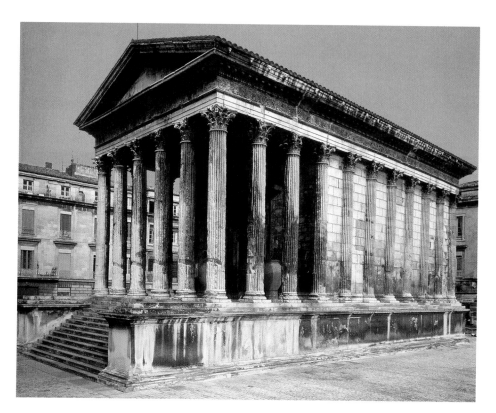

7-32 Maison Carrée, Nîmes, France, ca. 1–10 CE.

This exceptionally well preserved Corinthian pseudoperipteral temple in France, modeled on the Temple of Mars Ultor in Rome, exemplifies the conservative Neo-Classical Augustan architectural style.

Early Empire **177**

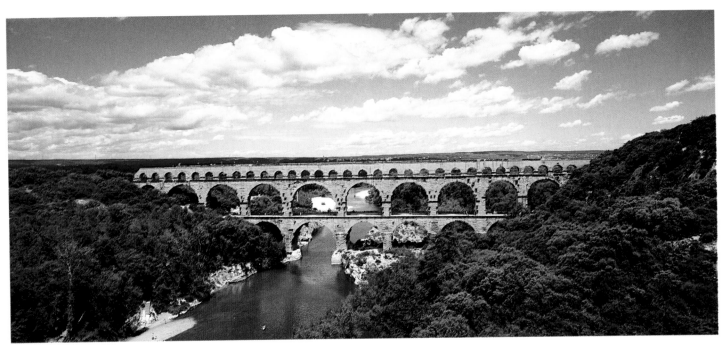

7-33 Pont-du-Gard, Nîmes, France, ca. 16 BCE.

Roman engineers constructed roads and bridges throughout the empire. This aqueduct bridge brought water from a distant mountain spring to Nîmes—about 100 gallons a day for each inhabitant.

Nemausus) in southern France (ancient Gaul). This exceptionally well preserved Corinthian pseudoperipteral temple, which dates to the opening years of the first century CE, is the best surviving example of the Augustan Neo-Classical architectural style.

An earlier Augustan project at Nîmes was the construction of the great aqueduct-bridge known today as the Pont-du-Gard (FIG. **7-33**). Beginning in the fourth century BCE, the Romans built aqueducts to carry water from mountain sources to their city on the Tiber River. As Rome's power spread through the Mediterranean world, its architects constructed aqueducts, roads, and bridges to serve colonies throughout the far-flung empire. The Pont-du-Gard demonstrates the skill of Rome's engineers. The aqueduct provided about 100 gallons of water a day for each inhabitant of Nîmes from a source some 30 miles away. The water was carried over the considerable distance by gravity alone, which required channels built with a continuous gradual decline over the entire route from source to city. The three-story bridge at Nîmes maintained the height of the water channel where the water crossed the Gard River. Each large arch spans some 82 feet and is constructed of blocks weighing up to two tons each. The bridge's uppermost level consists of a row of smaller arches, three above each of the large openings below. They carry the water channel itself. Their quickened rhythm and the harmonious proportional relationship between the larger and smaller arches reveal that the Roman engineer had a keen aesthetic as well as practical sense.

PORTA MAGGIORE Many aqueducts were required to meet the demand for water in the capital. Under the emperor Claudius (r. 41–54 CE), a grandiose gate, the Porta Maggiore (FIG. **7-34**), was constructed at the point where two of Rome's water lines (and two intercity trunk roads) converged. Its huge *attic* (uppermost story) bears a wordy dedicatory inscription that conceals the conduits of both aqueducts, one above the other. The gate is the outstanding example of the Roman *rusticated* (rough) masonry style. Instead of using the precisely shaped blocks Greek and Augustan architects preferred, the designer of the Porta Maggiore combined smooth and rusticated surfaces. These created an exciting, if eccentric, facade

with crisply carved pediments resting on engaged columns composed of rusticated drums.

NERO'S GOLDEN HOUSE In 64 CE, when Nero (r. 54–68 CE), stepson and successor of Claudius, was emperor, a great fire destroyed large sections of Rome. Architects carried out the rebuilding in accordance with a new code that required greater fireproofing, resulting in the widespread use of concrete, which was both cheap and fire resistant. Increased use of concrete gave Roman builders the opportunity to explore the possibilities opened up by the still relatively new material.

7-34 Porta Maggiore, Rome, Italy, ca. 50 CE.

This double gateway, which supports the water channels of two important aqueducts, is the outstanding example of Roman rusticated (rough) masonry, which was especially popular under Claudius.

The Golden House of Nero

Nero's Domus Aurea (FIG. 7-35), or Golden House, was a vast and notoriously extravagant country villa in the heart of Rome. The second-century CE Roman biographer Suetonius described it vividly:

> The entrance-hall was large enough to contain a huge statue [of Nero in the guise of Sol, the sun god, by Zenodorus; FIG. 7-2, no. 16], 120 feet high; and the pillared arcade ran for a whole mile. An enormous pool, like a sea, was surrounded by buildings made to resemble cities, and by a landscape garden consisting of ploughed fields, vineyards, pastures, and woodlands—where every variety of domestic and wild animal roamed about. Parts of the house were overlaid with gold and studded with precious stones and mother-of-pearl. All the dining-rooms had ceilings of fretted ivory, the panels of which could slide back and let a rain of flowers, or of perfume from hidden sprinklers, shower upon [Nero's] guests. The main

dining-room was circular, and its roof revolved, day and night, in time with the sky. Sea water, or sulphur water, was always on tap in the baths. When the palace had been decorated throughout in this lavish style, Nero dedicated it, and condescended to remark: "Good, now I can at last begin to live like a human being!"*

Suetonius's description is a welcome reminder that the Roman ruins tourists flock to see are but a dim reflection of the magnificence of the original structures. Only in rare instances, such as the Pantheon, with its marble-faced walls and floors (FIG. 7-51), can visitors experience anything approaching the architects' intended effects. Even there, much of the marble paneling is of later date, and the gilding is missing from the dome.

*Suetonius, *Nero*, 31. Translated by Robert Graves, *Suetonius: The Twelve Caesars* (New York: Penguin, 1957; illustrated edition, 1980), 197–198.

7-35 SEVERUS and CELER, section (*left*) and plan (*right*) of the octagonal hall of the Domus Aurea (Golden House) of Nero, Rome, Italy, 64–68 CE.

Nero's architects illuminated this octagonal room by placing an oculus in its concrete dome, and ingeniously lit the rooms around it by leaving spaces between their vaults and the dome's exterior.

After the great fire, Nero asked SEVERUS and CELER, two brilliant architect-engineers, to construct a grand new palace for him on a huge confiscated plot of fire-ravaged land near the Forum Romanum (see "The Golden House of Nero," above). Nero's Domus Aurea had scores of rooms, many adorned with frescoes (FIG. 7-22) in the Fourth Style, others with marble paneling or painted and gilded stucco reliefs. Structurally, most of these rooms, although built of concrete, are unremarkable. One octagonal hall (FIG. 7-35), however, stands apart from the rest and testifies to Severus and Celer's entirely new approach to architectural design.

The ceiling of the octagonal room is a dome that modulates from an eight-sided to a hemispherical form as it rises toward the *oculus*—the circular opening that admitted light to the room. Radiating outward from the five inner sides (the other three, directly or indirectly, face the outside) are smaller, rectangular rooms, three covered by barrel vaults, two others (marked by a broken-line X on the plan; FIG. 7-35, *right*) by the earliest known concrete groin vaults.

Severus and Celer ingeniously lit these satellite rooms by leaving spaces between their vaulted ceilings and the central dome's exterior. But the most significant aspect of the design is that here, for the first time, the architects appear to have thought of the walls and vaults not as limiting space but as shaping it.

Today, the octagonal hall no longer has its stucco decoration and marble *incrustation* (veneer). The concrete shell stands bare, but this serves to focus the visitor's attention on the design's spatial complexity. Anyone walking through the rooms sees that the central domed octagon is defined not by walls but by eight angled piers. The wide square openings between the piers are so large that the rooms beyond look like extensions of the central hall. The grouping of spatial units of different sizes and proportions under a variety of vaults creates a dynamic three-dimensional composition that is both complex and unified. Nero's architects were not only inventive but also progressive in their recognition of the malleable nature of concrete, a material not limited to the rectilinear forms of traditional architecture.

Spectacles in the Colosseum

Romans flocked to amphitheaters all over the Empire to see two main kinds of spectacles: gladiatorial combats and animal hunts.

Gladiators were professional fighters, usually slaves who had been purchased to train as hand-to-hand combatants in gladiatorial schools. Their owners, seeking to turn a profit, rented them out for performances. Beginning with Domitian, however, all gladiators who competed in Rome were state-owned to ensure that they could not be used as a private army to overthrow the government. Although every gladiator faced death every time he entered the arena, some had long careers and achieved considerable fame. Others, for example, criminals or captured enemies, were sent into the amphitheater without any training and without any defensive weapons. Those "gladiatorial games" were a form of capital punishment coupled with entertainment for the masses.

Wild animal hunts (*venationes*) were also immensely popular. Many of the hunters were also professionals, but often the hunts, like the gladiatorial games, were executions in thin disguise involving helpless prisoners who were easy prey for the animals. Sometimes no one would enter the arena with the animals. Instead, skilled archers shot the beasts with arrows from positions in the stands. Other times animals would be pitted against other animals—bears versus bulls, lions versus elephants, and such—to the delight of the crowds.

The Colosseum (FIG. 7-36) was the largest and most important amphitheater in the world, and the kinds of spectacles staged there were costlier and more impressive than those held anywhere else. There are even accounts of the Colosseum being flooded so that naval battles could be staged before an audience of tens of thousands, although some scholars have doubted that the arena could be made watertight or that ships could maneuver in the space available.

In the early third century, the historian Dio Cassius described the ceremonies Titus sponsored at the inauguration of the Colosseum in 80.

7-36 Aerial view of the Colosseum (Flavian Amphitheater), Rome, Italy, ca. 70–80 CE.

A complex system of concrete barrel vaults once held up the seats in the world's largest amphitheater, where 50,000 spectators could watch gladiatorial combats and wild animal hunts.

> There was a battle between cranes and also between four elephants; animals both tame and wild were slain to the number of nine thousand; and women . . . took part in despatching them. As for the men, several fought in single combat and several groups contended together both in infantry and naval battles. For Titus suddenly filled [the arena] with water and brought in horses and bulls and some other domesticated animals that had been taught to behave in the liquid element just as on land. He also brought in people on ships, who engaged in a sea-fight there. . . . On the first day there was a gladiatorial exhibition and wild-beast hunt. . . . On the second day there was a horse-race, and on the third day a naval battle between three thousand men, followed by an infantry battle. . . . These were the spectacles that were offered, and they continued for a hundred days.*

*Dio Cassius, *Roman History*, 66.25. Translated by Earnest Cary, *Dio's Roman History*, vol. 8 (Cambridge, Mass.: Harvard University Press, 1925), 311, 313.

The Flavians

Because of his outrageous behavior, Nero was forced to commit suicide in 68 CE, bringing the Julio-Claudian dynasty to an end. A year of renewed civil strife followed. The man who emerged triumphant in this brief but bloody conflict was Vespasian (r. 69–79 CE), a general who had served under Claudius and Nero. Vespasian, whose family name was Flavius, had two sons, Titus (r. 79–81 CE) and Domitian (r. 81–96 CE). The Flavian dynasty ruled Rome for more than a quarter century.

COLOSSEUM The Flavians left their mark on the capital in many ways, not the least being the construction of the Colosseum (FIGS. 7-2, no. 17, and 7-36), the monument that, for most people, still represents Rome more than any other building. In the past it was identified so closely with Rome and its empire that in the early Middle Ages there was a saying, "While stands the Colosseum, Rome shall stand; when falls the Colosseum, Rome shall fall; and when Rome falls—the World."[2] The Flavian Amphitheater, as it was known in its day, was one of Vespasian's first undertakings after becoming emperor. The decision to build the Colosseum was very shrewd politically. The site chosen was the artificial lake on the grounds of Nero's Domus Aurea, which engineers drained for the purpose. By building the new amphitheater there, Vespasian reclaimed for the public the land Nero had confiscated for his private pleasure and provided Romans with the largest arena for gladiatorial combats and other lavish spectacles that had ever been constructed. The Colosseum takes its name, however, not from its size—it could

1 in.

1 in.

hold more than 50,000 spectators—but from its location beside the Colossus of Nero (FIG. 7-2, no. 16), the huge statue at the entrance to his urban villa. Vespasian did not live to see the Colosseum in use. Titus completed and formally dedicated the amphitheater in 80 CE with great fanfare (see "Spectacles in the Colosseum," page 180).

The Colosseum, like the much earlier amphitheater at Pompeii (FIG. 7-13), could not have been built without concrete. A complex system of barrel-vaulted corridors holds up the enormous oval seating area. This concrete "skeleton" is apparent today to anyone who enters the amphitheater (FIG. 7-36). In the centuries following the fall of Rome, the Colosseum served as a convenient quarry for ready-made building materials. Almost all its marble seats were hauled away, exposing the network of vaults below. Hidden in antiquity but visible today are the arena substructures, which in their present form date to the third century. They housed waiting rooms for the gladiators, animal cages, and machinery for raising and lowering stage sets as well as animals and humans. Cleverly designed lifting devices brought beasts from their dark dens into the arena's bright light. Above the seats a great velarium, as at Pompeii (FIG. 7-14), once shielded the spectators. Poles affixed to the Colosseum's facade held up the giant awning.

The exterior travertine shell (FIG. 7-1) is approximately 160 feet high, the height of a modern 16-story building. Numbered entrances led to the cavea, where the spectators sat according to their place in the social hierarchy. The relationship of the 76 gateways to the tiers of seats within was carefully thought out and resembles the systems seen in modern sports stadiums. The decor of the exterior, however, had nothing to do with function. The facade is divided into four bands, with large arched openings piercing the lower three. Ornamental Greek orders frame the arches in the standard Roman sequence for multistoried buildings: from the ground up, Tuscan, Ionic, and then Corinthian. This sequence is based on the proportions of the orders, with the Tuscan viewed as capable of supporting the heaviest load. Corinthian pilasters (and between them the brackets for the wooden poles that held up the velarium) circle the uppermost story.

The use of engaged columns and a lintel to frame the openings in the Colosseum's facade is a variation of the scheme seen on the Etruscan Porta Marzia (FIG. 6-14) at Perugia. The Romans commonly used this scheme from Late Republican times on. Like the pseudoperipteral temple, which is an eclectic mix of Greek orders and Etruscan plan, this manner of decorating a building's facade combined Greek orders with an architectural form foreign to Greek post-and-lintel architecture, namely the arch. The Roman practice of framing an arch with an applied Greek order had no structural purpose, but it added variety to the surface. It also unified a multistoried facade by casting a net of verticals and horizontals over it.

FLAVIAN PORTRAITURE Vespasian was an unpretentious career army officer who desired to distance himself from Nero's extravagant misrule. His portraits (FIG. 7-37) reflect his much simpler tastes. They also made an important political statement. Breaking with the tradition Augustus established of depicting the Roman emperor as an eternally youthful god on earth, Vespasian's sculptors resuscitated the veristic tradition of the Republic, possibly at his specific direction. Although not as brutally descriptive as many Republican likenesses, Vespasian's portraits frankly recorded his receding hairline and aging, leathery skin—proclaiming his traditional Republican values in contrast to Nero's.

Portraits of people of all ages survive from the Flavian period, in contrast to the Republic, when only elders were deemed worthy of depiction. A portrait bust (FIG. 7-38) of a young woman is a case in point. Its purpose was to project not Republican virtues but rather idealized beauty—through contemporary fashion rather than by reference to images of Greek goddesses. The portrait is notable for its elegance and delicacy and for the virtuoso way the sculptor rendered the differing textures of hair and flesh. The elaborate Flavian coiffure,

Domitian erected this arch on the road leading into the Roman Forum to honor his brother, the emperor Titus, who became a god after his death. Victories fill the spandrels of the arcuated passageway.

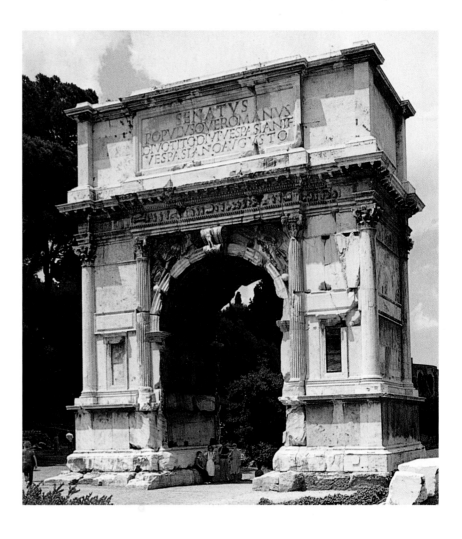

with its corkscrew curls punched out using a drill instead of a chisel, creates a dense mass of light and shadow set off boldly from the softly modeled and highly polished skin of the face and swanlike neck. The drill played an increasing role in Roman sculpture in succeeding periods and in time was used even for portraits of men, when much longer hair and full beards became fashionable.

ARCH OF TITUS When Titus died in 81 CE, only two years after becoming emperor, his younger brother, Domitian, succeeded him. Domitian erected an arch (FIGS. 7-2, no. 13, and 7-39) in Titus's honor on the Sacred Way leading into the Republican Forum Romanum (FIG. 7-2, no. 11). This type of arch, the so-called *triumphal arch,* has a long history in Roman art and architecture, beginning in the second century BCE. The term is something of a misnomer, however, because Roman arches celebrated more than just military victories. Freestanding arches, usually crowned by gilded-bronze statues, commemorated a wide variety of events, ranging from victories abroad to the building of roads and bridges at home.

The Arch of Titus is typical of the early triumphal arch and consists of one passageway only. As on the Colosseum, engaged columns frame the arcuated opening, but their capitals are the *Composite* type, an ornate combination of Ionic volutes and Corinthian acanthus leaves that became popular at about the same time as the Fourth Style in Roman painting. Reliefs depicting personified Victories (winged women, as in Greek art) fill the *spandrels* (the area between the arch's curve and the framing columns and entablature). A dedicatory inscription stating that the arch was erected to honor the god Titus, son of the god Vespasian, dominates the attic. Roman

emperors normally were proclaimed gods after they died, unless they ran afoul of the Senate and were damned. The statues of those who suffered *damnatio memoriae* were torn down, and their names were erased from public inscriptions. This was Nero's fate.

Inside the passageway of the Arch of Titus are two great relief panels. They represent the triumphal parade of Titus down the Sacred Way after his return from the conquest of Judaea at the end of the Jewish Wars in 70 CE. One of the reliefs (FIG. 7-40) depicts Roman soldiers carrying the spoils—including the sacred seven-branched candelabrum, the *menorah*—from the Temple in Jerusalem. Despite considerable damage to the relief, the illusion of movement is convincing. The parade moves forward from the left background into the center foreground and disappears through the obliquely placed arch in the right background. The energy and swing of the column of soldiers suggest a rapid march. The sculptor rejected the Classical low-relief style of the Ara Pacis (FIG. 7-31) in favor of extremely deep carving, which produces strong shadows. The heads of the forward figures have broken off because they stood free from the block. Their high relief emphasized their different placement in space compared with the heads in low relief, which are intact. The play of light and shadow across the protruding foreground and receding background figures enhances the sense of movement.

The panel (FIG. 7-41) on the other side of the passageway shows Titus in his triumphal chariot. The seeming historical accuracy of the spoils panel—it closely corresponds to the Jewish historian Josephus's contemporaneous description of Titus's triumph—gave way in this panel to allegory. Victory rides with Titus in the four-horse chariot and places a wreath on his head. Below her is a

7-40 Spoils of Jerusalem, relief panel from the Arch of Titus, Rome, Italy, after 81 CE. Marble, 7' 10" high.

The reliefs inside the bay of the Arch of Titus commemorate the emperor's greatest achievement—the conquest of Judaea. Here, Roman soldiers carry the spoils from the Jewish temple in Jerusalem.

7-41 Triumph of Titus, relief panel from the Arch of Titus, Rome, Italy, after 81 CE. Marble, 7' 10" high.

Victory crowns Titus in his triumphal chariot. Also present are personifications of Honor and Valor in this first known instance of the intermingling of human and divine figures in a Roman historical relief.

bare-chested youth who is probably a personification of Honor (*Honos*). A female personification of Valor (*Virtus*) leads the horses. These allegorical figures transform the relief from a record of Titus's battlefield success into a celebration of imperial virtues. Such an intermingling of divine and human figures occurs on the Republican Villa of the Mysteries frieze (FIG. 7-18) at Pompeii, but the Arch of Titus panel is the first known instance of divine beings interacting with humans on an official Roman historical relief. (On the Ara Pacis, FIG. 7-29, Aeneas and "Tellus" appear in separate framed panels, carefully segregated from the procession of living Romans.) The Arch of Titus was erected after the emperor's death, and its reliefs were carved when Titus was already a god. Soon afterward, however, this kind of interaction between mortals and immortals became a staple of Roman narrative relief sculpture, even on monuments honoring a living emperor.

HIGH EMPIRE

In the second century CE, under Trajan, Hadrian, and the Antonines, the Roman Empire reached its greatest geographic extent (MAP 7-1) and the height of its power. Rome's might was unchallenged in the Mediterranean world, although the Germanic peoples in Europe, the Berbers in Africa, and the Parthians and Persians in the Near East constantly applied pressure. Within the empire's secure boundaries, the Pax Romana meant unprecedented prosperity for all who came under Roman rule.

Trajan

Domitian's extravagant lifestyle and ego resembled Nero's. He demanded to be addressed as *dominus et deus* (lord and god) and so angered the senators that he was assassinated in 96 CE. The Senate chose the elderly Nerva, one of its own, as emperor. Nerva ruled for only 16 months, but before he died he established a pattern of succession by adoption that lasted for almost a century. Nerva picked Trajan, a capable and popular general born in Italica (Spain), as the next emperor. Trajan was the first non-Italian to rule Rome. Under Trajan, imperial armies brought Roman rule to ever more distant areas (MAP 7-1), and the imperial government took on ever greater responsibility for its people's welfare by instituting a number of farsighted social programs. Trajan was so popular that the Senate granted him the title *Optimus* (the Best), an epithet he shared with Jupiter (who was said to have instructed Nerva to choose Trajan as his successor). In Late Antiquity, Augustus, the founder of the Roman Empire, and Trajan became the yardsticks for success. The goal of new emperors was to be *felicior Augusto, melior Traiano* (luckier than Augustus, better than Trajan).

7-42 Aerial view of Timgad (Thamugadi), Algeria, founded 100 CE.

Timgad, like other new Roman colonies, was planned with great precision. Its strict grid scheme features two main thoroughfares, the cardo and the decumanus, with the forum at their intersection.

TIMGAD In 100 CE, Trajan founded a new colony for army veterans at Timgad, ancient Thamugadi (FIG. **7-42**), in what is today Algeria. Like other colonies, Timgad became the physical embodiment of Roman authority and civilization for the local population and served as a key to the Romanization of the provinces. The town was planned with great precision, its design resembling that of a Roman military encampment or *castrum.* (Scholars still debate which came first. The castrum may have been based on the layout of Roman colonies.) Unlike the sprawling unplanned cities of Rome and Pompeii, Timgad is a square divided into equal quarters by its two main streets, the cardo and the decumanus. They cross at right angles and are bordered by colonnades. Monumental gates once marked the ends of the two avenues. The forum is located at the point where the streets intersect. The quarters are subdivided into square blocks, and the forum and public buildings, such as the theater and baths, occupy areas sized as multiples of these blocks. The Roman plan is a modification of the Hippodamian plan of Greek cities (FIG. **5-76**), though more rigidly ordered.

The fact that most of these colonial settlements were laid out in the same manner, regardless of whether they were in North Africa, Mesopotamia, or England, expresses concretely the unity and centralized power of the Roman Empire at its height. But even the Romans could not regulate human behavior completely. As the aerial view reveals, when the population of Timgad grew sevenfold and burst through the Trajanic colony's walls, rational planning was ignored, and the city and its streets branched out haphazardly.

FORUM OF TRAJAN Trajan completed several major building projects in Rome, including the remodeling of the Circus Maximus (FIG. **7-2**, no. 2), Rome's giant chariot-racing stadium, and the construction of a vast new bathing complex near the Colosseum constructed on top of Nero's Golden House. His most important undertaking, however, was a huge new forum (FIGS. **7-2**, no. 7, and **7-43**), roughly twice the size of the century-old Forum of Augustus (FIG. **7-2**, no. 10)—even excluding the enormous market complex next to the forum. The new forum glorified Trajan's victories in his two wars against the Dacians (who lived in what is now Romania) and was paid for with the spoils of those campaigns. The architect

7-43 APOLLODORUS OF DAMASCUS, Forum of Trajan, Rome, Italy, dedicated 112 CE (James E. Packer and John Burge). (1) Temple of Trajan, (2) Column of Trajan, (3) libraries, (4) Basilica Ulpia, (5) forum, (6) equestrian statue of Trajan.

With the spoils from two Dacian wars, Trajan built Rome's largest forum. It featured an equestrian statue of the emperor, statues of Dacian captives, two libraries, and a basilica with clerestory lighting.

was Apollodorus of Damascus, Trajan's chief military engineer during the Dacian Wars. Apollodorus's plan incorporated the main features of most early forums (FIG. 7-12), except that a huge basilica, not a temple, dominated the colonnaded open square. The temple (completed after the emperor's death and dedicated to the newest god in the Roman pantheon, Trajan himself) was set instead behind the basilica. It stood at the rear end of the forum in its own courtyard, with two libraries and a giant commemorative column, the Column of Trajan (FIGS. 7-43, no. 2, and 7-44).

Entry to Trajan's forum was through an impressive gateway resembling a triumphal arch. Inside the forum were other reminders of Trajan's military prowess. A larger-than-life-size gilded-bronze equestrian statue of the emperor stood at the center of the great court in front of the basilica. Statues of captive Dacians stood above the columns of the forum porticos.

The Basilica Ulpia (Trajan's family name was Ulpius) was a much larger and far more ornate version of the basilica in the forum of Pompeii (FIG. 7-12, no. 3). As shown in FIG. 7-43, no. 4, it had *apses*, or semicircular recesses, on each short end. Two aisles flanked the nave on each side. In contrast to the Pompeian basilica, the entrances were on the long side facing the forum. The building was vast: about 400 feet long (without the apses) and 200 feet wide. Light entered through clerestory windows, made possible by elevating the timber-roofed nave above the colonnaded aisles. In the Republican basilica at Pompeii, light reached the nave only indirectly through aisle windows. The clerestory (used millennia before at Karnak in Egypt, FIG. 3-26) provided much better illumination.

COLUMN OF TRAJAN The Column of Trajan (FIG. 7-44) was probably also the brainchild of Apollodorus of Damascus. The idea of covering the shaft of a colossal freestanding column with a continuous spiral narrative frieze seems to have been invented for this monument, but it was often copied in antiquity, the Middle Ages (FIG. 11-25), and as late as the 19th century. Trajan's column is 128 feet high. It once featured a heroically nude statue of the emperor at the top. (The present statue of Saint Peter dates to the 16th century.) The tall pedestal, decorated with captured Dacian arms and armor, served as Trajan's tomb.

Scholars have likened the 625-foot band that winds around the column to an illustrated scroll of the type housed in the neighboring libraries (and that Lars Pulena holds on his sarcophagus, FIG. 6-15). The reliefs depict Trajan's two successful campaigns against the Dacians. The story unfolds in more than 150 episodes in which some 2,500 figures appear. The band increases in width as it winds to the top of the column, so that it is easier to see the upper portions. Throughout, the relief is very low so as not to distort the contours of the shaft. Paint enhanced the legibility of the figures, but a viewer still would have had difficulty following the narrative from beginning to end.

Much of the spiral frieze is given over to easily recognizable compositions such as those found on coin reverses and on historical relief panels: Trajan addressing his troops, sacrificing to the gods, and so on. The narrative is not a reliable chronological account of the Dacian Wars, as was once thought. The sculptors nonetheless accurately recorded the general character of the campaigns. Notably, battle scenes take up only about a quarter of the frieze. As is true of modern military operations, the Romans spent more time constructing forts, transporting men and equipment, and preparing for battle than fighting. The focus is always on the emperor, who appears throughout the frieze, but the enemy is not belittled. The Romans won because of their superior organization and more powerful army, not because they were inherently superior beings.

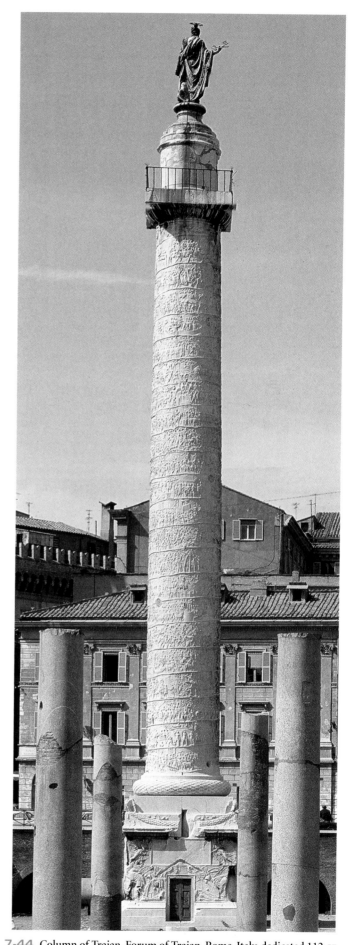

7-44 Column of Trajan, Forum of Trajan, Rome, Italy, dedicated 112 CE.

The spiral frieze of Trajan's column tells the story of the Dacian Wars in 150 episodes. All aspects of the campaigns were represented, from battles to sacrifices to road and fort construction.

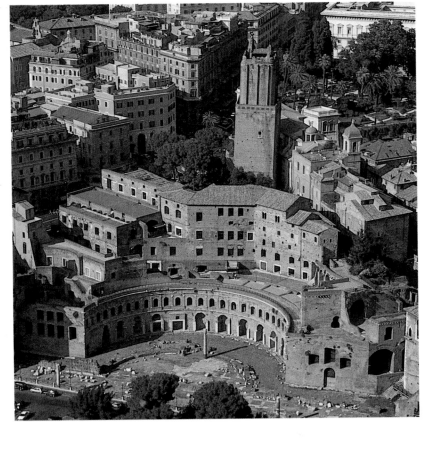

7-45 APOLLODORUS OF DAMASCUS, aerial view of the Markets of Trajan, Rome, Italy, ca. 100–112 CE.

Apollodorus of Damascus used brick-faced concrete to transform the Quirinal Hill overlooking Trajan's forum in Rome into a vast multilevel complex of barrel-vaulted shops and administrative offices.

MARKETS OF TRAJAN On the Quirinal Hill overlooking the forum, Apollodorus built the Markets of Trajan (FIGS. 7-2, no. 8, and 7-45) to house both shops and administrative offices. As earlier at Palestrina (FIG. 7-5), concrete made possible the transformation of a natural slope into a multilevel complex. Trajan's architect was a master of this modern medium as well as of the traditional stone-and-timber post-and-lintel architecture of the forum below. The basic unit was the *taberna*, a single-room shop covered by a barrel vault. Each taberna had a wide doorway, usually with a window above it that allowed light to enter a wooden inner attic used for storage. The shops were on several levels. They opened either onto a hemispherical facade winding around one of the great exedras of Trajan's forum, onto a paved street farther up the hill, or onto a great indoor market hall (FIG. 7-46) resembling a modern shopping mall. The hall housed two floors of shops, with the upper shops set back on each side and lit by skylights. Light from the same sources reached the ground-floor shops through arches beneath the great umbrella-like groin vaults (FIG. 7-6c) covering the hall.

ARCH OF TRAJAN, BENEVENTO In 109 CE, Trajan opened a new road, the Via Traiana, in southern Italy. Several years later the Senate erected a great arch (FIG. 7-47) honoring Trajan at the point where the road entered Benevento (ancient Beneventum). Architecturally, the Arch of Trajan at Benevento is almost identical

to Titus's arch (FIG. 7-39) in Rome, but relief panels cover both facades of the Trajanic arch, giving it a billboardlike function. Every inch of the surface heralded the emperor's achievements. In one panel, he enters Rome after a successful military campaign. In another, he distributes largesse to needy children. In still others, he is portrayed as the founder of colonies for army veterans and as the builder of a new port at Ostia, Rome's harbor at the mouth of the Tiber. The reliefs present Trajan as the guarantor of peace and security in the empire, the benefactor of the poor, and the patron of soldiers and merchants alike. In short, the emperor is all things to all people. In several of the panels, Trajan freely intermingles with

7-46 APOLLODORUS OF DAMASCUS, interior of the great hall, Markets of Trajan, Rome, Italy, ca. 100–112 CE.

The great hall of Trajan's markets resembles a modern shopping mall. It housed two floors of shops, with the upper ones set back and lit by skylights. Concrete groin vaults cover the central space.

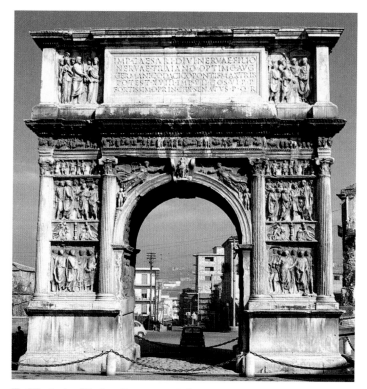

7-47 Arch of Trajan, Benevento, Italy, ca. 114–118 CE.

Unlike Titus's arch (FIG. 7-39), Trajan's has relief panels covering both facades, transforming it into a kind of advertising billboard featuring the emperor's many achievements on and off the battlefield.

1 in.

7-48 Portrait bust of Hadrian, from Rome, ca. 117–120 CE. Marble, 1′ 4¾″ high. Museo Nazionale Romano–Palazzo Massimo alle Terme, Rome.

Hadrian, a lover of all things Greek, was the first Roman emperor to wear a beard. His artists modeled his idealizing official portraits on Classical Greek statues like Kresilas's Pericles (FIG. 5-41).

divinities, and on the arch's attic (which may have been completed after his death and deification), Jupiter hands his thunderbolt to the emperor, awarding him dominion over Earth. Such scenes, depicting the "first citizen" of Rome as a divinely sanctioned ruler in the company of the gods, henceforth became the norm, not the exception, in official Roman art.

Hadrian

Hadrian, Trajan's chosen successor and fellow Spaniard, was a connoisseur and lover of all the arts as well as an author and architect. He greatly admired Greek culture and traveled widely as emperor, often in the Greek East. Everywhere he went, statues and arches were set up in his honor.

HADRIANIC PORTRAITURE More portraits of Hadrian exist today than of any other emperor except Augustus. Hadrian, who was 41 years old at the time of Trajan's death and who ruled for more than two decades, is always depicted in his portraits as a mature adult who never ages. Hadrian's portraits (FIG. 7-48) more closely resemble Kresilas's portrait of Pericles (FIG. 5-41) than those of any Roman emperor before him. Fifth-century BCE statues also provided the prototypes for the idealizing official portraits of Augustus, but the Augustan models were Greek images of young athletes. The models for Hadrian's artists were Classical statues of mature Greek men. Hadrian himself wore a beard—a habit that, in its Roman context, must be viewed as a Greek affectation. Beards then became the norm for all subsequent Roman emperors for more than a century and a half.

PANTHEON Soon after Hadrian became emperor, work began on the Pantheon (FIGS. 7-2, no. 5, and 7-49), the temple of all the gods, one of the best-preserved buildings of antiquity and most

7-49 Pantheon, Rome, Italy, 118–125 CE.

Originally, the approach to Hadrian's "temple of all gods" in Rome was from a columnar courtyard. Like a temple in a Roman forum (FIG. 7-12), the Pantheon stood at one narrow end of the enclosure.

7-50 Restored cutaway view (*left*) and lateral section (*right*) of the Pantheon, Rome, Italy, 118–125 CE (John Burge).

The Pantheon's traditional facade masked its revolutionary cylindrical drum and its huge hemispherical dome. The interior symbolized both the orb of the earth and the vault of the heavens.

influential designs in architectural history. The Pantheon reveals the full potential of concrete, both as a building material and as a means for shaping architectural space. Originally, visitors approached the Pantheon from a columnar courtyard, and the temple itself, like temples in Roman forums, stood at one narrow end of the enclosure (FIG. **7-50,** *left*). Its facade of eight Corinthian columns—almost all that could be seen from ground level in antiquity—was a bow to tradition. Everything else about the Pantheon was revolutionary. Behind the columnar porch is an immense concrete cylinder covered by a huge hemispherical dome 142 feet in diameter. The dome's top is also 142 feet from the floor (FIG. **7-50,** *right*). The design is thus based on the intersection of two circles (one horizontal, the other vertical) so that the interior space can be imagined as the orb of the earth and the dome as the vault of the heavens.

If the Pantheon's design is simplicity itself, executing that design required all the ingenuity of Hadrian's engineers. They built up the cylindrical drum level by level using concrete of varied composition. Extremely hard and durable basalt went into the mix for the foundations, and the builders gradually modified the "recipe" until, at the top, featherweight pumice replaced stones to lighten the load. The dome's thickness also decreases as it nears the oculus, the circular opening 30 feet in diameter that is the only light source for the interior (FIG. **7-51**). The use of *coffers* (sunken decorative panels) lessened the dome's weight without weakening its structure. The coffers further reduced the dome's mass and also provided a handsome pattern of squares within the vast circle. Renaissance drawings suggest that each coffer once had a glistening gilded-bronze rosette at its center, enhancing the symbolism of the dome as the starry heavens.

Below the dome, much of the original marble veneer of the walls, niches, and floor has survived. In the Pantheon, visitors can get a sense, as almost nowhere else, of how magnificent the interiors of Roman concrete buildings could be. But despite the luxurious skin of the Pantheon's interior, the sense experienced on first entering the structure is not the weight of the enclosing walls but the space they enclose. In pre-Roman architecture, the form of the enclosed space was determined by the placement of the solids, which did not so much shape space as interrupt it. Roman architects were the first to conceive of architecture in terms of units of space that could be

7-51 Interior of the Pantheon, Rome, Italy, 118–125 CE.

The coffered dome of the Pantheon is 142 feet in diameter and 142 feet high. The light entering through its oculus forms a circular beam that moves across the dome as the sun moves across the sky.

Hadrian and Apollodorus of Damascus

Dio Cassius, a third-century CE senator who wrote a history of Rome from its foundation to his own day, recounted a revealing anecdote about Hadrian and Apollodorus of Damascus, architect of the Forum of Trajan (FIG. 7-43):

> Hadrian first drove into exile and then put to death the architect Apollodorus who had carried out several of Trajan's building projects. . . . When Trajan was at one time consulting with Apollodorus about a certain problem connected with his buildings, the architect said to Hadrian, who had interrupted them with some advice, "Go away and draw your pumpkins. You know nothing about these problems." For it so happened that Hadrian was at that time priding himself on some sort of drawing. When he became emperor he remembered this insult and refused to put up with Apollodorus's outspokenness. He sent him [his own] plan for the temple of Venus and Roma [FIG. 7-2, no. 14], in order to demonstrate that it was possible for a great work to be conceived without his [Apollodorus's] help,

and asked him if he thought the building was well designed. Apollodorus sent a [very critical] reply. . . . [The emperor did not] attempt to restrain his anger or hide his pain; on the contrary, he had the man slain.*

The story says a great deal both about the absolute power Roman emperors wielded and about how seriously Hadrian took his architectural designs. But perhaps the most interesting detail is the description of Hadrian's drawings of "pumpkins." These must have been drawings of concrete domes like the one in the Serapeum (FIG. 7-52) at Hadrian's Tivoli villa. Such vaults were too adventurous for Apollodorus, or at least for a public building in Trajanic Rome, and Hadrian had to try them out later at home at his own expense.

*Dio Cassius, *Roman History*, 69.4.1–5. Translated by J. J. Pollitt, *The Art of Rome, c. 753 B.C.–A.D. 337: Sources and Documents* (New York: Cambridge University Press, 1983), 175–176.

7-52 Canopus and Serapeum, Hadrian's Villa, Tivoli, Italy, ca. 125–128 CE.

Hadrian was an architect and may have personally designed some buildings at his private villa at Tivoli. The Serapeum features the kind of pumpkin-shaped concrete dome the emperor favored.

shaped by the enclosures. The Pantheon's interior is a single unified, self-sufficient whole, uninterrupted by supporting solids. It encloses visitors without imprisoning them, opening through the oculus to the drifting clouds, the blue sky, the sun, and the gods. In this space, the architect used light not merely to illuminate the darkness but to create drama and underscore the interior shape's symbolism. On a sunny day, the light that passes through the oculus forms a circular beam, a disk of light that moves across the coffered dome in the course of the day as the sun moves across the sky itself. Escaping from the noise and torrid heat of a Roman summer day into the Pantheon's cool, calm, and mystical immensity is an experience almost impossible to describe and one that should not be missed.

HADRIAN'S VILLA, TIVOLI Hadrian, the amateur architect, was not the designer of the Pantheon, but the emperor was deeply involved with the construction of his private country villa at Tivoli. One of his projects there was the construction of a pool and

an artificial grotto, called the Canopus and Serapeum (FIG. 7-52), respectively. Canopus was an Egyptian city connected to Alexandria by a canal. Its most famous temple was dedicated to the god Serapis. Nothing about the Tivoli design, however, derives from Egyptian architecture. The grotto at the end of the pool is made of concrete and has an unusual pumpkin-shaped dome that Hadrian probably designed himself (see "Hadrian and Apollodorus of Damascus," above). Yet, in keeping with the persistent eclecticism of Roman art and architecture, Greek columns and marble copies of famous Greek statues lined the pool, as would be expected from a lover of Greek art. The Corinthian colonnade at the curved end of the pool, however, is of a type unknown in Classical Greek architecture. The colonnade not only lacks a superstructure but has *arcuated* (curved or arched) lintels, as opposed to traditional Greek horizontal lintels, between alternating pairs of columns. This simultaneous respect for Greek architecture and willingness to break its rules are typical of much Roman architecture of the High and Late Empire.

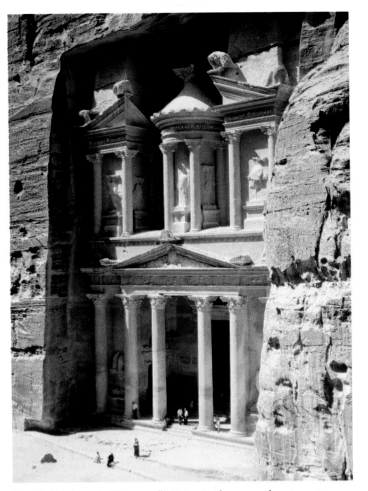

7-53 Al-Khazneh ("Treasury"), Petra, Jordan, second century CE.

This rock-cut tomb facade is a prime example of Roman "baroque" architecture. The designer used Greek architectural elements in a purely ornamental fashion and with a studied disregard for Classical rules.

AL-KHAZNEH, PETRA An even more extreme example of what many scholars have called Roman "baroque" architecture (because of the striking parallels with 17th-century Italian buildings; see Chapter 19) is the second-century CE tomb nicknamed Al-Khazneh, the "Treasury" (FIG. **7-53**), at Petra, Jordan. It is one of the most elaborate of many tomb facades cut into the sheer rock faces of the local rose-colored mountains. As at Hadrian's villa, Greek architectural elements are used here in a purely ornamental fashion and with a studied disregard for Classical rules.

The tomb's facade is more than 130 feet high and consists of two stories. The lower story resembles a temple facade with six columns, but the columns are unevenly spaced and the pediment is only wide enough to cover the four central columns. On the upper level, a temple-within-a-temple sits on top of the lower temple. Here the facade and roof split in half to make room for a central tholoslike cylinder, which contrasts sharply with the rectangles and triangles of the rest of the design. On both levels, the rhythmic alternation of deep projection and indentation creates dynamic patterns of light and shadow. At Petra, as at Tivoli, the architect used the vocabulary of Greek architecture, but the syntax is new and distinctively Roman. In fact, the design recalls some of the architectural fantasies painted on the walls of Roman houses—for example, the tholos seen through columns surmounted by a broken pediment (FIG. **7-19**, *right*) in the Second Style cubiculum from Boscoreale.

Ostia

The average Roman, of course, did not own a luxurious country villa and was not buried in a grand tomb. About 90 percent of Rome's population of close to one million lived in multistory apartment blocks (*insulae*). After the great fire of 64 CE, these were brick-faced concrete buildings. The rents were not cheap, as the law of supply and demand in real estate was just as valid in antiquity as it is today. Juvenal, a Roman satirist of the early second century CE, commented that people willing to give up chariot races and the other diversions Rome had to offer could purchase a fine home in the countryside "for a year's rent in a dark hovel" in a city so noisy that "the sick die mostly from lack of sleep."[3] Conditions were much the same for the inhabitants of Ostia, Rome's harbor city. After its new port opened under Trajan, Ostia's prosperity increased dramatically and so did its population. A burst of building activity began under Trajan and continued under Hadrian and throughout the second century CE.

APARTMENT HOUSES Ostia had many multistory insulae (FIG. **7-54**). Shops occupied the ground floors. Above were up to four floors of apartments. Although many of these were large, they had neither the space nor the light of the typical Pompeian private domus (see "The Roman House," page 167). In place of peristyles, insulae had only narrow light wells or small courtyards. Consequently, instead of looking inward, large numbers of glass windows faced the city's noisy streets. The residents cooked their food in the hallways. Only deluxe apartments had private toilets. Others shared latrines, often on a different floor from the apartment. Still, these insulae were quite similar to modern apartment houses, which also sometimes have shops on the ground floor.

7-54 Model of an insula, Ostia, Italy, second century CE. Museo della Civiltà Romana, Rome.

Rome and Ostia were densely populated cities, and most Romans lived in multistory brick-faced concrete insulae (apartment houses) with shops on the ground floor. Private toilet facilities were rare.

7-55 Neptune and creatures of the sea, detail of a floor mosaic in the Baths of Neptune, Ostia, Italy, ca. 140 CE.

Black-and-white floor mosaics were very popular during the second and third centuries. The artists conceived them as surface decorations, not as illusionistic compositions meant to rival paintings.

Another strikingly modern feature of these multifamily residences is their brick facades, which were not concealed by stucco or marble veneers. When a classical motif was desired, builders could add brick pilasters or engaged columns, but always left the brick exposed. Ostia and Rome have many examples of apartment houses, warehouses, and tombs with intricate moldings and contrasting colors of brick. In the second century CE, brick came to be appreciated as attractive in its own right.

BATHS OF NEPTUNE Although the decoration of Ostian insulae tended to be more modest than that of the private houses of Pompeii, the finer apartments had mosaic floors and painted walls and ceilings. The most popular choice for elegant pavements at Ostia in both private and public edifices was the black-and-white mosaic. One of the largest and best-preserved examples is in the so-called Baths of Neptune, named for the grand mosaic floor (FIG. 7-55) showing four seahorses pulling the Roman god of the sea across the waves. Neptune needs no chariot to support him as he speeds along, his mantle blowing in the strong wind. All about the god are other sea denizens, positioned so that wherever a visitor enters the room, some figures appear right side up. The second-century artist rejected the complex polychrome modeling of figures seen in Pompeian mosaics such as *Battle of Issus* (FIG. 5-70) and used simple black silhouettes enlivened by white interior lines. Roman artists conceived black-and-white mosaics as surface decorations, not as three-dimensional windows, and thus they were especially appropriate for floors.

ISOLA SACRA The tombs in Ostia's Isola Sacra cemetery were usually constructed of brick-faced concrete, and the facades of these houses of the dead resembled those of the contemporary insulae of the living. These were normally communal tombs, not the final resting places of the very wealthy. Many of them were adorned with small painted terracotta plaques immortalizing the activities of middle-class merchants and professional people. A characteristic example (FIG. 7-56) depicts a vegetable seller behind a counter. The artist had little interest in the Classical-revival style of contemporary imperial art and tilted the counter forward so that the observer can see the produce clearly. Such scenes of daily life appear on Roman funerary reliefs all over Europe. They were as much a part of the artistic legacy to the later history of Western art as the monuments of the Roman emperors, which until recently were the exclusive interest of art historians.

1 in.

7-56 Funerary relief of a vegetable vendor, from Ostia, Italy, second half of second century CE. Painted terracotta, 1′ 5″ high. Museo Ostiense, Ostia.

Terracotta plaques illustrating the activities of middle-class merchants frequently adorned Ostian tomb facades. In this relief of a vegetable seller, the artist tilted the counter to display the produce clearly.

High Empire **191**

The Antonines

Early in 138 CE, Hadrian adopted the 51-year-old Antoninus Pius (r. 138–161 CE). At the same time, he required that Antoninus adopt Marcus Aurelius (r. 161–180 CE) and Lucius Verus (r. 161–169 CE), thereby assuring a peaceful succession for at least another generation. When Hadrian died later in the year, the Senate proclaimed him a god, and Antoninus Pius became emperor. Antoninus ruled the Roman world with distinction for 23 years. After his death and deification, Marcus Aurelius and Lucius Verus became the Roman Empire's first co-emperors.

COLUMN OF ANTONINUS PIUS Shortly after Antoninus Pius's death, Marcus and Lucius erected a memorial column in his honor. Its pedestal has a dedicatory inscription on one side and a relief illustrating the *apotheosis* (FIG. 7-57), or ascent to Heaven, of Antoninus and his wife Faustina the Elder on the opposite side. On the adjacent sides are two identical representations of the *decursio* (FIG. 7-58), or ritual circling of the imperial funerary pyre.

The two figural compositions are very different. The apotheosis relief remains firmly in the Classical tradition with its elegant, well-proportioned figures, personifications, and single ground line corresponding to the panel's lower edge. The Campus Martius (Field of Mars), personified as a youth holding the Egyptian obelisk that stood in that area of Rome, reclines at the lower left corner. Roma (Rome personified) leans on a shield decorated with the she-wolf suckling Romulus and Remus (compare FIG. 6-11). Roma bids

7-57 Apotheosis of Antoninus Pius and Faustina, pedestal of the Column of Antoninus Pius, Rome, Italy, ca. 161 CE. Marble, 8′ 1½″ high. Musei Vaticani, Rome.

This representation of the apotheosis (ascent to Heaven) of Antoninus Pius and Faustina is firmly in the Classical tradition with its elegant, well-proportioned figures, personifications, and single ground line.

1 ft.

7-58 Decursio, pedestal of the Column of Antoninus Pius, Rome, Italy, ca. 161 CE. Marble, 8′ 1½″ high. Musei Vaticani, Rome.

In contrast to FIG. 7-57, the Antonine decursio reliefs break sharply with Classical art conventions. The ground is the whole surface of the relief, and the figures stand on floating patches of earth.

1 ft.

farewell to the couple being lifted into the realm of the gods on the wings of a personification of uncertain identity. All this was familiar from earlier scenes of apotheosis. New to the imperial repertoire, however, was the fusion of time the joint apotheosis represents. Faustina had died 20 years before Antoninus Pius. By depicting the two as ascending together, the artist wished to suggest that Antoninus had been faithful to his wife for two decades and that now they would be reunited in the afterlife.

The decursio reliefs (FIG. 7-58) break even more strongly with Classical convention. The figures are much stockier than those in the apotheosis relief, and the panel was not conceived as a window onto the world. The ground is the whole surface of the relief, and marching soldiers and galloping horses alike stand on floating patches of earth. This, too, had not occurred before in imperial art, only in plebeian art (FIG. 7-10). After centuries of following the rules of Classical design, elite Roman artists and patrons finally became dissatisfied with them. When seeking a new direction, they adopted some of the non-Classical conventions of the art of the lower classes.

MARCUS AURELIUS Another break with the past occurred in the official portraits of Marcus Aurelius, although his images retain the pompous trappings of imperial iconography. In a larger-than-life-size gilded-bronze equestrian statue (FIG. **7-59**), the emperor possesses a superhuman grandeur and is much larger than any normal human would be in relation to his horse. Marcus stretches out his right arm in a gesture that is both a greeting and an offer of clemency. Some evidence suggests that beneath the horse's raised right foreleg an enemy once cowered, begging the emperor for mercy. Marcus's portrait owed its preservation throughout the Middle Ages to the fact that it was mistakenly thought to portray Constantine, the first Christian emperor of Rome. Most ancient bronze statues were melted down for their metal value, because Christians regarded them as impious images from the pagan world. Even today, after centuries of new finds, only a few bronze equestrian statues survive. The type was, however, often used for imperial portraits—an equestrian statue of Trajan stood in the middle of his forum (FIG. 7-43, no. 6). Perhaps more than any other statuary type, the equestrian portrait expresses the Roman emperor's majesty and authority.

This message of supreme confidence is not conveyed, however, by the portrait head of Marcus's equestrian statue or any of the other portraits of the emperor in the years just before his death. Portraits of aged emperors were not new (FIG. 7-37), but Marcus's were the first ones in which a Roman emperor appeared weary, saddened, and even worried. For the first time, the strain of constant warfare on the frontiers and the burden of ruling a worldwide empire show in the emperor's face. The Antonine sculptor ventured beyond Republican verism, exposing the ruler's character, his thoughts, and his soul for all to see, as Marcus revealed them himself in his *Meditations*, a deeply moving philosophical treatise setting forth the emperor's personal worldview. This was a major turning point in the history of ancient art, and, coming as it did when the Classical style was being challenged in relief sculpture (FIG. 7-58), it marked the beginning of the end of Classical art's domination in the Greco-Roman world.

ORESTES SARCOPHAGUS Other profound changes also were taking place in Roman art and society at this time. Beginning under Trajan and Hadrian and especially during the rule of the Antonines, Romans began to favor burial over cremation. This reversal of funerary practices may reflect the influence of Christianity and

7-59 Equestrian statue of Marcus Aurelius, from Rome, Italy, ca. 175 CE. Bronze, 11′ 6″ high. Musei Capitolini, Rome.

In this equestrian portrait of Marcus Aurelius as omnipotent conqueror, the emperor stretches out his arm in a gesture of clemency. An enemy once cowered beneath the horse's raised foreleg.

other Eastern religions, whose adherents believed in an afterlife for the human body. Although the emperors themselves continued to be cremated in the traditional Roman manner, many private citizens opted for burial. Thus they required larger containers for their remains than the ash urns that were the norm until the second century CE. This in turn led to a sudden demand for sarcophagi, which are more similar to modern coffins than are any other ancient type of burial container.

Greek mythology was one of the most popular subjects for the decoration of these sarcophagi. In many cases, especially in the late second and third centuries CE, the Greek heroes and heroines were given the portrait features of the Roman men and women interred in the marble coffins. These private patrons were following the model of imperial portraiture, where emperors and empresses frequently masqueraded as gods and goddesses and heroes and heroines (see "Role Playing in Roman Portraiture," page 174). An early example of the type (although it lacks any portraits) is the sarcophagus

7-60 Sarcophagus with the myth of Orestes, ca. 140–150 CE. Marble, 2′ 7½″ high. Cleveland Museum of Art, Cleveland.

Under the Antonines, Romans began to favor burial over cremation, and sarcophagi became very popular. Themes from Greek mythology, such as the tragic saga of Orestes, were common subjects.

(FIG. 7-60) now in Cleveland, one of many decorated with the story of the tragic Greek hero Orestes. All the examples of this type use the same basic composition. Orestes appears more than once in every case. Here, at the center, Orestes slays his mother Clytaemnestra and her lover Aegisthus to avenge their murder of his father Agamemnon, and then, at the right, takes refuge at Apollo's sanctuary at Delphi (symbolized by the god's tripod).

The repetition of sarcophagus compositions indicates that sculptors had access to pattern books. In fact, sarcophagus production was a major industry during the High and Late Empire. Several important regional manufacturing centers existed. The sarcophagi produced in the Latin West, such as the Cleveland Orestes sarcophagus, differ in for-

mat from those made in the Greek-speaking East. Western sarcophagi have reliefs only on the front and sides, because they were placed in floor-level niches inside Roman tombs. Eastern sarcophagi have reliefs on all four sides and stood in the center of the burial chamber. This contrast parallels the essential difference between Etrusco-Roman and Greek temples. The former were set against the wall of a forum or sanctuary and approached from the front, whereas the latter could be reached (and viewed) from every side.

MELFI SARCOPHAGUS An elaborate example (FIG. 7-61) of a sarcophagus of the Eastern type comes from Rapolla, near Melfi in southern Italy. It was manufactured, however, in Asia Minor and

7-61 Asiatic sarcophagus with kline portrait of a woman, from Rapolla, near Melfi, Italy, ca. 165–170 CE. Marble, 5′ 7″ high. Museo Nazionale Archeologico del Melfese, Melfi.

Sarcophagi were produced in several regional centers. Western sarcophagi were decorated only on the front. Eastern sarcophagi, such as this one with a woman's portrait on the lid, have reliefs on all four sides.

Iaia of Cyzicus and the Art of Encaustic Painting

The names of very few Roman artists are known. Those that are tend to be names of artists and architects who directed major imperial building projects (Severus and Celer, Domus Aurea; Apollodorus of Damascus, Forum of Trajan), worked on a gigantic scale (Zenodorus, Colossus of Nero), or made precious objects for famous patrons (Dioscurides, gem cutter for Augustus).

An interesting exception to this rule is Iaia of Cyzicus. Pliny the Elder reported the following about this renowned painter from Asia Minor who worked in Italy during the Republic:

> Iaia of Cyzicus, who remained a virgin all her life, painted at Rome during the time when M. Varro [116–27 BCE; a renowned Republican scholar and author] was a youth, both with a brush and with a cestrum on ivory, specializing mainly in portraits of women; she also painted a large panel in Naples representing an old woman and a portrait of herself done with a mirror. Her hand was quicker than that of any other painter, and her artistry was of such high quality that she commanded much higher prices than the most celebrated painters of the same period.*

The *cestrum* Pliny mentioned is a small spatula used in *encaustic* painting, a technique of mixing colors with hot wax and then applying them to the surface. Pliny knew of encaustic paintings of considerable antiquity, including those of Polygnotos of Thasos (see Chapter 5, page 121). The best evidence for the technique, however, comes from Roman Egypt, where mummies were routinely furnished with portraits painted with encaustic on wooden panels (FIG. 7-62).

Artists applied encaustic to marble as well as to wood. According to Pliny, when Praxiteles was asked which of his statues he preferred, the fourth-century BCE Greek artist, perhaps the ancient world's greatest marble sculptor, replied: "Those that Nikias painted."† This anecdote underscores the importance of coloration in ancient statuary.

---

*Pliny the Elder, *Natural History*, 35.147–148. Translated by J. J. Pollitt, *The Art of Rome, c. 753 B.C.–A.D. 337: Sources and Documents* (New York: Cambridge University Press, 1983), 87.
†Pliny the Elder, *Natural History*, 35.133.

1 in.

7-62 Mummy portrait of a priest of Serapis, from Hawara (Faiyum), Egypt, ca. 140–160 CE. Encaustic on wood, $1' 4\frac{3}{4}'' \times 8\frac{3}{4}''$. British Museum, London.

In Roman times, the Egyptians continued to bury their dead in mummy cases, but painted portraits replaced the traditional masks. This portrait was painted in encaustic—colors mixed with hot wax.

---

attests to the vibrant export market for such luxury items in Antonine times. The decoration of all four sides of the marble box with statuesque images of Greek gods and heroes in architectural frames is distinctively Asiatic. The figures portrayed include Venus and the legendary beauty Helen of Troy. The lid portrait, which carries on the tradition of Etruscan sarcophagi (FIGS. 6-5 and 6-15), is also a feature of the most expensive Western Roman coffins. Here the deceased, a woman, reclines on a *kline* (bed). With her are her faithful little dog (only its forepaws remain at the left end of the lid) and Cupid (at the right). The winged infant-god mournfully holds a downturned torch, a reference to the death of a woman whose beauty rivaled that of his mother, Venus, and of Homer's Helen.

MUMMY PORTRAITS In Egypt, burial had been practiced for millennia. Even after the Kingdom of the Nile was reduced to a Roman province in 30 BCE, Egyptians continued to bury their dead in mummy cases (see "Mummification," Chapter 3, page 43). In Roman times, however, painted portraits on wood often replaced the traditional stylized portrait masks (see "Iaia of Cyzicus and the Art of Encaustic Painting," above). Hundreds of Roman mummy portraits have been preserved in the cemeteries of the Faiyum district. One of them (FIG. 7-62) depicts a priest of the Egyptian god Serapis, whose curly hair and beard closely emulate Antoine fashion in Rome. Such portraits, which mostly date to the second and third centuries CE, were probably painted while the subjects were still alive. This one exhibits the painter's refined use of the brush and spatula, mastery of the depiction of varied textures and of the play of light over the soft and delicately modeled face, and sensitive portrayal of the deceased's calm demeanor. Art historians use the Faiyum mummies to trace the evolution of portrait painting after Mount Vesuvius erupted in 79 CE (compare FIG. 7-25).

The Western and Eastern Roman sarcophagi and the mummy cases of Roman Egypt all served the same purpose, despite their differing shape and character. In an empire as vast as Rome's, regional differences are to be expected. As will be discussed later, geography also played a major role in the Middle Ages, when Western and Eastern Christian art differed sharply.

LATE EMPIRE

By the time of Marcus Aurelius, two centuries after Augustus established the Pax Romana, Roman power was beginning to erode. It was increasingly difficult to keep order on the frontiers, and even within the Empire the authority of Rome was being challenged. Marcus's son Commodus (r. 180–192 CE), who succeeded his father, was assassinated, bringing the Antonine dynasty to an end. The economy was in decline, and the efficient imperial bureaucracy was disintegrating. Even the official state religion was losing ground to Eastern cults, Christianity among them, which were beginning to gain large numbers of converts. The Late Empire was a pivotal era in world history during which the pagan ancient world was gradually transformed into the Christian Middle Ages.

The Severans

Civil conflict followed Commodus's death. When it ended, an African-born general named Septimius Severus (r. 193–211 CE) was master of the Roman world. He succeeded in establishing a new dynasty that ruled the Empire for nearly a half century.

SEVERAN PORTRAITURE Anxious to establish his legitimacy after the civil war, Septimius Severus adopted himself into the Antonine dynasty, declaring that he was Marcus Aurelius's son. It is not surprising, then, that official portraits of the emperor in bronze and marble depict him with the long hair and beard of his Antonine "father"—whatever Severus's true appearance may have been. That is also how he appears in the only preserved painted portrait of an em-

7-64 Portrait of Caracalla, ca. 211–217 CE. Marble, 1′ 2″ high. Metropolitan Museum of Art, New York.

Caracalla's suspicious personality is brilliantly captured in this portrait. The emperor's brow is knotted, and he abruptly turns his head over his left shoulder, as if he suspects danger from behind.

peror. The portrait (FIG. 7-63), discovered in Egypt and painted in *tempera* (pigments in egg yolk) on wood (as were many of the mummy portraits from Faiyum), shows Severus with his wife Julia Domna, the daughter of a Syrian priest, and their two sons, Caracalla and Geta. Painted imperial likenesses must have been quite common all over the empire, but their perishable nature explains their almost total loss.

The Severan family portrait is of special interest for two reasons beyond its survival. Severus's hair is tinged with gray, suggesting that his marble portraits—which, like all marble sculptures in antiquity, were painted—also may have revealed his advancing age in this way. (The same was very likely true of the marble likenesses of the elderly Marcus Aurelius.) The group portrait is also notable because the face of the emperor's younger son, Geta, was erased. When Caracalla (r. 211–217 CE) succeeded his father as emperor, he had his brother murdered and the Senate damn his memory. (Caracalla also ordered the death of his wife Plautilla.) The painted *tondo* (circular format, or *roundel*) portrait from Egypt is an eloquent testimony to that *damnatio memoriae* and to the long arm of Roman authority. This kind of defacement of a political rival's portrait is not new. Thutmose III of Egypt, for example, destroyed Hatshepsut's portraits (FIG. 3-21) after her death. But the Roman government employed damnatio memoriae as a political tool more often and more systematically than did any other civilization.

7-63 Painted portrait of Septimius Severus and his family, from Egypt, ca. 200 CE. Tempera on wood, 1′ 2″ diameter. Staatliche Museen, Berlin.

The only known painted portrait of an emperor shows Septimius Severus with gray hair. With him are his wife Julia Domna and their two sons, but Geta's head was removed after his damnatio memoriae.

CARACALLA In the Severan painted tondo, Caracalla is portrayed as a boy with curly Antonine hair. The portraits of Caracalla as emperor are very different. In the head illustrated here (FIG. 7-64), the sculptor brilliantly suggested the texture of the emperor's short hair and close-cropped beard through deft handling of the chisel and

7-65 Chariot procession of Septimius Severus, relief from the attic of the Arch of Septimius Severus, Lepcis Magna, Libya, 203 CE. Marble, 5′ 6″ high. Castle Museum, Tripoli.

A new non-naturalistic aesthetic emerged in later Roman art. In this relief from a triumphal arch, Septimius Severus and his two sons face the viewer even though their chariot is moving to the right.

incisions into the marble surface. More remarkable, however, is the moving characterization of Caracalla's suspicious nature, a further development from the groundbreaking introspection of the portraits of Marcus Aurelius. Caracalla's brow is knotted, and he abruptly turns his head over his left shoulder, as if he suspects danger from behind. The emperor had reason to be fearful. An assassin's dagger felled him in the sixth year of his rule. Assassination would be the fate of many Roman emperors during the turbulent third century CE.

LEPCIS MAGNA The hometown of the Severans was Lepcis Magna, on the coast of what is now Libya. In the late second and early third centuries CE, the Severans constructed a modern harbor there as well as a new forum, basilica, arch, and other monuments. The Arch of Septimius Severus has been rebuilt. It features friezes on the attic on all four sides. One frieze (FIG. 7-65) depicts the chariot procession of the emperor and his two sons on the occasion of their homecoming in 203. Unlike the triumph panel (FIG. 7-41) on the Arch of Titus in Rome, this relief gives no sense of rushing motion. Rather, it has a stately stillness. The chariot and the horsemen behind it are moving forward, but the emperor and his sons are detached from the procession and face the viewer. Also different is the way the figures in the second row have no connection with the ground and are elevated above the heads of those in the first row so that they can be seen more clearly.

Both the frontality and the floating figures were new to official Roman art in Antonine and Severan times, but both appeared long before in the private art of freed slaves (FIGS. 7-9 and 7-10). Once sculptors in the emperor's employ embraced these non-Classical elements, they had a long afterlife, largely (although never totally) displacing the Classical style the Romans adopted from Greece. As is often true in the history of art, the emergence of a new aesthetic was a by-product of a period of social, political, and economic upheaval. Art historians call this new non-naturalistic, more abstract style the Late Antique style.

BATHS OF CARACALLA The Severans were also active builders in the capital. The Baths of Caracalla (FIG. 7-66) in Rome were the greatest in a long line of bathing and recreational complexes

7-66 Plan of the Baths of Caracalla, Rome, Italy, 212–216 CE. (1) natatio, (2) frigidarium, (3) tepidarium, (4) caldarium, (5) palaestra.

Caracalla's baths could accommodate 1,600 bathers. They resembled a modern health spa and included libraries, lecture halls, and exercise courts in addition to bathing rooms and a swimming pool.

7-67 Frigidarium, Baths of Diocletian, Rome, ca. 298–306 CE (remodeled by MICHELANGELO as the nave of Santa Maria degli Angeli, 1563).

The groin-vaulted nave of the church of Santa Maria degli Angeli in Rome was once the frigidarium of the Baths of Diocletian. It gives an idea of the lavish adornment of imperial Roman baths.

erected with imperial funds to win the public's favor. Made of brick-faced concrete and covered by enormous vaults springing from thick walls up to 140 feet high, Caracalla's baths dwarfed the typical baths of cities and towns such as Ostia and Pompeii. The design was symmetrical along a central axis, facilitating the Roman custom of taking sequential plunges in warm-, hot-, and cold-water baths in, respectively, the *tepidarium, caldarium,* and *frigidarium.* The caldarium (FIG. 7-66, no. 4) was a huge circular chamber with a concrete drum even taller than the Pantheon's (FIGS. 7-49 to 7-51) and a dome almost as large. Caracalla's baths also had landscaped gardens, lecture halls, libraries, colonnaded exercise courts (*palaestras*), and a giant swimming pool (*natatio*). The entire complex covered an area of almost 50 acres. Archaeologists estimate that up to 1,600 bathers at a time could enjoy this Roman equivalent of a modern health spa. A branch of one of the city's major aqueducts supplied water, and furnaces circulated hot air through hollow floors and walls throughout the bathing rooms.

The Baths of Caracalla also featured stuccoed vaults, mosaic floors (both black-and-white and polychrome), marble-faced walls, and marble statuary. One statue on display was the 10-foot-tall copy of Lysippos's Herakles (FIG. 5-66), whose muscular body must have inspired Romans to exercise vigorously. The concrete vaults of the baths collapsed long ago, but visitors can get an excellent idea of what the central bathing hall, the frigidarium, once looked like from the nave (FIG. 7-67) of the church of Santa Maria degli Angeli in Rome, which was once the frigidarium of the later Baths of Diocle-

tian. The Renaissance interior (remodeled in the 18th century) of that church has, of course, many new elements foreign to a Roman bath, including a painted altarpiece. The ancient mosaics and marble revetment are long gone, but the present-day interior with its rich wall treatment, colossal columns with Composite capitals, immense groin vaults, and clerestory lighting gives a better sense of the character of a Roman imperial bathing complex than does any other building in the world. It takes a powerful imagination to visualize the original appearance of Roman concrete buildings from the woeful ruins of brick-faced walls and fallen vaults at ancient sites today, but Santa Maria degli Angeli makes the task much easier.

The Soldier Emperors

The Severan dynasty ended when Severus Alexander (r. 222–235 CE) was murdered. The next half century was one of almost continuous civil war. One general after another was declared emperor by his troops, only to be murdered by another general a few years or even a few months later. (In 238 CE, two co-emperors the Senate chose were dragged from the imperial palace and murdered in public after only three months in office.) In these unstable times, no emperor could begin ambitious architectural projects. The only significant building activity in Rome during the era of the "soldier emperors" occurred under Aurelian (r. 270–275 CE). He constructed a new defensive wall circuit for the capital—a military necessity and a poignant commentary on the decay of Roman power.

TRAJAN DECIUS If architects went hungry in third-century Rome, sculptors and engravers had much to do. The mint produced great quantities of coins (in debased metal) so that the troops could be paid with money stamped with the current emperor's portrait and not with that of his predecessor or rival. Each new ruler set up portrait statues and busts everywhere to assert his authority. The sculpted portraits of the third century CE are among the most moving ever made, as notable for their emotional content as they are for their technical virtuosity. Portraits of Trajan Decius (r. 249–251), such as the marble bust illustrated here (FIG. 7-68), show the emperor, who is best known for persecuting Christians, as an old man with bags under his eyes and a sad expression. In his eyes, which glance away nervously rather than engage the viewer directly, is the anxiety of a man who knows he can do little to restore order to an out-of-control world. The sculptor modeled the marble as if it were pliant clay, compressing the sides of the head at the level of the eyes, etching the hair and beard into the stone, and chiseling deep lines in the forehead and around the mouth. The portrait reveals the anguished soul of the man—and of the times.

TREBONIANUS GALLUS Decius's successor was Trebonianus Gallus (r. 251–253 CE), another short-lived emperor. In a larger-than-life-size bronze portrait (FIG. 7-69), Trebonianus appears in heroic nudity, as had so many emperors and generals before him. His physique is not, however, that of the strong but graceful Greek athletes Augustus and his successors admired so much. Instead, his is a wrestler's body with massive legs and a swollen trunk. The heavyset body dwarfs his head, with its nervous expression. In this portrait, the Greek ideal of the keen mind in the harmoniously proportioned body gave way to an image of brute force, an image well suited to the age of the soldier emperors.

THIRD-CENTURY SARCOPHAGI By the third century, burial of the dead had become so widespread that even the imperial family was practicing it in place of cremation. Sarcophagi were more popular than ever. An unusually large sarcophagus (FIG. 7-70), discovered in Rome in 1621 and purchased by Cardinal Ludovisi, is

7-68 Portrait bust of Trajan Decius, 249–251 CE. Marble, full bust 2′ 7″ high. Musei Capitolini, Rome.

This portrait of a short-lived "soldier emperor" depicts an older man with bags under his eyes and a sad expression. The eyes glance away nervously, reflecting the anxiety of an insecure ruler.

7-69 Heroic portrait of Trebonianus Gallus, from Rome, Italy, 251–253 CE. Bronze, 7′ 11″ high. Metropolitan Museum of Art, New York.

In this over-life-size heroically nude statue, Trebonianus Gallus projects an image of brute force. He has the massive physique of a powerful wrestler, but his face has a nervous expression.

7-70 Battle of Romans and barbarians (*Ludovisi Battle Sarcophagus*), from Rome, Italy, ca. 250–260 CE. Marble, 5′ high. Museo Nazionale Romano–Palazzo Altemps, Rome.

A chaotic scene of battle between Romans and barbarians decorates the front of this sarcophagus. The sculptor piled up the writhing, emotive figures in an emphatic rejection of Classical perspective.

7-71 Sarcophagus of a philosopher, ca. 270–280 CE. Marble, 4′ 11″ high. Musei Vaticani, Rome.

On many third-century sarcophagi, the deceased appears as a learned intellectual. Here, the seated Roman philosopher is the central frontal figure. His two female muses also have portrait features.

1 ft.

decorated on the front with a chaotic scene of battle between Romans and one of their northern foes, probably the Goths. The sculptor spread the writhing and highly emotive figures evenly across the entire relief, with no illusion of space behind them. This piling of figures is an even more extreme rejection of Classical perspective than was the use of floating ground lines on the pedestal of the Column of Antoninus Pius (FIG. 7-58). It underscores the increasing dissatisfaction Late Antique artists felt with the Classical style.

Within this dense mass of intertwined bodies, the central horseman stands out vividly. He wears no helmet and thrusts out his open right hand to demonstrate that he holds no weapon. Several scholars have identified him as one of the sons of Trajan Decius. In an age when the Roman army was far from invincible and Roman emperors were constantly felled by other Romans, the young general on the Ludovisi battle sarcophagus is boasting that he is a fearless commander assured of victory. His self-assurance may stem from his having embraced one of the increasingly popular Oriental mystery religions. On the youth's forehead is carved the emblem of Mithras, the Persian god of light, truth, and victory over death.

The insecurity of the times led many Romans to seek solace in philosophy. On many third-century sarcophagi, the deceased assumes the role of the learned intellectual. One especially large example (FIG. 7-71) depicts a seated Roman philosopher holding a scroll. Two standing women (also with portrait features) gaze at him from left and right, confirming his importance. In the background are other philosophers, students or colleagues of the central deceased teacher. The two women may be the deceased's wife and daughter, two sisters, or some other combination of family members. The composition, with a frontal central figure and two subordinate flanking figures, is typical of the Late Antique style. This type of sarcophagus became very popular for Christian burials. Sculptors used the wise-man motif not only to portray the deceased (FIG. 8-6) but also Christ flanked by his apostles (FIG. 8-7).

TEMPLE OF VENUS, BAALBEK The decline in respect for Classical art also can be seen in architecture. At Baalbek (ancient Heliopolis) in present-day Lebanon, the architect of the Temple of Venus (FIG. 7-72), following in the "baroque" tradition of the Treasury at Petra (FIG. 7-53), ignored almost every rule of Classical design. Although made of stone, the third-century building, with its circular domed cella set behind a gabled columnar facade, was in many ways a critique of the concrete Pantheon (FIG. 7-49), which by then had achieved the status of a classic. Many features of the Baalbek temple intentionally depart from the norm. The platform, for example, is scalloped all around the cella. The columns—the only known instance of *five*-sided Corinthian capitals with corresponding pentagonal bases—support a matching scalloped entablature (which serves to buttress the shallow stone dome). These concave forms and those of the niches in the cella walls play off against the cella's convex shape. Even the "traditional" facade of the Baalbek temple is eccentric. The unknown architect inserted an arch within the triangular pediment.

Diocletian and the Tetrarchy

In an attempt to restore order to the Roman Empire, Diocletian (r. 284–305 CE), whose troops proclaimed him emperor, decided to share power with his potential rivals. In 293 he established the *tetrarchy* (rule by four) and adopted the title of Augustus of the East. The other three *tetrarchs* were a corresponding Augustus of the West, and Eastern and Western Caesars (whose allegiance to the two Augusti was cemented by marriage to their daughters). Together, the four emperors ruled without strife until Diocletian retired in 305. Without his leadership, the tetrarchic form of government collapsed and renewed civil war followed. The division of the Roman Empire into eastern and western spheres survived, however. It persisted throughout the Middle Ages, setting the Latin West apart from the Byzantine East.

7-72 Restored view (*top*) and plan (*bottom*) of the Temple of Venus, Baalbek, Lebanon, third century CE.

This "baroque" temple violates almost every rule of Classical design. It has a scalloped platform and entablature, five-sided Corinthian capitals, and a facade with an arch inside the triangular pediment.

TETRARCHIC PORTRAITURE The four tetrarchs often were portrayed together, both on coins and in the round. Artists did not try to capture their individual appearances and personalities but sought instead to represent the nature of the tetrarchy itself—that is, to portray four equal partners in power. In the two pairs of porphyry (purple marble) portraits of the tetrarchs (FIG. **7-73**) that are now embedded in the southwestern corner of Saint Mark's in Venice, it is impossible to name the rulers. Each of the four emperors has lost his identity as an individual and been subsumed into the larger entity of the tetrarchy. All the tetrarchs are identically clad in cuirass and cloak. Each grasps a sheathed sword in the left hand. With their right arms they embrace one another in an overt display of concord. The figures, like those on the decursio relief (FIG. **7-58**) of the Column of Antoninus Pius, have large cubical heads on squat bodies. The drapery is schematic and the bodies are shapeless. The faces are emotionless masks, distinguished only by the beard on two of the figures

7-73 Portraits of the four tetrarchs, from Constantinople, ca. 305 CE. Porphyry, 4′ 3″ high. Saint Mark's, Venice.

Diocletian established the tetrarchy to bring order to the Roman world. In group portraits, artists always depicted the four co-rulers as nearly identical partners in power, not as distinct individuals.

(probably the older Augusti, distinguishing them from the younger Caesars). Nonetheless, each pair is as alike as freehand carving can achieve. In this group portrait, carved eight centuries after Greek sculptors first freed the human form from the formal rigidity of the Egyptian-inspired kouros stance, an artist once again conceived the human figure in iconic terms. Idealism, naturalism, individuality, and personality now belonged to the past.

PALACE OF DIOCLETIAN When Diocletian abdicated in 305, he returned to Dalmatia (roughly the area of the former Yugoslavia), where he was born. There he built a palace (FIG. **7-74**) for himself at Split, near ancient Salona on the Adriatic coast of Croatia. Just as Aurelian had felt it necessary to girdle Rome with fortress walls, Diocletian instructed his architects to provide him with a well-fortified suburban palace. The complex, which covers about 10 acres, has the layout of a Roman castrum, complete with watchtowers flanking the gates. It gave the emperor a sense of security in the most insecure of times.

Within the high walls, two avenues (comparable to the cardo and decumanus of a Roman city; FIG. **7-42**) intersected at the palace's center. Where a city's forum would have been situated, Diocletian's palace had a colonnaded court leading to the entrance to the

7-74 Restored view of the palace of Diocletian, Split, Croatia, ca. 298–306.

Diocletian's palace resembled a fortified Roman city (compare FIG. **7-42**). Within its high walls, two avenues intersected at the forumlike colonnaded courtyard leading to the emperor's residential quarters.

imperial residence, which had a templelike facade with an arch within its pediment, as in the Temple of Venus (FIG. **7-72**) at Baalbek. Diocletian wanted to appear like a god emerging from a temple when he addressed those who gathered in the court to pay homage to him. On one side of the court was a Temple of Jupiter. On the other side was Diocletian's *mausoleum* (FIG. **7-74**, *center right*), which towered above all the other structures in the complex. The emperor's huge domed tomb was a type that would become very popular in Early Christian times not only for mausoleums but eventually also for churches, especially in the Byzantine East. In fact, the tomb is a church today.

Constantine

An all-too-familiar period of conflict followed the short-lived concord among the tetrarchs that ended with Diocletian's abdication. This latest war among rival Roman armies lasted two decades. The eventual victor was Constantine I ("the Great"), son of Constantius Chlorus, Diocletian's Caesar of the West. After the death of his father, Constantine invaded Italy. In 312, at the battle of the Milvian Bridge to Rome, he defeated and killed Maxentius and took control of the capital. Constantine attributed his victory to the aid of the Christian god. The next year, he and Licinius, Constantine's coemperor in the East, issued the Edict of Milan, ending the persecution of Christians.

In time, Constantine and Licinius became foes, and in 324 Constantine defeated and executed Licinius near Byzantium (modern Istanbul, Turkey). Constantine, now unchallenged ruler of the whole Roman Empire, founded a "New Rome" at Byzantium and named it Constantinople ("City of Constantine"). In 325, at the Council of Nicaea, Christianity became the de facto official religion of the Roman Empire. From this point on, paganism declined rapidly. Constantinople was dedicated on May 11, 330, "by the commandment of

God," and in 337 Constantine was baptized on his deathbed. For many scholars, the transfer of the seat of power from Rome to Constantinople and the recognition of Christianity mark the end of antiquity and the beginning of the Middle Ages.

Constantinian art is a mirror of this transition from the classical to the medieval world. In Rome, for example, Constantine was a builder in the grand tradition of the emperors of the first, second, and early third centuries, erecting public baths, a basilica on the road leading into the Roman Forum, and a triumphal arch. But he was also the patron of the city's first churches (see Chapter 8).

ARCH OF CONSTANTINE Between 312 and 315, Constantine erected a great triple-passageway arch (FIGS. **7-2**, no. 15, and **7-75**) next to the Colosseum to commemorate his defeat of Maxentius. The arch was the largest erected in Rome since the end of the Severan dynasty. Much of the sculptural decoration, however, was taken from earlier monuments of Trajan, Hadrian, and Marcus Aurelius, and all of the columns and other architectural elements date to an earlier era. Sculptors refashioned the second-century reliefs to honor Constantine by recutting the heads of the earlier emperors with the features of the new ruler. They also added labels to the old reliefs, such as *Liberator Urbis* (liberator of the city) and *Fundator Quietus* (bringer of peace), references to the downfall of Maxentius and the end of civil war. The reuse of statues and reliefs on the Arch of Constantine has often been cited as evidence of a decline in creativity and technical skill in the waning years of the pagan Roman Empire. Although such a judgment is in large part deserved, it ignores the fact that the reused sculptures were carefully selected to associate Constantine with the "good emperors" of the second century. That message is underscored in one of the arch's few Constantinian reliefs. It shows Constantine on the speaker's platform in the Roman Forum between statues of Hadrian and Marcus Aurelius.

7-75 Arch of Constantine (south side), Rome, Italy, 312–315 CE.

Much of the sculptural decoration of Constantine's arch came from monuments of Trajan, Hadrian, and Marcus Aurelius. Sculptors recut the heads of the earlier emperors with Constantine's features.

In another Constantinian relief (FIG. 7-76), the emperor distributes largesse to grateful citizens who approach him from right and left. Constantine is a frontal and majestic presence, elevated on a throne above the recipients of his munificence. The figures are squat in proportion, like the tetrarchs (FIG. 7-73). They do not move according to any Classical principle of naturalistic movement but

1 ft.

7-76 Distribution of largesse, detail of the north frieze of the Arch of Constantine, Rome, Italy, 312–315 CE. Marble, 3′ 4″ high.

This Constantinian frieze is less a narrative of action than a picture of actors frozen in time. The composition's rigid formality reflects the new values that would come to dominate medieval art.

rather have the mechanical and repeated stances and gestures of puppets. The relief is very shallow, the forms are not fully modeled, and the details are incised. The frieze is less a narrative of action than a picture of actors frozen in time so that the viewer can distinguish instantly the all-important imperial donor (at the center on a throne) from his attendants (to the left and right above) and the recipients of the largesse (below and of smaller stature).

This approach to pictorial narrative was once characterized as a "decline of form," and when judged by the standards of Classical art, it was. But the composition's rigid formality, determined by the rank of those portrayed, was consistent with a new set of values. It soon became the preferred mode, supplanting the Classical notion that a picture is a window onto a world of anecdotal action. Comparing this Constantinian relief with a Byzantine icon (FIG. 9-18) reveals that the compositional principles of the Late Antique style are those of the Middle Ages. They were very different from—but not necessarily "better" or "worse" than—those of the Greco-Roman world. The Arch of Constantine is the quintessential monument of its era, exhibiting a respect for the past in its reuse of second-century sculptures while rejecting the norms of Classical design in its frieze, paving the way for the iconic art of the Middle Ages.

COLOSSUS OF CONSTANTINE After Constantine's victory over Maxentius, his official portraits broke with tetrarchic tradition as well as with the style of the soldier emperors, and resuscitated the Augustan image of an eternally youthful head of state. The most impressive of Constantine's preserved portraits is an eight-and-one-half-foot-tall head (FIG. 7-77), one of several marble fragments of a colossal enthroned statue of the emperor composed of a brick core, a wooden torso covered with bronze, and a head and limbs of marble. Constantine's artist modeled the seminude seated portrait on Roman images of Jupiter. The emperor held an orb (possibly surmounted by the cross of Christ), the symbol of global power, in his extended left hand. The nervous glance of third-century portraits is absent, replaced by a frontal mask with enormous eyes set into the broad and simple planes of the head. The emperor's personality is lost in this immense image of eternal authority. The colossal size, the likening of the emperor to Jupiter, the eyes directed at no person or thing of this world—all combine to produce a formula of overwhelming power appropriate to Constantine's exalted position as absolute ruler.

7-77 Portrait of Constantine, from the Basilica Nova, Rome, Italy, ca. 315–330 CE. Marble, 8′ 6″ high. Musei Capitolini, Rome.

Constantine's portraits revive the Augustan image of an eternally youthful ruler. This colossal head is one of several fragments of an enthroned Jupiter-like statue of the emperor holding the orb of world power.

BASILICA NOVA, ROME Constantine's gigantic portrait sat in the western apse of the Basilica Nova ("New Basilica," FIGS. 7-2, no. 12, and **7-78**), a project Maxentius had begun and Constantine completed. From its position in the apse, the emperor's image dominated the interior of the basilica in much the same way that enthroned statues of Greco-Roman divinities loomed over awestruck mortals who entered the cellas of pagan temples.

7-78 Restored cutaway view of the Basilica Nova, Rome, Italy, ca. 306–312 CE (John Burge).

The lessons learned in the construction of baths and market halls were applied to the Basilica Nova, where fenestrated concrete groin vaults replaced the clerestory of a traditional stone-and-timber basilica.

1 ft.

7-79 Aula Palatina (exterior), Trier, Germany, early fourth century CE.

The austere brick exterior of Constantine's Aula Palatina at Trier is typical of later Roman architecture. Two stories of windows with lead-framed panes of glass take up most of the surface area.

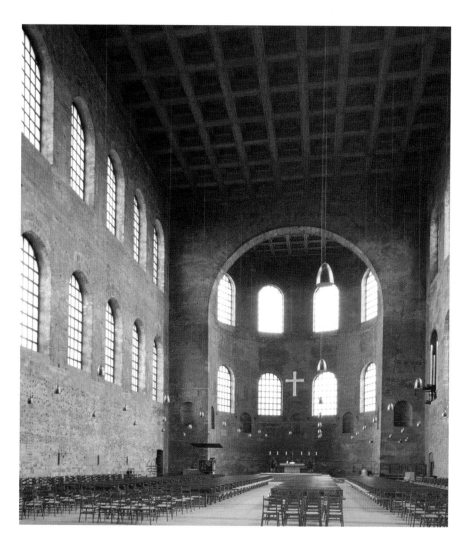

The Basilica Nova ruins never fail to impress tourists with their size and mass. The original structure was 300 feet long and 215 feet wide. Brick-faced concrete walls 20 feet thick supported coffered barrel vaults in the aisles. These vaults also buttressed the groin vaults of the nave, which was 115 feet high. The walls and floors were richly marbled and stuccoed. The reconstruction in FIG. 7-78 effectively suggests the immensity of the interior, where the great vaults dwarf even the emperor's colossal portrait. The drawing also clearly reveals the fenestration of the groin vaults, a lighting system akin to the clerestory of a traditional stone-and-timber basilica. Here, Roman builders applied to the Roman basilica the lessons learned in the design and construction of buildings such as Trajan's great market hall (FIG. 7-46) and the Baths of Diocletian (FIG. 7-67).

AULA PALATINA, TRIER At Trier (ancient Augusta Treverorum) on the Moselle River in Germany, the imperial seat of Constantius Chlorus as Caesar of the West, Constantine built a new palace complex. It included a basilica-like audience hall, the Aula Palatina (FIG. 7-79), of traditional form and materials. The Aula Palatina measures about 190 feet long and 95 feet wide and has an austere brick exterior, which was enlivened somewhat by highlighting in grayish white stucco. The use of lead-framed panes of glass for the windows enabled the builders to give life and movement to the blank exterior surfaces.

Inside (FIG. 7-80), the audience hall was also very simple. Its flat, wooden, coffered ceiling is some 95 feet above the floor. The interior has no aisles, only a wide space with two stories of large windows that provide ample light. At the narrow north end, the main hall is divided from the semicircular apse (which also has a flat ceiling) by a so-called *chancel arch*. The Aula Palatina's interior is quite severe, although marble veneer and mosaics originally covered the arch and apse to provide a magnificent environment for the enthroned emperor. The design of both the interior and exterior has close parallels in many Early Christian churches.

7-80 Aula Palatina (interior), Trier, Germany, early fourth century CE.

The interior of the audience hall of Constantine's palace complex in Germany resembles a timber-roofed basilica with an apse at one end, but it has no aisles. The large windows provided ample illumination.

CONSTANTINIAN COINS The two portraits of Constantine on the coins in FIG. **7-81** reveal both the essential character of Roman imperial portraiture and the special nature of Constantinian art. The first (FIG. 7-81, *left*) was issued shortly after the death of Constantine's father, when Constantine was in his early 20s and his position was still insecure. Here, in his official portrait, he appears considerably older, because he adopted the imagery of the tetrarchs. Indeed, were it not for the accompanying label identifying this Caesar as Constantine, it would be impossible to know who was portrayed. Eight years later (FIG. 7-81, *right*)—after the defeat of Maxentius and the Edict of Milan—Constantine, now the unchallenged Augustus of the West, is clean-shaven and looks his actual 30 years of age, having rejected the mature tetrarchic look in favor of youth. These two coins should dispel any uncertainty about the often fictive nature of imperial portraiture and the ability of Roman emperors to choose any official image that suited their needs. In Roman art, "portrait" is often not synonymous with "likeness."

The later coin is also an eloquent testimony to the dual nature of Constantinian rule. The emperor appears in his important role as imperator, dressed in armor, wearing an ornate helmet, and carrying a shield bearing the enduring emblem of the Roman state—the she-wolf nursing Romulus and Remus (compare FIG. 6-11 and Roma's shield in FIG. 7-57). Yet he does not carry the scepter of the pagan Roman emperor. Rather, he holds a cross crowned by an orb. In addition, at the crest of his helmet, at the front, just below the grand plume, is a disk containing the *Christogram,* the monogram made up of *chi* (X), *rho* (P), and *iota* (I), the initial letters of Christ's name in Greek (compare the shield one of the soldiers holds in FIG. 9-10). Constantine was at once portrayed as Roman emperor and as a soldier in the army of the Lord. The coin, like Constantinian art in general, belongs both to the classical and to the medieval world.

7-81 Coins with portraits of Constantine. Nummus (*left*), 307 CE. Billon, diameter 1″. American Numismatic Society, New York. Medallion (*right*), ca. 315 CE. Silver, diameter 1″. Staatliche Münzsammlung, Munich.

These two coins underscore that portraits of Roman emperors are rarely true likenesses. On the earlier coin, Constantine appears as a bearded tetrarch. On the later coin, he appears eternally youthful.

THE ROMAN EMPIRE

MONARCHY AND REPUBLIC, 753–27 BCE

▌ According to legend, Romulus and Remus founded Rome in 753 BCE. In the sixth century, Etruscan kings ruled the city and Roman art was Etruscan in character.

▌ In the centuries following the establishment of the Republic (509–27 BCE), Rome conquered its neighbors in Italy and then moved into Greece, bringing exposure to Greek art and architecture.

▌ Republican temples combined Etruscan plans with the Greek orders, and houses had peristyles with Greek columns. The Romans, however, pioneered the use of concrete as a building material.

▌ The First Style of mural painting derived from Greece, but the illusionism of the Second Style is distinctly Roman.

▌ Republican portraits were usually superrealistic likenesses of elderly patricians and celebrated traditional Roman values.

Villa of the Mysteries, Pompeii,
ca. 60–50 BCE

EARLY EMPIRE, 27 BCE–96 CE

▌ Augustus (r. 27 BCE–14 CE) became the first Roman emperor after defeating Mark Antony and Cleopatra at Actium in 31 BCE.

▌ Augustan art revived the Classical style with frequent references to Periclean Athens. Augustus's ambitious building program made lavish use of marble, and his portraits always depicted him as an idealized youth.

▌ Under the Julio-Claudians (r. 14–68 CE), the full potential of concrete began to be realized in buildings such as the Golden House of Nero.

▌ The Flavian emperors (r. 69–96 CE) erected the Colosseum, Rome's first and largest amphitheater, and arches and other monuments celebrating their victory in Judaea.

▌ Pompeii and Herculaneum were buried in 79 CE during the eruption of Mount Vesuvius. During the last quarter century of the towns' existence, the Third and Fourth Styles were used to decorate the walls of houses.

Augustus as general, Primaporta,
ca. 20 BCE

Arch of Titus, Rome
after 81 CE

HIGH EMPIRE, 96–192 CE

▌ The Roman Empire reached its greatest extent under Trajan (r. 98–117 CE). The emperor's new forum and markets transformed the civic center of Rome. The Column of Trajan commemorated his two campaigns in Dacia in a spiral frieze with thousands of figures.

▌ Hadrian (r. 117–138 CE), emulating Greek statesmen and philosophers, was the first emperor to wear a beard. He built the Pantheon, a triumph of concrete technology.

▌ Under the Antonines (r. 138–192 CE), the dominance of Classical art began to erode, and imperial artists introduced new compositional schemes in relief sculpture and a psychological element in portraiture.

Pantheon, Rome,
118–125 CE

LATE EMPIRE, 193–337 CE

▌ In the art of the Severans (r. 193–235 CE), the Late Antique style took root. Artists represented the emperor as a central frontal figure disengaged from the action around him.

▌ During the chaotic era of the soldier emperors (r. 235–284 CE), artists revealed the anxiety and insecurity of the emperors in moving portraits.

▌ Diocletian (r. 284–305 CE) reestablished order by sharing power. Statues of the tetrarchs portray the four emperors as identical and equal rulers, not as individuals.

▌ Constantine (r. 306–337 CE) restored one-man rule, ended persecution of the Christians, and transferred the capital of the Empire from Rome to Constantinople in 330. The abstract formality of Constantinian art paved the way for the iconic art of the Middle Ages.

Arch of Constantine, Rome,
312–315 CE

NOTES

Introduction

1. Quoted in George Heard Hamilton, *Painting and Sculpture in Europe, 1880–1940,* 6th ed. (New Haven, Conn.: Yale University Press, 1993), 345.

2. Quoted in *Josef Albers: Homage to the Square* (New York: Museum of Modern Art, 1964), n.p.

Chapter 2

1. Translated by Françoise Tallon, in Prudence O. Harper et al., *The Royal City of Susa* (New York: Metropolitan Museum of Art, 1992), 132.

Chapter 3

1. Herodotus, *Histories,* 2.35.

2. The chronology adopted in this chapter is that of John Baines and Jaromír Malék, *Atlas of Ancient Egypt* (Oxford: Oxford University Press, 1980), 36–37. The division of kingdoms is that of, among others, Mark Lehner, *The Complete Pyramids* (New York: Thames & Hudson, 1997), 8–9, and David P. Silverman, ed., *Ancient Egypt* (New York: Oxford University Press, 1997), 20–39.

Chapter 4

1. Homer, *Iliad,* 2.466–649.

Chapter 5

1. Plutarch, *Life of Pericles,* 12.

2. Pliny, *Natural History,* 34.74.

3. Ibid., 36.20.

4. Lucian, *Amores,* 13–14; *Imagines,* 6.

5. Plutarch, *Moralia,* 335A–B. Translated by J. J. Pollitt, *The Art of Ancient Greece: Sources and Documents* (New York: Cambridge University Press, 1990), 99.

6. Pliny, *Natural History,* 35.110.

Chapter 7

1. Livy, *History of Rome,* 25.40.1–3.

2. Recorded by the Venerable Bede, the great English scholar, monk, and saint, who died in 735. Translated by Lord Byron in *Childe Harold's Pilgrimage* (1817), 4.145.

3. Juvenal, *Satires,* 3.225, 232.

GLOSSARY

à la grecque—French, "in Greek style."

abacus—The uppermost portion of the *capital* of a *column,* usually a thin slab.

abbess—See *abbey.*

abbey—A religious community under the direction of an abbot (for monks) or an abbess (for nuns).

abbot—See *abbey.*

abrasion—The rubbing or grinding of stone or another material to produce a smooth finish.

acropolis—Greek, "high city." In ancient Greece, usually the site of the city's most important temple(s).

additive light—Natural light, or sunlight, the sum of all the wavelengths of the visible *spectrum.* See also *subtractive light.*

additive sculpture—A kind of sculpture *technique* in which materials (for example, clay) are built up or "added" to create form.

adobe—The clay used to make a kind of sun-dried mud brick of the same name; a building made of such brick.

agora—An open square or space used for public meetings or business in ancient Greek cities.

aisle—The portion of a *basilica* flanking the *nave* and separated from it by a row of *columns* or *piers.*

ala (pl. **alae**)—A rectangular recess at the back of the *atrium* of a Roman house.

altar frontal—A decorative panel on the front of a church altar.

altarpiece—A panel, painted or sculpted, situated above and behind an altar. See also *retable.*

alternate-support system—In church architecture, the use of alternating wall supports in the *nave,* usually *piers* and *columns* or *compound piers* of alternating form.

Amazonomachy—In Greek mythology, the battle between the Greeks and Amazons.

ambo—A church *pulpit* for biblical readings.

ambulatory—A covered walkway, outdoors (as in a church *cloister*) or indoors; especially the passageway around the *apse* and the *choir* of a church. In Buddhist architecture, the passageway leading around the *stupa* in a *chaitya hall.*

amphiprostyle—A *classical* temple *plan* in which the *columns* are placed across both the front and back but not along the sides.

amphitheater—Greek, "double theater." A Roman building type resembling two Greek theaters put together. The Roman amphitheater featured a continuous elliptical *cavea* around a central *arena.*

amphora—An ancient Greek two-handled jar used for general storage purposes, usually to hold wine or oil.

amulet—An object worn to ward off evil or to aid the wearer.

antae—The molded projecting ends of the walls forming the *pronaos* or *opisthodomos* of an ancient Greek temple.

ante legem—Latin, "before the law." In Christian thought, the period before Moses received the Ten Commandments. See also *sub lege.*

apadana—The great audience hall in ancient Persian palaces.

apostle—Greek, "messenger." One of the 12 disciples of Jesus.

apotheosis—Elevated to the rank of gods, or the ascent to heaven.

apoxyomenos—Greek, "athlete scraping oil from his body."

apse—A recess, usually semicircular, in the wall of a building, commonly found at the east end of a church.

arcade—A series of *arches* supported by *piers* or *columns.*

arch—A curved structural member that spans an opening and is generally composed of wedge-shaped blocks (*voussoirs*) that transmit the downward pressure laterally. See also *thrust.*

Archaic—The artistic style of 600–480 BCE in Greece, characterized in part by the use of the *composite view* for painted and *relief* figures and of Egyptian stances for statues.

Archaic smile—The smile that appears on all *Archaic* Greek statues from about 570 to 480 BCE. The smile is the Archaic sculptor's way of indicating that the person portrayed is alive.

architrave—The *lintel* or lowest division of the *entablature;* also called the epistyle.

archivolt—The continuous molding framing an *arch.* In *Romanesque* or *Gothic* architecture, one of the series of concentric bands framing the *tympanum.*

arcuated—*Arch*-shaped.

arena—In a Roman *amphitheater,* the central area where bloody *gladiatorial* combats and other boisterous events took place.

armature—The crossed, or diagonal, *arches* that form the skeletal framework of a *Gothic rib vault.* In sculpture, the framework for a clay form.

arriccio—In *fresco* painting, the first layer of rough lime plaster applied to the wall.

ashlar masonry—Carefully cut and regularly shaped blocks of stone used in construction, fitted together without mortar.

atlantid—A male figure that functions as a supporting *column.* See also *caryatid.*

atmospheric perspective—See *perspective.*

atrium—The central reception room of a Roman house that is partly open to the sky. Also the open, *colonnaded* court in front of and attached to a Christian *basilica.*

attic—The uppermost story of a building, *triumphal arch,* or city gate.

attribute—(n.) The distinctive identifying aspect of a person, for example, an object held, an associated animal, or a mark on the body. (v.) To make an *attribution.*

attribution—Assignment of a work to a maker or makers.

axial plan—See *plan.*

baldacchino—A canopy on *columns,* frequently built over an altar. The term derives from *baldacco.*

baptism—The Christian bathing ceremony in which an infant or a convert becomes a member of the Christian community.

baptistery—In Christian architecture, the building used for *baptism,* usually situated next to a church. Also, the designated area or hall within a church for baptismal rites.

bar tracery—See *tracery.*

Baroque—The traditional blanket designation for European art from 1600 to 1750. The stylistic term *Baroque,* which describes art that features dramatic theatricality and elaborate ornamentation in contrast to the simplicity and orderly rationality of Renaissance art, is most appropriately applied to Italian art of this period. The term derives from *barroco.*

barrel vault—See *vault.*

base—In ancient Greek architecture, the molded projecting lowest part of *Ionic* and *Corinthian columns.* (*Doric* columns do not have bases.)

basilica—In Roman architecture, a public building for legal and other civic proceedings, rectangular in plan with an entrance usually on a long side. In Christian architecture, a church somewhat resembling the Roman basilica, usually entered from one end and with an *apse* at the other.

bas-relief—See *relief.*

battlement—A low parapet at the top of a circuit wall in a fortification.

bay—The space between two columns, or one unit in the *nave arcade* of a church; also, the passageway in an *arcuated* gate.

ben-ben—A pyramidal stone; a fetish of the Egyptian god Re.

benedictional—A Christian religious book containing bishops' blessings.

bilateral symmetry—Having the same forms on either side of a central axis.

bilingual vases—Experimental Greek vases produced for a short time in the late sixth century BCE; one side featured *black-figure* decoration, the other *red-figure.*

black-figure painting—In early Greek pottery, the silhouetting of dark figures against a light background of natural, reddish clay, with linear details *incised* through the silhouettes.

blind arcade—An *arcade* having no true openings, applied as decoration to a wall surface.

block statue—In ancient Egyptian sculpture, a cubic stone image with simplified body parts.

Book of Hours—A Christian religious book for private devotion containing prayers to be read at specified times of the day.

breviary—A Christian religious book of selected daily prayers and Psalms.

bucranium (pl. **bucrania**)—Latin, "bovine skull." A common motif in classical architectural ornament.

buon fresco—See *fresco.*

burin—A pointed tool used for *engraving* or *incising.*

buttress—An exterior masonry structure that opposes the lateral *thrust* of an *arch* or a *vault.* A *pier* buttress is a solid mass of masonry. A flying buttress consists typically of an inclined member carried on an arch or a series of arches and a solid buttress to which it transmits lateral *thrust.*

Byzantine—The art, territory, history, and culture of the Eastern Christian Empire and its capital of Constantinople (ancient Byzantium).

caduceus—In ancient Greek mythology, a magical rod entwined with serpents, the attribute of Hermes (Roman, Mercury), the messenger of the gods.

caldarium—The hot-bath section of a Roman bathing establishment.

caliph(s)—Islamic rulers, regarded as successors to Muhammad.

calligrapher—One who practices *calligraphy.*

calligraphy—Greek, "beautiful writing." Handwriting or penmanship, especially elegant writing as a decorative art.

came—A lead strip in a *stained-glass* window that joins separate pieces of colored glass.

campanile—A bell tower of a church, usually, but not always, freestanding.

canon—A rule, for example, of proportion. The ancient Greeks considered beauty to be a matter of "correct" proportion and sought a canon of proportion, for the human figure and for buildings. The fifth-century BCE sculptor Polykleitos wrote the *Canon,* a treatise incorporating his formula for the perfectly proportioned statue.

canon table—A concordance, or matching, of the corresponding passages of the four *Gospels* as compiled by Eusebius of Caesarea in the fourth century.

canopic jar—In ancient Egypt, the container in which the organs of the deceased were placed for later burial with the mummy.

capital—The uppermost member of a *column,* serving as a transition from the *shaft* to the *lintel.* In classical architecture, the form of the capital varies with the *order.*

Capitolium—An ancient Roman temple dedicated to the gods Jupiter, Juno, and Minerva.

cardo—The north-south street in a Roman town, intersecting the *decumanus* at right angles.

Caroline minuscule—The alphabet that *Carolingian* scribes perfected, from which the modern English alphabet was developed.

Carolingian (adj.)—Pertaining to the empire of Charlemagne (Latin, "Carolus Magnus") and his successors.

carpet page—In early medieval manuscripts, a decorative page resembling a textile.

cartoon—In painting, a full-size preliminary drawing from which a painting is made.

carving—A *technique* of sculpture in which the artist cuts away material (for example, from a stone block) in order to create a *statue* or a *relief.*

caryatid—A female figure that functions as a supporting *column.* See also *atlantid.*

castellum—See *westwork.*

casting—A sculptural *technique* in which the artist pours liquid metal, plaster, clay or another material into a *mold.* When the material dries, the sculptor removes the cast piece from the mold.

castrum—A Roman military encampment.

catacombs—Subterranean networks of rock-cut galleries and chambers designed as cemeteries for the burial of the dead.

cathedra—Latin, "seat." See *cathedral.*

cathedral—A bishop's church. The word derives from *cathedra,* referring to the bishop's chair.

cavea—Latin, "hollow place or cavity." The seating area in ancient Greek and Roman theaters and *amphitheaters.*

cella—The chamber at the center of an ancient temple; in a classical temple, the room (Greek, *naos*) in which the *cult statue* usually stood.

centaur—In ancient Greek mythology, a creature with the front or top half of a human and the back or bottom half of a horse.

centauromachy—In ancient Greek mythology, the battle between the Greeks and *centaurs.*

central plan—See *plan.*

cestrum—A small spatula used in *encaustic* painting.

chamfer—The surface formed by cutting off a corner of a board or post; a bevel.

chancel arch—The arch separating the chancel (the *apse* or *choir*) or the *transept* from the *nave* of a basilica or church.

chantry—An endowed chapel for the chanting of the mass for the founder of the chapel.

chaplet—A metal pin used in hollow-casting to connect the *investment* with the clay core.

charun—An Etruscan death demon.

chiaroscuro—In drawing or painting, the treatment and use of light and dark, especially the gradations of light that produce the effect of *modeling.*

chimera—A monster of Greek invention with the head and body of a lion and the tail of a serpent. A second head, that of a goat, grows out of one side of the body.

chisel—A tool with a straight blade at one end for cutting and shaping stone or wood.

chiton—A Greek tunic, the essential (and often only) garment of both men and women, the other being the *himation,* or mantle.

choir—The space reserved for the clergy and singers in the church, usually east of the *transept* but, in some instances, extending into the *nave.*

Christogram—The three initial letters (chi-rho-iota, or ☧) of Christ's name in Greek, which came to serve as a monogram for Christ.

chronology—In art history, the dating of art objects and buildings.

chryselephantine—Fashioned of gold and ivory.

cire perdue—See *lost-wax process.*

cista (pl. **cistae**)—An Etruscan cylindrical container made of sheet bronze with cast handles and feet, often with elaborately engraved bodies, used for women's toiletry articles.

city-state—An independent, self-governing city.

Classical—The art and culture of ancient Greece between 480 and 323 BCE. Lowercase *classical* refers more generally to Greco-Roman art and culture.

clerestory—The *fenestrated* part of a building that rises above the roofs of the other parts. The oldest known clerestories are Egyptian. In Roman *basilicas* and medieval churches, clerestories are the windows that form the *nave's* uppermost level below the timber ceiling or the *vaults.*

cloison—French, "partition." A cell made of metal wire or a narrow metal strip soldered edge-up to a metal base to hold *enamel,* semiprecious stones, pieces of colored glass, or glass paste fired to resemble sparkling jewels.

cloisonné—A decorative metalwork technique employing *cloisons;* also, decorative brickwork in later Byzantine architecture.

cloister—A monastery courtyard, usually with covered walks or *ambulatories* along its sides.

cluster pier—See *compound pier.*

codex (pl. **codices**)—Separate pages of *vellum* or *parchment* bound together at one side; the predecessor of the modern book. The codex superseded the *rotulus.* In *Mesoamerica,* a painted and inscribed book on long sheets of bark paper or deerskin coated with fine white plaster and folded into accordion-like pleats.

coffer—A sunken panel, often ornamental, in a *vault* or a ceiling.

collage—A composition made by combining on a flat surface various materials, such as newspaper, wallpaper, printed text and illustrations, photographs, and cloth.

colonnade—A series or row of *columns,* usually spanned by *lintels.*

colonnette—A thin *column.*

colophon—An inscription, usually on the last page, giving information about a book's manufacture. In Chinese painting, written texts on attached pieces of paper or silk.

color—The value, or tonality, of a color is the degree of its lightness or darkness. The intensity, or saturation, of a color is its purity, its brightness or dullness. See also *primary colors, secondary colors,* and *complementary colors.*

column—A vertical, weight-carrying architectural member, circular in cross-*section* and consisting of a *base* (sometimes omitted), a *shaft,* and a *capital.*

complementary colors—Those pairs of colors, such as red and green, that together embrace the entire spectrum. The complement of one of the three *primary colors* is a mixture of the other two.

compose—See *composition.*

Composite capital—A capital combining *Ionic* volutes and *Corinthian* acanthus leaves, first used by the ancient Romans.

composite view—A convention of representation in which part of a figure is shown in profile and another part of the same figure is shown frontally; also called twisted perspective.

composition—The way in which an artist organizes *forms* in an artwork, either by placing shapes on a flat surface or arranging forms in space.

compound pier—A *pier* with a group, or cluster, of attached *shafts,* or *responds,* especially characteristic of *Gothic* architecture.

conceptual representation—The representation of the fundamental distinguishing properties of a person or object, not the way a figure or object appears in space and light at a specific moment. See *composite view.*

concrete—A building material invented by the Romans and consisting of various proportions of lime mortar, volcanic sand, water, and small stones.

confraternity—In Late Antiquity, an association of Christian families pooling funds to purchase property for burial. In late medieval Europe, an organization founded by laypersons who dedicated themselves to strict religious observances.

congregational mosque—A city's main *mosque,* designed to accommodate the entire Muslim population for the Friday noonday prayer. Also called the great mosque or Friday mosque.

connoisseur—An expert in *attributing* artworks to one artist rather than another. More generally, an expert on artistic *style.*

consuls—In the Roman Republic, the two chief magistrates.

contour line—In art, a continuous line defining the outer shape of an object.

contrapposto—The disposition of the human figure in which one part is turned in opposition to another part (usually hips and legs one way, shoulders and chest another), creating a counterpositioning of the body about its central axis. Sometimes called "weight shift" because the weight of the body tends to be thrown to one foot, creating tension on one side and relaxation on the other.

corbel—A projecting wall member used as a support for some element in the superstructure. Also, courses of stone or brick in which each course projects beyond the one beneath it. Two such walls, meeting at the topmost course, create a corbeled *arch* or corbeled *vault.*

corbeled arch—See *corbel.*

corbeled vault—A *vault* formed by the piling of stone blocks in horizontal *courses,* cantilevered inward until the two walls meet in an *arch.*

Corinthian capital—A more ornate form than *Doric* or *Ionic;* it consists of a double row of acanthus leaves from which tendrils and flowers grow, wrapped around a bell-shaped *echinus.* Although this *capital* form is often cited as the distinguishing feature of the Corinthian *order,* no such order exists, in strict terms, but only this style of capital used in the *Ionic* order.

cornice—The projecting, crowning member of the *entablature* framing the *pediment;* also, any crowning projection.

corona civica—Latin, "civic crown." A Roman honorary wreath worn on the head.

course—In masonry construction, a horizontal row of stone blocks.

crenel—See *crenellation.*

crenellation—Alternating solid merlons and open crenels in the notched tops of walls, as in *battlements.*

crossing—The space in a *cruciform* church formed by the intersection of the *nave* and the *transept.*

cross vault—See *vault.*

crossing square—The area in a church formed by the intersection (*crossing*) of a *nave* and a *transept* of equal width, often used as a standard *module* of interior proportion.

crossing tower—The tower over the *crossing* of a church.

cruciform—Cross-shaped.

Crusades—In medieval Europe, armed pilgrimages aimed at recapturing the Holy Land from the *Muslims.*

crypt—A *vaulted* space under part of a building, wholly or partly underground; in churches, normally the portion under an *apse.*

cubiculum (pl. **cubicula**)—A small cubicle or bedroom that opened onto the *atrium* of a Roman house. Also, a chamber in an Early Christian *catacomb* that served as a mortuary chapel.

cuerda seca—A type of polychrome tilework used in decorating Islamic buildings.

cuirass—A military leather breastplate.

cult statue—The statue of the deity that stood in the *cella* of an ancient temple.

cuneiform—Latin, "wedge-shaped." A system of writing used in ancient Mesopotamia, in which wedge-shaped characters were produced by pressing a *stylus* into a soft clay tablet, which was then baked or otherwise allowed to harden.

cuneus (pl. **cunei**)—In ancient Greek and Roman theaters and *amphitheaters,* the wedge-shaped section of stone benches separated by stairs.

cutaway—An architectural drawing that combines an exterior view with an interior view of part of a building.

Cycladic—The prehistoric art of the Aegean Islands around Delos, excluding Crete.

Cyclopean masonry—A method of stone construction, named after the mythical *Cyclopes,* using massive, irregular blocks without mortar, characteristic of the Bronze Age fortifications of Tiryns and other *Mycenaean* sites.

Cyclops (pl. **Cyclopes**)—A mythical Greek one-eyed giant.

cylinder seal—A cylindrical piece of stone usually about an inch or so in height, decorated with an *incised* design, so that a raised pattern is left when the seal is rolled over soft clay. In the ancient Near East, documents, storage jars, and other important possessions were signed, sealed, and identified in this way. Stamp seals are an earlier, flat form of seal used for similar purposes.

Daedalic—The Greek *Orientalizing* sculptural style of the seventh century BCE named after the legendary artist Daedalus.

damnatio memoriae—The Roman decree condemning those who ran afoul of the Senate. Those who suffered damnatio memoriae had their memorials demolished and their names erased from public inscriptions.

decumanus—The east-west street in a Roman town, intersecting the *cardo* at right angles.

decursio—The ritual circling of a Roman funerary pyre.

Deësis—Greek, "supplication." An image of Christ flanked by the figures of the Virgin Mary and Saint John the Baptist, who intercede on behalf of humankind.

demos—Greek, "the people," from which the word *democracy* is derived.

demotic—Late Egyptian writing.

denarius—The standard Roman silver coin from which the word *penny* ultimately derives.

diagonal rib—See *rib.*

diaphragm arch—A transverse, wall-bearing *arch* that divides a *vault* or a ceiling into compartments, providing a kind of firebreak.

dictator—In the Roman Republic, the supreme magistrate with extraordinary powers, appointed during a crisis for a specified period. Julius Caesar eventually became *dictator perpetuo,* dictator for life.

dictator perpetuo—See *dictator.*

dipteral—See *peristyle.*

diptych—A two-paneled painting or *altarpiece;* also, an ancient Roman, Early Christian, or Byzantine hinged writing tablet, often of ivory and carved on the external sides.

disputatio—Latin, "logical argument." The philosophical methodology used in *Scholasticism.*

documentary evidence—In art history, the examination of written sources in order to determine the date of an artwork, the circumstances of its creation, or the identity of the artist(s) who made it.

doge—Duke; a ruler of the Republic of Venice, Italy.

dome—A hemispherical *vault;* theoretically, an *arch* rotated on its vertical axis. In *Mycenaean* architecture, domes are beehive-shaped.

domus—A Roman private house.

Doric—One of the two systems (or *orders*) invented in ancient Greece for articulating the three units of the elevation of a *classical* building—the platform, the *colonnade,* and the superstructure (*entablature*). The Doric order is characterized by, among other features, *capitals* with funnel-shaped *echinuses, columns* without *bases,* and a *frieze* of *triglyphs* and *metopes.* See also *Ionic.*

doryphoros—Greek, "spear bearer."

double monastery—A *monastery* for both monks and nuns.

dromos—The passage leading to a *tholos tomb.*

drum—One of the stacked cylindrical stones that form the *shaft* of a *column.* Also, the cylindrical wall that supports a *dome.*

echinus—The convex element of a *capital* directly below the *abacus.*

elevation—In architecture, a head-on view of an external or internal wall, showing its features and often other elements that would be visible beyond or before the wall.

emblema—The central framed figural panel of a *mosaic* floor.

embroidery—The technique of sewing threads onto a finished ground to form contrasting designs. Stem stitching employs short overlapping strands of thread to form jagged lines. Laid-and-couched work creates solid blocks of color.

enamel—A decorative coating, usually colored, fused onto the surface of metal, glass, or ceramics.

encaustic—A painting *technique* in which pigment is mixed with melted wax and applied to the surface while the mixture is hot.

engaged column—A half-round *column* attached to a wall. See also *pilaster.*

ensi—A Sumerian ruler.

entablature—The part of a building above the *columns* and below the roof. The entablature has three parts: *architrave, frieze,* and *pediment.*

entasis—The convex profile (an apparent swelling) in the *shaft* of a *column.*

Eucharist—In Christianity, the partaking of the bread and wine, which believers hold to be either Christ himself or symbolic of him.

evangelist—One of the four authors (Matthew, Mark, Luke, John) of the New Testament *Gospels.*

exedra—Recessed area, usually semicircular.

facade—Usually, the front of a building; also, the other sides when they are emphasized architecturally.

faience—A low-fired opaque glasslike silicate.

fan vault—See *vault.*

fauces—Latin, "jaws." In a Roman house, the narrow foyer leading to the *atrium.*

fenestrated—Having windows.

fenestration—The arrangement of the windows of a building.

feudalism—The medieval political, social, and economic system held together by the relationship between landholding *liege lords* and the *vassals* who were granted tenure of a portion of their land and in turn swore allegiance to the liege lord.

fibula (pl. **fibulae**)—A decorative pin, usually used to fasten garments.

findspot—Place where an artifact was found; provenance.

finial—A crowning ornament.

First Style mural—The earliest style of Roman mural painting. Also called the Masonry Style, because the aim of the artist was to imitate, using painted stucco relief, the appearance of costly marble panels.

Flamboyant—A Late French *Gothic* style of architecture superseding the *Rayonnant* style and named for the flamelike appearance of its pointed bar *tracery.*

flashing—In making *stained-glass* windows, fusing one layer of colored glass to another to produce a greater range of colors.

fleur-de-lis—A three-petaled iris flower; the royal flower of France.

florin—The denomination of gold coin of Renaissance Florence that became an international currency for trade.

flute or **fluting**—Vertical channeling, roughly semicircular in cross-*section* and used principally on *columns* and *pilasters.*

flying buttress—See *buttress.*

folio—A page of a manuscript or book.

foreshortening—The use of *perspective* to represent in art the apparent visual contraction of an object that extends back in space at an angle to the perpendicular plane of sight.

form—In art, an object's shape and structure, either in two dimensions (for example, a figure painted on a surface) or in three dimensions (such as a statue).

formal analysis—The visual analysis of artistic *form.*

forum—The public square of an ancient Roman city.

Fourth Style mural—In Roman mural painting, the Fourth Style marks a return to architectural illusionism, but the architectural vistas of the Fourth Style are irrational fantasies.

freedmen, freedwomen—In ancient and medieval society, men and women who had been freed from servitude, as opposed to having been born free.

freestanding sculpture—See *sculpture in the round.*

fresco—Painting on lime plaster, either dry (dry fresco, or fresco secco) or wet (true, or buon, fresco). In the latter method, the pigments are mixed with water and become chemically bound to the freshly laid lime plaster. Also, a painting executed in either method.

fresco secco—See *fresco.*

Friday mosque—See *congregational mosque.*

frieze—The part of the *entablature* between the *architrave* and the *cornice;* also, any sculptured or painted band in a building. See *register.*

frigidarium—The cold-bath section of a Roman bathing establishment.

genre—A style or category of art; also, a kind of painting that realistically depicts scenes from everyday life.

Geometric—The style of Greek art during the ninth and eighth centuries BCE, characterized by abstract geometric ornament and schematic figures.

gigantomachy—In ancient Greek mythology, the battle between gods and giants.

giornata (pl. **giornate**)—Italian, "day." The section of plaster that a *fresco* painter expects to complete in one session.

gladiator—An ancient Roman professional fighter, usually a slave, who competed in an *amphitheater.*

glaze—A vitreous coating applied to pottery to seal and decorate the surface; it may be colored, transparent, or opaque, and glossy or *matte.* In oil painting, a thin, transparent, or semitransparent layer applied over a color to alter it slightly.

glazier—A glassworker.

gold leaf—Gold beaten into tissue-paper-thin sheets that then can be applied to surfaces.

gorgon—In ancient Greek mythology, a hideous female demon with snake hair. Medusa, the most famous gorgon, was capable of turning anyone who gazed at her into stone.

Gospels—The four New Testament books that relate the life and teachings of Jesus.

Gothic—Originally a derogatory term named after the Goths, used to describe the history, culture, and art of western Europe in the 12th to 14th centuries. Typically divided into periods designated Early (1140–1194), High (1194–1300), and Late (1300–1500).

granulation—A decorative technique in which tiny metal balls (granules) are fused to a metal surface.

great mosque—See *congregational mosque.*

Greek cross—A cross with four arms of equal length.

grisaille—A monochrome painting done mainly in neutral grays to simulate sculpture.

groin—The edge formed by the intersection of two barrel *vaults.*

groin vault—See *vault.*

ground line—In paintings and reliefs, a painted or carved baseline on which figures appear to stand.

guild—An association of merchants, craftspersons, or scholars in medieval and Renaissance Europe.

hall church—See *Hallenkirche.*

Hallenkirche—German, "hall church." A church design favored in Germany, but also used elsewhere, in which the *aisles* rise to the same height as the *nave.*

Helladic—The prehistoric art of the Greek mainland (*Hellas* in Greek).

Hellas—The ancient name of Greece.

Hellenes (adj. **Hellenic**)—The name the ancient Greeks called themselves as the people of *Hellas.*

Hellenistic—The term given to the art and culture of the roughly three centuries between the death of Alexander the Great in 323 BCE and the death of Queen Cleopatra in 30 BCE, when Egypt became a Roman province.

henge—An arrangement of *megalithic* stones in a circle, often surrounded by a ditch.

heraldic composition—A *composition* that is symmetrical on either side of a central figure.

herm—A bust on a quadrangular *pillar.*

Hiberno-Saxon—An art style that flourished in the monasteries of the British Isles in the early Middle Ages. Also called Insular.

hierarchy of scale—An artistic convention in which greater size indicates greater importance.

hieroglyphic—A system of writing using symbols or pictures.

high relief—See *relief.*

Hijra—The flight of Muhammad from Mecca to Medina in 622, the year from which Islam dates its beginnings.

himation—An ancient Greek mantle worn by men and women over the *chiton* and draped in various ways.

Hippodamian plan—A city *plan* devised by Hippodamos of Miletos ca. 466 BCE, in which a strict grid was imposed on a site, regardless of the terrain, so that all streets would meet at right angles.

historiated—Ornamented with representations, such as plants, animals, or human figures, that have a narrative—as distinct from a purely decorative—function.

hubris—Greek, "arrogant pride."

hue—The name of a *color.* See also *primary colors, secondary colors,* and *complementary colors.*

humanism—In the *Renaissance,* an emphasis on education and on expanding knowledge (especially of *classical* antiquity), the exploration of individual potential and a desire to excel, and a commitment to civic responsibility and moral duty.

hydria—An ancient Greek three-handled water pitcher.

hypaethral—A building having no *pediment* or roof, open to the sky.

hypostyle hall—A hall with a roof supported by *columns.*

icon—A portrait or image; especially in Byzantine churches, a panel with a painting of sacred personages that are objects of veneration. In the visual arts, a painting, a piece of sculpture, or even a building regarded as an object of veneration.

iconoclasm—The destruction of religious or sacred images. In Byzantium, the period from 726 to 843 when there was an imperial ban on such images. The destroyers of images were known as iconoclasts. Those who opposed such a ban were known as iconophiles.

iconoclast—See *iconoclasm.*

iconography—Greek, the "writing of images." The term refers both to the content, or subject, of an artwork and to the study of content in art. It also includes the study of the symbolic, often religious, meaning of objects, persons, or events depicted in works of art.

iconophile—See *iconoclasm.*

iconostasis—Greek, "icon stand." In Byzantine churches, a screen or a partition, with doors and many tiers of *icons,* separating the sanctuary from the main body of the church.

illuminated manuscript—A luxurious handmade book with painted illustrations and decorations.

illusionism (adj. **illusionistic**)—The representation of the three-dimensional world on a two-dimensional surface in a manner that creates the illusion that the person, object, or place represented is three-dimensional. See also *perspective.*

imagines—In ancient Rome, wax portraits of ancestors.

imam—In Islam, the leader of collective worship.

imperator—Latin, "commander in chief," from which the word *emperor* derives.

impluvium—In a Roman house, the basin located in the *atrium* that collected rainwater.

in antis—In ancient Greek architecture, the area between the *antae.*

incise—To cut into a surface with a sharp instrument; also, a method of décoration, especially on metal and pottery.

incrustation—Wall decoration consisting of bright panels of different colors.

indulgence—A religious pardon for a sin committed.

insula (pl. **insulae**)—In Roman architecture, a multistory apartment house, usually made of brick-faced *concrete;* also refers to an entire city block.

Insular—See *Hiberno-Saxon.*

intensity—See *color.*

interaxial or **intercolumniation**—The distance between the center of the lowest *drum* of a *column* and the center of the next.

intercolumniation—See *interaxial.*

internal evidence—In art history, the examination of what an artwork represents (people, clothing, hairstyles, and so on) in order to determine its date. Also, the examination of the *style* of an artwork to identify the artist who created it.

International Style—A *style* of 14th- and 15th-century painting begun by Simone Martini, who adapted the French *Gothic* manner to Sienese art fused with influences from Northern Europe. This style appealed to the aristocracy because of its brilliant color, lavish costumes, intricate ornamentation, and themes involving splendid processions of knights and ladies. Also, a style of 20th-century architecture associated with Le Corbusier, whose elegance of design came to influence the look of modern office buildings and skyscrapers.

intonaco—In *fresco* painting, the last layer of smooth lime plaster applied to the wall; the painting layer.

investment—In hollow-casting, the final clay mold applied to the exterior of the wax model.

Ionic—One of the two systems (or *orders*) invented in ancient Greece for articulating the three units of the elevation of a *classical* building: the platform, the *colonnade,* and the superstructure (*entablature*). The Ionic order is characterized by, among other features, *volutes, capitals, columns* with *bases,* and an uninterrupted *frieze.*

iwan—In Islamic architecture, a *vaulted* rectangular recess opening onto a courtyard.

jambs—In architecture, the side posts of a doorway.

ka—In ancient Egypt, the immortal human life force.

Kaaba—Arabic, "cube." A small cubical building in Mecca, the Islamic world's symbolic center.

keep—A fortified tower in a castle that served as a place of last refuge.

kline (pl. **klinai**)—A couch or funerary bed. A type of *sarcophagus* with a reclining portrait of the deceased on its lid.

Koran—Islam's sacred book, composed of *surahs* (chapters) divided into verses.

kore (pl. **korai**)—Greek, "young woman." An *Archaic* Greek statue of a young woman.

kouros (pl. **kouroi**)—Greek, "young man." An *Archaic* Greek statue of a young man.

krater—An ancient Greek wide-mouthed bowl for mixing wine and water.

Kufic—An early form of Arabic script, characterized by angularity, with the uprights forming almost right angles with the baseline.

labyrinth—Maze. The English word derives from the mazelike plan of the *Minoan* palace at Knossos.

laid-and-couched work—See *embroidery.*

lamassu—Assyrian guardian in the form of a man-headed winged bull.

lancet—In *Gothic* architecture, a tall narrow window ending in a *pointed arch.*

landscape—A picture showing natural scenery, without narrative content.

lateral section—See *section.*

leading—In the manufacture of *stained-glass* windows, the joining of colored glass pieces using lead *cames.*

lectionary—A book containing passages from the *Gospels,* arranged in the sequence that they are to be read during the celebration of religious services, including the *Mass,* throughout the year.

lekythos (pl. **lekythoi**)—A flask containing perfumed oil; lekythoi were often placed in Greek graves as offerings to the deceased.

liege lord—In *feudalism,* a landowner who grants tenure of a portion of his land to a *vassal.*

line—The extension of a point along a path, made concrete in art by drawing on or chiseling into a *plane.*

linear perspective—See *perspective.*

lintel—A horizontal *beam* used to span an opening.

liturgy (adj. **liturgical**)—The official ritual of public worship.

loculi—Openings in the walls of *catacombs* to receive the dead.

longitudinal plan—See *plan.*

longitudinal section—See *section.*

lost-wax (cire perdue) process—A bronze-casting method in which a figure is modeled in wax and covered with clay; the whole is fired, melting away the wax (French, cire perdue) and hardening the clay, which then becomes a mold for molten metal.

low relief—See *relief.*

lunette—A semicircular area (with the flat side down) in a wall over a door, niche, or window; also, a painting or *relief* with a semicircular frame.

lux nova—Latin, "new light." Abbot Suger's term for the light that enters a *Gothic* church through *stained-glass* windows.

machicolated gallery—A gallery in a defensive tower with holes in the floor to allow stones or hot liquids to be dumped on enemies below.

madrasa—An Islamic theological college adjoining and often containing a *mosque.*

magus (pl. **magi**)—One of the three wise men from the East who presented gifts to the infant Jesus.

mandorla—An almond-shaped *nimbus* surrounding the figure of Christ or other sacred figure.

maniera—Italian, "style" or "manner." See *Mannerism.*

maniera greca—Italian, "Greek manner." The Italo-Byzantine painting style of the 13th century.

manor—In *feudalism,* the estate of a *liege lord.*

maqsura—In some *mosques,* a screened area in front of the *mihrab* reserved for a ruler.

martyr—A person who chooses to die rather than deny his or her religious belief. See also *saint.*

martyrium—A shrine to a Christian martyr *saint.*

Masonry Style—See *First Style mural.*

mass—The bulk, density, and weight of matter in *space.*

Mass—The Catholic and Orthodox ritual in which believers understand that Christ's redeeming sacrifice on the cross is repeated when the priest consecrates the bread and wine in the *Eucharist.*

mastaba—Arabic, "bench." An ancient Egyptian rectangular brick or stone structure with sloping sides erected over a subterranean tomb chamber connected with the outside by a shaft.

mausoleum—A monumental tomb. The name derives from the mid-fourth-century BCE tomb of Mausolos at Halikarnassos, one of the Seven Wonders of the ancient world.

meander—An ornament, usually in bands but also covering broad surfaces, consisting of interlocking geometric motifs. An ornamental pattern of contiguous straight lines joined usually at right angles.

medium (pl. **media**)—The material (for example, marble, bronze, clay, *fresco*) in which an artist works; also, in painting, the vehicle (usually liquid) that carries the pigment.

megalith (adj. **megalithic**)—Greek, "great stone." A large, roughly hewn stone used in the construction of monumental prehistoric structures.

megaron—The large reception hall and throne room in a *Mycenaean* palace, fronted by an open, two-columned porch.

mendicants—In medieval Europe, friars belonging to the Franciscan and Dominican orders, who renounced all worldly goods, lived by contributions of laypersons (the word *mendicant* means "beggar"), and devoted themselves to preaching, teaching, and doing good works.

menorah—In antiquity, the Jewish sacred seven-branched candelabrum.

merlon—See *crenellation.*

Mesolithic—The "middle" Stone Age, between the *Paleolithic* and the *Neolithic* ages.

Messiah—The savior of the Jews prophesied in the Old Testament. Christians believe that Jesus of Nazareth was the Messiah.

metamatics—The name Swiss artist Jean Tinguely gave to the motor-driven devices he constructed to produce instant abstract paintings.

metope—The square panel between the *triglyphs* in a *Doric frieze,* often sculpted in *relief.*

mihrab—A semicircular niche set into the *qibla* wall of a *mosque.*

minaret—A distinctive feature of *mosque* architecture, a tower from which the faithful are called to worship.

minbar—In a *mosque,* the *pulpit* on which the *imam* stands.

Minoan—The prehistoric art of Crete, named after the legendary King Minos of Knossos.

Minotaur—The mythical beast, half man and half bull, that inhabited the *labyrinth* of the *Minoan* palace at Knossos.

modeling—The shaping or fashioning of three-dimensional forms in a soft material, such as clay; also, the gradations of light and shade reflected from the surfaces of matter in space, or the illusion of such gradations produced by alterations of value in a drawing, painting, or print.

module (adj. **modular**)—A basic unit of which the dimensions of the major parts of a work are multiples. The principle is used in sculpture and other art forms, but it is most often employed in architecture, where the module may be the dimensions of an important part of a building, such as the diameter of a *column.*

mold—A hollow form for *casting.*

molding—In architecture, a continuous, narrow surface (projecting or recessed, plain or ornamented) designed to break up a surface, to accent, or to decorate.

monastery—A group of buildings in which monks live together, set apart from the secular community of a town.

monastic—Relating to life in a *monastery.*

monastic order—An organization of monks living according to the same rules, for example, the Benedictine, Franciscan, and Dominican orders.

monochrome (adj. **monochromatic**)—One color.

monolith (adj. **monolithic**)—A stone *column shaft* that is all in one piece (not composed of *drums*); a large, single block or piece of stone used in *megalithic* structures. Also, a colossal statue carved from a single piece of stone.

monotheism—The worship of one all-powerful god.

moralized Bible—A heavily illustrated Bible, each page pairing paintings of Old and New Testament episodes with explanations of their moral significance.

mortuary temple—In Egyptian architecture, a temple erected for the worship of a deceased *pharaoh.*

mosaic—Patterns or pictures made by embedding small pieces (*tesserae*) of stone or glass in cement on surfaces such as walls and floors; also, the technique of making such works.

mosaic tilework—An Islamic decorative technique in which large ceramic panels are fired, cut into smaller pieces, and set in plaster.

moschophoros—Greek, "calf bearer."

mosque—The Islamic building for collective worship. From the Arabic word *masjid*, meaning a "place for bowing down."

Mozarabic—Referring to the Christian culture of northern Spain during the time Islamic *caliphs* ruled southern Spain.

Muhaqqaq—A cursive style of Islamic *calligraphy*.

mullion—A vertical member that divides a window or that separates one window from another.

mummification—A technique used by ancient Egyptians to preserve human bodies so that they may serve as the eternal home of the immortal *ka*.

muqarnas—Stucco decorations of Islamic buildings in which stalactite-like forms break a structure's solidity.

mural—A wall painting.

Mycenaean—The prehistoric art of the Late *Helladic* period in Greece, named after the citadel of Mycenae.

mystery play—A dramatic enactment of the holy mysteries of the Christian faith performed at church portals and in city squares.

naos—See *cella*.

narthex—A porch or vestibule of a church, generally *colonnaded* or *arcaded* and preceding the *nave*.

natatio—The swimming pool in a Roman bathing establishment.

naturalism—The style of painted or sculptured representation based on close observation of the natural world that was at the core of the *classical* tradition.

nave—The central area of an ancient Roman *basilica* or of a church, demarcated from *aisles* by *piers* or *columns*.

nave arcade—In *basilica* architecture, the series of *arches* supported by *piers* or *columns* separating the *nave* from the *aisles*.

necropolis—Greek, "city of the dead." A large burial area or cemetery.

nemes—In ancient Egypt, the linen headdress worn by the *pharaoh*, with the *uraeus* cobra of kingship on the front.

Neolithic—The "new" Stone Age.

niello—A black metallic alloy.

nimbus—A halo or aureole appearing around the head of a holy figure to signify divinity.

Nun—In ancient Egypt, the primeval waters from which the creator god emerged.

nymphs—In *classical* mythology, female divinities of springs, caves, and woods.

oculus (pl. **oculi**)—Latin, "eye." The round central opening of a *dome*. Also, a small round window in a *Gothic cathedral*.

odalisque—A woman in a Turkish harem.

ogee arch—An *arch* composed of two double-curving lines meeting at a point.

ogive (adj. **ogival**)—The diagonal *rib* of a *Gothic vault*; a pointed, or Gothic, *arch*.

Olympiad—The four-year period defined by the staging of the Olympic Games in ancient Greece.

opere francigeno—See *opus francigenum*.

opisthodomos—In ancient Greek architecture, a porch at the rear of a temple, set against the blank back wall of the *cella*.

optical mixture—The visual effect of juxtaposed *complementary colors*.

opus francigenum—Latin, "French work." Architecture in the style of *Gothic* France; *opere francigeno* (adj.), "in the French manner."

opus modernum—Latin, "modern work." The late medieval term for *Gothic* art and architecture. Also called *opus francigenum*.

orant—In Early Christian art, a figure with both arms raised in the ancient gesture of prayer.

oratory—The church of a Christian *monastery*.

orbiculum—A disklike opening.

orchestra—Greek, "dancing place." In ancient Greek theaters, the circular piece of earth with a hard and level surface on which the performance took place.

order—In *classical* architecture, a style represented by a characteristic design of the *columns* and *entablature*. See also *superimposed orders*.

Orientalizing—The early phase of *Archaic* Greek art (seventh century BCE), so named because of the adoption of forms and motifs from the ancient Near East and Egypt. See also *Daedalic*.

orthogonal plan—The imposition of a strict grid *plan* on a site, regardless of the terrain, so that all streets meet at right angles. See also *Hippodamian plan*.

Ottonian (adj.)—Pertaining to the empire of Otto I and his successors.

oxidizing—The first phase of the ancient Greek ceramic firing process, which turned both the pot and the clay *slip* red. During the second (reducing) phase, the oxygen supply into the kiln was shut off, and both pot and slip turned black. In the final (reoxidizing) phase, the pot's coarser material reabsorbed oxygen and became red again, whereas the smoother slip did not and remained black.

palaestra—An ancient Greek and Roman exercise area, usually framed by a *colonnade*. In Greece, the palaestra was an independent building; in Rome, palaestras were also frequently incorporated into a bathing complex.

Paleolithic—The "old" Stone Age, during which humankind produced the first sculptures and paintings.

palette—A thin board with a thumb hole at one end on which an artist lays and mixes *colors*; any surface so used. Also, the colors or kinds of colors characteristically used by an artist. In ancient Egypt, a slate slab used for preparing makeup.

Pantokrator—Greek, "ruler of all." Christ as ruler and judge of heaven and earth.

papyrus—A plant native to Egypt and adjacent lands used to make paperlike writing material; also, the material or any writing on it.

parapet—A low, protective wall along the edge of a balcony, roof, or bastion.

parchment—Lambskin prepared as a surface for painting or writing.

parekklesion—The side chapel in a Byzantine church.

parthenos—Greek, "virgin." The epithet of Athena, the virgin goddess.

passage grave—A prehistoric tomb with a long stone corridor leading to a burial chamber covered by a great *tumulus*.

paten—A large shallow bowl or plate for the bread used in the *Eucharist*.

patrician—A Roman freeborn landowner.

patron—The person or entity that pays an artist to produce individual artworks or employs an artist on a continuing basis.

pebble mosaic—A *mosaic* made of irregularly shaped stones of various colors.

pectoral—An ornament worn on the chest.

pediment—In *classical* architecture, the triangular space (gable) at the end of a building, formed by the ends of the sloping roof above the *colonnade*; also, an ornamental feature having this shape.

pendant—The large hanging terminal element of a *Gothic* fan *vault*.

pendentive—A concave, triangular section of a hemisphere, four of which provide the transition from a square area to the circular base of a covering *dome*. Although pendentives appear to be hanging (pendant) from the dome, they in fact support it.

Pentateuch—The first five books of the Old Testament.

peplos—A simple, long belted garment of wool worn by women in ancient Greece.

period style—See *style*.

peripteral—See *peristyle*.

peristyle—In *classical* architecture, a *colonnade* all around the *cella* and its porch(es). A peripteral colonnade consists of a single row of *columns* on all sides; a dipteral colonnade has a double row all around.

Perpendicular—A Late English *Gothic* style of architecture distinguished by the pronounced verticality of its decorative details.

personal style—See *style*.

personification—An abstract idea represented in bodily form.

perspective (adj. **perspectival**)—A method of presenting an illusion of the three-dimensional world on a two-dimensional surface. In linear perspective, the most common type, all parallel lines or surface edges converge on one, two, or three vanishing points located with reference to the eye level of the viewer (the horizon line of the picture), and associated objects are rendered smaller the farther from the viewer they are intended to seem. Atmospheric, or aerial, perspective creates the illusion of distance by the greater diminution of color intensity, the shift in color toward an almost neutral blue, and the blurring of contours as the intended distance between eye and object increases.

pharaoh (adj. **pharaonic**)—An ancient Egyptian king.

physical evidence—In art history, the examination of the materials used to produce an artwork in order to determine its date.

pictograph—A picture, usually stylized, that represents an idea; also, writing using such means; also, painting on rock. See also *hieroglyphic*.

pier—A vertical, freestanding masonry support.

Pietà—A painted or sculpted representation of the Virgin Mary mourning over the body of the dead Christ.

pilaster—A flat, rectangular, vertical member projecting from a wall of which it forms a part. It usually has a *base* and a *capital* and is often *fluted*.

pillar—Usually a weight-carrying member, such as a *pier* or a *column*; sometimes an isolated, freestanding structure used for commemorative purposes.

pinakotheke—Greek, "picture gallery." An ancient Greek building for the display of paintings on wood panels.

pinnacle—In *Gothic* churches, a sharply pointed ornament capping the *piers* or flying *buttresses*; also used on church *facades*.

plan—The horizontal arrangement of the parts of a building or of the buildings and streets of a city or town, or a drawing or diagram showing such an arrangement. In an axial plan, the parts of a building are organized longitudinally, or along a given axis; in a central plan, the parts of the structure are of equal or almost equal dimensions around the center.

plane—A flat surface.

plate tracery—See *tracery*.

platero—See *Plateresque*.

plebeian—The Roman social class that included small farmers, merchants, and freed slaves.

pointed arch—A narrow *arch* of pointed profile, in contrast to a semicircular arch.

polis (pl. **poleis**)—An independent *city-state* in ancient Greece.

polytheism—The belief in multiple gods.

pontifex maximus—Latin, "chief priest." The high priest of the Roman state religion, often the emperor himself.

portico—A roofed *colonnade;* also an entrance porch.

post-and-lintel system—A system of construction in which two posts support a *lintel.*

predella—The narrow ledge on which an *altarpiece* rests on an altar.

prefiguration—In Early Christian art, the depiction of Old Testament persons and events as prophetic forerunners of Christ and New Testament events.

primary colors—Red, yellow, and blue—the *colors* from which all other colors may be derived.

princeps—Latin, "first citizen." The title Augustus and his successors as Roman emperor used to distinguish themselves from Hellenistic monarchs.

pronaos—The space, or porch, in front of the *cella,* or naos, of an ancient Greek temple.

proportion—The relationship in size of the parts of persons, buildings, or objects, often based on a *module.*

prostyle—A *classical* temple *plan* in which the *columns* are only in front of the *cella* and not on the sides or back.

provenance—Origin or source; findspot.

psalter—A book containing the Psalms.

pseudoperipteral—In Roman architecture, a pseudo-peripteral temple has a series of engaged *columns* all around the sides and back of the *cella* to give the appearance of a *peripteral colonnade.*

pulpit—A raised platform in a church on which a priest stands while leading the religious service.

punchwork—Tooled decorative work in *gold leaf.*

putto (pl. **putti**)—A cherubic young boy.

pylon—The wide entrance gateway of an Egyptian temple, characterized by its sloping walls.

qibla—The direction (toward Mecca) Muslims face when praying.

quadrant arch—An *arch* whose curve extends for one quarter of a circle's circumference.

quatrefoil—A shape or plan in which the parts assume the form of a cloverleaf.

radiating chapels—In medieval churches, chapels for the display of *relics* that opened directly onto the *ambulatory* and the *transept.*

radiocarbon dating—A method of measuring the decay rate of carbon isotopes in organic matter to determine the age of organic materials such as wood and fiber.

raking cornice—The *cornice* on the sloping sides of a *pediment.*

ramparts—Defensive wall circuits.

Rayonnant—The "radiant" style of *Gothic* architecture, dominant in the second half of the 13th century and associated with the French royal court of Louis IX at Paris.

red-figure painting—In later Greek pottery, the silhouetting of red figures against a black background, with painted linear details; the reverse of *black-figure painting.*

reducing—See *oxidizing.*

refectory—The dining hall of a Christian *monastery.*

regional style—See *style.*

register—One of a series of superimposed bands or *friezes* in a pictorial narrative, or the particular levels on which motifs are placed.

relics—The body parts, clothing, or objects associated with a holy figure, such as the Buddha or Christ or a Christian *saint.*

relief—In sculpture, figures projecting from a background of which they are part. The degree of relief is designated high, low (bas), or sunken. In the last, the artist cuts the design into the surface

so that the highest projecting parts of the image are no higher than the surface itself. See also *repoussé.*

relieving triangle—In *Mycenaean* architecture, the triangular opening above the *lintel* that serves to lighten the weight to be carried by the lintel itself.

reliquary—A container for holding *relics.*

Renaissance—French, "rebirth." The term used to describe the history, culture, and art of 14th- through 16th-century western Europe during which artists consciously revived the *classical* style.

renovatio—Latin, "renewal." During the *Carolingian* period, Charlemagne sought to revive the culture of ancient Rome (renovatio imperi Romani).

reoxidizing—See *oxidizing.*

repoussé—Formed in *relief* by beating a metal plate from the back, leaving the impression on the face. The metal sheet is hammered into a hollow *mold* of wood or some other pliable material and finished with a *graver.* See also *relief.*

respond—An engaged *column, pilaster,* or similar element that either projects from a *compound pier* or some other supporting device or is bonded to a wall and carries one end of an *arch.*

retable—An architectural screen or wall above and behind an altar, usually containing painting, sculpture, carving, or other decorations. See also *altarpiece.*

revetment—In architecture, a wall covering or facing.

rib—A relatively slender, molded masonry *arch* that projects from a surface. In *Gothic* architecture, the ribs form the framework of the *vaulting.* A diagonal rib is one of the ribs that form the **X** of a *groin vault.* A transverse rib crosses the *nave* or *aisle* at a 90-degree angle.

rib vault—A *vault* in which the diagonal and transverse *ribs* compose a structural skeleton that partially supports the masonry *web* between them.

ridgepole—The beam running the length of a building below the peak of the gabled roof.

Romanesque—"Roman-like." A term used to describe the history, culture, and art of medieval western Europe from ca. 1050 to ca. 1200.

rose window—A circular *stained-glass* window.

rotulus—The manuscript scroll used by Egyptians, Greeks, Etruscans, and Romans; predecessor of the *codex.*

roundel—See *tondo.*

rusticate (n. **rustication**)—To give a rustic appearance by roughening the surfaces and beveling the edges of stone blocks to emphasize the joints between them. Rustication is a technique employed in ancient Roman architecture, and was also popular during the *Renaissance,* especially for stone *courses* at the ground-floor level.

sacra rappresentazione (pl. **sacre rappresentazioni**)—Italian, "holy representation." A more elaborate version of a *mystery play* performed for a lay audience by a *confraternity.*

sacramentary—A Christian religious book incorporating the prayers priests recite during *Mass.*

saint—From the Latin word *sanctus,* meaning "made holy by God." Applied to persons who suffered and died for their Christian faith or who merited reverence for their Christian devotion while alive. In the Roman Catholic Church, a worthy deceased Catholic who is canonized by the pope.

sarcophagus (pl. **sarcophagi**)—Latin, "consumer of flesh." A coffin, usually of stone.

saturation—See *color.*

satyr—A Greek mythological follower of Dionysos having a man's upper body, a goat's hindquarters and horns, and a horse's ears and tail.

scarab—An Egyptian gem in the shape of a beetle.

Scholasticism—The *Gothic* school of philosophy in which scholars applied Aristotle's system of rational inquiry to the interpretation of religious belief.

school—A chronological and stylistic classification of works of art with a stipulation of place.

scriptorium (pl. **scriptoria**)—The writing studio of a *monastery.*

sculpture in the round—Freestanding figures, carved or modeled in three dimensions.

secco—Italian, "dry." See also *fresco.*

Second Style mural—The style of Roman mural painting in which the aim was to dissolve the confining walls of a room and replace them with the illusion of a three-dimensional world constructed in the artist's imagination.

secondary colors—Orange, green, and purple, obtained by mixing pairs of *primary colors* (red, yellow, blue).

section—In architecture, a diagram or representation of a part of a structure or building along an imaginary plane that passes through it vertically. Drawings showing a theoretical slice across a structure's width are lateral sections. Those cutting through a building's length are longitudinal sections. See also *elevation* and *cutaway.*

sedes sapientiae—Latin, "throne of wisdom." A Romanesque sculptural type depicting the Virgin Mary with the Christ Child in her lap.

senate—Latin senatus, "council of elders." The Senate was the main legislative body in Roman constitutional government.

serdab—A small concealed chamber in an Egyptian *mastaba* for the statue of the deceased.

Severe Style—The Early *Classical* style of Greek sculpture, ca. 480–450 BCE.

sexpartite vault—See *vault.*

shaft—The tall, cylindrical part of a *column* between the *capital* and the *base.*

signoria—The governing body in the Republic of Florence.

sinopia—A burnt-orange pigment used in *fresco* painting to transfer a *cartoon* to the *arriccio* before the artist paints the plaster.

siren—In ancient Greek mythology, a creature that was part bird and part woman.

skene—Greek, "stage." The stage of a *classical* theater.

skenographia—Greek, "scene painting"; the Greek term for *perspective* painting.

skiagraphia—Greek, "shadow painting." The Greek term for shading, said to have been invented by Apollodoros, an Athenian painter of the fifth century BCE.

slip—A mixture of fine clay and water used in ceramic decoration.

space—In art history, both the actual area an object occupies or a building encloses, and the *illusionistic* representation of space in painting and sculpture.

spandrel—The roughly triangular space enclosed by the curves of adjacent *arches* and a horizontal member connecting their vertexes; also, the space enclosed by the curve of an *arch* and an enclosing right angle. The area between the arch proper and the framing *columns* and *entablature.*

spectrum—The range or band of visible colors in natural light.

sphinx—A mythical Egyptian beast with the body of a lion and the head of a human.

springing—The lowest stone of an *arch,* resting on the *impost block.* In *Gothic vaulting,* the lowest stone of a diagonal or transverse *rib.*

squinch—An architectural device used as a transition from a square to a polygonal or circular base for a *dome*. It may be composed of *lintels, corbels,* or *arches*.

stained glass—In *Gothic* architecture, the colored glass used for windows.

stamp seal—See *cylinder seal*.

statue—A three-dimensional sculpture.

stave—A wedge-shaped timber; vertically placed staves embellish the architectural features of a building.

stele (pl. **stelae**)—A carved stone slab used to mark graves or to commemorate historical events.

stem stitching—See *embroidery*.

stigmata—In Christian art, the wounds Christ received at his crucifixion that miraculously appear on the body of a *saint*.

still life—A picture depicting an arrangement of inanimate objects.

stoa—In ancient Greek architecture, an open building with a roof supported by a row of *columns* parallel to the back wall. A covered *colonnade* or *portico*.

Stoic—A philosophical school of ancient Greece, named after the *stoas* in which the philosophers met.

strategos—Greek, "general."

strigil—A tool Greek athletes used to scrape oil from their bodies after exercising.

stucco—A type of plaster used as a coating on exterior and interior walls. Also used as a sculptural medium.

style—A distinctive artistic manner. Period style is the characteristic style of a specific time. Regional style is the style of a particular geographical area. Personal style is an individual artist's unique manner.

stylistic evidence—In art history, the examination of the *style* of an artwork in order to determine its date or the identity of the artist.

stylobate—The uppermost course of the platform of a *classical* Greek temple, which supports the *columns*.

stylus—A needlelike tool used in *engraving* and *incising*; also, an ancient writing instrument used to inscribe clay or wax tablets.

sub gracia—Latin, "under grace." In Christian thought, the period after the coming of Christ.

sub lege—Latin, "under the law." In Christian thought, the period after Moses received the Ten Commandments and before the coming of Christ. See also *sub gracia*.

subtractive light—The painter's light in art; the light reflected from pigments and objects. See also *additive light*.

subtractive sculpture—A kind of sculpture technique in which materials are taken away from the original mass; carving.

sultan—A *Muslim* ruler.

sunken relief—See *relief*.

Sunnah—The collection of the Prophet Muhammad's moral sayings and descriptions of his deeds.

superimposed orders—*Orders* of architecture that are placed one above another in an *arcaded* or *colonnaded* building, usually in the following sequence: *Doric* (the first story), *Ionic,* and *Corinthian*. Superimposed orders are found in later Greek architecture and were used widely by Roman and *Renaissance* builders.

surah—A chapter of the *Koran,* divided into verses.

symbol—An image that stands for another image or encapsulates an idea.

symmetria—Greek, "commensurability of parts." Polykleitos's treatise on his *canon* of proportions incorporated the principle of symmetria.

symposium—An ancient Greek banquet attended solely by men (and female servants and prostitutes).

taberna—In Roman architecture, a single-room shop usually covered by a barrel *vault*.

tablinum—The study or office in a Roman house.

tapestry—A weaving technique in which the *weft* threads are packed densely over the *warp* threads so that the designs are woven directly into the fabric.

technique—The processes artists employ to create *form,* as well as the distinctive, personal ways in which they handle their materials and tools.

tempera—A *technique* of painting using pigment mixed with egg yolk, glue, or casein; also, the *medium* itself.

templon—The columnar screen separating the sanctuary from the main body of a Byzantine church.

tephra—The volcanic ash produced by the eruption on the *Cycladic* island of Thera.

tepidarium—The warm-bath section of a Roman bathing establishment.

terracotta—Hard-baked clay, used for sculpture and as a building material. It may be *glazed* or painted.

tessera (pl. **tesserae**)—Greek, "cube." A tiny stone or piece of glass cut to the desired shape and size for use in forming a *mosaic*.

tetrarch—One of four corulers.

tetrarchy—Greek, "rule by four." A type of Roman government established in the late third century CE by Diocletian in an attempt to foster order by sharing power with potential rivals.

texture—The quality of a surface (rough, smooth, hard, soft, shiny, dull) as revealed by light. In represented texture, a painter depicts an object as having a certain texture even though the paint is the actual texture.

theatron—Greek, "place for seeing." In ancient Greek theaters, the slope overlooking the *orchestra* on which the spectators sat.

Theotokos—Greek, "she who bore God." The Virgin Mary, the mother of Jesus.

Third Style mural—In Roman mural painting, the style in which delicate linear fantasies were sketched on predominantly monochromatic backgrounds.

tholos (pl. **tholoi**)—A temple with a circular plan. Also, the burial chamber of a *tholos tomb*.

tholos tomb—In *Mycenaean* architecture, a beehive-shaped tomb with a circular plan.

thrust—The outward force exerted by an *arch* or a *vault* that must be counterbalanced by a *buttress*.

tonality— See *color*.

tondo (pl. **tondi**)—A circular painting or *relief* sculpture.

Torah—The Hebrew religious scroll containing the Pentateuch.

torque—The distinctive necklace worn by the Gauls.

tracery—Ornamental stonework for holding *stained glass* in place, characteristic of *Gothic* cathedrals. In plate tracery, the glass fills only the "punched holes" in the heavy ornamental stonework. In bar tracery, the stained-glass windows fill almost the entire opening, and the stonework is unobtrusive.

tramezzo—A screen placed across the *nave* of a church to separate the clergy from the lay audience.

transept—The part of a church with an axis that crosses the *nave* at a right angle.

transverse arch—An *arch* separating one *vaulted bay* from the next.

transverse barrel vault—In medieval architecture, a semicylindrical *vault* oriented at a 90-degree angle to the *nave* of a church.

transverse rib—See *rib*.

treasury—In ancient Greece, a small building set up for the safe storage of *votive offerings*.

trefoil—A cloverlike ornament or symbol with stylized leaves in groups of three.

tribune—In church architecture, a gallery over the inner *aisle* flanking the *nave*.

triclinium—The dining room of a Roman house.

trident—The three-pronged pitchfork associated with the ancient Greek sea god Poseidon (Roman, Neptune).

triforium—In a *Gothic* cathedral, the *blind arcaded* gallery below the *clerestory;* occasionally, the arcades are filled with *stained glass*.

triglyph—A triple projecting, grooved member of a *Doric frieze* that alternates with *metopes*.

trilithons—A pair of *monoliths* topped with a *lintel;* found in *megalithic* structures.

Trinity—In Christianity, God the Father, his son Jesus Christ, and the Holy Spirit.

tripod—An ancient Greek deep bowl on a tall three-legged stand.

triptych—A three-paneled painting, ivory plaque, or *altarpiece*. Also, a small, portable shrine with hinged wings used for private devotion.

trumeau—In church architecture, the *pillar* or center post supporting the *lintel* in the middle of the doorway.

tubicen—Latin, "trumpet player."

tumulus (pl. **tumuli**)—Latin, "burial mound." In Etruscan architecture, tumuli cover one or more subterranean multichambered tombs cut out of the local tufa (limestone). Also characteristic of the Japanese Kofun period of the third and fourth centuries.

tunnel vault—See *vault*.

turris—See *westwork*.

Tuscan column—The standard type of Etruscan *column*. It resembles ancient Greek *Doric* columns but is made of wood, is unfluted, and has a *base*. Also a popular motif in *Renaissance* and *Baroque* architecture.

twisted perspective—See *composite view*.

tympanum (pl. **tympana**)—The space enclosed by a *lintel* and an *arch* over a doorway.

typology—In Christian theology, the recognition of concordances between events, especially between episodes in the Old and New Testaments.

uraeus—An Egyptian cobra; one of the emblems of *pharaonic* kingship.

ushabti—In ancient Egypt, a figurine placed in a tomb to act as a servant to the deceased in the afterlife.

valley temple—The temple closest to the Nile River associated with each of the Great Pyramids at Gizeh in ancient Egypt.

value—See *color*.

vassal—In *feudalism,* a person who swears allegiance to a *liege lord* and renders him military service in return for tenure of a portion of the lord's land.

vault (adj. **vaulted**)—A masonry roof or ceiling constructed on the *arch* principle, or a concrete roof of the same shape. A barrel (or tunnel) vault, semicylindrical in cross-*section,* is in effect a deep arch or an uninterrupted series of arches, one behind the other, over an oblong space. A quadrant vault is a half-barrel vault. A groin (or cross) vault is formed at the point at which two barrel vaults intersect at right angles. In a ribbed vault, there is a framework of *ribs* or arches under the intersections of the vaulting sections. A sexpartite vault is one whose ribs divide the vault into six compartments. A fan vault is a vault characteristic of English *Perpendicular Gothic* architecture, in which radiating ribs form a fanlike pattern.

vaulting web—See *web*.

velarium—In a Roman *amphitheater,* the cloth awning that could be rolled down from the top of the *cavea* to shield spectators from sun or rain.

vellum—Calfskin prepared as a surface for writing or painting.

venationes—Ancient Roman wild animal hunts staged in an *amphitheater*.

veristic—True to natural appearance; superrealistic.

vita contemplativa—Latin, "contemplative life." The secluded spiritual life of monks and nuns.

volume—The *space* that *mass* organizes, divides, or encloses.

volute—A spiral, scroll-like form characteristic of the ancient Greek *Ionic* and the Roman *Composite capital*.

votive offering—A gift of gratitude to a deity.

voussoir—A wedge-shaped stone block used in the construction of a true *arch*. The central voussoir, which sets the arch, is called the keystone.

warp—The vertical threads of a loom or cloth.

web—The masonry blocks that fill the area between the *ribs* of a *groin vault*. Also called vaulting web.

wedjat—The eye of the Egyptian falcon-god Horus, a powerful *amulet*.

weld—To join metal parts by heating, as in assembling the separate parts of a *statue* made by *casting*.

westwork—German, "western entrance structure." The *facade* and towers at the western end of a medieval church, principally in Germany. In contemporary documents the westwork is called a castellum (Latin, "castle" or "fortress") or turris ("tower").

white-ground painting—An ancient Greek vase-painting *technique* in which the pot was first covered with a *slip* of very fine white clay, over which black *glaze* was used to outline figures, and diluted brown, purple, red, and white were used to color them.

ziggurat—In ancient Mesopotamian architecture, a monumental platform for a temple.

BIBLIOGRAPHY

This list of books is very selective but comprehensive enough to satisfy the reading interests of the beginning art history student and general reader. The resources listed range from works that are valuable primarily for their reproductions to those that are scholarly surveys of schools and periods or monographs on individual artists. The emphasis is on recent in-print books and on books likely to be found in college and municipal libraries. No entries for periodical articles appear, but the bibliography begins with a list of some of the major journals that publish art historical scholarship in English.

SELECTED PERIODICALS

African Arts
American Art
American Indian Art
American Journal of Archaeology
Antiquity
Archaeology
Archives of American Art
Archives of Asian Art
Ars Orientalis
Art Bulletin
Art History
Art in America
Art Journal
Artforum International
Burlington Magazine
Gesta
History of Photography
Journal of Roman Archaeology
Journal of the Society of Architectural Historians
Journal of the Warburg and Courtauld Institutes
Latin American Antiquity
Oxford Art Journal
Women's Art Journal

GENERAL STUDIES

Baxandall, Michael. *Patterns of Intention: On the Historical Explanation of Pictures.* New Haven, Conn.: Yale University Press, 1985.

Bindman, David, ed. *The Thames & Hudson Encyclopedia of British Art.* London: Thames & Hudson, 1988.

Boström, Antonia. *The Encyclopedia of Sculpture.* 3 vols. London: Routledge, 2003.

Broude, Norma, and Mary D. Garrard, eds. *The Expanding Discourse: Feminism and Art History.* New York: Harper Collins, 1992.

Bryson, Norman. *Vision and Painting: The Logic of the Gaze.* New Haven, Conn.: Yale University Press, 1983.

Bryson, Norman, Michael Ann Holly, and Keith Moxey. *Visual Theory: Painting and Interpretation.* New York: Cambridge University Press, 1991.

Büttner, Nils. *Landscape Painting: A History.* New York: Abbeville, 2006.

Chadwick, Whitney. *Women, Art, and Society.* 4th ed. New York: Thames & Hudson, 2007.

Cheetham, Mark A., Michael Ann Holly, and Keith Moxey, eds. *The Subjects of Art History: Historical Objects in Contemporary Perspective.* New York: Cambridge University Press, 1998.

Chilvers, Ian, and Harold Osborne, eds. *The Oxford Dictionary of Art.* 3d ed. New York: Oxford University Press, 2004.

Corbin, George A. *Native Arts of North America, Africa, and the South Pacific: An Introduction.* New York: Harper Collins, 1988.

Crouch, Dora P., and June G. Johnson. *Traditions in Architecture: Africa, America, Asia, and Oceania.* New York: Oxford University Press, 2000.

Curl, James Stevens. *Oxford Dictionary of Architecture and Landscape Architecture.* 2d ed. New York: Oxford University Press, 2006.

Encyclopedia of World Art. 17 vols. New York: McGraw-Hill, 1959–1987.

Fielding, Mantle. *Dictionary of American Painters, Sculptors, and Engravers.* 2d ed. Poughkeepsie, N.Y.: Apollo, 1986.

Fine, Sylvia Honig. *Women and Art: A History of Women Painters and Sculptors from the Renaissance to the 20th Century.* Rev. ed. Montclair, N.J.: Alanheld & Schram, 1978.

Fleming, John, Hugh Honour, and Nikolaus Pevsner. *The Penguin Dictionary of Architecture and Landscape Architecture.* 5th ed. New York: Penguin, 2000.

Frazier, Nancy. *The Penguin Concise Dictionary of Art History.* New York: Penguin, 2000.

Freedberg, David. *The Power of Images: Studies in the History and Theory of Response.* Chicago: University of Chicago Press, 1989.

Gaze, Delia., ed. *Dictionary of Women Artists.* 2 vols. London: Routledge, 1997.

Hall, James. *Illustrated Dictionary of Subjects and Symbols in Eastern and Western Art.* New York: Icon Editions, 1994.

Harris, Anne Sutherland, and Linda Nochlin. *Women Artists: 1550–1950.* Los Angeles: Los Angeles County Museum of Art; New York: Knopf, 1977.

Hauser, Arnold. *The Sociology of Art.* Chicago: University of Chicago Press, 1982.

Hults, Linda C. *The Print in the Western World: An Introductory History.* Madison: University of Wisconsin Press, 1996.

Kemp, Martin. *The Science of Art: Optical Themes in Western Art from Brunelleschi to Seurat.* New Haven, Conn.: Yale University Press, 1990.

Kostof, Spiro, and Gregory Castillo. *A History of Architecture: Settings and Rituals.* 2d ed. Oxford: Oxford University Press, 1995.

Kultermann, Udo. *The History of Art History.* New York: Abaris, 1993.

Lucie-Smith, Edward. *The Thames & Hudson Dictionary of Art Terms.* 2d ed. New York: Thames & Hudson, 2004.

Moffett, Marian, Michael Fazio, and Lawrence Wadehouse. *A World History of Architecture.* Boston: McGraw-Hill, 2004.

Murray, Peter, and Linda Murray. *A Dictionary of Art and Artists.* 7th ed. New York: Penguin, 1998.

Nelson, Robert S., and Richard Shiff, eds. *Critical Terms for Art History.* Chicago: University of Chicago Press, 1996.

Penny, Nicholas. *The Materials of Sculpture.* New Haven, Conn.: Yale University Press, 1993.

Pevsner, Nikolaus. *A History of Building Types.* London: Thames & Hudson, 1987. Reprint of 1979 ed.

———. *An Outline of European Architecture.* 8th ed. Baltimore: Penguin, 1974.

Pierce, James Smith. *From Abacus to Zeus: A Handbook of Art History.* 7th ed. Upper Saddle River, N.J.: Pearson Prentice Hall, 1998.

Placzek, Adolf K., ed. *Macmillan Encyclopedia of Architects.* 4 vols. New York: Macmillan, 1982.

Podro, Michael. *The Critical Historians of Art.* New Haven, Conn.: Yale University Press, 1982.

Pollock, Griselda. *Vision and Difference: Femininity, Feminism, and Histories of Art.* London: Routledge, 1988.

Preziosi, Donald, ed. *The Art of Art History: A Critical Anthology.* New York: Oxford University Press, 1998.

Read, Herbert. *The Thames & Hudson Dictionary of Art and Artists.* Rev. ed. New York: Thames & Hudson, 1994.

Reid, Jane D. *The Oxford Guide to Classical Mythology in the Arts 1300–1990s.* 2 vols. New York: Oxford University Press, 1993.

Roth, Leland M. *Understanding Architecture: Its Elements, History, and Meaning.* 2d ed. Boulder, Colo.: Westview, 2006.

Schama, Simon. *The Power of Art.* New York: Ecco, 2006.

Slatkin, Wendy. *Women Artists in History: From Antiquity to the 20th Century.* 4th ed. Upper Saddle River, N.J.: Prentice Hall, 2000.

Steer, John, and Antony White. *Atlas of Western Art History: Artists, Sites, and Monuments from Ancient Greece to the Modern Age.* New York: Facts on File, 1994.

Stratton, Arthur. *The Orders of Architecture: Greek, Roman, and Renaissance.* London: Studio, 1986.

Sutton, Ian. *Western Architecture: From Ancient Greece to the Present.* New York: Thames & Hudson, 1999.

Trachtenberg, Marvin, and Isabelle Hyman. *Architecture, from Prehistory to Post-Modernism.* 2d ed. Upper Saddle River, N.J.: Prentice Hall, 2003.

Turner, Jane, ed. *The Dictionary of Art.* 34 vols. New ed. New York: Oxford University Press, 2003.

Wittkower, Rudolf. *Sculpture Processes and Principles.* New York: Harper & Row, 1977.

Wren, Linnea H., and Janine M. Carter, eds. *Perspectives on Western Art: Source Documents and Readings from the Ancient Near East through the Middle Ages.* New York: Harper & Row, 1987.

Ancient Art, General

Aruz, Joan, and Ronald Wallenfels, eds. *Art of the First Cities: The Third Millennium BC from the Mediterranean to the Indus.* New York: Metropolitan Museum of Art, 2003.

Beard, Mary, and John Henderson. *Classical Art: From Greece to Rome.* New York: Oxford University Press, 2001.

Boardman, John. *The World of Ancient Art.* London: Thames & Hudson, 2006.

————, ed. *The Oxford History of Classical Art.* New York: Oxford University Press, 1997.

Clayton, Peter A., and Martin J. Price, eds. *The Seven Wonders of the Ancient World.* New York: Routledge, 1988.

Connolly, Peter, and Hazel Dodge. *The Ancient City: Life in Classical Athens and Rome.* New York: Oxford University Press, 1998.

De Grummond, Nancy Thomson, ed. *An Encyclopedia of the History of Classical Archaeology.* 2 vols. Westport, Conn.: Greenwood, 1996.

Dunbabin, Katherine. *Mosaics of the Greek and Roman World.* New York: Cambridge University Press, 1999.

Gates, Charles. *Ancient Cities: The Archaeology of Urban Life in the Ancient Near East and Egypt, Greece, and Rome.* London: Routledge, 2003.

Kampen, Natalie B., ed. *Sexuality in Ancient Art.* New York: Cambridge University Press, 1996.

Lexicon Iconographicum Mythologiae Classicae. 10 vols. Zurich: Artemis, 1981–1999.

Ling, Roger. *Ancient Mosaics.* Princeton, N.J.: Princeton University Press, 1998.

Lloyd, Seton, and Hans Wolfgang Muller. *Ancient Architecture: Mesopotamia, Egypt, Crete.* New York: Electa/Rizzoli, 1980.

Oliphant, Margaret. *The Atlas of the Ancient World: Charting the Great Civilizations of the Past.* New York: Simon & Schuster, 1992.

Onians, John. *Classical Art and the Cultures of Greece and Rome.* New Haven, Conn.: Yale University Press, 1999.

Renfrew, Colin, and Paul G. Bahn. *Archaeology: Theories, Methods, and Practices.* London: Thames & Hudson, 1991.

Stillwell, Richard, William L. MacDonald, and Marian H. McAllister, eds. *The Princeton Encyclopedia of Classical Sites.* Princeton, N.J.: Princeton University Press, 1976.

Trigger, Bruce. *Understanding Early Civilizations: A Comparative Study.* New York: Cambridge University Press, 2003.

Ward-Perkins, John B. *Cities of Ancient Greece and Italy: Planning in Classical Antiquity.* Rev. ed. New York: Braziller, 1987.

Wolf, Walther. *The Origins of Western Art: Egypt, Mesopotamia, the Aegean.* New York: Universe, 1989.

Chapter 1:
Art before History

Bahn, Paul G. *The Cambridge Illustrated History of Prehistoric Art.* New York: Cambridge University Press, 1998.

Bahn, Paul G., and Jean Vertut. *Journey through the Ice Age.* Berkeley: University of California Press, 1997.

Beltrán, Antonio, ed. *The Cave of Altamira.* New York: Abrams, 1999.

Burl, Aubrey. *Great Stone Circles.* New Haven, Conn.: Yale University Press, 1999.

Chauvet, Jean-Marie, Eliette Brunel Deschamps, and Christian Hillaire. *Dawn of Art: The Chauvet Cave.* New York: Abrams, 1996.

Chippindale, Christopher. *Stonehenge Complete.* New York: Thames & Hudson, 1994.

Cunliffe, Barry, ed. *The Oxford Illustrated Prehistory of Europe.* New York: Oxford University Press, 1994.

Hodder, Ian. *The Leopard's Tale: Revealing the Mysteries of Çatalhöyük.* London: Thames & Hudson, 2006.

Kenyon, Kathleen M. *Digging up Jericho.* New York: Praeger, 1974.

Leroi-Gourhan, André. *The Dawn of European Art: An Introduction to Paleolithic Cave Painting.* Cambridge: Cambridge University Press, 1982.

Marshack, Alexander. *The Roots of Civilization: The Cognitive Beginnings of Man's First Art, Symbol and Notation.* 2d ed. Wakefield, R.I.: Moyer Bell, 1991.

Pfeiffer, John E. *The Creative Explosion: An Inquiry into the Origins of Art and Religion.* New York: Harper & Row, 1982.

Renfrew, Colin, ed. *British Prehistory: A New Outline.* London: Noyes, 1975.

Ruspoli, Mario. *The Cave of Lascaux: The Final Photographs.* New York: Abrams, 1987.

Scarre, Chris. *Exploring Prehistoric Europe.* New York: Oxford University Press, 1998.

Wainwright, Geoffrey. *The Henge Monuments: Ceremony and Society in Prehistoric Britain.* London: Thames & Hudson, 1990.

White, Randall. *Prehistoric Art: The Symbolic Journey of Humankind.* New York: Abrams, 2003.

Chapter 2:
The Ancient Near East

Akurgal, Ekrem. *Art of the Hittites.* New York: Abrams, 1962.

Allen, Lindsay. *The Persian Empire.* Chicago: University of Chicago Press, 2005.

Amiet, Pierre. *Art of the Ancient Near East.* New York: Abrams, 1980.

Bahrani, Zainab. *The Graven Image: Representation in Babylonia and Assyria.* Philadelphia: University of Pennsylvania Press, 2003.

Bienkowski, Piotr, and Alan Millard, eds. *Dictionary of the Ancient Near East.* Philadelphia: University of Pennsylvania Press, 2000.

Collon, Dominique. *Ancient Near Eastern Art.* Berkeley: University of California Press, 1995.

————. *First Impressions: Cylinder Seals in the Ancient Near East.* 2d ed. London: British Museum, 1993.

————. *Near Eastern Seals.* Berkeley: University of California Press, 1990.

Crawford, Harriet. *Sumer and the Sumerians.* New York: Cambridge University Press, 1991.

Curatola, Giovanni. *The Art and Architecture of Mesopotamia.* New York: Abbeville, 2007.

Curtis, John E. *Ancient Persia.* Cambridge, Mass.: Harvard University Press, 1990.

Curtis, John E., and Julian E. Reade. *Art and Empire: Treasures from Assyria in the British Museum.* New York: Metropolitan Museum of Art, 1995.

Curtis, John E., and Nigel Tallis. *Forgotten Empire: The World of Ancient Persia.* Berkeley: University of California Press, 2005.

Frankfort, Henri. *The Art and Architecture of the Ancient Orient.* 5th ed. New Haven, Conn.: Yale University Press, 1996.

Ghirshman, Roman. *The Arts of Ancient Iran: From Its Origins to the Time of Alexander the Great.* New York: Golden, 1964.

————. *Persian Art: The Parthian and Sassanian Dynasties, 249 BC–AD 651.* New York: Golden, 1962.

Gunter, Ann C., ed. *Investigating Artistic Environments in the Ancient Near East.* Washington, D.C.: Arthur M. Sackler Gallery, 1990.

Harper, Prudence O., Joan Aruz, and Françoise Tallon, eds. *The Royal City of Susa: Ancient Near Eastern Treasures in the Louvre.* New York: Metropolitan Museum of Art, 1992.

Lloyd, Seton. *The Archaeology of Mesopotamia: From the Old Stone Age to the Persian Conquest.* London: Thames & Hudson, 1984.

Macqueen, James G. *The Hittites and Their Contemporaries in Asia Minor.* Rev. ed. New York: Thames & Hudson, 1986.

Meyers, Eric M., ed. *The Oxford Encyclopedia of Archaeology in the Near East.* 5 vols. New York: Oxford University Press, 1997.

Moortgat, Anton. *The Art of Ancient Mesopotamia.* New York: Phaidon, 1969.

Oates, Joan. *Babylon.* Rev. ed. London: Thames & Hudson, 1986.

Parrot, André. *The Arts of Assyria.* New York: Golden, 1961.

————. *Sumer: The Dawn of Art.* New York: Golden, 1961.

Porada, Edith. *Man and Images in the Ancient Near East.* Wakefield, R.I.: Moyer Bell, 1995.

Porada, Edith, and Robert H. Dyson. *The Art of Ancient Iran: Pre-Islamic Cultures.* Rev. ed. New York: Greystone, 1969.

Postgate, J. Nicholas. *Early Mesopotamia: Society and Economy at the Dawn of History.* London: Routledge, 1992.

Potts, Daniel T. *The Archaeology of Elam: Formation and Transformation of an Ancient Iranian State.* New York: Cambridge University Press, 1999.

Reade, Julian E. *Assyrian Sculpture.* Cambridge, Mass.: Harvard University Press, 1999.

————. *Mesopotamia.* Cambridge, Mass.: Harvard University Press, 1991.

Roaf, Michael. *Cultural Atlas of Mesopotamia and the Ancient Near East.* New York: Facts on File, 1990.

Russell, John M. *Sennacherib's Palace without Rival at Nineveh.* Chicago: University of Chicago Press, 1991.

Saggs, H.W.F. *Babylonians*. London: British Museum, 1995.

Sasson, Jack M., ed. *Civilizations of the Ancient Near East*. 4 vols. New York: Scribner, 1995.

Snell, Daniel C. *Life in the Ancient Near East: 3100–332 BC*. New Haven, Conn.: Yale University Press, 1997.

Strommenger, Eva, and Max Hirmer. *5,000 Years of the Art of Mesopotamia*. New York: Abrams, 1964.

Zettler, Richard L., and Lee Horne. *Treasures from the Royal Tombs of Ur*. Philadelphia: University of Pennsylvania Museum of Archaeology and Anthropology, 1998.

CHAPTER 3:
EGYPT UNDER THE PHARAOHS

Arnold, Dieter. *Building in Egypt: Pharaonic Stone Masonry*. New York: Oxford University Press, 1991.

Arnold, Dorothea. *The Royal Women of Amarna*. New York: Metropolitan Museum of Art, 1996.

———. *When the Pyramids Were Built: Egyptian Art of the Old Kingdom*. New York: Rizzoli, 1999.

Baines, John, and Jaromír Málek. *Atlas of Ancient Egypt*. New York: Facts on File, 1980.

Bard, Kathryn A. *An Introduction to the Archaeology of Ancient Egypt*. Oxford: Blackwell, 2007.

———, ed. *Encyclopedia of the Archaeology of Ancient Egypt*. London: Routledge, 1999.

Bianchi, Robert S. *Cleopatra's Egypt: Age of the Ptolemies*. Brooklyn: Brooklyn Museum, 1988.

———. *Splendors of Ancient Egypt from the Egyptian Museum, Cairo*. London: Booth-Clibborn, 1996.

Capel, Anne K., and Glenn E. Markoe, eds. *Mistress of the House, Mistress of Heaven: Women in Ancient Egypt*. New York: Hudson Hills, 1996.

D'Auria, Sue, Peter Lacovara, and Catharine H. Roehrig. *Mummies and Magic: The Funerary Arts of Ancient Egypt*. Boston: Museum of Fine Arts, 1988.

Davis, Whitney. *The Canonical Tradition in Ancient Egyptian Art*. New York: Cambridge University Press, 1989.

Egyptian Art in the Age of the Pyramids. New York: Abrams, 1999.

Hawass, Zahi. *Valley of the Golden Mummies*. New York: Abrams, 2000.

Ikram, Salima, and Aidan Dodson. *The Mummy in Ancient Egypt: Equipping the Dead for Eternity*. New York: Thames & Hudson, 1998.

Kemp, Barry J. *Ancient Egypt: Anatomy of a Civilization*. 2d ed. New York: Routledge, 2006.

Kozloff, Arielle P., and Betsy M. Bryan. *Egypt's Dazzling Sun: Amenhotep III and His World*. Cleveland: Cleveland Museum of Art, 1992.

Lange, Kurt, and Max Hirmer. *Egypt: Architecture, Sculpture, and Painting in Three Thousand Years*. 4th ed. London: Phaidon, 1968.

Lehner, Mark. *The Complete Pyramids: Solving the Ancient Mysteries*. New York: Thames & Hudson, 1997.

Mahdy, Christine, ed. *The World of the Pharaohs: A Complete Guide to Ancient Egypt*. London: Thames & Hudson, 1990.

Málek, Jaromír. *Egypt: 4,000 Years of Art*. New York: Phaidon, 2003.

———. *Egyptian Art*. London: Phaidon, 1999.

———, ed. *Egypt: Ancient Culture, Modern Land*. Norman: University of Oklahoma Press, 1993.

Redford, Donald B. *Akhenaton, the Heretic King*. Princeton, N.J.: Princeton University Press, 1984.

———, ed. *The Oxford Encyclopedia of Ancient Egypt*. 3 vols. New York: Oxford University Press, 2001.

Reeves, C. Nicholas. *The Complete Tutankhamun: The King, the Tomb, the Royal Treasure*. London: Thames & Hudson, 1990.

Robins, Gay. *The Art of Ancient Egypt*. Cambridge, Mass.: Harvard University Press, 1997.

———. *Egyptian Painting and Relief*. Aylesbury: Shire, 1986.

———. *Proportion and Style in Ancient Egyptian Art*. Austin: University of Texas Press, 1994.

———. *Women in Ancient Egypt*. London: British Museum, 1993.

Romer, John. *Valley of the Kings: Exploring the Tombs of the Pharaohs*. New York: Holt, 1994.

Russmann, Edna R. *Egyptian Sculpture: Cairo and Luxor*. Austin: University of Texas Press, 1989.

Schäfer, Heinrich. *Principles of Egyptian Art*. Rev. ed. Oxford: Clarendon, 1986.

Schulz, Regina, and Matthias Seidel, eds. *Egypt: The World of the Pharaohs*. Cologne: Könemann, 1999.

Shafer, Byron E., ed. *Temples of Ancient Egypt*. Ithaca, N.Y.: Cornell University Press, 1997.

Shaw, Ian, and Paul Nicholson. *The Dictionary of Ancient Egypt*. London: British Museum, 1995.

Silverman, David P., ed. *Ancient Egypt*. New York: Oxford University Press, 1997.

Smith, William Stevenson, and William Kelly Simpson. *The Art and Architecture of Ancient Egypt*. Rev. ed. New Haven, Conn.: Yale University Press, 1998.

Weeks, Kent R., ed. *Valley of the Kings*. Vercelli: White Star, 2001.

Wildung, Dietrich. *Egypt: From Prehistory to the Romans*. Cologne: Taschen, 1997.

CHAPTER 4:
THE PREHISTORIC AEGEAN

Barber, R. L. N. *The Cyclades in the Bronze Age*. Iowa City: University of Iowa Press, 1987.

Betancourt, Philip P. *A History of Minoan Pottery*. Princeton, N.J.: Princeton University Press, 1965.

Cadogan, Gerald. *Palaces of Minoan Crete*. London: Methuen, 1980.

Chadwick, John. *The Mycenaean World*. New York: Cambridge University Press, 1976.

Cullen, Tracey, ed. *Aegean Prehistory: A Review*. Boston: Archaeological Institute of America, 2001.

Demargne, Pierre. *The Birth of Greek Art*. New York: Golden, 1964.

Dickinson, Oliver P.T.K. *The Aegean Bronze Age*. New York: Cambridge University Press, 1994.

Doumas, Christos. *Thera, Pompeii of the Ancient Aegean: Excavations at Akrotiri, 1967–1979*. New York: Thames & Hudson, 1983.

———. *The Wall-Paintings of Thera*. Athens: Thera Foundation, 1992.

Fitton, J. Lesley. *Cycladic Art*. Cambridge, Mass.: Harvard University Press, 1989.

———. *The Discovery of the Greek Bronze Age*. London: British Museum, 1995.

Forsyth, Phyllis Young. *Thera in the Bronze Age*. New York: Peter Lang, 1997.

Getz-Preziosi, Patricia. *Sculptors of the Cyclades: Individual and Tradition in the Third Millennium BC*. Ann Arbor: University of Michigan Press, 1987.

Graham, James W. *The Palaces of Crete*. Princeton, N.J.: Princeton University Press, 1987.

Hampe, Roland, and Erika Simon. *The Birth of Greek Art: From the Mycenaean to the Archaic Period*. New York: Oxford University Press, 1981.

Higgins, Reynold. *Minoan and Mycenaean Art*. Rev. ed. New York: Thames & Hudson, 1997.

Hood, Sinclair. *The Arts in Prehistoric Greece*. New Haven, Conn.: Yale University Press, 1992.

Immerwahr, Sarah A. *Aegean Painting in the Bronze Age*. University Park: Pennsylvania State University Press, 1990.

MacGillivray, J. A. *Minotaur: Sir Arthur Evans and the Archaeology of the Minoan Myth*. New York: Hill and Wang, 2000.

Marinatos, Nanno. *Art and Religion in Thera: Reconstructing a Bronze Age Society*. Athens: Mathioulakis, 1984.

Marinatos, Spyridon, and Max Hirmer. *Crete and Mycenae*. London: Thames & Hudson, 1960.

McDonald, William A., and Carol G. Thomas. *Progress into the Past: The Rediscovery of Mycenaean Civilization*. 2d ed. Bloomington: Indiana University Press, 1990.

Preziosi, Donald, and Louise A. Hitchcock. *Aegean Art and Architecture*. New York: Oxford University Press, 1999.

Taylour, Lord William. *The Mycenaeans*. London: Thames & Hudson, 1990.

Vermeule, Emily. *Greece in the Bronze Age*. Chicago: University of Chicago Press, 1972.

Warren, Peter. *The Aegean Civilisations from Ancient Crete to Mycenae*. 2d ed. Oxford: Elsevier-Phaidon, 1989.

CHAPTER 5:
ANCIENT GREECE

Arias, Paolo. *A History of One Thousand Years of Greek Vase Painting*. New York: Abrams, 1962.

Ashmole, Bernard. *Architect and Sculptor in Classical Greece*. New York: New York University Press, 1972.

Berve, Helmut, Gottfried Gruben, and Max Hirmer. *Greek Temples, Theatres, and Shrines*. New York: Abrams, 1963.

Biers, William. *The Archaeology of Greece: An Introduction*. 2d ed. Ithaca, N.Y.: Cornell University Press, 1996.

Boardman, John. *Athenian Black Figure Vases*. Rev. ed. New York: Thames & Hudson, 1985.

———. *Athenian Red Figure Vases: The Archaic Period*. New York: Thames & Hudson, 1988.

———. *Athenian Red Figure Vases: The Classical Period*. New York: Thames & Hudson, 1989.

———. *Early Greek Vase Painting, 11th–6th Centuries BC*. New York: Thames & Hudson, 1998.

———. *Greek Sculpture: The Archaic Period*. Rev. ed. New York: Thames & Hudson, 1985.

———. *Greek Sculpture: The Classical Period*. New York: Thames & Hudson, 1987.

———. *Greek Sculpture: The Late Classical Period and Sculpture in Colonies and Overseas*. New York: Thames & Hudson, 1995.

———. *The Parthenon and Its Sculpture*. Austin: University of Texas Press, 1985.

Camp, John M. *The Archaeology of Athens*. New Haven, Conn.: Yale University Press, 2001.

Carpenter, Thomas H. *Art and Myth in Ancient Greece*. New York: Thames & Hudson, 1991.

Charbonneaux, Jean, Roland Martin, and François Villard. *Archaic Greek Art*. New York: Braziller, 1971.

———. *Classical Greek Art*. New York: Braziller, 1972.

———. *Hellenistic Art*. New York: Braziller, 1973.

Coldstream, J. Nicholas. *Geometric Greece*. New York: St. Martin's, 1977.

Coulton, J. J. *Ancient Greek Architects at Work*. Ithaca, N.Y.: Cornell University Press, 1982.

Fullerton, Mark D. *Greek Art*. New York: Cambridge University Press, 2000.

Haynes, Denys E. L. *The Technique of Greek Bronze Statuary*. Mainz: von Zabern, 1992.

Houser, Caroline. *Greek Monumental Bronze Sculpture*. New York: Vendome, 1983.

Hurwit, Jeffrey M. *The Art and Culture of Early Greece, 1100–480 BC*. Ithaca, N.Y.: Cornell University Press, 1985.

———. *The Athenian Acropolis: History, Mythology, and Archaeology from the Neolithic Era to the Present*. New York: Cambridge University Press, 1999.

Jenkins, Ian. *Greek Architecture and Its Sculpture*. Cambridge, Mass.: Harvard University Press, 2006.

———. *The Parthenon Frieze*. Austin: University of Texas Press, 1994.

Lawrence, Arnold W., and R. A. Tomlinson. *Greek Architecture*. Rev. ed. New Haven, Conn.: Yale University Press, 1996.

Martin, Roland. *Greek Architecture: Architecture of Crete, Greece, and the Greek World*. New York: Electa/Rizzoli, 1988.

Mattusch, Carol C. *Classical Bronzes: The Art and Craft of Greek and Roman Statuary*. Ithaca, N.Y.: Cornell University Press, 1996.

———. *Greek Bronze Statuary from the Beginnings through the Fifth Century BC*. Ithaca, N.Y.: Cornell University Press, 1988.

Mee, Christopher, and Tony Spawforth. *Greece: An Oxford Archaeological Guide*. New York: Oxford University Press, 2001.

Morris, Sarah P. *Daidalos and the Origins of Greek Art*. Princeton, N.J.: Princeton University Press, 1992.

Osborne, Robin. *Archaic and Classical Greek Art*. New York: Oxford University Press, 1998.

Palagia, Olga. *The Pediments of the Parthenon*. Leiden: E. J. Brill, 1993.

———, ed. *Greek Sculpture: Functions, Materials, and Techniques in the Archaic and Classical Periods*. New York: Cambridge University Press, 2006.

Palagia, Olga, and Jerome J. Pollitt. *Personal Styles in Greek Sculpture*. New York: Cambridge University Press, 1996.

Pedley, John Griffiths. *Greek Art and Archaeology*. 4th ed. Upper Saddle River, N.J.: Prentice Hall, 2007.

Pollitt, Jerome J. *Art and Experience in Classical Greece*. New York: Cambridge University Press, 1972.

———. *Art in the Hellenistic Age*. New York: Cambridge University Press, 1986.

———. *The Art of Ancient Greece: Sources and Documents*. 2d ed. New York: Cambridge University Press, 1990.

Pugliese Carratelli, G. *The Greek World: Art and Civilization in Magna Graecia and Sicily*. New York: Rizzoli, 1996.

Reeder, Ellen D., ed. *Pandora: Women in Classical Greece*. Baltimore: Walters Art Gallery, 1995.

Rhodes, Robin F. *Architecture and Meaning on the Athenian Acropolis*. New York: Cambridge University Press, 1995.

Richter, Gisela M. *The Portraits of the Greeks*. Rev. ed. by R.R.R. Smith. Ithaca, N.Y.: Cornell University Press, 1984.

Ridgway, Brunilde S. *The Archaic Style in Greek Sculpture*. 2d ed. Chicago: Ares, 1993.

———. *Fifth-Century Styles in Greek Sculpture*. Princeton, N.J.: Princeton University Press, 1981.

———. *Fourth-Century Styles in Greek Sculpture*. Madison: University of Wisconsin Press, 1997.

———. *Hellenistic Sculpture I: The Styles of ca. 331–200 BC*. Madison: University of Wisconsin Press, 1990.

———. *Hellenistic Sculpture II: The Styles of ca. 200–100 BC*. Madison: University of Wisconsin Press, 2000.

———. *Prayers in Stone: Greek Architectural Sculpture*. Berkeley: University of California Press, 1999.

———. *Roman Copies of Greek Sculpture: The Problem of the Originals*. Ann Arbor: University of Michigan Press, 1984.

———. *The Severe Style in Greek Sculpture*. Princeton, N.J.: Princeton University Press, 1970.

Robertson, Martin. *The Art of Vase-Painting in Classical Athens*. New York: Cambridge University Press, 1992.

———. *A History of Greek Art*. Rev. ed. 2 vols. New York: Cambridge University Press, 1986.

———. *A Shorter History of Greek Art*. New York: Cambridge University Press, 1981.

Shapiro, H. Alan. *Art and Cult in Athens under the Tyrants*. Mainz: von Zabern, 1989.

———. *Myth into Art: Poet and Painter in Classical Greece*. New York: Routledge, 1994.

Smith, R. R. R. *Hellenistic Sculpture*. New York: Thames & Hudson, 1991.

Spawforth, Tony. *The Complete Greek Temples*. London, Thames & Hudson, 2006.

Spivey, Nigel. *Greek Art*. London: Phaidon, 1997.

Stansbury-O'Donnell, Mark D. *Pictorial Narrative in Ancient Greek Art*. New York: Cambridge University Press, 1999.

Stewart, Andrew. *Art, Desire, and the Body in Ancient Greece*. New York: Cambridge University Press, 1997.

———. *Greek Sculpture: An Exploration*. 2 vols. New Haven, Conn.: Yale University Press, 1990.

Wycherley, Richard E. *How the Greeks Built Cities*. New York: Norton, 1976.

CHAPTER 6:
THE ETRUSCANS

Banti, Luisa. *The Etruscan Cities and Their Culture*. Berkeley: University of California Press, 1973.

Barker, Graeme, and Tom Rasmussen. *The Etruscans*. Oxford: Blackwell, 1998.

Boethius, Axel. *Etruscan and Early Roman Architecture*. 2d ed. New Haven, Conn.: Yale University Press, 1978.

Bonfante, Larissa, ed. *Etruscan Life and Afterlife: A Handbook of Etruscan Studies*. Detroit: Wayne State University Press, 1986.

Brendel, Otto J. *Etruscan Art*. 2d ed. New Haven, Conn.: Yale University Press, 1995.

Cristofani, Mauro. *The Etruscans: A New Investigation*. London: Orbis, 1979.

De Grummond, Nancy Thomson. *Etruscan Myth, Sacred History, and Legend*. Philadelphia: University of Pennsylvania Museum, 2006.

Haynes, Sybille. *Etruscan Civilization: A Cultural History*. Los Angeles: J. Paul Getty Museum, 2000.

Heurgon, Jacques. *Daily Life of the Etruscans*. London: Weidenfeld & Nicolson, 1964.

Pallottino, Massimo. *The Etruscans*. Harmondsworth: Penguin, 1978.

Richardson, Emeline. *The Etruscans: Their Art and Civilization*. Rev. ed. Chicago: University of Chicago Press, 1976.

Ridgway, David, and Francesca Ridgway, eds. *Italy before the Romans*. New York: Academic, 1979.

Spivey, Nigel. *Etruscan Art*. New York: Thames & Hudson, 1997.

Spivey, Nigel, and Simon Stoddart. *Etruscan Italy: An Archaeological History*. London: Batsford, 1990.

Sprenger, Maja, Gilda Bartoloni, and Max Hirmer. *The Etruscans: Their History, Art, and Architecture*. New York: Abrams, 1983.

Steingräber, Stephan. *Abundance of Life: Etruscan Wall Painting*. Los Angeles: J. Paul Getty Museum, 2006.

Torelli, Mario, ed. *The Etruscans*. New York: Rizzoli, 2001.

CHAPTER 7:
THE ROMAN EMPIRE

Anderson, James C., Jr. *Roman Architecture and Society*. Baltimore: Johns Hopkins University Press, 1997.

Andreae, Bernard. *The Art of Rome*. New York: Abrams, 1977.

Bianchi Bandinelli, Ranuccio. *Rome: The Center of Power: Roman Art to AD 200*. New York: Braziller, 1970.

———. *Rome: The Late Empire: Roman Art AD 200–400*. New York: Braziller, 1971.

Brendel, Otto J. *Prolegomena to the Study of Roman Art*. New Haven, Conn.: Yale University Press, 1979.

Claridge, Amanda. *Rome: An Oxford Archaeological Guide*. New York: Oxford University Press, 1998.

Clarke, John R. *The Houses of Roman Italy, 100 BC–AD 250*. Berkeley: University of California Press, 1991.

Cornell, Tim, and John Matthews. *Atlas of the Roman World*. New York: Facts on File, 1982.

D'Ambra, Eve. *Roman Art*. New York: Cambridge University Press, 1998.

———, ed. *Roman Art in Context*. Upper Saddle River, N.J.: Prentice Hall, 1994.

Dobbins, John J., and Pedar Foss, eds. *The World of Pompeii*. London: Routledge, 2007.

Gazda, Elaine K., ed. *Roman Art in the Private Sphere*. Ann Arbor: University of Michigan Press, 1991.

Grant, Michael. *Cities of Vesuvius: Pompeii and Herculaneum*. Harmondsworth: Penguin, 1976.

Hannestad, Niels. *Roman Art and Imperial Policy*. Aarhus: Aarhus University Press, 1986.

Henig, Martin, ed. *A Handbook of Roman Art*. Ithaca, N.Y.: Cornell University Press, 1983.

Kent, John P. C., and Max Hirmer. *Roman Coins*. New York: Abrams, 1978.

Kleiner, Diana E. E. *Roman Sculpture*. New Haven, Conn.: Yale University Press, 1992.

Kleiner, Diana E. E., and Susan B. Matheson, eds. *I Claudia: Women in Ancient Rome*. New Haven, Conn.: Yale University Art Gallery, 1996.

Kleiner, Fred S. *A History of Roman Art*. Belmont, Calif.: Wadsworth, 2007.

Kraus, Theodor. *Pompeii and Herculaneum: The Living Cities of the Dead*. New York: Abrams, 1975.

Lancaster, Lynne. *Concrete Vaulted Construction in Imperial Rome*. New York: Cambridge University Press, 2006.

Ling, Roger. *Roman Painting*. New York: Cambridge University Press, 1991.

L'Orange, Hans Peter. *The Roman Empire: Art Forms and Civic Life*. New York: Rizzoli, 1985.

MacCormack, Sabine G. *Art and Ceremony in Late Antiquity*. Berkeley: University of California Press, 1981.

MacDonald, William L. *The Architecture of the Roman Empire I: An Introductory Study*. Rev. ed. New Haven, Conn.: Yale University Press, 1982.

———. *The Architecture of the Roman Empire II: An Urban Appraisal*. New Haven, Conn.: Yale University Press, 1986.

———. *The Pantheon: Design, Meaning, and Progeny*. Cambridge, Mass.: Harvard University Press, 1976.

Mazzoleni, Donatella. *Domus: Wall Painting in the Roman House.* Los Angeles: J. Paul Getty Museum, 2004.

McKay, Alexander G. *Houses, Villas, and Palaces in the Roman World.* Ithaca, N.Y.: Cornell University Press, 1975.

Nash, Ernest. *Pictorial Dictionary of Ancient Rome.* 2d ed. 2 vols. New York: Praeger, 1962.

Pollitt, Jerome J. *The Art of Rome, 753 BC–AD 337: Sources and Documents.* Rev. ed. New York: Cambridge University Press, 1983.

Richardson, Lawrence, Jr. *A New Topographical Dictionary of Ancient Rome.* Baltimore: Johns Hopkins University Press, 1992.

———. *Pompeii: An Architectural History.* Baltimore: Johns Hopkins University Press, 1988.

Sear, Frank. *Roman Architecture.* Rev. ed. Ithaca, N.Y.: Cornell University Press, 1989.

Stambaugh, John E. *The Ancient Roman City.* Baltimore: Johns Hopkins University Press, 1988.

Taylor, Rabun. *Roman Builders.* New York: Cambridge University Press, 2003.

Toynbee, Jocelyn M. C. *Death and Burial in the Roman World.* London: Thames & Hudson, 1971.

Wallace-Hadrill, Andrew. *Houses and Society in Pompeii and Herculaneum.* Princeton, N.J.: Princeton University Press, 1994.

Ward-Perkins, John B. *Roman Architecture.* New York: Electa/Rizzoli, 1988.

———. *Roman Imperial Architecture.* 2d ed. New Haven, Conn.: Yale University Press, 1981.

Wilson-Jones, Mark. *Principles of Roman Architecture.* New Haven, Conn.: Yale University Press, 2000.

Wood, Susan. *Roman Portrait Sculpture AD 217–260.* Leiden: E. J. Brill, 1986.

Yegül, Fikret. *Baths and Bathing in Classical Antiquity.* Cambridge, Mass.: MIT Press, 1992.

Zanker, Paul. *Pompeii: Public and Private Life.* Cambridge, Mass.: Harvard University Press, 1998.

———. *The Power of Images in the Age of Augustus.* Ann Arbor: University of Michigan Press, 1988.

CREDITS

*The author and publisher are grateful to the proprietors and custodians of various works of art
for photographs of these works and permission to reproduce them in this book.
Sources not included in the captions are listed here.*

INDEX

Boldface names refer to artists. Page numbers in italics refer to illustrations.